DISCARD

D0081489

Trade unions and democracy

Published in our
centenary year
≈ **2004** ≈
MANCHESTER
UNIVERSITY
PRESS

PERSPECTIVES ON DEMOCRATIZATION

The series presents critical texts on democratization processes and democratic theory. Written in an accessible style, the books are theoretically informed and empirically rich, and examine issues critical to the establishment, extension and deepening of democracy in different political systems and contexts. Important examples of successful democratization processes, as well as reasons why experiments in democratic government fail, are some of the issues analysed in the series. The books in the series make an important contribution to the ongoing debates about democracy, good governance and democratization.

series editors: SHIRIN M. RAI and WYN GRANT

already published

Democratization through the looking-glass
PETER BURNELL (editor)

Democracy as public deliberation
MAURIZIO PASSERIN D'ENTRÈVES (editor)

Globalizing democracy
KATHERINE FIERLBECK

Terrorism and democratic stability
JENNIFER S. HOLMES

Democratizing the European Union
CATHERINE HOSKYNS and MICHAEL NEWMAN (editors)

Democracy in Latin America
GERALDINE LIEVESLEY

Mainstreaming gender, democratizing the state?
SHIRIN RAI (editor)

Trade unions and democracy

Strategies and perspectives

MARK HARCOURT AND GEOFFREY WOOD editors

MANCHESTER UNIVERSITY PRESS

Manchester and New York

distributed exclusively in the USA by Palgrave

Copyright © Manchester University Press 2004

While copyright in the volume as a whole is vested in Manchester
University Press, copyright in individual chapters belongs to their
respective authors, and no chapter may be reproduced wholly or in part
without the express permission in writing of both author and publisher.

Published by Manchester University Press
Oxford Road, Manchester M13 9NR, UK
and Room 400, 175 Fifth Avenue, New York, NY 10010, USA
www.manchesteruniversitypress.co.uk

Distributed exclusively in the USA by
Palgrave, 175 Fifth Avenue, New York,
NY 10010, USA

Distributed exclusively in Canada by
UBC Press, University of British Columbia, 2029 West Mall,
Vancouver, BC, Canada V6T 1Z2

British Library Cataloguing-in-Publication Data
A catalogue record for this book is available from the British Library

Library of Congress Cataloging-in-Publication Data applied for

ISBN 0 7190 6978 5 *hardback*

First published 2004
13 12 11 10 09 08 07 06 05 04   10 9 8 7 6 5 4 3 2 1

Typeset
by Action Publishing Technology Ltd, Gloucester
Printed in Great Britain
by Bell & Bain Limited, Glasgow

FLORIDA GULF COAST
UNIVERSITY LIBRARY

Contents

Figures and tables

Figures

Tables

Notes on contributors

Chris Brewster is Professor of International Human Resource Management at Henley Management College, UK.

Pauline Dibben lectures in Human Resource Management at Middlesex University, London.

Matt Flynn is Research Officer at PSC and a PhD student at Cranfield University.

John Godard is Professor of Industrial Relations at the IH Asper School of Business, University of Manitoba, Canada.

Mark Harcourt is Professor in the Department of Strategic Management at Waikato University, Hamilton, New Zealand.

Richard W. Hurd is Professor of Labor Studies at Cornell University, Ithaca, New York.

Phil James is Professor of Employment Regulation at Middlesex University, London.

Kamel Mellahi is Lecturer in Strategic Management at Loughborough University, Loughborough.

Neal Ollett is a PhD student at the School of Industrial Relations, and the Graduate School of Management at Griffith University, Australia.

Dave Peetz is Associate Professor in the School of Industrial Relations at Griffith University, Australia.

Mike Rigby is Principal Lecturer at South Bank University Business School, South Bank University.

Ian Roper is Senior Lecturer in Employment Relations at Middlesex University in London.

Roger Smith is Principal Lecturer at South Bank University Business School, South Bank University.

Eddie Webster is Professor and Director of the Sociology of Work Unit (SWOP) at the University of Witwatersrand, Johannesburg.

Julianne Whiteley works for Daimler Chrysler, and is a former postgraduate student of Rhodes University, South Africa.

Geoffrey Wood is Professor of Comparative HRM at Middlesex University, and Overseas Associate of the University of Witwatersrand.

1

Introduction – trade unions and democracy: possibilities and contradictions

GEOFFREY WOOD

This book seeks to explore the role of trade unions as products of, and agents for democracy. In dealing with unions and democracy, one is, of course, looking at two closely related issues. Firstly, there is the extent to which unions may, as civil society agents, promote democracy within wider society in the case of authoritarian regimes and/or when formal structures for democratic pluralism seem moribund or semi-functional, as watchdogs protecting hard won democratic gains, or as partners to an accommodation between competing interest groups. Secondly, there are questions of internal union democracy, the tensions between rank-and-file and leadership, and the effects of strategic deals or alliances on internal accountability.

The crisis facing established democratic institutions in the advanced societies has been widely noted. In response, there has been increasing interest in the role of civil society actors, ranging from established socio-political collectives to new grassroots organizations. On the one hand, conventional wisdom holds that organized labour in the advanced societies remains locked in a cycle of political marginalization and decline. On the other hand, unions continue to represent a significant component of society within most industrialized countries. Indeed, in many cases, they have demonstrated a capacity for effective renewal and for co-ordinating their efforts with other civil society actors as part of the current groundswell of public opinion against the neo-liberal orthodoxy.

Globalization, unions and democracy

The term 'globalization' is widely deployed and little understood. For the purposes of this volume, it can be taken to refer to the process of the unification of markets and of consumer taste, increasingly mobile investor capital, and rapid technological change that has taken place since the mid-1970s (Wood and Brewster 2002). This has placed renewed pressures on firms to enhance their competitiveness; as their power to set prices is eroded in the face of intense competition, profitability increasingly depends on cutting the costs of inputs, making labour repressive policies highly attractive. Large scale unemployment has returned in many industrialized market economies, whilst massive job losses have become a feature of the 'shock therapy' adjustment policies inflicted on emerging markets (Hyman 2003).

Most of the subsequent chapters devote specific attention to globalization's consequences, either implicitly or explicitly. As noted by John Godard, the effects of this have been particularly pronounced in countries such as the United States, where institutional support for organized labour has always been limited (chapter 8). Unions have been poor in matching the capacity for mobility exhibited by trans-national corporations; attempts to promote trans-national solidarity have had limited impact to date (chapter 7). Again, even when unions deploy innovative new recruitment tactics, there is considerable evidence to suggest that these are most successful in the case of jobs that cannot be readily relocated to a more labour repressive locale.

Hence, unions are directly affected by the forces of 'globalization' in both the political sphere, and at the workplace. As governments attempt to deal with both the increasing disorder of the global economy and the heightened power of trans-national corporations, the political environment has become very much more unfavourable to organized labour. In some cases, this has led to the role of unions as social partners being eroded (Hyman 2003; chapters 3 and 15). Secondly, the adoption of more hard-line policies by firms, and the shrinking of formal employment in traditional areas of union activity in many developed and transitional economies has greatly magnified the retention challenge; in many countries, unions are heavily pressed to retain existing members, a challenge perhaps as difficult and important as initial recruitment (Verma *et al.* 2002: 377; cf. chapters 7, 8 and 11).

Consequently, the forces associated with 'globalization' pose specific challenges to the capacity of unions to represent working people; they make both firms and national institutions less responsive to pressures from both the factory floor and community. Within the workplace, the strengthening of the hand of management has resulted in the erosion of traditional forms of collective representation in favour of productivity centred partnership deals (chapter 15). Within the polity, the role of unions has been similarly weakened, as governments have become less receptive to the interests of organized labour (chapters 2, 3, 4 and 5).

Yet, 'globalization' is a contested process. Whilst the fortunes of unions are closely bound up with changes in the global economy, the persistence of national difference underscores the extent to which the strategic choices made by unions remain vital (chapters 8, 11, 16; Hyman 2003). As Verma *et al.* (2002: 382) note, unions need to constantly explore alternative strategies and structures to take advantage of inevitable economic crises and restructuring. In reality, 'globalization' is both a 'connecting' and 'disconnecting' process (chapter 6). Whilst increasing global competition may prompt certain firms and sectors to deploy innovative forms of work organization, this often also entails downsizing; increasing numbers of new jobs are temporary and insecure, locking their incumbents into the periphery of the labour market (382). Unions need to both meet 'pent up' demands for representation and make it easier for recruits to remain members when they switch jobs, and move to increasingly insecure occupations (Verma *et al.* 2002: 382; chapters 6 and 9).

Whilst the 1998 International Labour Organization (ILO) 'Declaration on Fundamental Principles and Rights at Work' is founded on the assumption that the ability of workers to form unions and to engage in collective bargaining is a fundamental human right, in reality, few employers voluntarily concede this (Friedman 2003: xvi). Indeed, a growing number of economies found their international competitiveness on labour repression, a repressiveness that is rarely confined to the shopfloor. There is no international mechanism to enforce ILO Conventions, or even to ensure that they are endorsed by individual national governments (Moody 1997: 252). Nor is there any other international body with the ability to secure international labour rights (253). Hence, the securing of organizational rights worldwide depends on the efforts of the labour movement, human rights organizations and their allies. However, lobbying to link labour rights with trade agreements may result in the former being linked with protectionism. Perhaps, a more fertile ground for campaigning is on specific grassroots issues, bringing together clusters of labour activists from different nations, building on common ground between the local and the trans-national (chapter 16 and conclusion).

Is too much democracy bad for you? Reconciling internal and external democracy

Much of the literature on trade unions and democracy rests on the assumption that internal union democracy is detrimental to wider social democracy and vice versa (Baccaro 2001). This viewpoint can be divided into three distinct sub-schools of thought. Firstly, drawing on the American political science, writers such as Wagner have argued that democratic pressures from below could lead to government being overloaded by excess demands (Crouch 1979). This can lead to a 'political trade' cycle emerging; governments increasingly are forced to offer 'bribes' to gain popular support. This would include increasing public spending to unsustainable levels.

Wagner's somewhat bleak conclusion was that for a pluralist democracy to work, rank-and-file pressure has to be somehow disarmed (Crouch 1979). Similarly, Huntington argued that the relationships between interest groups and governments could become strained; excessive demands can overstress the authorities (Huntington 1968). Again, Lipset (1977; Baccaro 2001) suggested that strong union democracy is likely to be detrimental to wider social democracy. The former is likely to result in 'irresponsible' short-term demands for resources, which are likely to make for a volatile and unstable polity. These concerns were shared by Dunlop (1975) who held that unions have a vested interest in reining in interests antithetical to the wider social system; a functional part of the social whole, they play a vital role in limiting and channelling popular decision making, and ensuring that the polity is not ceaselessly buffeted by demands from below.

Secondly, writers on neo-corporatism have argued that, for a social accord to work, 'centralized bodies representing the interests of labour, business and the state must be able to strike a deal, and have the moral and/or legal authority to carry their constituents with them' (Harcourt and Wood 2003). In its post-war variants, corporatism ('neo-corporatism') builds on the common ground between key interest groupings in society, reconciling their interests in a context where basic individual liberties are preserved (Baccaro 2001). However, under neo-corporatism, not only must there be a dominant union federation capable of mediating the demands of individual unions, but it must be capable of reining in potentially rebellious constituents, making them stick to a deal (Regini 1986; Schmidt and Reissert 1991). Whilst unions depend on effectively representing their members in order to retain their support – and to make deals on their behalf – they also have to exercise coercion, both to keep the rank and file in line (in order that any deal the union makes is honoured) and to discourage individuals from selfishly pursuing their own interests (Olson 1982; chapter 2).

Thirdly, and more recently, the literature on social partnerships involving unions suggests that, again, enterprise-level deals with managers are predicated on the organizational mediation of rank-and-file pressures. Workplace-level social partnerships between managers and employees seem to receive particular emphasis in Britain (see Bacon and Storey 2000: 407). Such partnerships are not necessarily characterized by an absence of conflict; rather, conflict becomes institutionalized, with established mechanisms for conflict resolution that do not endanger the existing workplace order (Kirichenko and Koudyukin 1993: 43). While they potentially allow unions – and those they represent – a greater say in workplace governance, it can be argued that, in practice, such deals have done little to advance democracy at either the industrial or the social level. As many writers have correctly pointed out, the willingness of unions to commit themselves to such partnerships – in effect, helping management pull their chestnuts out of the fire – is a product of union weakness (cf. Bacon and Storey 2000). Gall (2003a: 92) argues that such deals often involve the imposition of 'anti-disruption' or similar measures, aimed at limiting the range of choices open to workers. Moreover, work place level social partnership deals have often proved fragile or ineffective. Much trumpeted partnership agreements have often failed to rescue companies from subsequent financial crises, good examples being Hyundai and Rover (Guest 2001: 103).

Squaring the circle? Internal and external democracy

In contrast, more radical theories of unions and democracy have tended to see internal and external democracy as reconcilable; to advance genuine social democracy, unions must, themselves, be democratic. Whilst the Leninist tradition would suggest that the latter should be on 'democratic centralist' lines, involving subordination to a vanguard party, later accounts have suggested that vibrant grassroots democracy provides the surest path to union revitalization. Hence, external activities, efforts and outreach need to involve the ranks and workplace activists from the start (Moody 1997; cf. Gall 2003b). Democracy represents the foundation of union strength; lively internal democracy makes for organizational vibrancy, and provides a sound foundation for outreach (Moody 1997: 4).

Actions by unions to 'determine their own destinies' incorporate both wider social and a workplace dimension. The former may involve both participation in the politics of the streets, and alliances or trade-offs at the commanding heights. At workplace level, the struggle for union recognition is not only one aimed at material outcomes, but also incorporates procedural goals, aimed at giving employees a greater say in the organization of work and the ability to constrain the actions of management (Gall 2003b:18; Wood 1998).

But, how may internal democracy be sustained? Michels' classic account on the inevitability of oligarchy holds that union leaders will inevitably become bureaucrats, able to entrench their positions into one of a semi-permanent elite (Michels 1972; see chapter 2). More recently, writers such as Desai (2002) have argued that union leaders will inevitably face co-optation into the ruling elite – or irrelevance – unless the union is firmly rooted in the community, with power being decentralized to the lowest possible level. Any accommodation with the status quo entails unacceptable compromise; unions become bound to maintaining the existing order and are forced to sacrifice the long-term interests of the poor.

Other writers, such as Southall and Wood (1999), have argued that unions inevitably have to make a range of often-awkward strategic choices, such as the forging of alliances with other groupings. This will inevitably involve some trade-offs between influence and autonomy (1999; Valenzuela 1992: 60–63). Whilst this may mean that more radical agendas for social transformation may be sacrificed to gain short-term concessions from capital, such choices allow unions to make real gains in difficult climates. This does not necessarily mean an abandonment of internal democracy, but rather the mediating of a plethora of grassroots pressures in such a manner as to successfully promote the interests of current and potential members.

The contemporary literature on union strategic choice argues that the differing fortunes of organized labour in different national contexts can partially be explained through real decisions made at key historical moments (cf. Hyman 1997). Whilst union membership has declined in most of the advanced societies, the uneven nature of the decline, and the robust performance of individual unions in extremely adverse consequences underscores the importance of strategic vision.

As Frege and Kelly (2003: 12) note, the strategic choices made by unions are shaped by the institutional context, identity, and the strategies adopted towards them by employers, and the state and political parties. These mould the manner in which grassroots concerns and organizational outcomes are framed and articulated. Whilst a highly repressive 'climate of little hope' will inevitably be detrimental to unions, weaker manifestations of injustice and/or where there seems some hope of social change inevitably heighten latent feelings of deprivation, leading to an upsurge of shopfloor militancy (cf. Davies 1978). The latter is particularly likely when workers perceive a close linkage between workplace and wider social injustice, and blame at least a proportion of their misfortunes on management (Kelly 1998).

Whilst this may make for effective political or social movement unionism, it may be difficult for unions to institutionalize gains, or mediate competing demands from the shopfloor. Unions can, in such contexts, develop into a viable force for social democracy, or become locked into a kind of grassroots anti-politics, unable to advance a progressive agenda beyond sporadic attacks on the worst excesses of capital. Conversely, effective centralized collective bargaining and/or corporatism may secure the status and influence of unions at both workplace and societal level. However, this may also make for a certain lack of dynamism, and an inability to represent marginal categories of labour (cf. Harcourt and Wood 2003; Wood and Harcourt 2001). In both these instances, the outcomes at least in part depend on the real strategic choices open to union leaders and their constituents.

Trade unions and democracy

Following on this introduction, the book is organized into seven thematic sections, dealing with related issues such as internal democracy, organizing non-traditional constituents, the role of unions in wider society, and the possibilities for broadening participation and new forms of engagement.

Thematic section 1: trade unions and the crisis of democracy

How are unions to advance a democratic agenda, both internally and externally? Both neo-classical and systems theories of trade unions have tended to prioritize the development and institutionalization of the latter at the expense of the former. Meanwhile, both theories of bureaucracy and elite theory concede inevitable tendencies towards formalization and a lack of accountability. Although Weber believed that the latter could be reined in through entrenched mechanisms for accountability and recall (Giddens 1979: 181), as noted earlier, Michels (1972) believed such tendencies were extremely difficult to check. Whilst the ultra-left tradition remains cynical as to the ability of unions under capitalism to make real gains or effect meaningful compromises, a more pragmatic critical tradition, encompassing writers from Miliband (1972) to the regulation theorists (Jessop 2001) has held that the contradictory nature of contemporary capitalism makes it possible for workers to extract meaningful concessions from capitalism, and develop those aspects of state and economy that allow both for the operation of markets and active institutional mediation in the pursuit of macro-economic stability and equity. Chapter 2 concludes that the latter perspective highlights the manner in which 'unions can both serve as an effective mechanism for articulating the concerns of the rank and file, and in promoting more accountable and sustainable macro-economic policies', mediating the worst excesses of the market, and providing a real way forward from the present and persistent macro-economic volatility.

Chapter 3 looks at the effects of neo-liberal reforms on the political sphere, and, more specifically, on the institutions and practices of democracy. It contrasts the neo-liberal policy mix, which is inherently rigid and relies on hierarchically organized governmental institutions staffed by ideological homogenous acolytes with neo-corporatist alternatives. In contrast, social accords are inherently democratic, given their inclusive nature, the emphasis on trade-offs and mutually beneficial agreements, and their promotion of democratic rights such as the freedoms of expression and association. In chapter 4, Ian Roper explores the relationship between the crisis of participation and account-ability in formal politics, and the coterminous decline of trade unions, and possible alternatives to neo-liberalism. It is concluded that 'third way' solutions are unlikely to resolve the present malaise in representivity; rather, it is vital to consider new ways of reclaiming and enhancing the role of the public sphere, both within and beyond formal state structures.

Thematic section 2: unionization in a fragmented world: organizing non-traditional constituencies

Postmodern accounts of the labour movement are founded on the assumption that the traditional conception of the working class has become fragmented into a mosaic of competing identities around gender, sexuality, locale and ethnicity (Kelly 1998: 144; Moody 1997: 122). Such accounts incorporate an implicit assumption that, under classic modernity, there was a 'golden age' of working-class solidarity, which has become fractured in the age of hyperreality (Moody 1997: 144; Wood 1997). However, as Moody (1997: 144) notes, there is little evidence that such a 'golden age' ever existed; whilst in many national contexts, unions were relatively strong in the 1950s and 1960s, internal discrimination against ethnic minorities and women was widespread. The assumption that the 'normal employee' was male discounted high levels of female participation in certain industries, such as textiles (Hyman 2003). Again, a higher proportion of females confined to the home did not mean that the working class was immune to gender issues, simply that they were manifested in different forms (Moody 1997: 144). Whilst the rise of gender and sexual identity movements has resulted in a range of non-economic lifestyle issues being placed on the agenda, these are not necessarily antithetical – and, in some cases may be complementary – to class identity (Kelly 1998: 122). Nonetheless, whilst cleavages on the lines of gender, ethnicity and sexual identity are not new to the labour movement, it is evident that the traditional male dominated order is increasingly untenable. In order to attract and retain members in an age of accelerating membership turnover, unions have to be seen to be more responsive to the needs and concerns of existing and potential members. This will entail existing structures of internal democracy being revisited, which may entail the development of new sections of the labour movement specifically focused on servicing the needs of key constituencies (cf. chapter 10) and/or closer alliances with community movements (cf. chapters 6, 12 and 16).

There is considerable evidence to suggest that atypical employment situations – such as part-time, agency and other temporary forms of work, self-employment, and structural unemployment – have become more common (Hyman 2003). Hence, union identities and strategies based on labour market perspectives of the 'mass worker', founded on a standard model of full-time employment, an assumed degree of job security and limited occupational mobility, are no longer tenable. Instead, unions need to identify programmes with which horizontally and vertically differentiated groupings of workers can identify (2003).

In chapter 5, Phil James notes that, whilst union decline, at least in part, can be ascribed to fluctuations in the business cycle and more hard-line governmental and employer policies, it also represents a product of far-reaching changes in labour market composition. The latter would encompass the decline of traditional manufacturing occupations and the growing importance of service sector activity, rise of non-standard work, and increasing employment in the SME sector. In response, unions have devoted increasing attention towards developing new outreach and recruitment strategies tailored to the needs of such categories of organized labour. Strategies adopted include partnership initiatives, the adoption of the organizing model and political campaigning. Whilst, James argues, it is perhaps too soon to judge the effectiveness of such strategies, which will be partially moulded by surrounding political, economic and industrial relations contexts, they highlight the potentially mutually supporting linkage between an ability to successfully represent the concerns of key constituencies and effective outreach.

In chapter 6, Eddie Webster explores the challenges facing unions in bringing highly marginalized categories of labour into the organizational fold. Based on the case of informal sector workers in the South African city of Durban, this chapter both highlights the limits of conventional outreach strategies, and the need for unions to reach out to, and build links with, members of such categories of labour. The global spread of neo-liberal policies has resulted in the shrinking of formal employment in most developing countries; unions have to contend with the diminishment of traditional constituencies. The increasing amount of informal and highly insecure work has created a 'crisis of representation', as trade unions 'lose their capacity to provide a voice for the new poor'. This necessitates a rethink of the entire conceptual framework as to what constitutes a worker. Those engaged in informal occupations may lack an employer (or indeed anyone to bargain with), but do 'not have access to any productive resources or assets' and are forced to sell their labour power. Exploring new forms of outreach to informal workers is necessary both on the grounds of representivity and equity: 'labour needs to broaden its constituency and form alliances with groups outside of the traditional unions in the formal sector ... the future of the labour movement and the organization of informal workers depends on such a coalition'.

Thematic section 3: the changing impact and strength of the labour movement in the advanced societies

As Frege and Kelly (2003: 9–12) note, there is a real need to progress contemporary debates beyond endless contestations as to the real reason underlying union decline. Yet, it is clear the relative strength of unions matters for democracy. The rise of unions within the advanced societies in most cases took place coterminously with the rise of the broadening of the mainstream democratic discourse, and with a greater emphasis being placed on a social and redistributive political agenda. As Giddens (1981) notes, the real gains made by the working classes in the advanced societies in the 1950s and 1960s was at least in part due to union activity. Union activity demonstrated that divergent class interests could, at least temporarily, be accommodated within plural democracy. As Friedman (2003: xv) notes, 'with a strong union in the workplace, autocracy gives way to democracy'. Again, within much of Western Europe, unions played a vital role in the evolution of institutional forms that underpinned viable manifestations of social democracy.

The declining fortunes of unions, particularly pronounced in the Anglo-Saxon world, has been associated with the increasing power of large corporations, the weakening of the public sphere and widening social inequality. The latter developments have both 'hollowed out' and weakened the nature of formal democratic discourse (Anderson 2000). Unions could play a major role in the re-enrergization of public life, but this is contingent on the ability to effectively articulate grassroots concerns, and to reach out to the growing body of the unorganized (Moody 1997; Wood and Psoulis 2001).

In chapter 7, Mike Rigby, Roger Smith and Chris Brewster make the case that there is insufficient evidence to suggest that union decline in the advanced societies is cyclical, or likely to be reversed in the foreseeable future. Yet, they reiterate that trade unions have been one of the 'bulwarks of a democratic society, in and beyond the workplace'. Within Western Europe they remain embedded in the central institutional fabric within the advanced societies, and they are likely to continue to play an important role in democratic processes. Western European unions were central forces in the development of democracy, the welfare state, and, more recently, have positively impacted on debates and policy interventions surrounding labour market reform. However, they face the challenge in securing a long-term role in an expanding European Union that incorporates East European states with very different organizational traditions, and in reaching out to, and effectively articulating, the needs of, categories of labour where union penetration is slight or declining.

In examining the cases of the United States and Canada, John Godard notes that whilst the Canadian context is considerably more conducive to union activity than the US one, in both cases, unions face serious long-term challenges in attracting, retaining, and effectively representing members (chapter 8). Godard highlights the similarities and differences between the US and Canada, and the relationship between political and economic forces, and the relative fortunes of unions. If unions are to recover, broader social mobilization is vital; whilst mobilization may be facilitated by long-term economic swings (cf. Kelly 1998), it is heavily dependent on 'the development of an effective strategy and ultimately paradigm for enhancing employment rights and the quality of the work experience in general'.

In chapter 9, Rick Hurd provides a critical appraisal of the organizing model for union renewal. He argues that there is very much more to union renewal than effective recruitment and an emphasis on mobilization. Above all, unions need to devote more attention to the complexities of organizational change, expanding member education, overcoming conservatism amongst staff members and leadership, balancing representation and organizing, and real strategic planning. Without radical institutional change, attempts at mobilization will do little more 'than stir excitement', whilst an adverse external environment can easily 'overwhelm individual campaign victories'. Hurd concludes that the organizing model has been far less successful than is commonly believed; hence, the aims and strategies of union renewal need to be rethought, if unions are to regain their position within the advanced societies.

Thematic section 4: the changing impact and strength of the labour movement: cases from emerging economies

Within a number of emerging markets, most notably South Africa, Brazil and South Korea, unions played a central role in relatively recent struggles against authoritarianism, have retained significant mass followings, and remain committed to advancing a specifically working-class agenda inside and outside the workplace. Yet, in all three instances, unions have battled to define an alternative political project following on democratization, and, in some cases, membership has begun to flatten out, or decline. The relative fortunes of unions in these contexts is of considerable importance, not only as key civil society actors articulating an agenda geared towards the poor, but also as potential spearheads of a new labour internationalism, imparting a fresh vibrancy into their Western counterparts (Moody 1997).

In chapter 10, Dave Peetz and Neal Ollett provide a critical appraisal of the relative strength and capacity of the South Korean labour movement. The story of South Korean unions is one of both great strength and weakness: 'Unions' vertical co-ordinating capacity is very strong as a result of the deep articulation between national, industry and local levels. Yet horizontal co-ordinating capacity is very weak'. The latter is due to divisions between two major union federations. Again, established unions have battled to reach out to marginal categories of labour. The latter has led to an emergence of a new strand of unionism, women's unions. The latter remain relatively small and vulnerable, but challenge the way mainstream unions think about female peripheral workers (cf. chapter 6). Whilst the importance of unions in the struggle for democratization is not to be underestimated, they face the further challenge of broadening the base of effective representation both within the workplace and without. In chapter 11, Julianne Whitely provides an overview of the changing fortunes of organized labour in Zimbabwe and South Africa. Whilst in both countries unions managed to establish a powerful national presence in adverse circumstances, they now have to contend with the challenge posed by the reduction in the number of formal sector jobs as a result of neo-liberal reforms and, in the case of Zimbabwe, chronic political instability.

Thematic section 5: unions and politics – political engagement and social movement unionism

In seeking to advance the interests of their members – and broaden the base of democratic participation in decision making both within and without the workplace – unions have the choice of forging close alliances with political parties or developing an alternative political role outside the realm of mainstream party politics. The latter may entail either a completely independent social movement unionism role, or one that is predicated on building alliances with like-minded grassroots organizations. Social movement unionism asserts the primacy of democracy as a source of union power and vision (Moody 1997: 4). It shares the organizing models concern with reaching out to vulnerable and hitherto unorganized sections of the labour market, but sees this as a source of strength, rather than an end in itself (Moody 1997: 4).

In chapter 12, Pauline Dibben provides an overview of contemporary manifestations of social movement unionism. This chapter stresses that effective social movement unionism depends on democratic participation (Moody 1997) and/or strong grassroots linkages (Waterman 1993), with the organizational project being infused with a sense of injustice (cf. Kelly

1998), most specifically against unrestrained international capitalism, and the neo-liberal ideological hegemony. To Dibben, the project of social movement unionism is vested with a certain urgency. Unless the ongoing marginalization of the most vulnerable is reversed and they are drawn into the labour movement, unions will be left with little more to do other than organizing 'insider' categories of labour in a kind of business unionism.

In chapter 13, Phil James explores the differing relationships unions can have with political parties, current trends, and the likely future trajectories of such relationships. It is argued that the constitutional nature – or otherwise of such links – does not provide a reliable indicator of the closeness of union–party relationships or the degree of influence that unions can exert within parties; 'the influence that unions wield over parties can be seen to be affected by a range of, often inter-related, factors, including the degree of ideological congruency that exists between the union movement, on the one hand, and the party, on the other'. Whilst a long-term trend has been towards the weakening of union–political party linkages, in some contexts, this may stabilize around a new equilibrium.

Thematic section 6: democracy within the union

As Gall (2003b: 18) notes, the struggle for union recognition at the workplace represents both a means and an end; it is aimed not only at gaining more favourable employment contracts, but also at assisting workers in gaining a real say in workplace governance. Recognition represents a key component of industrial democracy and 'has both a democratizing and civilizing effect on society'.

Matt Flynn, Chris Brewster, Roger Smith and Mike Rigby argue that the present crisis of organized labour has forced 'unions to re-examine some very traditional concepts of participative democracy, with unions seeking to link membership involvement in union activities to involvement in decision-making' (chapter 14). Nor is this rethinking retrogressive; unions have been forced to come to terms with structural weaknesses and make their activities more accessible to a wider range of members and potential members.

Thematic section 7: partnership and strategic alternatives

Unions face the possibility of advancing their cause through reaching accommodations with employers, the state and other social actors. Such accommodations may take place at a range of levels, from the workplace through to the commanding heights. To proponents, they may help unions entrench their position, allow for the greater democratization of working life, and/or allow input into the highest levels of macro-economic policy. On the other hand, they may entail reduced levels of grassroots accountability and result in unions sacrificing their interests – and a rich tradition of struggle – in return for the meaningless concessions that ever more firmly bind them to an unjust status quo.

Chapter 15 introduces the widely disparate forms which 'social partnerships' assume, the reasons behind the emergence of such deals, and their durability and likely outcome from a business systems theory perspective. It is concluded that contemporary social partnerships in the 'Anglo-Saxon' economies represent thinly veiled attempts to promote the legitimacy of management, and are likely neither to prove durable nor to significantly broaden workplace democracy.

Chapter 16 explores the possibilities for alternative forms of strategic engagement between unions and other social actors – given the palpable limitations of workplace-level partnerships – and the extent to which these could contribute to a regeneration of the European social model. However, a new form of social democracy is only possible if corporate interests are impelled in this direction through the mass mobilization of new social movements and/or if all credible alternatives are exhausted. The concluding chapter further develops some of the themes and issues raised in preceding chapters and explores possible strategies for future renewal.

Conclusion

Many of the contributions in this volume are infused with a 'pessimistic realism'; they underscore the real challenges facing Western unions coping with the legacy of decades of numerical decline, and those faced by their counterparts in emerging economies as a result of far-reaching economic restructuring. However, they also highlight the importance of activism and organization, the vitality of internal debates and need for unions to impact on both formal political discourses, and in the politics of the streets.

References

Anderson, P. 2000. 'Renewals', *New Left Review*, 1, 239: 5–24.

Baccaro, L. 2001. 'Union Democracy Revisited', *Economic and Industrial Democracy*, 22, 2: 183–210.

Bacon, N. and Storey, J. 2000. 'New Employment Strategies in Britain: Towards Individualism or Partnership?', *British Journal of Industrial Relations*, 38, 3: 407–427.

Crouch, C. 1979. 'The State, Capital and Liberal Democracy', in Crouch, C. (ed.), *State and Economy in Contemporary Capitalism*. London: Croom Helm.

Davies, J. C. 1978. 'Why Do Revolutions Occur?', in Lewis, P., Potter, D. and Castles, F. (eds.), *The Practice of Comparative Politics*. London: Longman.

Desai, A. 2002. *We Are the Poors: Community Struggles in Post-Apartheid South Africa*. New York: Monthly Review Press.

Dunlop, J. T. 1975. 'Political Systems and Industrial Relations', in Barrett, B., Beishon, J. and Rhodee, E. (eds.), *Industrial Relations and Wider Society*. Drayton: Collier-Macmillan.

Frege, C. and Kelly, J. 2003. 'Union Revitilization Strategies in Comparative Perspective', *European Journal of Industrial Relations*, 9, 1: 7–24.

Friedman, S. 2003. 'Preface', in Gall, G. (ed.), *Union Organizing: Campaigning for Union Recognition*. London: Routledge.

Gall, G. 2003a. 'Employer Opposition to Union Recognition', in Gall, G. (ed.), *Union Organizing: Campaigning for Union Recognition*. London: Routledge.

—— 2003b. 'Introduction', in Gall, G. (ed.), *Union Organizing: Campaigning for Union Recognition*. London: Routledge.

Giddens, A. 1979. *Capitalism and Modern Social Theory: An Analysis of the Writings of Marx, Durkheim, and Max Weber*. Cambridge: Cambridge University Press.

—— 1981. *The Class Structure of the Advanced Societies*. London: Unwin.

Guest, D. 2001. 'Industrial Relations and Human Resource Management', in Storey, J. (ed.), *Human Resource Management*. London: Thomson Learning.

Harcourt, M. and Wood, G. 2003. 'Under What Circumsances Do Social Accords Work?', *Journal of Economic Issues* (in print).

Huntingdon, S. 1968. *Political Order in Changing Societies*. London: Yale University Press.

Hyman, R. 1997. 'Trade Unions and Interest Representation in the Context of Globalization', *Transfer*, 3: 515–533.

—— 2003. 'An Emerging Agenda for Trade Unions', *Labournet*. www.labournet.de/diskussion/gewerkschaft/hyman.html

Jessop, B. 2001. 'Series Preface', in Jessop, B. (ed.), *Developments and Extensions: Regulation Theory and the Crisis of Capitalism, Volume 5*. London: Edward Elgar.

Kelly, J. 1998. *Rethinking Industrial Relations: Mobilization, Collectivism and Long Waves*. London: Routledge.

Kirichenko, O. and Koudyukin, P. 1993. 'Social Partnerships in Russia: The First Steps', *Economic and Industrial Democracy*, 14: 43–55.

Lipset, M. 1977. *Union Democracy*. New York: Free Press.

Michels, R. 1972. 'Power in the Party', in Worsley, P. (ed.), *Problems of Modern Sociology*. London: Penguin.

Miliband, R. 1972. *Parliamentary Socialism*. London: Merlin.

Moody, K. 1997. *Workers in a Lean World*. London: Verso.

Olson, M. 1982. *The Rise and Decline of Nations: Economic Growth, Stagflation and Social Rigidities*. New Haven: Yale University Press.

Regini, M. 1986. 'Political Bargaining in Western Europe During the Crisis of the 1980s', in Jacobi, O., Jessop, B., Kastendiek, H. and Regini, M. (eds.), *Economic Crisis, Trade Unions and the State*. London: Croom Helm.

Schmidt, G. and Reissert, B. 1991. 'On the Institutional Conditions of Effective Labour Market Policies', in Matzner, E. and Streeck, W. (eds.), *Beyond Keynesianism: The Socio-Economics of Production and Full Employment*. Aldershot: Edward Elgar.

Southall, R. and Wood, G. 1999. 'The Congress of South African Trade Unions, the ANC and the Election: Whither the Alliance?', *Transformation*, 38: 68–83.

Valenzuela, J. S. 1992. 'Labour Movements and Political Systems', in Regini, M. (ed.), *The Future of Labour Movements*. London: Sage.

Verma, A., Kochan, T. A. and Wood, S. 2002. 'Union Decline and Prospects for Revival', *British Journal of Industrial Relations*, 40, 3: 373–384.

Waterman, P. 1993. 'Social-Movement Unionism: A New Union Model for a New World Order?', *Review*, 16, 3: 245–278.

Wood, G. 1997. 'The Delirium of Change: Giles Deleuze's Optimistic Postmodernism', *Koers*, 62, 2: 1–12.

—— 1998. *Trade Union Recognition: Cornerstone of the New South African Employment Relations*. Johannesburg: International Thompson.

Wood, G. and Brewster, C. 2002. 'Decline and Renewal in the British Labour Movement', *Society in Transition*, 33, 2: 241–258.

Wood, G. and Harcourt, M. 2001. 'The Consequences of Neo-Corporatism: A Syncretic Analysis', *International Journal of Sociology and Social Policy*, 20, 8: 1–22.

Wood, G. and Psoulis, C. 2001. 'Globalization, Democratization and Organized Labor in Transitional Economies: The Case of the Congress of South African Trade Unions', *Work and Occupations*, 28, 3: 293–314.

2

Trade unions and theories of democracy

GEOFFREY WOOD

Theories of democracy are relevant in understanding both the manner in which trade unions are governed, and the extent to which they may, through actively representing a specific constituency, broaden accountability within a society. The latter is of particular importance in an age of declining participation in national elections, and where large corporations have seemingly overshadowed the powers of national governments.

The rational choice tradition

This tradition rests on the assumptions central to neo-classical economics: that society is made up rational profit-seeking individuals whose behavioural patterns can be readily quantified. In traditional rational choice theory, democratization is seen to be a historical accident as a result of: 'a dispersion of forces and resources that makes it impossible for any one leader or group to overpower all the others' (Olson 2000: 134).

If it is not possible to divide society into small autocracies, each contending for resources, then the alternative, 'work[ing] out a framework for mutual toleration' between the principal interest groupings in society is likely to be realized (Olson 2000: 134). However, such arrangements will be tenuous unless on-going trade offs can be made, and potentially disruptive grassroots elements reined in.

But, how do such interest groupings come into being and persist, if society is indeed composed of rational utility maxi-mizing individuals each pursuing their own good? If all individuals are equally concerned with optimizing their individual utilities, why do they sometimes subordinate their interests to a collective goal, when there may be real benefits attached to 'freeriding'? (cf. Olson 1982). For example, people may gain the benefits of joining a union without joining it if the union already enjoys widespread support, 'freeriding' on the efforts of others. But, if everybody seeks to 'freeride', the union will soon collapse. To Olson, the solution is two-fold. Firstly, unions will seek to ensure that the benefits they offer are 'private goods'; in other words, exclusively for the benefit of their members, such as access to a particular craft, or to a particular set of 'friendly society' benefits (Kelly 1998: 68). Secondly, there is what is sometimes referred to as the 'Olsonian trap'; whilst unions depend on effectively representing their members in order to retain their support, they also have to exercise coercion, both to keep the rank and file in line (in order that any deal the union makes is honoured) and to discourage freeriding. As Olson and Kahkonen (2002: 27) assert:

> individuals in any large group do not have an automatic incentive to contribute to or act in the interest of their group and large groups will only be able to organize and act in their common interest only if they are able to work out 'selective incentives' or punishments and rewards, that apply to individuals whether they do or do not share in the costs of organization and action on behalf of the group.

Thus, whilst inherently a means of representation, to survive, unions must in some way be anti-democratic. Yet, as Kelly (1998: 77) notes, many successful strikes seem to involve no visible picketing or other forms of collective action to intimidate non-strikers; in other words, solidarity does not necessarily seem contingent on coercion. Secondly, where unions have relied on compulsory membership either via legislation or a closed shop, they have often proved considerably weaker than unions that relied on active recruitment (Kelly 1998: 79; Moody 1997).

In recent years, the rational choice tradition has tended to fragment, between, on the one hand, neo-liberal 'fundamentalists' who argue that individual rights are paramount, and those who deploy rational choice more as a methodological tool than a specific theoretical frame of reference. To orthodox neo-liberals, the principal aims of the state should simply be to uphold such rights (cf. Nozick 1984), the 'ultraminimalist' state favoured by Milton Friedman and other neo-liberal proponents of unfettered free markets (Wood 2003). To proponents of rights based approaches, the duties of the firm are, hence, limited: shareholders have a right to fair return on their investment, and employees a right for their employment contract to be correctly implemented, but, of course, the latter should be accorded no specific legal protection to engage in collective action or organization (Wood 2003). Rather, employee collectives would constitute 'market imperfections', which would inevitably dilute the right of management to effectively manage. By exercising coercion on both their rank and file, and on the firm, unions of necessity, encroach on individual liberties; they are essentially anti-democratic.

Conversely, the more pragmatic rational choice school of thought focuses on the possibilities it accords in terms of econometric modelling, without making too many ideological assumptions as to the role of trade unions in societies. This viewpoint is reflected in many articles in leading journals such as *Industrial Relations* and *Industrial and Labor Relations Review*, and makes no close-ended assumptions as to the contradictions between union activity and democracy. However, it still largely rests upon many of Olson's fundamental assumptions, above all, on the distinctions between private and public goods. Unions will try to maximize the benefits accruing to their members, and seek to deter freerider behaviour by limiting their availability to those persistently outside the fold; in this sense, unions are in the business of exclusive rather than broadly inclusive social betterment.

Systems theory

On of the most influential critiques of rational choice theory was provided by Talcott Parsons, who rejected the notion that rational self-action could provide the basis for collective order and action (Lane 1998: 8). Rather, collectivism is underpinned by solidarity, identified with institutionalized shared values, fulfilling the primary function of defining the obligations of loyalty the individual had to the collective (8). In other words, common values and norms provide the basis for trust. Democracy is thus not just about compromise and coexistence between self-serving individuals, but a mechanism by which concerns may be articulated, whilst reinforcing shared values and beliefs. These assumptions provided the basis for the pluralist tradition in industrial relations thinking.

Dunlop (1975: 364) argues that there is continuing interaction between industrial relations systems participants and wider society; conflict and co-operation between the different industrial relations actors is often designed to impact on political power within society. Trade unions operate within a wider social context, and shape and are reshaped by the wider political system (364). There is a close relationship between what trade unions do, and the broader political system (364). Under Stalinist rule in Eastern Europe, unions served as little more than conveyor belts for state policy. In the United States, unions have greater freedom of action than their former Soviet counterparts did, but have far fewer legal rights than unions in Western Europe do. The wider society similarly determines who union leaders are; they may be imposed by a political party, or selected by socially acceptable forms of election and predetermined standards of office. Moreover, societies may allow little or much scope for independent decision making (Dunlop 1975: 366). Certain political systems may permit considerable diversity in union policy; others may constrain or seek to stifle brands of unionism that are antithetical to the status quo, an example being the case of the United States for most of the twentieth century. However, in most instances, unions form part of an existing social order than a serious challenger thereto; workplace conflict represents the competition of specific interest groupings operating within an overall systemic framework. Moreover, in democratic states, unions and other civil society groupings play a vital mediating role, ensuring that the polity remains responsive to the will of the populace, without being constantly buffeted by changes in popular opinion.

Unions represent an economic, political and social institution (Flanders 1975: 24). They are a collective attempt to regulate aspects of the employment relationship, which may have implications within and without the firm. However, systems approaches seek to impart a predictability to union behaviour which accords little room for the expression of interests that may be antithetical to the wider social order. Moreover, they only accord limited attention as to why the system is held together and reconstituted (Fox 1975: 259). Indeed, it can be argued that the systems approach denies the importance of strategic choices made by unions and the members that compose them (Kochan, quoted in Kelly 1998: 19). Whilst, as Kelly (1998: 19) notes, strategic choices may be constrained or remade by power imbalances between the different groupings, such contestations may be a lot more dynamic than the systems approach would suggest. Conflict may be just as present as social harmony between and within collectives (Lane 1998: 9); unions may represent a more dynamic instrument for redressing power imbalances in society in favour of the less endowed than systems theory would suggest.

Weber and after: the contradictions of representation

To Max Weber, structures for democratic representation are closely related to the rise of the bureaucracy; the former depends on rational and formal codes governing behaviour (Wood 2003). Yet, there is a central tension between democratization and the bureaucratization process; for democratic rights to be exercised, additional bureaucratic structures are needed (Giddens 1979: 180; Wood 2003). Democracy requires the impersonal selection of individuals to fill leadership posts, a process that will necessarily result in reduced accountability (Giddens 1979: 180). Direct democracy is not possible in mass societies (or in large organizations); at best, representational democracy is the only viable option. Yet, under universal suffrage, leaders must have a degree of charisma, stimulating 'Caesarist' tendencies in leaders, be they of political parties or unions. However, these pressures can be kept in check through the promotion of open debate and mechanisms whereby leaders who overstep the mark might be brought to book; democracy is not only about representation, but the existence of effective structures to ensure accountability, and to allow for recall (181; Wood 2003).

A rather more pessimistic vision is that of Robert Michels (1972: 185). Michels shares Weber's concerns on the inevitable counter-democratic tendencies inherent in the process of bureaucratization. However, to Michels, these tendencies are virtually impossible to check, and are present in all bureaucracies, even trade unions and socialist political organizations (Lee and Worsley 1972: 181; Michels 1972: 186–187). In becoming bureaucrats, leaders are distanced from the grassroots; because of their organizational power, they are able to resist challenges to their leadership and become a semi-permanent elite (181). This process Michels referred to as the 'iron law of oligarchy'.

Elite theories

To Vilfred Pareto, all social orders are characterized by the exercise of power of a minority over a majority; this is a natural characteristic of the human condition (Aron 1950: 1–11). Elites are subject to change; this is particularly true of formal democracies. However, there is always a minority who hold the key positions in society, and who will control a disproportionate share of national resources (1–11). Whilst democratization may allow greater room for regulated contestation between different sections of the elite, and for peaceful political succession, it can also result in leadership becoming weak with no material benefit for the mass of society. On the one hand, attempts by unions and other civil society groupings to promote greater social equity are likely be prove stillborne. On the other, unions are prone to their own internal tendencies towards elitism, echoing Michels' vision of the inevitability of oligarchy.

The radical tradition

Engels (1952) saw trade unions as playing a potentially revolutionary role; no matter how limited their activities were, they attacked the very basis of capital accumulation. However, whilst employers vigorously opposed early attempts at unionization, eventual recognition brought with it a sometimes uneasy cohabitation; it seems that unions could co-exist with capitalism, whilst the latter proved considerably flexible in accommodating workplace resistance.

   These developments led Lenin (1933) to dismiss the possibility that trade unions could make any meaningful gains under capitalism; as part of the system, they had no real opportunity to serve as a democratic voice for employees within or without the workplace. These concerns are echoed by current ultra-leftists, who argue that any form of democratic participation by the mass of society under

capitalism must thus be little more than a fraud (Callinicos 1997).
This insistence seemed increasingly untenable, given that the
1950s and 1960s saw gains in the material conditions of the
working class within the advanced societies, partially driven by
union activity (Giddens 1981). As Kelly (1998: 134) notes, if one
focuses on the omnipotence of capital, it is difficult to explain how
unions make any gains at all.

A further problem with the ultra-left perspective, is that it
fails to come to terms with the authoritarian side of the Leninist
tradition. The alleged need for unified strategic responses to the
centralized forces of monopoly capitalism (Harman 1998) can
provide an excuse for authoritarianism and the use of violence
against those who breach discipline.[1]

To some writers in the Althusserian/ French structuralist
Marxist tradition, the ability of organized labour reflects the
relative autonomy of the capitalist state (Crouch 1979). Under
capitalism, different fractions or segments of the ruling class
compete, allowing for real – albeit temporary – social compromises with unions (Strinati 1982). Nonetheless, structural
Marxists historically discounted the possibilities for real reform
driven by mass action (Crouch 1979).

More pragmatic accounts, such as that of Ralph Miliband,
suggest that different state forms matter; there is a world of
difference between capitalist authoritarianism (examples being
Pinochet's Chile and apartheid South Africa), and liberal democracies. The latter state is relatively autonomous, inherently
flexible, and, hence, more stable than its authoritarian counterparts (Crouch 1979; Miliband 1972). The system does indeed
impart significant power to the working class and its collectives,
enabling real gains to be made, even if the overall capitalist
framework remains in place (Crouch 1979: 29; Miliband 1972;
Wood 2003). The apparent pliability of the capitalist state
underscores the need to break with structuralist Marxism, and
develop a more dynamic state theory that reflects the realities of
liberal democracy, recognizing the fact that trade unions can
force real concessions from capitalism. Even within unions, it is
possible for workers to withdraw legitimacy from an unresponsive leadership, and vest it in shop stewards, and other unofficial
leaders of 'low level collectives' (Salamon 1987: 146). In this
manner, what union representatives actually do at plant level
may be closely in line with rank-and-file wishes and aspirations,
even if national leadership is largely accountable.

Other writers in the radical tradition have departed from Marxism to alternative enlightenment approaches, most notably Jurgen Habermas of the Frankfurt school (Wood 2003). Many aspects of Habermas's work have much in common with earlier thinkers such Max Weber in his emphasis on the relationship between the rational discourse and social progress; if there is room for the former, social progress is possible on incremental lines, a good example being the European welfare state of the 1950s and 1960s (Habermas 1989; Wood 2003). For example, a system of social accords, involving negotiation between organized labour, business and the state, may allow the interests of each constituency to be effectively represented on an ongoing basis (cf. Matzner and Streeck 1991). Democratization represents an ongoing project, rather than a completed process; within formal democracies there is generally space for gradual improvements in the way they operate.

Postmodernism

Postmodern theories of trade unions and industrial relations tend to fall into two categories: theorists of domination and post-industrialists. The first is probably closer to postmodernism's radical origins. For example, to Giles Deleuze, all of society is emeshed in a complex web of power relations; established social actors represent more a reflection of existing reality than a viable force for change. Real progress would involve a deformalization of social relationships, with interactions being purpose orientated, and not regulated or bound by the complexities of social norms, routines, and underlying power networks (see Deleuze and Guattari 1988: 380; Wood 2003). Once grassroots minorities break free from the 'plane of capital' from seeing themselves in terms of other groupings in society, it is possible to completely escape existing power networks; change is possible through 'local deserters' not established collectives (472; Wood 2003). Postmodernists in this camp would view unions as both part of the system, and a further mechanism of domination; the alternative would be to create more open structures for people to 'speak for themselves', a vision inspired by Michel Foucault's predictably ineffectual grouping working for penal reform (cf. Poster 1984).

The second strand draws heavily on Alvin Toffler's (1973) conceptions of post-industrial society and similar works in this genre. To postmodernists in this camp, the postmodern age represents a distinct new epoch; these changes penetrate political, social and economic life. Traditional manufacturing declines, to be replaced by new forms of information work. The tyranny of the factory breaks down to be replaced by new post-fordist forms of production. Post-fordism is, of course, a rather diverse concept, and has been appropriated by a number of different theoretical schools (cf. Sayer 2001: 43). However, to postmodernists in this camp, it represents part of a broader process of social change, and is founded on a redefinition of product philosophy, manufacturing technology, work design and personnel policies (Kern and Schumann 2001). The large factory is replaced by new spatial (and often virtual) forms, with old hierarchies of authority being replaced by more participative and flatter forms of workplace governance, opening the way for faster responses to a rapidly changing and less coherent world. As the roots of conflict between capital and labour decline, the role of unions becomes increasingly superfluous. Moreover, no longer do unions represent the working class, but rather an increasingly hetrogenous grouping (Kelly 1998: 116). Hence, unions are no longer able to offer a coherent voice, speaking out against capitalism. However, whilst postmodernists do correctly point to some long-term changes in economic life, the scale and universality of such changes can be disputed (Kelly 1998: 120). For example, firms may infuse some aspects of flexibility to gain economies of both scale and scope, whilst retaining many of the characteristics of mass production. Increasing diversity in the workforce may lead to both a proliferation of concerns and a sharing of interests in many key areas (Kelly 1998: 120).

Unions, democracy and the third way

The 'third way' perspective of Anthony Giddens, closely associated with New Labour, argues for more localized partnerships. Giddens (2000: 4) asserts that the major social questions of the first half of the twentieth century revolved around the effects of industrialization, and of politically accommodating the working class, and, hence, the labour movement. This led to neo-corpo-ratism, associated with formal tripartite structures, characterized by historic compromises between labour, capital and the state (4). However, given the increasing failures of large centralized institutions, Giddens (2000: 4) argues that there is a need to move away from 'bureaucratic top down approaches' favoured by the left. Individuals have to take responsibility for their own fate: this underscores the need to create a favourable climate for wealth creation, rather than simply emphasizing distribution (4). Within this context, unions should seek to build partnerships with management, aimed at promoting long term profitability, tempered with accountability. What is envis-aged is an emphasis on the mutual responsibilities of employers and employees, with unions and managers engaging in ongoing dialogue 'to introduce change, improve productivity and resolve disputes' (490). This desire is advocated in legislation enacted by the Labour government in Britain, including the Fairness at Work legislation, and through the 1999 Partnership Initiative, the latter providing some funding for new partnership arrange-ments (Guest 2001: 104). Social partnerships have received broad backing from the British labour movement (Beardwell and Holden 2001:490). However, this may simply reflect the vulner-ability of unions, and the desire to retain some vestiges of support from the state and employers (490).

Critics of the new social partnerships have argued that such deals are more likely to be motivated by the exigencies of prof-itability rather than fairness or democracy, and amount to little more than an emasculation of the labour movement (cf. Breitenfellner 1997). Within the factory, unions become bound to the managerial agenda, and outside to a project that does little to ameliorate the excesses of neo-liberalism. Indeed, Stuart Hall argues that the third way does little to constrain the conse-quences of unrestrained markets, and in particular rising social inequality (see Giddens 2000: 11). Fairness at Work legislation may have reversed 'some of the iniquities established under and by previous Conservative administrations' (Gall 2003: 1). Most notably, the 1999 Employment Relations Act allows for unions to acquire statutory recognition when they gain the support of the majority of employees at a specific workplace (1). But, it can be argued that these measures represent more of a redress for past wrongs, than real steps towards a more inclusivist future. Indeed, Moody (1997:122) argues that 'neo-liberal social democrats' are only distinguishable from their right-wing counterparts in that they favour gradualism rather than radical deregulation.

Contemporary institutionalist accounts

As Sabel (1997: 179) notes, the decline of unions, and hence, the failure of collective bargaining in most of the advanced societies, belies the Durkheimian notion that the increased complexity of the division of labour promotes mutual dependence and hence, the development of shared social goals. However, this does not imply that the relentless pursuit of self-interest can provide the basis for progress; rather, self-interest 'appears at war with itself', equally prone to paralyzing selfishness as mutually bene-ficial co-operation. Humans are social animals, who depend on advancing gains through co-operation cemented by trust (179). When the cumulative effects of individual transactions become burdensome, they seek to jointly regulate their affairs. Ultimately through such actions, state policy may be influenced, reshaping the conditions of private transactions (182). In turn, this ultimately leads to the discovery or creation of new prob-lems of collective action, as discontent with existing arrangements mounts (183). Thus, social collectives such as unions are inevitable in complex societies, and play a vital role in ensuring that both firms and wider social structures are responsive to the needs of individuals. Should the former fail, they may be replaced with others, or reinvent themselves in a modified form. Unions represent an agent of accountability, albeit one subject to change or reconstitution. However, the need for unions or similar collectives will always exist, and play a vital role in mediating the interests and concerns of individu-als with broader socio-economic happenings.

Moreover, unless they are subject to some or other form of institutional mediation, markets themselves are inherently unstable and likely to result in gross social inequality (Boyer and Hollingsworth 1997: 434). Markets are only efficient when they are channelled towards clear political and social aims, and 'contained and tamed by a variety of political and social institu-tions' (435). Social systems of production remain embedded within national institutional forms and orbits of trust (437). Differences in national institutional frameworks are likely to both reflect and result in variations in trust relations and in differing forms of representation and social action. Similarly, at regional level forms of co-ordination may characterize particular industrial districts. Hence, markets are embedded in social and political institutions at both national and regional levels (436).

Given the above, unions can play a vital role in mediating the excesses of markets, and reconciling the activities of firms with the very real social needs of stability and equity. Yet, the extent to which unions can achieve this must, of necessity vary greatly from context to context. The diffusion of more flexible forms of production may result in either dualistic or inclusive systems (Hirst and Zeitlin 1997: 224). Under a dualistic system, advanced regional economies increasingly opt out of national regulationary regimes. This results in better work and conditions of work for a coterie of inside workers, but leaves the system open to external macro-economic shocks, and disruption from outsiders. Moreover, such high value added areas of economic activity characterized by flexible forms of production, are supplemented by the activities of 'low value added' firms, often located on the geographical periphery, and characterized by more traditional production paradigms.

Within a dualistic system, unions are presented with a stark choice. They might either confine their activities to representing 'insiders', which, perforce, will lead to a restricted range of concerns, and, within a flexible production regime, inevitably lead to partnership deals with management. The latter may broaden the base of democratic participation in decision making regarding the social organization of work. However, it will constrain the possibility for independent action; democracy may become more meaningful at the micro-level, but at all levels more confined. Alternatively unions may seek to draw together labour market outsiders in a broad social movement project, serving as a voice for the marginalized. However, this would impose its own organizational problems. These may include a lack of legal protection, the insecurity of tenure of potential members and the lack of a social welfare safety net, and the relatively unskilled nature of work in 'outsider' areas of economic activity – sub-contracting, new forms of unskilled service work, and traditional forms of fordist, low value added production. Such dualism is a key characteristic of the Anglo-American model, or what is sometimes referred to as a compartmentalized business system (Whitley 2000).

Under a more inclusive system, firms and industrial districts are integrated into national welfare systems of training and reinsurance, with the gradual extension of more flexible forms of production to less successful regions and groups (Whitley 2000). Such systems are characterized by relatively high levels of trust and cooperation between individuals and organizations. Parties form alliances with their own kind; employers in relatively united employer associations, employee collectives in industrial unions and national-level federations (Marsden 1998: 187). The resultant interchange between employer and employee collectives is likely to incorporate a focus on co-operation, rather than simply competition (Whitley 1997: 236). Such systems are likely to include corporatist deals between unions and employers at national level and negotiated forms of work organization at plant level (such as via works councils), allowing high levels of worker discretion. They are likely to be underpinned by highly institutionalized forms of interchange that may diminish the possibility for spontaneity, with demands that are palpably asystemic being quickly reined in. However, they do allow for union members to express their will at a range of levels: plant, industry, national, and via formal political processes. The latter can be both indirectly via a union-linked social democratic party, and directly at the polls. Multiple forms of participation allow unions and their members to switch their demands to different levels, should one form of participation prove ineffective. However, at most levels, democratic grassroots participation is likely to be indirect, with 'dysfunctional' demands being filtered out (cf. Marsden 1998), whilst labour market outsiders remain firmly outside this virtuous tent (Casey and Gold 2000).

Heightened global competition, and increasing overcapacity in production has forced both manufacturing and service sector firms into progressive rounds of relentless cost-cutting, which has, inevitably, placed inclusivist models under great strain (Brenner 2002). In essence, the question emerges as to whether economies can afford the luxury of inclusivism, given the potential ability of less inclusivist models to seize short-term competitive advantages on the grounds of cost in key areas. Against this must be considered the higher levels of social solidarity – epitomized by the nature of interchange and trust, and lower levels of inequality – typically encountered in such systems (Sako 1998; Wood and Harcourt 2001). Furthermore, inclusivist systems have retained higher proportion of 'good' jobs, characterized by relatively high skills profiles and security of tenure, in established industries (Brenner 2002). However, perhaps the raison d'etre of such systems is the possibility for the further broadening of democracy in an age of declining participation in formal electoral processes.

Contemporary institutionalist accounts, most notably the Parisian regulation school, highlights the close linkage between the economic and the social, in contrast to neo-liberals who discount the worth of the latter (Jessop 2001a: 422). What sets these accounts apart too is a renewed interest in governance mechanisms – including collectives, networks and alliances – which co-ordinate economic activity (423). Such mechanisms do not only operate at the level of the state; politics and democratic participation potentially reside at a range of levels. Renewed interest in governance in part reflects concern as to the increasingly visible limitations of the Anglo-American model and earlier crisis of the conventional Keynesian model (425).

As Hollingsworth notes, the process of reconciling social demand with production involves of necessity a range of governing institutions, going beyond the employment contract on the one hand, and formal state structures on the other (Jessop 2001a: 426). In other words, regulation is very much more than either top-down juridico-political regulation or an enforcement of contractual liabilities. Nor does this entail a return to earlier systems thinking; contemporary institutionalist thinking encompasses issues such as the self-organization of systems (rather than primarily their interaction with other systems) and how they are 'steered' (governed, guided or managed: Jessop 2001a: 427). There are many and varied struggles over the constitution of such objects; regulation and governance are never totally successful, and are always subject to reformation (428). States, markets and intermediate mechanisms of governance are always open to failure; this results in the institutional centre of gravity periodically shifting (438). A contemporary trend has been for the state to become hollowed out, with issues and capacities being shifted to both the trans-national and sub-national levels (Macleod 2001: 547). The impact of unions at each of these levels, and the ability to respond to change in institutional centres of gravity is contingent on organizational forms, the nature of alliances forged, active strategic choices made, and the nature and course of both internal contestations and external struggles. Identity and subject are multi-faceted; the concerns of union members may involve intersections of class, ethnicity, gender, culture and space. Potentially, this allows for an expansion of the political discourse, for new compromises and new modes of development (Jessop 2001b: 523). Lipietz places great emphasis on grassroots alliances between broad social movements as the basis for the cultivation of civic virtues, given the seeming lack of responsiveness of formal democratic institutions (Jessop 2001c: xxii).

Trade unions and the crisis of democracy

Numerous critical writers, including Perry Anderson (2000) and Noreena Hertz (2001), have argued that the power of large corporations has led to the 'death of democracy'. As governments become increasingly unwilling or unable to restrain the worst excesses of the market, democratic participation becomes increasingly meaningless; people are denied a real choice of policies even under multi-partyism.

Two possible conclusions can be drawn from these developments. The first is that the institutional centre has irrevocably shifted away from the state. Formal democratic participation is in effect a broken telephone. Castells (1998) argues that:

> So there is democracy, which is a very important thing, but once we elect our representatives, they have very little capacity to really influence the events along the lines of what they promised to do. The relationship between whom I vote for and what he or she is able to do for me becomes very indirect ... we are seeing a growing voiding of representative democracy in the sense of the ability to make a difference in our lives. It's not that democracy is finished, it's only that the relationship between political representation and what happens in my life is more and more remote and indirect.

Castells argues that the inevitable response to this is the rise of new social movements, grassroots organizations uniting people around issues of common concern when formal structures of democratic participation are seen as unresponsive (Castells 1998). Whilst arguing that movements have a vital role to play in society, Castells cautions that there is a danger that they may degenerate into narrow and intolerant sectionalist organizations, the future should be in new grassroots alliances. By forging new links with like-minded community organizations, but providing a class vision and context, unions can continue to impact on events (Moody 1997: 276).

Social movement unionism aims to represent members not only through collective bargaining, but as Gindin suggests, 'in the fight for everything that affects working people in their communities and country' (Moody 1997: 275). 'In social movement unionism neither unions nor their members are passive in any sense. Unions take an active lead in the streets, as well as in politics' (Moody 1997: 276).

It is argued that democracy is closely related to a union's capacity to mobilize and act. Democracy becomes a means for building solidarity, ensuring accountability, and for devising appropriate strategies (Moody 1997: 276). Social movement unions are characterized by vibrant and internal debate, even over difficult and potentially divisive issue; union members can only reach out to broader constituencies if they are activated through involvement in shaping the union's agenda at both workplace and social levels (277). However, union democracy does not come from nowhere; it is something that has to be fought for, often against established and entrenched union elites; however, the fight for internal union democracy is a necessary precursor to the struggle for greater participation and accountability in wider society (277).

Alternatively, it could be argued that institutions remain nested; the state remains of importance, but coexists with emerging trans-national actors and institutions, and regional formations and interest groupings (Boyer and Hollingsworth 1997). This raises issues such as the acceptability of such complex – and seemingly unaccountable – forms of institutional ordering to the public, the role of existing states in challenging the erosion of their authority, and the extent to which social solidarity is being eroded by the market. However, the lesson of history is that 'taming the market has always been more rewarding over the long term than myopically following it' (477). Imaginative collective forms of coordination can challenge and address the most important political and social issues of the age (477). This would suggest that unions should retain the capacity to engage at a range of levels, at the workplace, in the community, at governmental level, and through both new forms of partnership and established tools of collective action.

Democracy and democratic representation is a contested process both within the union, and in articulating its members' interests in wider society. This would seem to indicate the need for a new theory of democracy – and for practical organizational tools based thereon – for governing both union organization and wider institutions 'nested in a complex world' (cf. Boyer and Hollingsworth 1997: 477).

Conclusion

As ostensibly the collective voice of their members, what unions do is inherently bound up with questions of democracy. This concerns both the extent to which union leaders accurately represent the wishes of, and are accountable to, the rank and file, and the manner in which they can ensure that these interests are represented within and without the workplace. To neo-liberals the effects of these challenges are necessarily contradictory; to be effective at all but the most micro-level, union leaders have to constantly reign in their membership. This 'Olsonian trap' means that unions are only in a position to negotiate or reach deals with other collectives if they can force their members to keep to any agreements made. In contrast, the Leninist tradition is equally dismissive of unions but for a different reason; they are inherently a feature of the capitalist system unless guided by a vanguardist party. Whilst many postmodernists have dismissed unions as yet another tool of domination by the status quo others have suggested that they have become irrelevant owing to new forms of work organization, participation and involvement.

However, there are a range of other accounts that are rather more optimistic about both the internal and external dimensions of union democracy, ranging from social movement theories to regulationist accounts. What these theories have in common is a belief that unions can both serve as an effective mechanism for articulating the concerns of the rank and file, and in promoting more accountable and sustainable macroeconomic policies. They reflect the renewed interest in the potential of civil society groupings given the seeming sclerosis of formal political institutions in the advanced societies, and the present crises of neo-liberalism.

Note

1 For example, whilst often upheld as a model for shopfloor democracy, the South African independent unions do not have an unblemished record in this regard. On the one hand, there are remarkably high levels of participation in union meetings, with elections for office bearers being regularly held. On the other hand, at times violence has been used to enforce unity, whilst there are instances where specific categories of worker (such as migrants dwelling in hostels) have deliberately sought to exclude others. It could be argued that, in the bleak years of the late apartheid era, it was necessary for the opposition to be closely unified in opposing the combined forces of capital and the apartheid state. However, this would ascribe a unity to both capital and the ruling group that was, at certain historic moments, lacking. Moreover, in certain cases, the strategic use of violence, such as during the 1997 railways workers strike, caused organized labour to lose the moral high ground, providing the apartheid state with excuses to mount a bloody counter-attack.

References

Anderson, P. 2000. 'Renewals', *New Left Review*, 1, 239: 5–24.

Aron, R. 1950. 'Social Science and the Ruling Class', *British Journal of Sociology*, 1, 1: 5–11.

Beardwell, I. and Holden, L. 2001. *Human Resource Management: A Contemporary Approach*. London: Prentice Hall.

Boyer, R. and Hollingsworth, J. R. 1997. 'From National Embeddedness to Spatial and Institutional Nestedness', in Hollingsworth, J. R. and Boyer, R. (eds.), *Contemporary Capitalism: the Embeddedness of Institutions*. Cambridge: Cambridge University Press.

Breitenfellner, A. 1997. 'Global Unionism: a Potential Player', *International Labour Review*, 136, 4: 531–555.

Brenner, R. 2002. *The Boom and the Bubble: The US in the World Economy*. London: Verso.

Callinicos, A. 1997. 'Where Does Political Power Lie?', *International Socialist Review*, 206: www.isf.org.uk.

Casey, B. and Gold, M. 2000. *Social Partnerships and Economic Performance*. Cheltenham: Edward Elgar.

Castells, M. 1998. 'Interview conducted by Bregtje van der Haak', *DNW*, September.

Crouch, C. 1979. 'The State, Capital and Liberal Democracy', in Crouch, C. (ed.), *State and Economy in Contemporary Capitalism*. London: Croom Helm.

Deleuze, G. and Guattari, F. 1988. *A Thousand Plateaus*. Minneapolis: University of Minnesota Press.

Dunlop, J. T. 1975. 'Political Systems and Industrial Relations', in Barrett, B., Beishon, J. and Rhodee, E. (eds.), *Industrial Relations and Wider Society*. Drayton: Collier-Macmillan.

Engels, F. 1952. *The Condition of the Working Class in Britain in 1844*. London: Allen and Unwin.

Flanders, A. 1975. 'Industrial Relations: What Is Wrong with the System?', in Barrett, B., Beishon, J. and Rhodee, E. (eds.), *Industrial Relations and Wider Society*. Drayton: Collier-Macmillan.

Foucault, M. 1979. *Discipline and Punish*. Harmondsworth: Penguin.

Fox, A. 1975. 'Ideologies of Managers and Collectives', in Barrett, B., Beishon, J. and Rhodee, E. (eds.), *Industrial Relations and Wider Society*. Drayton: Collier-Macmillan.

Gall, G. 2003. 'Introduction', in Gall, G. (ed.), *Union Organizing: Campaigning for Union Recognition*. London: Routledge.

Giddens, A. 1979. *Capitalism and Modern Social Theory: an Analysis of the Writings of Marx, Durkheim, and Max Weber*. Cambridge: Cambridge University Press.

—— 1981. *The Class Structure of the Advanced Societies*. London: Unwin.

—— 2000. *The Third way and Its Critics*. Cambridge: Polity.

Guest, D. 2001. 'Industrial Relations and Human Resource Management', in Storey, J. (ed.), *Human Resource Management*. London: Thomson Learning.

Habermas, J. 1989. *The New Conservatism*. Cambridge: Polity.

Harman, C. 1998. 'For Democratic Centralism', *International Socialism Journal*, 80: www.isf.org.uk.

Hertz, L. 2001. *The Silent Takeover: Global Capitalism and the Death of Democracy*. London: Heinemann.

Hirst, P. and Zeitlin, J. 1997. 'Flexible Specialization: Theory and Evidence in the Analysis of Institutional Change', in Hollingsworth, J. R. and Boyer, R. (eds.), *Contemporary Capitalism: The Embeddedness of Institutions*. Cambridge: Cambridge University Press.

Jessop, B. 2001a. 'The Regulation Approach, Governance and Post-Fordism: Alternative Perspectives on Economic and Political Change?', in Jessop, B. (ed.), *Developments and Extensions: Regulation Theory and the Crisis of Capitalism*, Volume 5. London: Edward Elgar.

—— 2001b. 'Twenty Years of the Parisian Regulation Approach: The Paradox of Success Abroad and Failure at Home', in Jessop, B. (ed.), *Developments and Extensions: Regulation Theory and the Crisis of Capitalism*, Volume 5. London: Edward Elgar.

—— 2001c. 'Series Preface', in Jessop, B. (ed.), *Developments and Extensions: Regulation Theory and the Crisis of Capitalism*, Volume 5. London: Edward Elgar.

Kelly, J. 1998. *Rethinking Industrial Relations: Mobilization, Collectivism and Long Waves*. London: Routledge.

Kern, H. and Schumann, M. 2001. 'New Concepts of Production in West German Plants', in Jessop, B. (ed.), *Regulationist Perspectives on Fordism and Post-Fordism: Regulation Theory and the Crisis of Capitalism*, Volume 3. London: Edward Elgar.

Lane, C. 1998. 'Theories and Issues in the Study of Trust', in Lane, C. and Bachman, R. (eds.), *Trust Within and Between Organizations*. Oxford: Oxford University Press.

Lee, J. and Worsley, P. 1972. 'The Politics of Inequality', in Worsley, P. (ed.),

Problems of Modern Sociology. London: Penguin.

Lefebvre, R. 1966. *The Sociology of Karl Marx*. London: Penguin.

Lenin, V. I. 1933. *The State and Revolution*. Bournemouth: The Little Lenin Library.

Macleod, G. 2001. 'Globalizing Parisian Thought Waves', in Jessop, B. (ed.), *Developments and Extensions: Regulation Theory and the Crisis of Capitalism, Volume 5*. London: Edward Elgar.

Marsden, D. 1998. 'Understanding the Role of Interfirm Institutions in Sustaining Trust within the Employment Relationship', in Lane, C. and Bachman, R. (eds.), *Trust Within and Between Organizations*. Oxford: Oxford University Press.

Matzner, E. and Streeck, W. 1991. 'Towards a Socio-Economics of Employment in a Post-Keynesian Economy', in Matzner, E. and Streeck, W. (eds.), *Beyond Keynesianism: the Socio-Economics of Production and Full Employment*. Aldershot: Edward Elgar.

Michels, R. 1972. 'Power in the Party', in Worsley, P. (ed.), *Problems of Modern Sociology*. London: Penguin.

Miliband, R. 1972. *Parliamentary Socialism*. London: Merlin.

Moody, K. 1997. *Workers in a Lean World*. London: Verso.

Nozick, R. 1984. 'Moral Consciousness and Distributive Justice', in Sandel, M. (ed.), *Liberalism and Its Critics*. Oxford: Basil Blackwell.

Olson, M. 1982. *The Rise and Decline of Nations: Economic Growth, Stagflation and Social Rigidities*. New Haven: Yale University Press.

—— 2000. 'Dictatorship, Democracy and Development', in Olson, M. and Kahkonen, S. (eds.), *The Not-So-Dismal Science: A Broader View of Economies and Societies*. Oxford: Oxford University Press.

Olson, M. and Kahkonen, S. 2002. 'Introduction: The Broader View', in Olson, M. and Kahkonen, S. (eds.), *The Not-So-Dismal Science: A Broader View of Economies and Societies*. Oxford: Oxford University Press.

Poster, M. 1984. *Foucault, Marxism and History*. Cambridge: Polity.

Sabel, C. 1997. 'Constitutional Orders: Trust Building and Response to Change', in Hollingsworth, J. R. and Boyer, R. (eds.), *Contemporary Capitalism: The Embeddedness of Institutions*. Cambridge: Cambridge University Press.

Sako, M. 1998. 'Does Trust Improve Business Performance?', in Lane, C. and Bachman, R. (eds.), *Trust Within and Between Organizations*. Oxford: Oxford University Press.

Salamon, M. 1987. *Industrial Relations*. New York:Prentice Hall.

Sayer, A. 2001. 'Postfordism in Question', in Jessop, B. (ed.), *Regulationist Perspectives on fordism and Post-fordism: Regulation Theory and the Crisis of Capitalism, Volume 3*. London: Edward Elgar.

Strinati, D. 1982. *Capitalism, the State and Industrial Relations*. London: Croom Helm.

Toffler, A. 1973. *Future Shock*. London: Pan.

Whitley, R. 1997. 'The Social Regulation of Work Systems', in Whitley, R. and Kristensen, P. H., *Governance at Work: The Social Regulation of Economic Relations*. Oxford: Oxford University Press.

—— 2000. *Divergent Capitalisms*. Oxford: Oxford University Press.

Wood, G. 2003. 'Participation, State, Economy and Society', in Burnell, P. (ed.), *Democratization Through the Looking Glass*. Manchester: Manchester University Press.

Wood, G. and Harcourt, M. 2001. 'The Consequences of Neo-Corporatism: A Syncretic Analysis', *International Journal of Sociology and Social Policy*, 20, 8: 1–22.

Wright, E. O. 1999. 'Metatheoretical Foundation of Charles Tilly's Durable Inequality', revised version of paper presented at the Social Science History Conference, Chicago, Ill., 20 November.

3

Neo-liberal reforms and accords: are they compatible with democracy?

MARK HARCOURT

Since the early 1980s, many countries across the globe have experimented with neo-liberal reforms, which have entailed reducing state intervention in the economy and freeing individuals and private corporations to set prices and determine outputs. Much is known about the often very negative impacts of these reforms on incomes, unemployment, and poverty. Much less discussed are the effects of these reforms on the political sphere, particularly the institutions and practices of democracy. Even less is known about the alternatives to neo-liberal reform and how they might affect the political sphere. This chapter seeks to redress this imbalance by comparing the orthodox, neo-liberal reform strategy with a more heterodox alternative, based on compromises between peak bodies representing capital, labour, the state, and other groups and formalized in national-level agreements called pacts or accords.

The chapter starts with a description of neo-liberalism and the particular types of neo-liberal reforms which the International Monetary Fund (IMF) and World Bank have urged many developing countries to implement. It then articulates the basic incongruities between neo-liberal reform and democracy, and how the various institutions characterizing the latter have had to be suspended, marginalized, or undermined to facilitate adoption of the former. Having established the political shortcomings of neo-liberal reform, the chapter moves on to define and describe accords. Next, it deals with the fundamental compatibility of accord negotiation with democratic processes and values. The chapter also outlines how internal democracy within the peak bodies that negotiate accords can actually improve popular acceptance of, and support for, accords. Finally, empirical evidence is used to establish the many economic benefits of accords.

What is neo-liberal economic reform?

The Anglo-Saxon, developed market economies, particularly Britain, Canada and the USA, have long been the embodiment of a neo-liberal or orthodox economic order, in the sense that economic development has been the primary preserve of private firms and individuals, freely interacting via product and factor markets. In neo-liberal societies, the state plays a relatively residual and passive role. It supports the private arrangements firms and individuals enter into by providing a legal framework for contract enforcement and dispute mediation and adjudication. It also provides an income floor, a so-called safety net, for those individuals who are unable to 'make it' on their own in a market economy. The state also regulates certain aspects of economic activity, such as health and safety, where asymmetrical access to information renders one party (usually the worker or consumer) vulnerable to exploitation by the other (usually the firm). However, the state's broader role in economic development remains stunted. In particular, the state plays little or no role in fostering one sector over another. Incentives for economic development, such as they are, tend to be non-specific. For instance, research and development tax credits may be made available to all firms. Furthermore, the state interferes relatively rarely in setting prices or mandating levels of production or manipulating either of these through subsidies.

Anglo-Saxon societies, which were already among the most neo-liberal in the world in the late 1970s, have embraced an even more purist version of the neo-liberal creed since then. In the USA, for instance, a handful of industries, such as trucking, airlines and finance, which had been regulated, have now been deregulated. In the UK, several organisations, which had been in government hands, have been privatized. Chief among these have been British Gas, British Steel, British Telecom and British Airways.

The swing to neo-liberal policies has not been confined to the richer Anglo-Saxon countries. Many poorer countries have adopted neo-liberal policies, often at the behest of the International Monetary Fund, the World Bank, Washington-based bureaucrats with connections to the major private lenders, or a combination of all three. In fact, so powerful have these groups been in setting the development agenda in many less developed countries (LDCs) that they have been collectively referred to as the 'Washington Consensus'. In many cases, access to both public and private loans and foreign aid has been made contingent, at least to some extent, on implementing a neo-liberal economic strategy.

In the poorer parts of the world, a neo-liberal strategy has typically involved a combination of the following elements. First, to qualify for IMF assistance, LDCs have been required to pursue tight monetary and fiscal policies aimed at delivering low inflation, a reduction in government deficits and eventually debt as well, and a balance of payments in the national income accounts. These policies are supposed to work by deflating aggregate demand, thereby reducing the public's appetite for imports and alleviating price and wage pressures in overly-tight markets. Other aspects of the policy mix include a fixed nominal exchange rate to prevent import prices from increasing and feeding into domestic inflation.

Second, to qualify for World Bank assistance, LDCs are normally forced to implement what has been called a Structural Adjustment Program of microeconomic reforms. These reforms typically entail liberalizing product and factor markets of government interference and control. For instance, international trade is liberalized by eliminating quotas and reducing and homogenizing tariffs, with the eventual goal being free trade. Capital markets are liberalized by lifting ceilings on interest rates and by allowing capital to move freely across international borders through the abolition of foreign exchange controls. Labour markets are liberalized by eliminating statutory protections against dismissal, lowering or eliminating minimum wages, and by removing institutions which favour unionization or provide unions with labour market influence. The effects of the tax system on economic activity are also neutralized, often by replacing a morass of excise and sales taxes with a one-size-fits-all value-added tax. Finally, government-owned enterprises are privatized, and their subsidies phased out.

Neo-liberalism: is it anti-democratic?

Many scholars (see Austin 2000; Pickel 1993) have long argued that authoritarian regimes are better able to carry out neo-liberal reforms than their democratic counterparts for the following reasons. First, democratic regimes are 'weaker' than authoritarian ones. The process of legislating reforms in a democracy requires multiple readings of proposed laws, and extensive select committee hearings. All of this makes passing legislation to enact reforms a slow and arduous process. Within a given timeframe, even those democratic regimes with a mandate to implement reforms achieve less than their authoritarian counterparts (Pickel 1993).

Second, political business cycle theorists have long argued that democratic regimes are ultimately answerable to the public, and so rational politicians, interested in re-election, are highly susceptible to populist pressures (Lindbeck 1976; Nordhaus 1975; Tufte 1978). Neo-liberal policies ordinarily involve obvious, painful sacrifices over the short term. Workers lose their jobs; firms go bankrupt; real wages fall; profits are squeezed. In contrast, the economic gains of reform are less certain, take longer to materialize, and are spread out over a number of years. New industries, new companies, and new jobs take longer to create than old ones do to destroy. With a three- or five-year electoral cycle, democratic governments can count on being in office long enough to take the blame for any costs of reform, but not long enough to take the credit for any benefits. As a result, democratic governments naturally seek re-election by pursuing policies whose gains are immediate and obvious and whose costs are delayed and subtle. Any government that tries to reform is likely to be ousted by any opposition party or parties, which advocate more populist policies.

Populist pressures are likely to be particularly acute, where highly organized rentier groups can mobilize people and resources to oppose unpopular, neo-liberal policies (see, for example, Crisp 1998). Rentier groups are groups that earn economic rent as a result of state policies. For instance, manufacturing firms in many developing countries earn economic rents, because their monopoly positions in domestic product markets are maintained by high tariffs and heavy government subsidies, which protect them from foreign and domestic competition, respectively (see, for example, Crisp 1998). Such groups often bear the brunt of structural adjustment, and earn none of the expected gains. They therefore have strong incentives to fight any microeconomic reform which threatens their interests.

In contrast, beneficiaries of neo-liberal reform, such as exporters, are unlikely to be as large or as organized, at least in terms of a highly regulated and protected economy's current configuration of industries and organizations. Moreover, given the diffuse and long-term nature of the benefits received, they may not even identify themselves as potential beneficiaries. If a neo-liberal program involves important stabilization elements, such as fiscal retrenchment and monetary tightening, they may even see themselves as net losers of reform. Paradoxically, a united opposition to the short-term pain of neo-liberal reforms may make allies of the long-term losers and winners of reform.

Several large-scale empirical studies provide support for political business cycle (PBC) theory by showing strong links in the timing of populist, 'feel good' policies and elections. For instance, the evidence indicates that fiscal deficits (Block 2002; Moyo 1999; Schuknecht 1996, 2000; Shi and Svensson 2000), government capital expenditures (Khemani 2000), road construction (Khemani 2000), government consumption spending (Ames 1987; Shi and Svensson, 2000), and the money supply (Block 2002; Fouda 1997) tend to rise in election years, whereas taxes tend to fall (Khemani 2000). Moreover, these sorts of findings hold for a diverse range of developed and developing countries (Moyo 1999; Shi and Svensson 2000), including several in Africa (Block 2002; Fouda 1997), Latin America (Ames 1987), and Asia (Khemani 2000).

The experiences of many countries, which have experimented with far-reaching neo-liberal reforms, also bear out the predictions of the theorists. Reforms have often been initiated by despotic regimes, and then partially or fully unravelled by their democratic successors, yielding to strong populist pressures. The cases of Ghana and Turkey are illustrative. In Ghana, the reforms began in 1983 under the auspices of Flight Lieutenant Jerry Rawlings, the nation's military dictator. The budget deficit was reduced by cutting food and other subsidies and reducing spending on health and education. The currency was devalued, price controls on many manufactured goods abolished, and some firms privatized. The changes were not popular, but this made little difference to a regime which tolerated little public dissent and had few, if any, avenues for interest group consultation and participation around issues of policy choice, design, and implementation. In addition, as an unelected politician, Rawlings was willing to take the long view, believing that the public would eventually embrace reform if they waited long enough to see its positive effects. A return to restricted democratic rule in 1992 and full democratic rule in 1996 have led to a slowing down, and even reversal, of some reforms. The elected government has not been immune to populist pressures, particularly given the promises of opposition parties. In 1993, for instance, civil servants were given a highly inflationary increase in pay, in part to win their favour. Government spending increased, particularly in the rural areas, to help retain the support of farmers. However, the main pillars of a reform program remain, in part to secure continued funding from the IMF (Jeong 1998).

Turkey's experiences with economic reform have been similar. With the return of military rule during 1980–83, the country embarked on an aggressive and initially highly successful reform process. Reforms were continued from 1983 to 1987 by a highly centralized civilian administration, led by Turgut Ozal, in semi-democratic conditions, where the main political parties remained banished. A large legislative majority, party discipline, strong executive powers, and the support of an apolitical technocratic elite all helped to insulate Ozal from populist pressures during his term of office. However, with the return of full democracy after 1987, the previously banned, traditional parties re-emerged as major political forces. The political system subsequently fragmented, with multiple parties vying for popular support. In the 1990s, successive, weak, coalition governments had neither the will nor the inclination to continue with many of the reforms (Sayari 1996/97).

The importance of authoritarian governance is not limited to overtly authoritarian regimes. Paradoxically, several influential economists are strong advocates of political democracy, but in combination with undemocratic government institutions (Marangos 2002). Authoritarian decision making, unencumbered by democratic accountability processes, is seen as helpful to the adoption of neo-liberal policies even within democracies (Marangos 2002). In many countries, unelected agencies have been specially created to implement important parts of a reform program, often at the behest of the pundits. In addition, key decision rules, sometimes enshrined in statutes or even constitutions, have been put in place to protect reforms from the tinkering tendencies of elected officials and their minions. Nowhere is this perhaps more apparent than with monetary policy. Independent central banks have been created in countries as diverse as Chile, Peru, Estonia, Hungary, Poland, New Zealand, and Singapore (Grabel 2000; Quispe-Agnoli 2001). Many of these have legally mandated inflation targets which their chief executives are contractually obliged to achieve. Some countries, such as Ecuador, El Salvador, and Panama, have adopted the US dollar as their currency, thereby abdicating any domestic discretion over monetary policy (Quispe-Agnoli 2001). Others, like Argentina, have adopted currency boards, with similar effects (Quispe-Agnoli 2001).

Other aspects of authoritarian governance have also helped established democracies with their neo-liberal reforms, as the examples of New Zealand and Venezuela make clear. For the New Zealand case, Nagel (1998) has argued that the pace and scale of neo-liberal reforms were only made possible by undemocratic features of its political and governmental systems. At the time, the first-past-the-post voting system gave the Labour Party a free hand to implement reforms, without having to make compromises with a potentially troublesome coalition partner. The unicameral legislature and the absence of a presidential veto made it easy to pass new legislation. The unitary system of government meant that there were no provincial or state governments, with primary or sole jurisdiction over the design of key policy areas and the control of key programme expenditures. The central government was therefore free to enact new legislation in any aspect of economic or social activity. The conventions of party discipline and cabinet solidarity also ensured that a majority of parliamentarians voted for any new bill, as long as a majority of cabinet members, as few as 11 ministers, were supportive. In the absence of judicial review and a formal constitution, there were also no major legal barriers to carrying out what many now refer to as a neo-liberal revolution. In implementing the reforms, the Labour government was aided by a unified group of very willing and ideologically committed technocrats in its most powerful ministry, the Treasury Department (Ministry of Finance). Finally, Nagel (1998) has argued that, in some respects, the reforms were even shielded from the most important democratic accountability process, namely that associated with the ballot box. In 1984, in the election leading up to the first set of reforms, the public was never told, and had no reason to suspect, given the party's social democratic past, that Labour favoured reform. In 1987, Labour was elected again, but this time because a high proportion of otherwise disapproving voters were still prepared to vote 'Labour' for the party's highly appealing social policies: homosexual law reform, Maori land claims, women's rights, environmental protection and nuclear disarmament.

From 1989 to 1993, another long-standing democracy, Venezuela, also experimented with anti-democratic measures to implement neo-liberal reforms (Crisp 1998). President Carlos Andres Perez knew that the Venezuelan Congress would either delay or halt his reform program. For this reason, he used presidential decrees rather than legislative enactments to push through most of his reforms. For instance, import licences, agricultural subsidies, and some restrictions on foreign direct investment were eliminated; tariffs were reduced; and some public firms were corporatized in preparation for privatization, all without explicit enactments by Congress. Perez also realized that the organized labour and capital interests, which dominated the governing boards of most of Venezuela's public-sector organizations, would resist any type of reform. As a result, he created a parallel bureaucracy of new agencies, staffed by apolitical technocrats and reform-minded academics, to implement his neo-liberal policies (Crisp 1998).

Popular resistance to the Venezuelan reforms was intense. The elimination of price controls on public transit set off major riots on 27 February 1989. The president's administration responded with brutal suppression, resulting in hundreds of deaths (Crisp 1998: 22). There were two coup attempts, one in February and the other in November of 1992 (Crisp 1998: 22). Most of Congress actively opposed the president at every turn. A law making the central bank independent took years to pass. Tax reforms were never enacted while Perez was in office (Crisp 1998). In the end, Congress deposed Perez in 1993 on trumped-up corruption charges (Rey 1993 cited in Crisp 1998). Perez's successor, Rafael Caldera, abandoned many of the reforms, and reverted to a populist programme of price controls and large budget deficits.

What is the accord alternative?

Accords have no single definition. However, pundits do argue that accords share several key characteristics. First, accords are national-level pacts between the state, union federations and possibly also employer federations. Second, their negotiation is characterized by the making of trade-offs among the parties; outcomes are not simply imposed by one party on another. The stress is on establishing agreement, making compromises, and furthering understanding of contrary viewpoints. Third, accords ordinarily have major national, social and economic goals, including unemployment, poverty, inflation and deficit reduction among others. Fourth, goal accomplishment typically involves the negotiated trade-offs mentioned above. For example, the state might consent to pension improvements in return for union promises of wage moderation.

Accords: are they democratic?

Accords are, by their nature, inherently democratic. Non-governmental organizations (NGOs) representing 'the people' are brought directly into the policy design and implementation process. In particular, NGOs representing the larger, and potentially most affected, groups are involved in making and carrying out policies. In many neo-corporatist societies, the accord negotiation process was originally limited to just a few NGOs: the major employer and union federations. Although these usually covered a high proportion of employees and employers, it would still be a fair criticism to say that, in the past, NGOs involved in accord negotiations only stood for producer interests. Nevertheless, in more recent years, NGOs that represent the unemployed, the poor, women and the green movement have not been left out of accord negotiations. Together, these NGOs act for a broad cross-section of the public and its multi-faceted interests as producers, consumers and ordinary citizens. Policy is not driven solely by the ideological predilections of a small, narrowly focused group of academics and bureaucrats, working in one government ministry or agency.

The decision-making process associated with accords is also inherently democratic. NGOs do not simply dictate policies to passive politicians, whose acquiescence is ensured through a combination of campaign funding, media manipulation and trade union or corporate indoctrination. On the contrary, NGOs must deal with other NGOs, representing perhaps diametrically opposed interests. Capital must deal with labour, for example. This means that any deal must be brokered through a negotiation process, where the various actors make compromises and trade-offs among themselves to reach an agreement. The state is far from passive in these proceedings, often playing an active, facilitative role in using inducements, and possibly even threats, to push negotiations towards a particular set of outcomes.

Accords also strengthen democracy by promoting some of the freedoms necessary to its underlying functioning. In particular, the involvement of NGOs in policy formulation provides individuals and groups with opportunities to exercise their freedoms of association and expression, and encourages them to get organized, if they are not already, so that they can make use of these freedoms. Without such opportunities for involvement, these freedoms are likely to remain nothing more than 'paper freedoms', which exist in a constitutional sense but which are rarely exercised in practice.

Accord negotiation also helps to consolidate nascent democratic rule in nations more used to authoritarianism. It gives radical groups on both the left and right some influence on the policy process, and therefore less reason to want to overthrow democratic institutions through violent revolution or coup. It provides a highly institutionalized way to vent anger towards, and frustration with, one's opponents, without the need to 'take to the streets'. Finally, it co-opts radical groups by having them assume partial responsibility for negotiated policies and any negative outcomes they may generate. In serving these functions, accords have eased the transition to democratic rule in several former dictatorships, perhaps most noteworthy of which was Spain in the 1970s (Foweraker 1987; Martinez Lucio 1991; Rigby and Lawlor 1994).

Accords: do they promote democracy within NGOs?

Accords may well promote and strengthen political democracy in the wider society, but do they encourage and support democracy within NGOs? Neo-corporatist scholars (see, for example, Goldthorpe 1984; Schmitter and Lehmbruch 1979) have addressed this issue by examining the operation of democratic processes within the labour movement, but their analyses could just as easily apply to any democratically structured NGOs. In general, most of these theorists have traditionally argued that highly centralized negotiations among peak-level organizations representing labour, capital, and the state necessarily undermine or restrict internal union democracy. However, more recently, Baccaro has developed and empirically substantiated a more convincing view, which posits that internal union democracy, although far from being a prerequisite, actually facilitates central negotiations among labour, capital, and the state (Baccaro 2000, 2001a, 2001b, 2002). These two contradictory perspectives are outlined below.

In the traditional, neo-corporatist view, union leaders must be free to negotiate with the other social partners, the state and the employers, unencumbered by procedures which hold the leaders accountable to their membership. This means that democratic processes are generally weak and ineffectual. For instance, elections are infrequent. Most senior union officials are appointed by union leaders rather than elected by members. Decision making is heavily centralized, with the union leaders making the lion's share of the most important decisions. Major issues are not subject to ratification votes. There are few, if any, forums where members can 'voice' opposition to formal policies proposed by the leaders (see, for example, Goldthorpe 1984; Schmitter and Lehmbruch 1979).

Limits on 'voice' are not, however, enough. Limits on members' freedom of action are also necessary. For instance, disgruntled members should not have the freedom to 'vote with their feet' by exiting a union they are unhappy with to join another union more willing to act as a members' advocate. Likewise, they should not have the freedom to take action which might undermine an accord by, for example, engaging in strike activity for higher wages without their leaders' approval. Finally, and perhaps most importantly, they should not be in a position to leave the union movement altogether, and opt for an individual contract with their employer. Allowing any of these actions to take place would enable members to use the threat of exit to pressure their leaders into acting more in accordance with members' wishes.

Why are anti-democratic measures even needed? Neo-corporatist scholars have claimed that union leaders are intellectually better able to understand national, economic issues, and the roles that unions can play in securing superior economic outcomes, than the more sectarian, occupation- and industry-focused rank and file. Furthermore, union leadership roles naturally place the holders of these roles in a better position to see the 'big picture', whereas the rank and file tend to be preoccupied by everyday, shopfloor issues of little consequence to the wider public (Streeck 1982). In addition, the successful negotiation of national-level agreements is assumed to be in the self-interests of union leaders. After all, such agreements can give union leaders power and influence, politically, as well as celebrity status while in the media's eye. A high-profile impact on the national economy might also pave the way for political office and even a directorship with a large corporation (Sabel 1981).

Neo-corporatist scholars acknowledge that social accords can be in the interests of union members. The benefits an accord can provide in terms of jobs, social welfare improvements, and tax cuts may far outweigh the benefits of a nominal wage increase, especially one that is eroded by the price inflation caused by a general increase in nominal wages. However, Olson (1965 and 1982) was the first to recognize that what is in the interests of workers as a collective is not necessarily in their interests as individuals. The fact is that many of the benefits afforded through social accords are 'public goods', in the sense that making them available to one makes them available to all. For instance, the advantages of a macroeconomic environment characterized by low inflation are generally available to anyone living and working in that kind of environment. A worker who does not agree to a modest wage increase stands to benefit as much from low inflation as other workers whose agreement to modest wage increases helped generate the low inflation. Each worker also knows that, if his or her union secures a relatively high wage increase for its members, this will have an imperceptibly small impact on national price inflation. In most countries, individual unions, and the employers they bargain with, are simply too small in relation to the overall size of the economy to have any measurable effect on macro-economic variables like inflation and unemployment (Calmfors and Driffil 1988). For these reasons, an individual trade unionist will want to 'freeride' (Tarantelli 1986). She will want her union leaders to pursue an aggressive negotiating stance, and make no concessions on wages. Since all rational trade unionists will think this way, democratically controlled unions will prove reluctant to any form of wage moderation in an accord. As a result, accords are only feasible in those situations where union leaders are shielded from the demands of the rank and file. They are therefore incompatible with all but the most residual forms of union democracy (Crouch 1982).

Despite the appeal of these arguments, they are not corroborated by the empirical evidence. On the one hand, there are certainly examples of countries with democratic union movements, which have had limited successes with accords. The United Kingdom's short-lived experimentation with pacts, or social concertation, in the 1970s is one such case. On the other hand, there are certainly other countries which have combined democratic unions with a highly successful track record of longstanding accords. Norway and Sweden are typical of this group (Lange 1984).

Baccaro (2000, 2001a, 2001b, 2002) convincingly argues for the contrary position, that internal democracy facilitates, rather than hinders, the process of forming and sustaining a social accord. The differences between the Baccaro and neo-corporatist viewpoints start with their conception of the union member. In the traditional view, a member only cares about the substantive outcomes of a union leader's decision. The only substantive outcomes that matter are those which affect the member's welfare in the short term (see, for example, Goldthorpe 1984; Schmitter and Lehmbruch 1979). Furthermore, the nature of the relationships between decision, substantive outcomes, and members' welfare are also well-understood and known in advance. As a result, determining membership support or opposition is a relatively simple exercise; any decision that does not self-evidently improve the welfare of most members in the short term will be opposed.

Baccaro's conception of the union member is more realistic, if more complicated. Members' concerns are multidimensional. In particular, members care about procedural fairness as an end in itself, where the 'rightness' of any decision is judged at least partially in terms of how it was arrived at (Baccaro 2000, 2001a, 2001b, 2002). All else equal, decisions made in a fair manner are more likely to be supported than decisions made in an unfair manner. What is a fairly made decision? A fairly made decision is one which typically allows those whose lives are most likely to be affected by the decision, some degree of influence in the decision-making process. At its most basic, it means keeping affected parties informed of developments in the decision-making process. At its most involved, it means having the affected parties make the decision themselves.

None of this implies that substantive outcomes are totally irrelevant. On the contrary, they are still very important, but members have both ethical and pragmatic concerns about these outcomes. Ethical concerns are those which pertain to the member's basic sense of 'right' and 'wrong', whether, in principle, the decision has appropriate or inappropriate consequences for others. Pragmatic concerns are self-interested and focus on the implications of the decision for the individual member. Unlike in the traditional perspective, these concerns embrace both short-term and long-term considerations. However, many of these consequences are not well understood in advance. Members are bounded rational; they do not have the time, resources, or mental processing capacity to accurately assess the consequences of any and all aspects of every decision. Instead, they must rely on others for information, making them open to persuasion (Baccaro 2001a, 2001b).

What are the implications of Baccaro's analysis for the compatibility of union democracy and accord implementation? Union decisions arrived at through democratic processes are more likely to be viewed as procedurally fair and therefore acceptable to the membership, even when these decisions involve deleterious consequences for some members. Votes are particularly important to creating perceptions of procedural fairness in democratic organizations. As such, they play a major legitimization role: any leader who represents the majority can credibly claim to have a popular mandate to pursue a particular course of action. In contrast, leaders who represent minority views can only credibly claim to represent the 'will of the people', when that will has not yet been expressed through a vote but has been expressed through the mass rallies and protests of a vocal minority. In Italy, for example, Baccaro (2000, 2002) shows that leaders were able to legitimize national-level accords on wage indexation in 1983 and 1993 and pension reform in 1995 by holding referenda, in which a majority of voters expressed support for each accord. In the absence of similar referenda in 1984 and 1992 over wage indexation and 1994 over pension reform, radical, opposition groups credibly claimed, in the absence of evidence to the contrary, that their mass rallies and demonstrations indicated popular opposition to the accords. When referenda were used, opposition was muted and the accords were adopted with minimum fuss. When referenda were not used, protests were widespread, often large in scale, and sometimes violent. Leaders misinterpreted these events as indicative of the popular mood, and so the accords were shelved.

Trade union members may or may not vote for an accord. Many may follow their short-term interests and decide that the short-term sacrifices they are called upon to make are not worth the long-term benefits they and other groups receive in return. Other unionists may decide the opposite by placing their long-term interests, or the interests of others, ahead of their short-term interests. Theory cannot tell us what union members are likely to think or do (Baccaro 2001a, 2001b).

Bounded rationality also means that many trade unionists are unlikely to have highly developed, and totally informed, opinions about the issues. Many may be open to changing their preferences on the basis of new information from credible sources. Trade union leaders are likely to be important sources of such information. Their credibility with the membership may also be strong, particularly if they have nothing to personally gain by supporting one position over another. Consultative processes associated with union democracy, such as union meetings and informal interactions with shop stewards, afford union leaders with opportunities to communicate new information to members and convince them to change their views. In particular, these consultative processes can act as a means to communicate important information, perhaps unknown or misunderstood by members, on the long-term benefits of accords and their positive implications for third parties, such as the poor and unemployed (Baccaro 2001a, 2001b).

Baccaro (2001a, 2001b) has illustrated this 'deliberative' function of democracy, in swaying the membership to change their voting intentions, in a comparison of two very similar automobile parts manufacturing plants, owned by Fiat and located in southern Italy. In both plants, union members were asked to relinquish their Saturday overtime pay in exchange for promises of more jobs and major investments in plant and machinery to ensure each plant's long-term commercial viability. In one plant, the union's vote on management's proposals was preceded by consultations and discussions between union leaders and members. The leaders used these interactions to clarify and highlight the long-term advantages of greater employment security, associated with the new investment, and the union members' ethical obligation to create more jobs for their high-unemployment community. The union leaders established their credibility to speak on these issues by promising to be personally available for work on Saturdays, despite the lack of overtime pay, and by promising to ensure that none of their unemployed relatives applied for any of the new jobs. Many of the union members were swayed by the leaders' arguments and therefore changed their voting intentions. A majority voted for management's proposal, choosing new jobs and investment rather than overtime pay on Saturday. In the second plant, by contrast, the vote was not preceded by any major interactions between leaders and members. Members remained largely unconcerned about the new jobs and unaware or ill-informed about their own future job security. As a result, short-term, self-interested concerns about the more obvious loss of overtime pay pre-occupied the minds of most. Management's proposal was consequently rejected.

Accords: are they a practical economic alternative to neo-liberal reform?

Are accords a practical and preferable alternative to neo-liberal economic reform? The answer for many countries is likely to be 'yes', especially given the more draconian neo-liberal alternatives on offer. However, measuring the economic and social effects of accords is necessarily problematic, as with any macro-economic policy. Cross-country comparisons are always difficult. There are often external factors, beyond a single country's control or influence, which drive major changes in economic performance. These include changes in the terms of trade, shifts in international interest rates, political instability in neighbouring countries, and swings in commodity prices. However, the limited empirical evidence does indicate that accords can provide major economic and social benefits, especially when compared to neo-liberal policies (Wood and Harcourt 2000).

Neo-corporatist societies, where accords have been relatively commonplace and enduring, have been relatively successful at creating jobs and maintaining low unemployment rates (Cameron 1984; Freeman 1988; Henley and Tsakalotos 1992; Newell and Symons 1987). One reason for this success is the relatively high priority, reflected in high expenditures, given to active labour market policies (Kraft 1998). These are policies to stimulate labour demand in high-unemployment regions and industries through recruitment subsidies; policies to stimulate labour supply in shortage occupations through public training on a massive scale; and policies to better match labour supply and demand by having state agencies act as large-scale recruitment agencies (Harcourt 1996). Another reason for this success is the anti-inflationary impact of wage restraint, oftentimes delivered through an accord, which has allowed these countries to avoid employment-destroying and unemployment-creating, restrictive monetary policies as a cure for inflation. For instance, neo-corporatist Austria has had more success than any other nation in the OECD in maintaining low rates of inflation, without recourse to unemployment-generating, tight monetary policies (Iverson 1999: 152).

Neo-corporatist societies also tend to out-perform their neo-liberal competitors in creating so-called 'good' jobs (see, for example, Broersma 1996: 1004). In contrast, neo-liberal regimes have created mainly 'bad' jobs, jobs that pay only marginally above the minimum wage, offer few, if any, fringe benefits, and are either temporary or part-time (Moody 1997). Employers in neo-liberal societies have used their not inconsiderable managerial prerogatives to take advantage of high and rising unemployment by lowering pay and worsening working conditions. In the United States, the quintessential neo-liberal society, approximately 25 per cent of the workforce now works in insecure jobs paying less than poverty level wages (< US$17,000), a figure many times higher than in most of Western Europe (Brenner 2002: 236).

Neo-corporatist societies have also been relatively successful at delivering high levels of social and economic equality, levels which have been maintained or even improved since the mid-1970s (Barrell and Genre 1999; Corvers and van Veen 1995; Gottschalk 1993; Green et al. 1994; Schlutter 1997). They do this in two very different ways. First, they maintain large welfare states which pay generous benefits to unemployed, sick, disabled, or retired members of society, individuals who, for the most part, lack the wealth required to provide themselves with income from other sources. Second, neo-corporatist societies generally maintain highly centralized wage-bargaining regimes, which have lowered wage differentials across industries and removed wages at the bottom end of the labour market from downward competitive pressures. In contrast, many neo-liberal societies have reduced their welfare states, often as part of a fiscal stabilization initiative, with sometimes dramatic negative effects on the incomes of the very poorest parts of society. Likewise, several neo-liberal societies have deregulated and decentralized their labour markets, often by reducing or eliminating the rights of unions, and thereby exposed their least-skilled workers to downward competitive pressures on wages, emanating in many cases from a high-unemployment environment.

Neo-corporatist societies have also been relatively effective at fighting inflation (Al-Marhubi and Willett 1995; Casey and Gold 2000: 87; Cukierman and Lippi 1999; Hicks and Kenworthy 1998: 1654–1659; Newell and Symons 1987). Much of this success can be attributed to the wage restraint negotiated through social accords (Newell and Symons 1987; Sachs and Bruno 1985). After the first oil crisis, most neo-liberal regimes initially tolerated the rise in inflation with an accommodative monetary policy. Some attempts were made to lower inflation through, for instance, wage and price controls, but these efforts were, with some notable exceptions, unsuccessful. In the end, the US and UK governments tired of these gradualist approaches and opted for 'shock treatment' by using high interest rates to engineer a recession, push up unemployment, and thereby moderate wage demands. The policy has been a success, but many would argue that the cure, higher unemployment, deepening poverty, higher crime, and fiscal crisis, was worse than the disease (inflation).

Conclusions

Neo-liberal reforms can clearly involve major economic costs in terms of lost output, higher unemployment, lower incomes, and increased poverty, at least over the short to medium term. Their implementation and continuation can just as clearly involve major political costs in terms of promoting non-democratic, governmental institutions to supplant or sideline more conventional and democratic institutions. Purist versions of neo-liberal reform offer no scope for major compromises to appease the diverse range of interest groups that exist in any polity. Nor do they offer the prospect that policies might be tailored to suit the unique cultural, social, geographical, and economic conditions of particular countries. As a result, the neo-liberal policy mix is inherently rigid and so relies on monolithic, hierarchically organized governmental institutions, staffed by ideologically homogeneous individuals, for its implementation.

In contrast, accords are inherently democratic. Accord negotiation is inclusive, in the sense that it can potentially accommodate many interested groups. Accord negotiation is consensual; the parties make compromises with each other to arrive at some mutually acceptable agreement. Accords promote democratic rights and freedoms, such as the freedoms of expression and association. In fact, the exercise of these freedoms helps to ensure that different groups contribute, in positive ways, to the accord negotiation process rather than later stand in the way of its implementation.

The procedural aspects of accord development are not their only claim to superiority. The empirical evidence indicates that accords deliver major economic benefits. These can include: lower inflation, lower unemployment, lower wage inequality, and lower poverty among others. This record compares favourably with some of the disastrous outcomes of neo-liberalism, especially in the developing countries. Even when successful, neo-liberal reforms seem incapable of delivering macro-economic stability and growth in the absence of worsening poverty and inequality.

References

Al-Marhubi, F. and Willett, T. 1995. 'The Anti-Inflationary Influence of Corporatist Structures and Central Bank Independence: The Importance of the Hump Hypothesis', *Public Choice*, 84: 153–162.

Ames, B. 1987. *Political Survival: Politicians and Public Policy in Latin America*. Berkeley, Calif.: University of California Press.

Arestis, P. and Marshall, M. 1995. 'Obstacles to, and Strategies for the Achievment of Full Employment', in Arestis, P. and Marshall, M. (eds.), *The Political Economy of Full Employment: Conservatism, Corporatism and Institutional Change*. Aldershot: Edward Elgar.

Austin, G. 2000. 'Markets, Democracy and African Economic Growth', *The Round Table*, 357: 543–555.

Baccaro, L. 2000. 'Centralized Collective Bargaining and the Problem of "Compliance": Lessons from the Italian Experience', *Industrial and Labor Relations Review*, 53, 4: 579–601.

—— 2001a. '"Aggregative" and "Deliberative" Decision-Making Procedures: a Comparison of Two Southern Italian Factories', *Politics and Society*, 29, 2: 243–271.

—— 2001b. 'Union Democracy Revisited: Decision-Making Procedures in the Italian Labour Movement', *Economic and Industrial Democracy*, 22, 2: 183–210.

—— 2002. 'Negotiating the Italian Pension Reform with the Unions: Lessons for Corporatist Theory', *Industrial and Labor Relations Review*, 55, 3: 413–431.

Barrell, R. and Genre, V. 1999. 'Employment Strategies of Europe: Lessons from Denmark and the Netherlands', *National Institute Economic Review*, 168: 82–98.

Block, S. 2002. 'Political Business Cycles, Democratization, and Economic Reform: The Case of Africa', *Journal of Development Economics*, 67, 205–228.

Brenner, R. 2002. *The Boom and the Bubble: the US in the World Economy*. London: Verso.

Broersma, L. 1996. 'The Effect of Wage Restraint on Labour Market Flows', *Applied Economics*, 28: 999–1007.

Calmfors, L. and Driffil, J. 1988. 'Centralization of Wage Bargaining', *Economic Policy*, 6: 14–61.

Cameron, D. 1984. 'Social Democracy, Corporatism, Labour Quiescence and the Representation of Economic Interest in Advanced Capitalist Society', in Goldthorpe, J. (ed.), *Order and Conflict in Contemporary Capitalism*. Oxford: Clarendon Press.

Casey, B. and Gold, M. 2000. *Social Partnerships and Economic Performance*. Cheltenham: Edward Elgar.

Corvers, F. and van Veen, T. 1995. 'On the Measurement of Corporatism', *Labour*, 9, 3: 423–442.

Crisp, B. 1998. 'Lessons from Economic Reform in the Venezuelan Democracy', *Latin American Research Review*, 33, 1: 7–41.

Crouch, C. 1982. *The Logic of Collective Action*. London: Fontana.

Cukierman, A. and Lippi, F. 1999. 'Central Bank Independence, Centralization of Wage Bargaining, Inflation and Unemployment: Theory and Some Evidence', *European Economic Review*, 43: 1395–1434.

Fouda, S. 1997. 'Political Monetary Cycles and Independence of the Central Bank in a Monetary Union: An Empirical Test for a BEAC Franc Zone Member', *Journal of African Economics*, 6, 1: 112–131.

Foweraker, J. 1987. 'Corporatist Strategies and the Transition to Democracy in Spain', *Comparative Politics*, 20: 57–72.

Freeman, R. 1988. 'Evaluating the European View That the United States Has No Unemployment Problem', *American Economic Review*, 78, 2: 294–299.

Goldthorpe, J. 1984. *Order and Conflict in Contemporary Capitalism*. Oxford: Clarendon Press.

Gottschalk, P. 1993. 'Changes in Inequality and Family Income in Seven Industrialized Countries', *American Economic Review*, 73, 2: 136–142.

Grabel, I. 2000. 'The Political Economy of "Policy Credibility": The Newclassical Macroeconomics and the Remaking of Emerging Economies', *Cambridge Journal of Economics*, 24, 1: 1–19.

Green, F., Henley, A. and Tsakalotos, E. 1994. 'Income Inequality in Corporatist and Liberal Economies: A Comparison of Trends within OECD Countries', *International Review of Economics*, 8, 3: 303–331.

Harcourt, M. 1996. 'Unemployment Reduction in Canada: Lessons from Japan and Sweden', *Relations Industrielles*, 51, 1: 177–202.

Henley, A. and Tsakalotos, E. 1992. 'Corporatism and the European Labour Market after 1992', *British Journal of Industrial Relations*, 30, 4: 567–586.

Hicks, A. and Kenworthy, L. 1998. 'Cooperation and Political Economic Performance in Affluent Democratic Capitalism', *American Journal of Sociology*, 103, 6: 1631–1672.

Iverson, T. 1999. *Contested Economic Institutions*. Cambridge: Cambridge University Press.

Jeong, H. 1998. 'Economic Reform and Democratic Transition in Ghana', *World Affairs*, 160, 4: 218–230.

Khemani, S. 2000. 'Effect of Electoral Accountability on Economic Policy in India', *Annual Bank Conference on Development Economics*. Washington, DC: World Bank.

Kraft, K. 1998. 'An Evaluation of Active and Passive Labour Market Policy', *Applied Economics*, 30: 783–793.

Lange, P. 1984. 'Union Democracy and Liberal Corporatism: Exit, Voice, and Wage Regulation in Postwar Europe'. Centre for International Studies, Western Societies Program, Cornell University, Occasional Paper No. 16.

Layard, R., Nickell, S. and Jackman, R. 1994. *Unemployment: Macroeconomic Performance and the Labor Market*. Oxford: Oxford University Press.

Lindbeck, A. 1976. 'Stabilization Policies in Open Economies with Endogenous Politicians', *American Economic Review Papers and Proceedings*: 1–19.

Marangos, J. 2002. 'A Political Economy Approach to the Neoclassical Model of Transition', *American Journal of Economics and Sociology*, 61, 1: 259–276.

Martinez Lucio, M. 1991. 'Employer Identity and the Politics of the Labour Market in Spain', *West European Politics*, 14: 41–55.

Moody, K. 1997. *Workers in a Lean World*. London: Verso.

Moyo, D. 1999. *The Determinants of Public Savings in Developing Countries: Working Paper*. Oxford: Oxford University Press.

Nagel, J. 1998. 'Social Choice in a Pluralitarian Democracy: The Politics of Market Liberalization in New Zealand', *British Journal of Political Science*, 28: 223–267.

Newell, A. and Symons, J. 1987. 'Corporatism, Laissez-Faire and the Rise in Unemployment', *European Economic Review*, 31: 567–614.

Nordhaus, W. 1975. 'The Political Business Cycle', *Review of Economic*

Studies, 42: 169–190.

Olson, M. 1965. *The Logic of Collective Action*. Cambridge, Mass.: Harvard University Press.

—— 1982. *The Rise and Decline of Nations: Economic Growth, Stagflation and Social Rigidities*. New Haven, Conn.: Yale University Press.

Pickel, A. 1993. 'Authoritarianism or Democracy? Marketization as a Political Problem', *Policy Sciences*, 26: 139–163.

Quispe-Agnoli, M. 2001. 'Monetary Policy Alternatives for Latin America', *Federal Reserve Bank of Atlanta Economic Review*, 86, 3: 43–54.

Rey, J. C. 1993. 'La crisis de la legitimidad en Venezuela y el enjuiciamiento y remocion de Carlos Andres Perez de la Presidencia de la Republica', *Boletin Electoral Latinoamericano*, 9: 67–112.

Rigby, M. and Lawlor, T. 1994. 'Spanish Trade Unions 1986-1994: Life after National Agreements', *Industrial Relations Journal*, 25: 258–271.

Sabel, C. 1981. 'The Internal Politics of Trade Unions', in Berger, S. (ed.). *Organizing Interests in Western Europe*. New York: Cambridge University Press.

Sachs, J. and Bruno, M. 1985. *Econimics of Worldwide Stagflation*. Oxford: Basil Blackwell.

Sayari, S. 1996/97. 'Political Parties, Party Systems, and Economic Reforms: The Turkish Case', *Studies in Comparative International Development*, 31, 4: 29–45.

Schlutter, C. 1997. 'On the Performance of Social Benefit Systems', *Economic Journal*, 107, 441: 489–502.

Schmitter, P. C. and Lehmbruch, G. 1979. *Trends towards Corporatist Intermediation*. London: Sage.

Schuknecht, L. 1996. 'Political Business Cycles and Fiscal Policies in Developing Countries', *Kyklos*, 49, 2: 155–170.

—— 2000. 'Fiscal Policy Cycles and Public Expenditure in Developing Countries', *Public Choice*, 102,1: 113–128.

Shi, M. and Svensson, J. 2000. *Conditional Political Business Cycles: Theory and Evidence*. New York: Development Research Group, World Bank.

Streeck, W. 1982. 'Organizational Consequences of Corporatist Cooperation in West German Labor Unions', in Lehmbruch, G. and Schmitter, P. (eds.), *Patterns of Corporatist Policy-making*. Beverly Hills, Calif.: Sage.

Tarantelli, E. 1986. 'The Regulation of Inflation and Unemployment', *Industrial Relations*, 25, 1: 1–15.

Tufte, E. 1978. *Political Control of the Economy*. Princeton, N.J.: Princeton University Press.

Wood, G. and Harcourt, M. 2000. 'The Consequences of Neo-Corporatism: A Syncretic Analysis', *International Journal of Sociology and Social Policy*, 20, 8: 1–22.

4

Trade unions and democracy: can the 'third way' recast the link?

IAN ROPER

This chapter examines the relationship between the apparent 'crisis of democracy' and a parallel decline in the fortunes of unions. More specifically, it traces the rise of union influence in society coinciding with the rise in participative democracy in the first half of the twentieth century; and the subsequent decline in union influence coinciding with the seeming antipathy towards representative democratic institutions at the dawn of the twenty-first century. These developments in the fortunes of unions and democracy are closely linked to the economic and political programmes put into place by governments inspired by the ideologies of – what we would now call – neo-liberalism. Principally, these ideologies are based upon the belief that society was under attack from an increasingly bloated public sector, fed by overloaded public expectations promoted by overly powerful interest groups – chiefly trade unions. The concern being raised now is that the apparent success in suppressing these expectations has led to widespread apathy; that people's expectations of government are now so low that government may face a legitimation crisis equal and opposite to that identi-fied by radical observers in the 1970s (Gough 1979; Habermas 1975; O'Connor 1973). Thus, rather than there being a crisis based on too many demands being made on the state, there may now be a crisis of legitimacy on the continuing existence of democratic institutions at all. Against this background, the 'third way' has recently emerged as the self-proclaimed cham-pion of the centre-left, claiming to be able to revive the fortunes of participative democracy. This strategy is based upon a retreat from all the associations that its social democratic predecessors had with 'big government'.

This chapter will trace these various events and assess the

credibility of the third way's prescription for reviving democracy. Special attention will be paid to a recent contribution by Peter Ackers on the role that trade unions may have within this 'third way' relationship between unions and democratic renewal.

Tracing the crisis in representative and participatory democracy

The notion that there is a 'crisis of democracy' is widespread. It has been variously ascribed to apathy, to passive contentment, to a 'hollowing-out' of democracy. The problem has been attributed to the hegemony of conservative politics over a long period of time; a problem that has not abated with the revival of centre-left ascendancy in the mid 1990s (Anderson 2001). The fundamental 'problem' is that where representative parliamentary democracy is longstanding – i.e. in the 'old democracies' (Nohlen 2002) – there has been a slow but continuous decline in general political *participation*. This decline has been in terms of voter turnout, of political involvement within constitutional political parties, and in participation within political, community or sectional interest groups. From a classical pluralist perspective, these indicators of declining political participation in the democratic process could be assumed to be interdependent, in which case there could be seen to be a consistent trend toward disengagement; be this for reasons of apathy or anomie.

A key indicator is voter turnout. Low and declining voter turnout has been a long-term trend in the US. Similarly in the UK, low turnout was widely recognized as being the single most significant challenge to the Blair government's landslide victory in 2001. In France, the considerable shock that followed the short-lived success of far right Le Pen – at the expense of Jospin, eliminated in the first round of the 2002 presidential election – was at least partly attributed to the combination of low voter turnout and antipathy toward the mainstream candidates by the French electorate. Table 4.1 indicates the extent of the falling interest in participation in elections in a selection of countries.

Consistent with this trend is the equally uncontested and well-documented trend towards disengagement in membership of, and participation in, trade union activity in these countries. There has been a growth in political participation in certain

Table 4.1 Election turnout

Country	Number of elections since 1945	Average voter turnout (per cent) 1945–1980	Voter turnout 1980–2000				
			1980 (per cent)	1980 (rank)	2000 (per cent)	per cent change 2000 (rank)	1980–2000
Australia	22	84.2	83.97	3	81.75a	2	−2.22
Canada	18	82.6	64.53	8	54.64	9	−9.89
France	15	67.3	63.92	9	59.86b	5	−4.06
Germany	14	80.2	81.84	4	75.32a	3	−6.52
Italy	15	92.0	92.75c	1	84.92d	1	−7.83
Japan	22	68.7	74.70	7	59.02	6	−15.68
Korea	10	72.9	78.42e	5	55.74	8	−22.68
Sweden	17	84.1	86.94c	2	77.72a	4	−9.22
UK	16	73.8	75.06c	6	57.56d	7	−17.50
USAf	28	47.7	52.56	10	49.27	10	−3.29

Source: Adini, Ballington, J., Brians, C., Louner, S., Nohlen, D., Norris, P., Notosusanto, S., Sullivan, K. and Urritia, E. 2002. *Voter Turnout Since 1945: a Global Report.* Stockholm: International IDEA.
Notes: [a] = 1998; [b] =1997; [c] = 1979; [d] = 2001; [e] = 1981; [f] = presidential election

'new democracies' (ibid) and this can be strongly linked with the presence of visible, active and growing union movements.[1] Because participation in unions is – in the classical pluralist sense – an indicator of a strong participatory democracy, the simultaneous decline in unions and in electoral participation is unlikely to be a coincidence when we can, at the same point in time, witness the clamour for democratic participation coupled with increased union activity in countries such as South Africa, Korea and Brazil. Indeed these simultaneous trends cannot be separated from the spatial shifts in global economic activity. The extent to which the developed world is subject to deindustrialization – which is far from being consensus – is not because of some post-capitalist shift to some leisure-based society; it is because of uneven industrialization elsewhere. This process, with the growth in deregulated free trade zones and the like, is explicitly linked to the neoliberal globalisation project and largely based upon an international division of labour. Yet, in these developing countries, industrialization goes hand in hand with increased union activism (against great odds) and raised expectations for participatory democracy, issues that are intertwined under the banner of global social movement unionism, for example (Lambert and Webster 2001). This is somewhat paradoxical for neo-liberal assertions about development, democracy and collectivism: it seems that in these models for deregulated intensive industrialization, there remains a strong desire for collective representation, participative democracy and for protection against the harshest aspects of unrestrained managerial prerogative. The ideological underpinning of the current global neo-liberal hegemony can be traced back to the political project of restoring profitability in the advanced economies, in the face of the perceived threat from organized labour and 'democratic overload', as we shall now see.

Democracy and unions in the twentieth century: the forward march of labour

Hobsbawm (1981) famously detected the 'forward march of labour' being 'halted' before it became evident that British trade unionism was about to be subject to its greatest ever period of decline. However true his comment at the time of writing it, there is no dispute that for most of the twentieth century, organized labour was moving forward in terms of its role as a 'progressive force' in society; and that this role began to be seriously challenged in the last part of the century. At the outset of the twentieth century, the labour movement was growing in confidence and was widely viewed as being an indicator of progress in the industrialized world.[2] This confidence was exhibited by key examples. The British labour movement was traditionally characterized as being overly insular in its preoccupation with defending sectional occupational interests at the expense of broader social aims (Hyman 2001). Yet in 1900 'the industrial wing' of the British labour movement was ambitious enough to create its 'political wing' – the Labour Party – to further its wider social agendas: the great majority of unions in Britain have been institutionally tied to the Labour Party ever since. In Europe, different patterns emerged. Unions polarizing around either radical socialist, communist or syndicalist agendas; or around more conservative religion-based movements (France, Italy, Spain, Germany). Unions also forged close relationships with varying forms of workers' parties and social democratic parties – notably the SPD in Germany and the CGT in France.

In the US, early hopes that the American Federation of Labor (AFL) had of its role in society were gradually dampened. This lack of a workers' voice in society was compounded by the failure to establish any credible American workers' or socialist party in this period. Despite this, unions' political clout improved significantly in the 1930s. Here, unions increasingly demonstrated their credibility and resilience through the historic battles to become established in the vertically integrated corporations of what is now frequently termed 'early fordism' (Aglietta 1979). This credibility was further legitimized by the unions' more formal association with the Democratic Party during the New Deal. In all cases, then, labour was on the move and it was either pushing a reformist agenda or pushing a radical agenda.

The premise that organized labour positively contributes to democracy depends on the definition of democracy – which will remain a contested issue. However, if we restrict our definition to a minimal one, meaning representative democracy in the liberal-democratic tradition, the following fundamental characteristics can be assumed (Goodwin 2002):

- supremacy of the people;
- the consent of the governed as the basis of legitimacy;
- the rule of law: peaceful methods of conflict resolution;
- the existence of a common good or public interest;
- the value of the individual as a rational, morally active citizen;
- equal civil rights for all individuals.

To this list we could also add the classical pluralist notion that representative democracy should also require 'a right to form relatively independent associations or organizations, including independent political parties and interest groups' (Dahl 1982, paraphrased by Etzioni-Halevy 1997: 268). Between the 1950s and 1970s – the golden age of pluralist ascendancy in the social sciences in the west – union participation in the democratic process was assumed to be automatic. During this period, the forebears of what we would now label neo-liberalism identified unions as the threat to democracy.[3]

Neo-liberalism and unions: a problem *for* democracy or a problem *of* democracy?

Unions have been ascribed the role of 'enemy of democracy' by their critics – whose interests have been challenged by unions –

throughout their history. On a global scale, the ideological direction and political control of union confederations were seen as an important vessel for pursuing both sides of the Cold War (Munck 2002). In the post-war developed world, this ideological opposition to unions was crude and subsumed within more 'pragmatic' approaches to accommodating the demands of organized labour. On the whole, labour was accommodated through one form of compromise or another. Thus, from the 1930s, the Swedish corporatist model of social democracy was based upon strong union densities and supportive institutional arrangements (Hammarström and Nilsson 1998). In Britain the creation of the post-war welfare state settlement has been universally attributed to a recognition of the strength of organized labour at that point in time. In Germany, the restructuring of a strong labour movement after 1945 was seen as a key element in guaranteeing the future democracy of the Bundesrepublic. Even in the US, the legitimacy of organized labour was not challenged by the Cold War rhetoric of McCarthyism.[4] And even in the strictly non-democratic Spain of Franco, trade unions continued to operate effectively and formed part of the social basis on which democracy would eventually be constructed in the 1970s.

From 1980, however, unions' most ardent ideological adversaries assumed political ascendancy in Britain and the US, leading to a wider neo-liberal hegemony in the way that unions came to be viewed by a broader range of international institutions. The knock-on effects of the macro-economic policies pursued in these two countries had repercussions elsewhere. Although the significant economic effects stemmed from the US (in terms of the impact that structural changes to the US economy have as global economic hegemon), the symbolic political message (on facing-down unions, privatization and labour-market deregulation) was exported from Britain. The emergence of a more sophisticated approach to problematizing the role of organized labour within civil society coincided with the political ascendancy of populist anti-union governments in high profile countries, directly challenging the pluralist consensus on the role of unions in society.

The collection of theories and assumptions mobilized against unions can generally be bundled together under the banner of 'the new right'. These theories and assumptions are indisputably the theoretical forebears of what we now define as neo-liberalism. All have different, and often contradictory, prescriptions on the issue of unions and of the state (Gamble 1994). Yet they all form the basis upon which political and economic decisions have been based, that have had an impact on unions and on political participation. The most influential of these new right theories are those espoused by F. A. Hayek, Milton Friedman and those associated with 'public choice' theory (Dunleavy and O'Leary 1987; Gamble, 1994; Mishra 1984).

Hayek started the assault on full employment, the welfare state and the role of unions in society unfashionably early; on the eve of the post-war Keynsian consensus. Hayek's views were based on the unions' alleged role as a coercive restriction of labour supply in the economy; and as an irresponsible influence on government that would, in turn, increasingly resort to plundering resources from other areas of civil society. Even at this stage, Hayek proposed drastic countermeasures for union intransigence to structural adjustments in a peacetime economy:

> If, then, the trade unions successfully resist any lowering of the wages of the particular groups in question, there will be only two alternatives open: either coercion will have to be used, i.e. certain individuals will have to be selected for compulsory transfer to other and relatively less well paid positions, or those who can no longer be employed at the relatively high wages they have earned during the war must be allowed to remain unemployed till they are willing to accept work at a relatively lower wage. (Hayek 1944: 153–154)

Two observations stem from this. First, there is a paradox in this statement if we accept that Hayek placed highest priority on the primacy of individual freedom under the law. What is being suggested is that the market would be unable to effect the most desirable (from Hayek's point of view) outcome and that state coercion would be required to save the market from its own dysfunctions, even at the expense of individual freedom. This indicates that the neo-liberal view of the nightwatchman state is not one of non-interventionism per se, but, rather, it is one concerned with regulating the activities of those rational actors (workers who collude to protect their best interests) that do not fit easily with the voluntarist assumptions in neo-liberal democracy. A second observation from Hayek's comment, above, is that Hayek's recommendation – not taken up in 1945 in the developed world – accurately defines the kind of pre-conditions that international financial institutions routinely place on structural adjustment programmes being offered to developing nations in the new century (Saul 1997).

A second source for anti-union, new right theory was the monetarist school, who were first taken seriously during the economic crises of the 1970s. For Friedman (1968), the 'union problem' was one of unions operating as a means by which workers' expectations are raised beyond what would be the 'natural' equilibrium wage rate, so leading to a wage–price inflationary cycle. Friedman argued that the artificial stimulation of the economy through government deficit financing was ultimately doomed to failure. The inflated wage expectations of workers, aided by 'monopolistic' trade unions, continually forced the price of labour above its natural clearing rate. The solution, for monetarists, was for the cycle to be broken. Government was to focus exclusively (in terms of economic policy) on ensuring that monetary supply matched (and did not exceed) economic growth. Within this zero-sum scenario, people would be expected to behave according to 'rational expectations': employers would be curtailed from being able to pay the demanded wage increases and inflation would fall; falling inflation would then further curtail the demand for wage increases. In addition – and most crucially – unions' ability to coerce employers into settling above the natural clearing rate would need to be curtailed.

Another source of critique came in the form of seeing unions as acting as a 'selfish elite' preserving the interests of labour market insiders (largely skilled, mobilized blue-collar workers) at the expense of society as a whole and labour market outsiders (principally, the unemployed). The most articulate version of this assertion was provided by Mancur Olson (1971). This particular thesis was the basis by which unions could be, in the quasi-scientific language of 'rational choice', formally linked to the demise of freedom and efficiency.

A further influence on new right thinking is that of public choice theory. Public choice suggests that the state acts as an inefficient allocator of resources because its decision making is driven by 'bureau-maximizing' tendencies within the state who broker political interests competing for resources. This is often exacerbated by the electoral cycle whereby macro-economic policy is geared to produce short-term reductions in unemployment and taxation, only to manifest themselves later, in reversal and in increased inflation. This is exacerbated by the unrealistic expectations of politically motivated (as opposed to the more 'rational' economically motivated) interest groups. This all leads to government overload: too many demands on limited resources, all being distorted by the electoral cycle. Unions, particularly public sector unions, were identified as the chief beneficiary of this process by the 1970s. For public choice, such discretionary decision-making powers should be removed from public bureaucracy and political interests and placed within the sphere of consumer sovereignty, where competition tempers such wasteful behaviour. Public choice, then, provides the new right with its central rationale for privatization and deregulation.

The effects of the new right ascendancy on unions

During the 1980s and 1990s union membership declined in most of the industrialized world. Table 4.2 shows the fall in union membership densities during this period.

Table 4.2 Union density

Country	Union density (per cent)		Union density growth (per cent)	Rank order of union density	
	1985	1995	1985–95	1985	1995
Australia	46	33	−28	2	4
Canada	35	35	0	6	3
France	15	11	−27	9	10
Germany	36	30	−16	5	5
Italy	42	38	−10	4	2
Japan	29	24	−18	7	7
Korea	12	14	+17	10	9
Sweden	86	83	−3	1	1
UK	45	29	−35	3	6
USA	18	15	−17	8	8

Source: Derived from ILO in Ross, P., Bamber, G. and Whitehouse, G. 1998. 'Appendix – Employment, Economics and Industrial Relations: Comparative Statistics', in G. Bamber and R. Lansbury (eds), *International and Comparative Employment Relations*, 3rd edn. London: Sage.

The long-term effects of hostile governments on unions have been well documented. In the case of Britain, the new right inspired legislative assault on unions (Brown 1997; MacInnes,

1987; Martin *et al.*, 1995; Miller and Steele 1993) coincided with the economic restructuring of the economy (financial and employment deregulation, and privatization). What has been described as the 'surprising' decline of an entrenched union movement in Britain (Pencavel 2003) following an onslaught of neo-liberal legislation, is significant as an indicator of what could happen to equally entrenched movements elsewhere.

In the US, where direct state intervention in the internal affairs of unions was not a feature of the 'Reaganomics' experiment of the early 1980s, a similar downward trend in union membership has also been recorded. However, it is worth noting Godard's (1997) comment that government economic policies affecting worker expectations are at least as potent as those directly affecting unions' themselves:

> ... governments can follow one or both of two primary strategies to address the labour 'problem'. The first is to attempt to transform the institutions, and hence the system of industrial relations, through pro-employer legislative actions, directly weakening the labour movement's ability to organize and bargain effectively. The second strategy is to alter materially the conditions under which the system functions without changing the system itself, through the adoption of economic policies which (among other things) lower the expectations of workers and increase their fear of job loss. (Godard 1997: 416)

So deregulation, privatization and other policies more closely associated with 'public choice' and with the curtailment of 'big government', could be seen as at least as important a determinant of union fortunes as those policies explicitly affecting the activities of unions per se. This may explain similar declines experienced in other Anglo-Saxon countries, which pursued similar macro-economic policies while introducing less explicitly union-hostile policies than in Britain or the US.[5] Of course, it would be true to say that this political neo-liberal hegemony in the Anglo-Saxon world was not present in other developed economies and thus not responsible for the similar decline in union membership. In Western Europe, where the industrial relations 'social dialogue' was maintained along parameters governed by a Christian Democrat/Social Democrat political consensus throughout the 1980s and 1990s (Hyman 2001), and latterly through developments in the Social Chapter regulatory agenda from the EU, union membership levels also fell in every country bar Sweden (Visser 1996). However, wider macro-economic conditions (rising unemployment, structural changes to the composition of the labour market) that hit Europe over this period were affected, at least partly, by the increased mobility of capital, prompting arguments between those bemoaning Europe's inflexible labour market as being responsible for low job growth, and those concerned with tightening regulations to deter the practice of 'social dumping'. The former position has been formally supported by the now prescribed policy from what Hutton (2002) describes as the 'handmaidens of conservatism', the International Monetary Fund and the World Bank, that had switched allegiance from international Keynesianism to the (monetarist) 'Washington Consensus' during the 1970s.

Those governments with their anti-union rhetoric have long gone; but the core assumptions underlying them have become orthodoxy; among political opponents, domestically and internationally. Ultimately then, it is the theories and assumptions which underpin populist anti-union government policy that are of greater importance than the policies and governments themselves. In this sense, the response of the unions' traditional political allies has been important in defining the current agenda for the unions' role – and potential role – in the reconstituting of active and participatory democracy.

An attempt to revive union inclusion in the political system via corporatism would not seem to be a viable option. During the 1970s there was some movement in Britain toward northern European corporatist models (Austria, and Scandinavia) in the government's attempts to incorporate capital and labour via incomes policies. There were even attempts to introduce German-style mechanisms for codetermination. On both counts the unions were as opposed to the challenge to their independence and prime organizing principle of maintaining free collective bargaining as were employers over the potential challenge to the managerial prerogative (Taylor 1993). However, even though British unions – and the TUC in particular – have moved considerably towards favouring a 'social Europe' agenda from the 1990s, union densities have also declined in those EU countries where such regulated market economies have traditionally dominated.

Renewing democratic participation: neo-pluralism and the third way

The apparent inability of corporatist approaches to reviving either unions or democracy has been progressively giving way to revisionist strategies by union friendly parties in the developed world. In the case of Britain, the trajectory of the Labour Party has fluctuated from 1983's stringent opposition to the social market/social democrat/Christian democrat compromise – for it being a sop to business interests; to its courting of the EU Social Chapter agenda in 1992; to its recent moderate scepticism of the social market concept – now for being too 'inflexible' to accommodate the needs of UK employers (Hall *et al.* 2002; Smith and Morton 2001). This last shift reflects a move inspired by an attempt to reposition the 'progressive' centre left under the banner of the 'third way'. Indeed, it is claimed that the future of the centre-left in politics internationally is the third way; and that 'we are all third wayers now' (Reich 1999). It is certainly true that there has been some convergence in thinking among some political parties of the centre left. The ('New') Labour Party in Britain openly mimicked the political rebranding exercise carried out in the US by the ('New') Democrats in the 1990s. In terms of providing a rigorous grounding for the third way, beyond an aspirational catch-phrase intended to indicate 'moderation', some intellectual heavyweights, notably Anthony Giddens, have been brought in to add to its credibility. However, as a blueprint for social democratic politics in general, there is no real evidence that the 'third way' has exported well. There has been some suggestion that the German SPD and the Spanish Socialists may be swayed. Blair made appeals to go the third way to the ANC in South Africa. Since the demise of the Clinton presidency in the US, however, the third way appears less hegemonic. Even so, the third way remains influential. Ludlam *et al.* (2002) note the convergence between Labour and the Democrats on their respective links with the unions – in both cases a conscious distancing.

For Giddens (1998), the 'third way' is a response to five dilemmas that face orthodox social democracy. In relation to the trade unions and democracy, the crucial dilemmas are those relating to globalization and individualism. On globalization, Giddens contends that globalization challenges the capacity of autonomous decision making within nation states. However, he further suggests that third way politics 'should not identify globalization with a blanket endorsement of free trade. Free trade can be an engine of economic development, but given the socially and culturally destructive power of markets, it's wider consequences need always to be scrutinized' (Giddens 1998: 65).

The individualism that Giddens identifies is one that asserts the libertarian politics of the 1960s as much as the self-interested consumerism of the 1990s. The dilemma of individualism is that the legitimacy of democracy is potentially challenged if the institutions of the state do not face up to people's raised expectations. Presumably unions, being based on the principle of collectivism, face the same dilemma (Bacon and Storey 1996).

On both of these issues, however, the third way position of balancing the 'opportunities' and 'threats' posed by these developments is unclear. It is not clear, for example, how a balanced view of dealing with globalization can be approached: how can 'being realistic' about only pursuing policy options that cannot be undermined by unrestricted capital mobility, be balanced with not reifying markets above cultural and social values? A similar conceptual problem exists in separating individualism as a social reality from individualism as an ideology. Reifying individualism poses the danger of legitimizing those vested interests that claim to promote 'freedom' in terms of a branded lifestyle; but who do so at the expense of those who lose out through the uneven impacts of the international division of labour, as Klein (2000) most popularly demonstrates.

The third way has thus far proven ineffective as a solution for the decline in democratic participation and remains problematic as a potential framework for any renewed vibrancy of unions' participation therein. Despite these problems the third way is, at the moment at least, an influential agenda. Its influence and content has been met by understandable scepticism within organized labour, not least because third way advocates have tried to dissociate themselves from organized labour. However, a version of the third way that may be more digestible for organized labour is that being offered in the form of neo-pluralism and has most recently been articulated by Ackers (2002).

Neo-pluralism, itself, is not a new analytical framework. Indeed it has been ascribed to a number of approaches dealing with the apparent failures of the classical pluralism of Dahl and others, to deal with their conservative and radical critics

(Dunleavy and O'Leary 1987). Ackers' contribution should be seen more by a desire to break out of what are becoming increasingly outdated methods of analysis prevalent in (particularly British) industrial relations (Martin *et al.* 1995). The traditional pluralist frame of reference – concentrating on institutions, mechanisms and arrangements used in regulating collective bargaining – has become an increasingly untenable means for assessing developments in this area, when it is these very institutions that are subject to change.

The focus of Ackers' contribution is concerned not only with how to reframe the nature of employment relations, but also with tentative steps on how to redefine the role of organized labour in society in a manner that does not resort to a Marxist frame of reference – Kelly's (1998) in particular. In his argument, Ackers makes a claim for neo-pluralism to become the organizing framework in which to integrate unions, workplace and community. The basis of Ackers' neo-pluralist approach is that the concept of employment relations needs to widen its remit beyond the narrow economistic focus on the institutions and practices of collective bargaining, as has been the norm under the systems-oriented emphases in the pluralist approaches of Flanders and Fox (to which we should also add Dunlop, 1958). To this end, Ackers proposes that employment relations be extended outward to incorporate wider social institutions whose legitimacy is under threat from neo-liberalism. Key emphases are placed on neo-pluralism's capacity to engage with the issues of values, ethics and community to which pluralist employment relations had been unwilling to engage:

> Neo-pluralism is pluralism freed of Clegg's self-denying ordinance regarding ethics. And with it the illusion that a social science paradigm can simply 'describe society'. It does not introduce any startling new theoretical revelations into sociological thinking. Rather, it revives Durkheim's fundamental question about how moral communities and social institutions can bond work and society together.' (Ackers 2002: 15)

Ackers places particular emphasis on the institution of the family and also on other institutions that hark back to times when unions were more involved in mutual aid projects in the communities in which they were themselves grounded. The means by which neo-pluralism may be able to deliver on reviving these institutions is not, in itself, clear. Third way policy prescriptions and an emphasis on workplace 'partnership' between management and unions is the nearest Ackers gets. This seems to be placing a lot of faith in enlightened employers and in the ability and willingness of the leaders of macro-level institutions. To date, any such support from these quarters seems to be severely lacking. This points to a general problem with Ackers' position. It is not so much that neo-pluralism is 'soft on power' (p. 17) – though it is – it is that there does not appear to be any organizing principle or base from which to mobilize a new ethical hegemony around stakeholding. If the answer lies in re-establishing a community base from which unions could reconnect with civil society, it is unclear what distinctive contribution neo-pluralism would have to make in this. In the past, links between unions and their local community were prevalent – yet, ironically, were based upon singular self-interested projects, be they socialist, syndicalist, social-democratic, or religious. The alternative to this – mobilization around values without recourse to the singular pursuit of interests – is no different to the generic notion of a voluntary community-based association that Hayek has explicitly felt happy to endorse (Hayek 1976: 151).

In some ways Ackers' view that employment relations requires a greater consideration of the other aspects that make up worker and organizational priorities is correct and in some ways it is not. It is correct that issues outside work affect people's identities and motives. However, this is a truism and does not, in itself, help us to determine the weight that any one issue, extraneous to the employment relationship, should be given in employment relations. Under this definition, any aspect of human activity *could* be a legitimate focus of attention. In this sense, what Ackers is describing is sociology per se. More specifically, Ackers notes the family and community-based organizations as key institutions for such a focus. But why these? If pluralism is seen as an inadequate frame of reference for studying employment relations because of the self-evident decline in institutional arrangements such as collective bargaining, then why is the family being uncritically introduced as a basis for democratic renewal in employment relations? If unions need a new frame of reference that addresses current realities, then the institution of the nuclear family would seem an unlikely candidate. It is, perhaps, the single institution that has suffered a greater decline in the developed world that that of unions. Conceptually, reifying the family as a unit of analysis seems – to paraphrase Ackers' own criticism of Kelly again – to have missed some key developments in sociology over recent decades. Paradoxically, these developments are reflected in the increasing presence of women in the workforce and the subsequent undermining of 'traditional' gender roles within the family as well as at work (Wheelock 1990). What may well be legitimate, in any reformulation of unions role in society, would be a greater recognition of the effects of the changing gender composition of the (paid) workforce and how this interlinks with the domestic sphere; what is often described in the more neutral managerial jargon as 'work–life balance'.

Ackers' desire to redefine what the scope of employment relations should be in a modern context is correct. With regards to neo-pluralism, however, he is, to quote his own critique of Kelly, 'looking in the wrong place . . . for a framework that can deliver on these . . . promises' (15). Ackers' correctly identifies that much of the preoccupation of conventional IR is based around practices and institutions that have been so undermined (as we have noted). Collective bargaining, conflict resolution processes, joint consultation etc. continue to play a part in the regulation of the employment relationship, but cannot be assumed to be the organizing principle for the majority. The problem, for Ackers, of Kelly's approach – or any Marxist approach for that matter – is the emphasis on conflict as the defining characteristic of the employment relationship, and the overemphasis on workers and the workplace as being at the focal point of the employment relationship. The problem with the neo-pluralist alternative is that while it claims to supplement the focus on interests with that of interests and values, on close examination it seems preoccupied solely with values. In such a scenario it is unclear how interests could be articulated by the weaker party if they are expected to be seeking common interests? Paradoxically, Ackers' description of (conflict based) IR pluralism looks more like what, in political science, was being termed neo-pluralism; whereas Ackers' prescription of (IR) neo-pluralism looks more like the classical pluralism of Dahl.

Conclusions: unions and democracy now

From the liberal-democratic/classical pluralist definition of democracy, then, 'modern' democracy – i.e. that under neo-liberalism – seems to be lacking in a number of respects. The 'primacy of the unfettered market' now places constraints on most of these democratic/pluralist prerequisites. While equal civil rights, the supremacy of law and the value of the individual are compatible with the neo-liberal world view, they are so only (as, indeed, they always were) in the partial sense that socio-economic circumstances make access to these freedoms relative; on the above points some are clearly 'more equal than others'. The other democratic prerequisites are more constrained. The 'supremacy of the people' is now curtailed by the proviso that any democratic mandate must be compatible with the adherence to a variety of external constraints imposed by supranational institutions such as the WTO, the IMF and the World Bank. The 'consent of the governed', as the previously mentioned decline in voter turnout indicates, is increasingly open to challenge if we assume that 'consent' is measured by the proactive endorsement of the people through their participation in the process. The 'existence of a common good' is now fundamentally challenged in a range of ways. Its most crude expression is found in Thatcher's dictum that 'there is no such thing as society; there are only individuals and families'.

Despite appeals by 'third way' politics to reclaiming 'society' from the new right – as a *moral* ideal – 'the public good' remains contingent upon the constraints imposed by the necessities of the global economy. The most tangible expression of 'the public good' within the polity, remains the continuing existence of publicly funded, publicly accountable and publicly owned public services. This, as a principle, is now explicitly challenged by the third way. Even here, pragmatism plays its part. It remains unclear in the politics of the 'third way', how much the desire to abandon an adherence to the public provision of public services is based on pressure from (for example) the WTO and how much is due to the creation of commercially invigorated public service industries that will be able to capture overseas 'public sector markets', once they have been prised open by the General Agreement on Trade Services (GATS).

Notes

1 It should also be noted that participation in 'new social movements' may not be well represented by these trends. This issue, and its link to trade

unions and democracy, is more fully explored in chapter 10.

2 For various reasons, the growing strength of organized labour was viewed favourably by revolutionary Marxists, syndicalists, social democrats, 'workerists', Fabian socialists and liberals.

3 Specifically, it was 'liberty' that was the chief concern of the neo-liberal thinkers, but 'democracy' was often conflated with 'liberty' in these times.

4 During the McCarthyite witch hunts, union activists were challenged but not unions themselves. Indeed Ronald Reagan used his position as leader of the Screen Actors Guild as a platform for his anti-communism.

5 Although the experience in Canada has, for most of this period, been an acknowledged exception.

References

Ackers, P. 2002. 'Reframing Employment Relations: The Case for Neo-pluralism', *Industrial Relations Journal*, 33, 1: 2–19.

Adini, J., Ballington, J., Brians, C., Lounev, S., Nohlen, D., Norris, P., Notosusanto, S. Sullivan, K. and Urritia, E. 2002. *Voter Turnout Since 1945: A Global Report*. Stockholm: International IDEA.

Aglietta, M. 1979. *A Theory of Capitalist Regulation*. London: NLB.

Anderson, P. 2001. 'US Elections: Testing Formula Two', *New Left Review*, 8: 8–22.

Bach, S. 1999. 'Europe. Changing Public Service Employment Relations', in Bach, S., Bordogna, L., Della Rocca, G. and Winchester, D. (eds.), *Public Service Employment Relations in Europe. Transformation, Modernization or Inertia?* London: Routledge.

Bacon, N. and Storey, J. 1996. 'Individualism and Collectivism and the Changing Role of Trade Unions', in Ackers, P. and Smith, P. (eds.), *The New Workplace and Trade Unionism*. London: Routledge.

Brown, W., Deakin, S. and Ryan, P. 1997. 'The Effects of British Industrial Relations Legislation 1979–97', *National Institute Economic Review*, July: 69–83.

Dunleavy, P. and O'Leary, P. 1987. *Theories of the State: the Politics of Liberal Democracy*. Basingstoke: Macmillan.

Dunlop, J. 1958. *Industrial Relations Systems*. Carbondale: Southern Illinois University Press.

Etzioni-Helevy, E. (ed.) 1997. *Classes and Elites in Democracy and Democratization*. New York: Garland.

Friedman, M. 1968. 'The Role of Monetary Policy', *American Economic Review*, 58, 1: 1–17.

Gamble, A. 1994. *The Free Economy and the Strong State: The Politics of Thatcherism*, 2nd edn. Basingstoke: Macmillan.

Giddens, A. 1998. *The Third Way: The Renewal of Social Democracy*. Cambridge: Polity.

Godard, J. 1997. 'Managerial Strategies, Labour and Employment Relations and the State: The Canadian Case and Beyond', *British Journal of Industrial Relations* 35, 3: 399–426.

Goodwin, B. 2002. *Using Political Ideas*. Chichester: Wiley.

Gough, I. 1979. *The Political Economy of the Welfare State*. London: Macmillan.

Habermas, J. 1975. *Legitimation Crisis*. Boston: Beacon Press.

Hall, M., Broughton, A., Carley, M. and Sisson, K. 2002. *Works Councils for the UK? Assessing the Impact of EU Consultation Directive*. London: Industrial Relations Services.

Hammarström, O. and Nilsson, T. 1998. 'Employment Relations in Sweden', in Bamber, G. and Lansbury, R. (eds.), *International and Comparative Employment Relations*, 3rd edn. London: Sage.

Hayek, F. A. 1944. *The Road to Serfdom*. London: Routledge & Kegan Paul.

—— 1976. *Law, Legislation and Liberty*, Volume 2. London: Routledge & Kegan Paul.

Hobsbawm, E. 1981. *The Forward March of Labour Halted*. London: Verso.

Hutton, W. 2002. *The World We're In*. London: Little, Brown.

Hyman, R. 2001. *Understanding European Trade Unionism: Between Market, Class and Society*. London: Sage.

IDEA (n.d.) *Voter Turnout* www.idea/int/vt/index.cfm.

Kelly, J. 1998. *Rethinking Industrial Relations: Mobilization, Collectivism and Long Waves*. London: Routledge.

Klein, N. 2000. *No Logo: No Space, No Jobs*. London: Flamingo.

Lambert, R. and Webster, E. 2001. 'Southern Unionism and the New Labour Internationalisms', in Waterman, P. and Wills, J. (eds.), *Place, Space and the New Labour Internationalisms*. Oxford: Blackwell.

Lindblom, C. 1977. *Politics and Markets: The World's Political Economic Systems*. New York: Basic Books.

Ludlam, S., Bodah, M. and Coates, D. 2002. 'Trajectories of Solidarity: Changing Union–Party Linkages in the UK and the USA', *British Journal of Politics and International Relations*, 4, 2: 222–244.

MacInnes, J. 1987. *Thatcherism at Work*. Milton Keynes: Open University Press.

Martin, R., Smith, P., Fosh, P., Morris, H. and Undy, R. 1995. 'The Legislative Reform of Union Government 1979–94', *Industrial Relations Journal*, 26,2: 146–155.

Miller, K. and Steele, M. 1993. 'Employment Legislation, Thatcher and After', *Industrial Relations Journal*, 24, 3: 224–233.

Mishra, R. 1984. *The Welfare State in Crisis: Social Thought and Social Change*. Brighton: Wheatsheaf.

Munck, R. 2002. *Globalisation and Labour: The New Great Transformation*. London: Zed Books.

Nohlen, D. 2002. 'Political Participation in New and Old Democracies', in Pinter, R. P. and Gratschew, M. (eds.), *Voter Turnout Since 1945: A Global Report*. Stockholm: International IDEA.

O'Connor, J. 1973. *The Fiscal Crisis of the State*. New York: St Martin's Press.

Olson, M. 1971. *The Logic of Collective Action*. Cambridge, Mass.: Harvard University Press.

Pencavel, J. 2003. 'The Surprising Retreat of Union Britain', in Blundell, R.,

Card, D. and Freeman, R. (eds.), *Seeking a Premier League Economy*. Chicago: University of Chicago Press.

Pintor, R. and Gratschew, M. 2002. *Voter Turnout Since 1945: A Global Report*. Stockholm: International Institute for Democracy and Electoral Assistance.

Reich, R. 1999. 'We Are All Third Wayers Now', *The American Prospect*, 10, 43.

Ross, P., Bamber, G. and Whitehouse, G. 1998. 'Appendix: Employment, Economics and Industrial Relations: Comparative Statistics', in Bamber, G. and Lansbury, R. (eds.), *International and Comparative Employment Relations*, 3rd edn. London: Sage.

Saul, J. 1997. 'For Fear of Being Old Fashioned: Liberal Democracy vs Popular Democracy in Southern Africa', *Review of African Political Economy*, 72: 219–236.

Sklair, L. 2001. *The Transnational Capitalist Class*. Oxford: Blackwell.

Smith, P. and Morton, G. 2001. 'New Labour's Reform of Britain's Employment Law: the Devil is Not Only in the Detail but in the Values and Policy Too', *British Journal of Industrial Relations*, 39, 1: 119–138.

Taylor, R. 1993. *The Trade Unions Question in British Politics*. Oxford: Blackwell.

Visser, J. 1996. 'Traditions and Transitions in Industrial Relations: A European View, in D. Van Ruysseveldt and J. Visser (eds), *Indistrial Relations in Europe: Traditions and Transitions*. London: Sage.

Visser, J., Kochan, T. and Wood, S. 2002. 'Editor's Introduction to Special Edition on Union Decline and Prospects for Revival', *British Journal of Industrial Relations*, 40, 3: 373–384.

Wheelock, J. 1990. *Husbands at Home: the Domestic Economy in a Post-Industrial Economy*. London: Routledge.

5

Trade unions and non-standard employment

PHIL JAMES

Trade union membership has declined substantially across much, but not all, of the industrialized world (Ross *et al.* 1998). A variety of factors, the significance of which vary from country to country, have been identified as contributing to this pattern of decline, by both prompting membership loss and creating barriers to union recruitment (Waddington 2002). These include business cycle effects, the adoption of policies by employers aimed at undermining and excluding union organization, often through attempts to individualize employment relationships, and the pursuit by governments of legislative and other programmes that are intended to have a similar impact. Significantly for the present chapter, they also encompass a number of changes in the composition of employment, notably a shift of employment away from primary and manufacturing sectors towards private services, a growth of employment in smaller establishments and organizations, a rise in female labour market participation, a proportionate rise in the importance of non-manual work and, more particularly, an increase in various forms of non-standard employment.

These compositional changes are to some extent interrelated, as the close connection between part-time and female employment demonstrates. That said, there is no question that the rise of non-standard employment has constituted an important challenge to the development and maintenance of trade union organization and membership, particularly in the growing sectors of employment, and one that, in policy terms, unions have sought to address. Indeed, because of its connection to the other compositional changes detailed above, the extent to which unions are able to rise to meet this challenge has fundamental implications for the future health and vitality of the union movement internationally.

The chapter proceeds as follows. Initially, attention is paid to the meaning of the term 'non-standard employment' and the scale and growing significance of its place in the labour market. Following this, attention turns to the levels of union membership among non-standard workers and the potential that exists for these to be increased. This discussion, then, leads on to a critical examination of the strategies that unions have been adopting to secure such an increase.

Non-standard employment: its meaning and significance

The term non-standard employment is difficult to define precisely, although it is clearly intended to denote forms of employment that differ from 'standard' types. However, what constitutes 'standard' employment is problematic. For example, a common approach is to say that standard employment is 'full-time' and 'permanent' (Bradley *et al*. 2000). However, these two latter terms create definitional difficulties. Thus, the use of the word permanent is something of a misnomer since all, or virtually all, employment contracts can be legally terminated by an employer, with the result that it is more appropriate to use the phase 'open-ended' employment. In a similar vein, different approaches can be adopted with regard to the specification of the number of working hours that must be worked for a job to be defined as full-time. For example, in Canada the relevant threshold is 30 hours per week whereas in the United States it is 35 hours.

To confuse the matter further, marked differences also exist with regard to how countries define temporary employment (Tucker 2002). In addition, some authors prefer to define non-standard or 'contingent' employment in terms of its 'precariousness' and hence exclude from it part-time work on the grounds that, at least in some countries, a large proportion of this has a degree of permanence akin to that of full-time workers on open-ended contracts (Gallie *et al*. 1996; Heery *et al*. 2000b). These different definitional approaches lead to significantly different estimates of the scale of non-standard employment. For example, in the United States, the Bureau of Labor Statistics (BLS), which excludes part-time work when estimating the size of the 'contingent' workforce, suggests that such employment constitutes around 4 per cent of the total work-force, whereas the General Accounting Office (GAO), which does not, puts the figure at 30 per cent (BLS 2001; GAO 2000).

Nevertheless, notwithstanding these definitional problems, there is widespread agreement that the the period since the 1980s has seen a substantial growth internationally in the use of employment that is not full-time and open-ended, although there is evidence that the distribution of this expansion between the various categories of non-standard work varies considerably between countries (International Labour Organization 1997; Organization for Economic Co-operation and Development 2002). For example, in the USA the number of temporary workers grew by nearly 400 per cent in the period 1983–93 (Weinbaum 1999) and an upward trend in the use of this type of work has also been apparent in some European economies. However, this rising trend has, as can be seen from table 5.1, not been apparent in other countries. Thus, in Britain the proportion of the workforce consisting of temporary workers actually declined between 1985 and 1990 and, although it subsequently rose in the period to 1998, still stood only at the level that existed in the mid-1980s (Nolan and Slater 2002).

Table 5.1 Temporary employment across Europe (per cent temporary employees)

	1985	1990	1998
Spain	15.6	29.8	32.9
Finland	10.5	11.5	17.7
Portugal	14.4	18.3	17.3
France	4.7	10.5	13.9
Greece	21.1	16.5	13.0
Sweden	11.9	10.0	12.9
Germany	10.0	10.5	12.3
Netherlands	7.5	7.6	12.7
Denmark	12.3	10.8	10.1
Italy	4.8	5.2	8.6
Ireland	7.3	8.5	9.2
UK	7.0	5.2	7.1
Belgium	6.9	5.3	7.8

Source: Nolan, P. and Slater, G. 2002. 'The Labour Market: History, Structure and Prospects', in P. Edwards (ed.), *Industrial Relations: Theory and Practice*, 2nd edn. Oxford: Blackwell.

Trade union membership and non-standard employment

Not all international data show union membership to be lower among those engaged in the various types of non-standard employment. In Sweden, for example, it has been noted that the density of union membership among part-timers is almost as high as that for full-timers (Kjellberg 1998). Overall, however, it does generally reveal such a pattern (Mangan 2000). In the case of Britain, for example, workplace and labour force survey data (see table 5.2) shows this to be the case in respect of both temporary and part-time workers (Millward *et al.* 2000; Waddington 2002). Indeed, some econometric analyses have suggested that the growth in part-time employment is one of the factors that has contributed directly to union membership decline (Waddington 1992).

Table 5.2 Union density in Great Britain by category of employee

Category of employee	Union density (per cent) 1991	Union density (per cent) 1999
Full-time employees	42	33
Part-time employees	33	20
Permanent employees	38	31
Temporary employees	17	18

Source: Adapted from Waddington, J. 2002. 'Trade Union Organization', in P. Edwards (ed.), *Industrial Relations: Theory and Practice*, 2nd edn, Oxford: Blackwell.

Such findings, given the likelihood that non-standard work patterns will remain a significant and possibly growing, feature of the labour market in many countries, inevitably raise concerns about future trends in union membership.[1] At the same time, these fears should not be exaggerated. Thus, in Britain, not all econometric analysis has found a statistically significant association between the growth of part-time employment and union membership decline (Carruth and Disney 1988). Findings from the British workplace industrial/employee relations surveys conducted over the period 1980–98 point to a lack of a clear linear relationship between these two variables (Millward *et al.* 2000) and the extent of part-time employment has not been found to be a significant influence on variations in inter-industry levels of unionization (Bain and Elsheikh 1979; Richardson and Catlin 1979). Furthermore, it has been argued that the lower rates of unionization among part-time workers do not, in large part, stem from their holding less positive attitudes towards union membership and hence having a lower propensity to unionize. Rather, they largely reflect the barriers that they face in accessing union membership and related weaknesses in union recruitment strategies and activities (Gallie *et al.* 1996).

A number of British studies has obtained a range of evidence that is broadly compatible with this latter viewpoint. For example, one survey of non-members in part-time employment, conducted for the Union of Shop, Distributive and Allied Workers (USDAW), failed to find a marked antipathy among them towards unions, but, instead, found that the main reason for non-membership was the absence of any invitation to join (Frieze 1987). These findings, in turn, would seem to fit with the fact that the majority of female part-time workers are employed in sectors and occupations where rates of union density and recognition are relatively low (Walters 2002) and to be echoed by survey findings which indicate that the two most important determinants of union membership among such workers are the presence of workplace union representatives and past, favourable, experiences of unions (Sinclair 1995). This last finding is, furthermore, itself reinforced by a study of members of the British public sector union UNISON which found that part-time workers were less likely than full-time ones to express satisfaction with a number of aspects of local union organization, including contact with branch officers and shop stewards, and the location and timing of union meetings (Waddington and Kerr 1999).

Unions, at least in the case of part-time workers, do not necessarily face fundamental attitudinal barriers to the greater recruitment of non-standard workers. This does not, however, mean that such workers have the same views as full-time workers on open-ended contracts regarding what they want from unions and what factors therefore influence their decisions to both join unions and remain in membership. This is illustrated by another recent study which found that, in terms of their reasons for joining, part-time workers were more likely than their full-time counterparts to stress the provision of mutual support when they have a problem at work and access to free legal services and were less likely to make reference to the obtaining of improved pay and conditions (Waddington and Whitson 1997).

Non-standard workers: the potential for recruitment

At one level, some research findings indicate that the difficulties that unions face in recruiting non-standard workers are a reflection of a more general weakness in union recognition and organization in the areas of the economy where they work. In other words, lower levels of membership are a reflection of the problems unions have faced in expanding into those sectors of the economy where employment has been growing and where they have historically been poorly organized: a view that is given added weight by the fact that Waddington and Whitson (1997) found that part-time union members were much more likely to have joined as a result of informal recruitment methods or as a result of a recommendation from their management, rather than via contacts with lay and full-time union representatives and officials. At another level, however, the available evidence suggests that, as well as addressing these more structural problems of union organization, unions also need to take action to ensure that their policies and methods are perceived as relevant and appropriate by non-standard workers.

The scale of these problems and the challenges they create for unions are clearly significant and care must consequently be taken not to underestimate the difficulties they pose in terms of extending union membership among non-standard workers. Nevertheless, the evidence available on the employment conditions and experiences of non-standard workers suggests that unions have an opportunity to explain the value of union membership to them.

Several British-based surveys have explored the working conditions and experiences of temporary and part-time workers and compared them with those on full-time, open-ended, contracts (Cully et al. 1999; Gallie et al. 1998). Their findings do not paint a picture of universal disadvantage. For example, it has been found that part-time workers often work under less pressure than their full-time counterparts and generally do not perceive their employment to be less secure.[2] They do, however, in general indicate a fairly consistent pattern of employment disadvantage in terms of such matters as pay, benefits, consultation by managers, opportunities for career development and training, and scope for exercising skill and discretion at work.

These British findings are broadly replicated in a number of international studies. Furthermore, a number of other studies have also revealed non-standard employment status to be associated with poorer standards of health and safety and higher levels of work-related injuries and illness (Mangan 2000). For example, a large-scale Swedish survey of both permanent and various categories of non-permanent workers found that the latter were less likely to consider that they had sufficient knowledge of their work environment, and were more likely to feel that they had been neglected with regard to the training and instructions that were considered essential for them to implement job tasks in a 'good way' (Aronsson 1999). More generally, the second European survey of the working environment revealed that agency workers and those on fixed term contracts were significantly more likely to undertake work involving repetitive tasks, repetitive movements and painful or tiring working positions – all factors associated with musculoskeletal disorders (European Foundation for the Improvement of Living and Working Conditions 1997).

The labour market disadvantage suffered by non-standard workers clearly offers unions the potential to 'sell themselves' as a means of addressing it. At the same time, this 'sales opportunity' is far from straightforward for two main reasons. Firstly, because of the likely resistance of employers to attempts to extend union membership and organization to such workers, particularly given the fact, as noted earlier, that many of them are employed in sectors and organizations with little history of trade union representation (Kelly and Waddington 1995). Secondly, because of the fact that non-standard workers cannot be safely assumed to consider themselves to be 'subjectively' disadvantaged. For example, the authors of one British study found that, although suffering from relatively inferior working conditions and experiences compared with full-timers, part-time workers tended to feel more fairly treated at work, to be more likely to consider that workplace managers encouraged skills development, to rate management higher in terms of employee involvement and support for work life balance and to possess higher levels of job satisfaction (Cully *et al.* 1999).

The first of these problems is, of course, part of the previously mentioned more general difficulty that unions face in extending their membership base into such areas of employment growth as the private-sector services and small and medium sized enterprises: a problem that reflects the long recognized point that workers are more likely to join unions where an employer already recognizes unions (Bain 1970). As regards the second problem, this would appear to suggest that union recruitment strategies need to go beyond offering non-standard workers a means of combating their inferior position and extend to making them more aware of the injustices they face and their right to expect more equitable and better treatment.

Union recruitment strategies and their impact

It is fair to say that trade unions internationally were slow to respond to the changing labour market conditions and related membership losses they faced from the end of the 1970s (see e.g. International Labour Organization 1997). Gradually, as the years went by and membership losses increased, however, a number of countervailing strategies were developed, some of which focused specifically on non-standard workers, and others of which were concentrated on overcoming barriers to recruitment more generally: a concentration that, as the preceding paragraph highlighted, cannot be discounted in terms of its relevance and value to the extension of union organization to those employed on non-standard terms and conditions. These strategies can be viewed as falling into five broad, but to some extent interrelated, categories: the offering of individual benefit packages; the according of a greater and more strategic emphasis on member recruitment; actions to better address non-standard workers' interests and concerns; campaigning for legal frameworks that support member recruitment and employer recognition and embody more favourable rights for non-standard workers; and the development of approaches aimed at engendering greater employer willingness to voluntarily grant unions' negotiating rights.

Below, the nature of these strategies are outlined and consideration given to their potential and actual usefulness as a means of increasing union membership among the various types of non-standard employment.

Individual benefit packages

Historically, trade unions have always offered various types of individual benefits to members. Indeed, the provision of welfare benefits, such as the provision of financial support during sickness and unemployment, represented an important function of some of the early trade unions. However, the importance attached to the provision of such support has generally declined over time as a result of the advent of state social security systems.[3]

For the trade union movements in Britain and the United States, the decline in membership that occurred from the end of the 1970s, together with a belief in some quarters that this was associated with a growth of more individualist, and less collectivist, orientations on the part of workers, led to a renewed interest in the role that individual benefits could play in attracting new members, particularly in new areas of employment growth, such as non-standard work (Williams 1997; Hurd 2002). In fact, some commentators argued that they could be used as a basis for a fundamental re-conceptualization of the role and functions of trade unions in which members were viewed as consumers of individual services and had a relationship with their unions akin to that between the Automobile Association (AA) and its members (Bassett and Cave 1993). As a consequence, a variety of unions sought to increase the range of individual benefits they made available to members. For example, a number of unions launched credit cards, provided discounted personal insurance cover, developed or increased union training and educational opportunities, offered personal pension plans, improved access to free legal advice and marketed competitively priced mortgages and package holidays.

The making available of 'portable' benefits of this type, as well as other labour market services, such as the provision of training opportunities and the operation of employment agencies, has been noted to potentially have an important role to play in attracting the more precarious types of non-standard workers, such as temporary and self-employed ones, into union membership (Cobble 1997; Osterman 1999). Certainly, a number of unions, both in Britain and the United States, which have traditionally catered for members engaged in freelance and related work, have placed considerable weight on the provision of such benefits and services (Heery *et al.* 2000a; Osterman 1999).

That said, subsequent studies have suggested that this shift in approach has generally been relatively unsuccessful in attracting new recruits (Sapper 1991; Williams 1997). They have therefore cast some doubt on the extent to which there has been a marked shift towards the adoption of more individualistic orientations on the part of non-standard workers, as well as workers more generally: doubt that, in the case of Britain, has been reinforced by social attitude survey evidence (Kelly 1998). Nevertheless, the provision of individual benefits does have some role to play and not only in those unions which have historically catered for self-employed workers, since they would seem to be both valued and extensively used by members (Williams 1997).

Orientation towards recruitment

Attaching more importance to the provision of individual benefits reflects a more general attempt on the part of union movements to adopt a greater and more systematic focus on recruitment (Hurd 2002; Wood and Brewster 2002). This focus can be seen at both the level of trade union confederations and the level of individual unions.

In a number of countries central union confederations have taken steps to re-orientate their activities and purpose to encompass a greater emphasis on both campaigning and the development of union organization and membership (Industrial Relations Services 1997). These reforms have commonly embodied the taking of action to work with wider community and pressures groups on joint campaigns involving wider social and political issues (see chapter 11) and the development of new internal policies and infrastructures designed to support and expand union organizing. In this latter area, for example, an important feature of the work undertaken by union confederations in Australia, Britain, the Netherlands and the United States has been the establishment of academies that are used to train a cadre of new union organizers who can be subsequently employed by individual unions (Heery, et al. 2000a; Hurd 2002; Industrial Relations Services 1997).

With regard to individual unions, there is also evidence that there have been widespread attempts to review and revise recruitment strategies. New recruitment campaigns (and associated publicity and marketing activities), some of which have been explicitly aimed at non-standard workers, have been launched. Steps have been taken to increase the attention paid to recruitment by lay workplace representatives and full-time officials. Central responsibilities for recruitment have some-times been established or strengthened, and systems also sometimes put in place to monitor the implementation and effects of the new arrangements. In some unions, attempts have also been made, at both national and local levels, to support this greater attention to reducing the time paid officials spend on 'servicing' existing members by pursuing an 'organizing model' under which local trade union organizations are helped and encouraged to become more self-sufficient, thereby increasing the time that the officials have to focus on supporting the recruitment of new members (see chapter 7).

It is not possible to reach firm conclusions about how effec-tive these various changes have been in supporting the extension of membership, either generally or in respect of non-standard workers in particular. The available evidence, however, suggests that, perhaps, inevitably, their implementation has sometimes been difficult. For example, in both the United States and Britain there has been a degree of resistance among some affili-ates to central confederations taking a more active role in the area (Fletcher and Hurd 1998; Heery et al. 2000b). Recruitment campaigns have sometimes not been adequately resourced and co-ordinated (Mason and Bain 1991), and full-time officials have not always been able or willing to devote more time to recruit-ment issues (Kelly and Heery 1989). In addition, there is also some evidence that unions have sometimes focused their efforts more on consolidating their strength in sectors and occupations where they are already well established, rather than extending recruitment strategies to non-standard workers. For example, one British survey of 56 unions utilized 24 different methods to represent the interests of various categories of non-standard worker and found that in virtually all cases these methods had only been utilized by a minority of the unions concerned (Heery et al. 2002). In addition, such action was further found to be concentrated in unions that already had relatively high propor-tions of part-time and temporary workers in membership. This hesitancy to expand the focus of recruitment is, perhaps, to some extent understandable, at least in economies such as the United States and Britain where collective bargaining is predom-inantly carried out on a decentralized enterprise basis rather than at the multi-employer, sectoral level.

Willman (1989), in respect of Britain, has pointed out that

unions can, at least in the short term (see below), broadly adopt three different strategies towards the recruitment of new members: (1) seek to recruit non-members in non-organized workplaces; (2) seek to recruit members in existing organized workplaces; and (3) seek to recruit employers and thereby gain access to their workforces in this way.[4] All of these strategies clearly can be and are pursued by unions. However, Willman argues that they are likely to vary in their cost-effectiveness, and hence the extent to which they divert resources away from the servicing of existing members, with (1) being less cost-effective than (2) and (2) less cost effective than (3).[5]

Willman's analysis, moreover, does seem to accord to some extent with current union organizing attempts in Britain. Certainly, British evidence suggests that union efforts to gain employer recognition focus on firms with union members and no recognition agreements, on companies where they had been derecognized but retain high levels of membership and on firms with recognition covering part of a company or a workforce but not the whole. In contrast, because of the perceived costs and time involved, far less attention is being paid to companies and workplaces where there is neither recognition nor union membership (Oxenbridge et al. 2002).

Nevertheless, the above problems should not be taken to imply that unions have not, at the aggregate level, been doing more to make themselves attractive and accessible to non-standard workers, as well as other unorganized groups. There is, furthermore, some evidence that a vigorous and well-organized approach regarding their recruitment can be successful. In the United States, for example, union inspired attempts to organize graduate student teaching assistants and janitors, many of whom are on non-standard forms of employment, have met with a good deal of success (Bronfenbrenner et al. 1998; Hurd 2002).

Recruiting the employer

Willman has, then, argued that the 'recruitment of the employer' represents the most cost-effective approach to expanding union membership. Whether this argument is correct or not, it is the case that from the 1980s onwards unions in a number of countries, including Britain and the United States, have sought to adopt, at least publicly, more conciliatory and co-operative stances towards unorganized employers which have emphasized the mutual benefits that can stem from the establishment of a union presence (Fletcher and Hurd 1999; Hurd 2002; Wood and Brewster 2002). In Britain, for example, some unions in the 1980s produced glossy marketing brochures that stressed the willingness to work with the employer to improve competiteness via such means as greater labour flexibility, collaboration in the area of training, and a commitment to avoid disruption, through the conclusion of 'no strike' agreements under which all disputes would be resolved by arbitration (Lewis 1990). More recently, this approach has been conceptualized under the umbrella of 'partnership', reflecting the present Labour government's commitment to this somewhat vague and imprecise concept (Tailby and Winchester 2000).

There have been examples where this more conciliatory approach appears to have engendered employer willingness to accord recognition, sometimes even before a workforce has been fully recruited, but there is little evidence to suggest that this has expanded union membership among non-standard workers. However, anaedotal evidence from Britain indicates, if anything, that most such agreements are in 'traditional' sectors and do not therefore involve non-standard workers. As a result, they did not generally act to extend union recognition into the growing private services sector of the economy.[6]

Moreover, whatever the cost-effective virtues of this employer-based approach to membership expansion, it does carry the danger that unions will compete with each other to appear attractive to employers and in doing so obtain recognition agreements that are heavily weighted in the employer's favour, for example, by providing that negotiations will be conducted by elected company councils that consist of both union and non-union representatives. Such a fear may be countered by the argument that, once recognized, unions will then have a base to subsequently strengthen their position: a view that demonstrates that 'partnership' and 'organizing' models of union activity are not necessarily mutually exclusive, but may be used in a sequential way. However, the vailidity of this argument is far from certain, particularly given the danger that a 'top down' approach to the establishment of employer recognition runs the risk that the resulting workplace union organization may end up being highly reliant on 'servicing' support from union full-time officials: a situation which, somewhat ironically, Willman, in a later piece of work, has noted can lead to workplace organizations being a 'net importer', rather than 'exporter', of funds to the wider union. Furthermore, such a reliance on external servicing may result in what Boxall and Haynes (1997) have described as 'paper tiger' unionism: that is a weak form of workplace unionism that is unlikely to provide an effective basis of 'worker voice' and hence may yield results that are not seen to be impressive by either potential or current members.[7]

At the same time, these dangers need to be set alongside the fact that the earlier mentioned study by Oxenbridge, *et al.* (2002) also found evidence to suggest that non-union employers, when confronted with 'adversarial' organizing campaigns, tend to respond in a hostile manner. It would therefore seem that unions, in seeking to expand employer recognition, frequently occupy a position somewhere between a 'rock and a hard place'.[8]

Meeting non-standard workers' interests and concerns

Reference was made earlier, in relation to part-time workers, that their needs and interests may differ in certain respects from those of full-time ones. In a similar vein, attention has been drawn to the fact that women, ethnic minority workers, among whom union membership is often relatively low, and also temporary workers may have interests that differ somewhat from those of full-time and 'permanent' male workers. For example, Heery *et al.* (2000a) have pointed out that, in contrast to workers with a stable relationship with an employer, temporary and self-employed workers are likely to have a greater interest in the regulation of the external, rather than internal, labour market via such means as the specification of a framework of minimum terms and conditions and the provision of access to training and development.

An important dimension of union responses to the growth of non-standard employment has therefore been to revamp internal governmental structures and bargaining agendas in order to better address the concerns and interests of such workers. These responses have encompassed a number of elements, including the reserving of seats on executive committees for representatives of women, the establishment of special conferences, advisory bodies and committees for women and ethnic minorities, the establishment of bargaining objectives, such as the establishment of *pro rata* terms and conditions for non-standard workers, and the provision of training for negotiators.

Internationally, relatively little systematic information exists on the extent to which unions have made use of such strategies, although, as the earlier quoted research by Heery *et al.* (2002) indicates, it would seem that in Britain they have generally been used by small minorities of unions. As regards their impact on recruitment, scant evidence also exists and that which does is sometimes rather contradictory. For example, while union equality structures have been found to often occupy a rather marginal role (Colgan and Ledwith 2002), it is noticeable that the British Trade Union Congress's campaign to improve the rights of part-time workers stemmed from an initiative on the part of its equality committee. In addition, Heery *et al.* (2002) have found a significant and positive correlation between the scale of union activity aimed at addressing the needs of part-time and temporary workers and the presence of a women's or equality committee or conference.

At the same time, it needs to be recognized that union initiatives of the type discussed in this section, even if pursued, are likely to face two sets of important constraints. Firstly, the existence of tensions between the interests of non-standard and standard workers: tensions that may contradictorilly arise, for example, either because of concerns on the part of the latter that the use of the former type of staff will undermine existing terms and conditions and job security (Carre *et al.* 1994) or because the employment of such workers on inferior terms is seen as a means of enhancing future job security. Secondly, the difficulties that unions in countries in which enterprise-based unionism predominates face in addressing the wide external labour market needs of temporary and self-employed workers.[9]

Political campaigning

Political action to aid union recruitment has involved two different strategies. The first is lobbying for legal frameworks that assist unions in representing workers and securing recognition from employers. The second concerns campaigning for legal rights for workers, both out of principle and as a means of demonstrating the values and positive role of unions.

The first of these strands is addressed in detail in chapter 13 and is consequently not explored here. As regards the second, it should be noted that the period since the 1980s has seen unions in a variety of countries seeking and often obtaining, greater legal protection for various categories of non-standard workers, as well as for women. Examples of such campaigning include US union calls made to the Dunlop Commission, for improved legal rights for 'contingent' workers (Commission on the Future of Worker–Management Relations 1995), the pressure exerted by the British TUC for enhanced legal protection for part-time workers (Heery 1996) and the efforts of the European Trades Union (ETUC) in supporting the adoption of European directives concerning part-time, agency, fixed-term and temporary work. However, as laudable as these campaigns and related successes are, it is far from clear whether they have served to support the creation of a more favourable view of trade unionism and also acted to encourage more non-standard workers to join. In fact, some commentators have argued, on the contrary, that the establishment of a stronger base of individual employment rights runs the risk of, ironically, reducing the perceived need for unions among workers.

Conclusion

A significant growth in non-standard employment has occurred in much of the industrialized world since the 1980s. This growth has posed important challenges for trade unions, directly, because levels of union membership among such workers are typically lower, and indirectly, because, it is itself intimately connected with a number of other shifts in the composition of employment, including a rise in female labour force participation and a growth in the importance of the private services sector as a source of work.

In response to these challenges unions have adopted a number of strategies to improve member recruitment, some of which have focussed specifically on non-standard workers and others of which, although more broadly based, have potential implications for the recruitment of such workers because of their relevance to some of the other compositional changes mentioned above. These strategies can be viewed as falling into five broad, but overlapping, categories: the offering of individual benefit packages; the according of a greater and more strategic emphasis on member recruitment; actions to better address non-standard workers interests and concerns; campaigning for legal frameworks that support member recruitment and employer recognition and embody more favourable rights for non-standard workers; and the development of approaches aimed at engendering greater employer willingness to voluntarily grant union negotiating rights.

These developments have occurred against a backdrop of evidence which suggests that non-standard workers are not fundamentally antithetical towards joining unions and indicates that workers of this type frequently experience working conditions less favourable than other workers. Unions thus have an opportunity to 'sell themselves' as an avenue through which this unfavourable treatment can be addressed: although it apparently does not automatically follow that non-standard workers consider themselves to be the subject of such treatment. To date, the success of such strategies, in terms of expanding union membership among non-standard workers, is far from proven. What is, nevertheless, clear, is that their development and implementation has often been problematic.

In part, this is because non-standard workers, particularly those engaged in temporary work, are likely to have different concerns and interests from those employed on 'standard' employment contracts. Moreover, unions face a number of internal problems in both resourcing and mobilizing support for the adoption and operationalization of new recruitment strategies. These problems reflect concerns about the potential for such strategies to harm the ability of union officials and representatives to adequately service existing members and possible tensions between the interests of non-standard and 'full-time' workers. They also stem from doubts concerning the cost–benefit trade-off associated with according a higher priority to the recruitment of non-standard workers, particularly where they work in occupations and sectors which themselves have been traditionally poorly organized by unions.

For unions operating in economies where decentralized enterprise bargaining, predominates, this issue of cost-effectiveness is, perhaps, likely to be particularly problematic for two reasons. Firstly, because such bargaining, by definition, does not provide a platform for the regulation of the wider external labour market: an issue that is likely to be of relevance to temporary and freelance workers. Secondly, because in order to deliver benefits to members unions need to be able to secure bargaining rights from individual employers. Consequently, the issue of how best to obtain such rights cannot easily be divorced from the more general one of how to increase recruitment among poorly organized groups of workers, including non-standard ones.

In broad terms, different unions and different groupings within unions, adopt rather different positions to the issue of how best to obtain recognition from employers. One perspective is that the best way forward is to adopt a 'partnership' or 'joint governance' approach which embodies a willingness to work jointly with employers on a 'win–win' basis. Another eschews this approach and instead places an emphasis on the adoption of a more confrontational, 'organizing' one that is premised on the view that union renewal can only be achieved through the creation of combative workplace union organizations that have the capacity to challenge employer interests and agendas (Fairbrother 2000). In between these two viewpoints, would seem to sit a third, less 'pure', 'horses for courses', option within which the 'partnership' and 'organizing' models are not seen as mutually exclusive, but rather as part of a continuum encompassing differing degrees of 'co-operativeness' and 'adversarialism' that can be utilized in a tactical way, dependent on the attitudes and responses of particular employers.

These different positions can all be viewed as having potential advantages and disadvantages. However, the differences between them should not be overly exaggerated. For, to return to the cost-effectiveness issue, the co-operative, partnership approach itself is only likely to be financially viable for many unions if it, ultimately, leads to the development of reasonably self-sufficient workplace union organizations. In large part, therefore, the 'organizing and 'partnership' approaches, in practice, do not, necessarily, differ greatly in terms of their ultimate goals. Rather, they differ in terms of how this goal is best achieved, with the former approach stressing the advantages of gaining employer support as a means of developing effective workplace union organizations and the latter seeing the creation of such organizations as being more likely to arise in workforces that have developed a collective consciousness and solidarity through industrial struggles with employers.

In summary, unions have widely recognized the need to increase their recruitment among non-standard workers and have taken a variety of actions to achieve this. It, nevertheless, remains, at this stage, an open question as to how successful they have been and will be, in achieving this objective.[10] It also remains a question for debate as to which types of strategies are likely to most effectively contribute to its achievement and how far their relative values differ, both generally and between different national economies as a result of variations in the surrounding political, economic and industrial relations contexts.

Notes

1 A further point to note about this is that there is a danger in assuming that any upward trends in the use of non-standard work will necessarily continue. For example, survey data in Britain has revealed that the proportion of employees occupying permanent jobs rose from 88 to 92 per cent over the years 1992–2000. It further reveals that during this same period the proportion of workers employed on fixed term contracts of between one and three years duration and temporary contracts of less than 12 months fell from five to 2.8 per cent and 7.2 to 5.5 per cent respectively. See Taylor (undated).

2 Gallie *et al.* (1998) found, in contrast, that temporary workers on contracts of less than 12 months were likely to report higher levels of job insecurity. However, they also found that this was not the case with those who were on contracts of one to three years duration and that these longer-term workers also did not report the various other types of disadvantage reported by part-timers and their shorter-term temporary counterparts.

3 An important qualification to this general point is the role that unions play in administering government financed unemployment and other social security benefits in countries such as Belgium, Denmark, Finland and Sweden (see Kjellberg 1998).

4 Willman, in fact, distinguished a fourth strategy, namely to merge with other unions. However, this option has been excluded here due to the fact that it is not exclusively concerned with the recruitment of new members. It must, nevertheless, be acknowledged that, insofar as such mergers generate economies of scale, they potentially do provide the basis for enhanced recruitment activities in the future.

5 It has been argued that this potentially adverse 'trade-off' between expenditure on recruitment and the servicing of existing members can be, at least be partially ameliorated by unions critically reviewing their internal structures and modes of operating in order to obtain efficiency savings (Wood and Brewster, 2000). One way of obtaining such savings has been noted to be the engendering of greater self-sufficiency on the part of workplace union organizations in order to provide full-time offi-

cers with more time to spend on the recruitment of new members (Fletcher and Hurd 1999).

6 This said, it should be noted that a number of unions did manage to obtain recognition from the temporary employment agency Manpower. It should also be noted, in connection with this, that related developments concerning the representation of temporary agency workers have occurred in the Netherlands (see Visser 1998).

7 This point, in the case of Britain, is given some added weight by recent research that revealed widespread concerns on the part of union officials that a new right provided to workers under the Employment Relations Act 1999, to be represented in formal disciplinary and grievance hearings, whether or not a union was recognized at their workplace, that they would be 'deluged with calls for help from individual members and would be unable to respond due to a lack of resources' (Oxenbridge et al. 2002).

8 The findings of Oxenbridge et al. further suggest that in response to this situation unions are, against the background of Britain's new statutory framework on union recognition, tending to concentrate on trying to build up membership levels prior to seeking recognition, rather than seeking to 'recruit the employer' through the adoption of accommodative concessions. It may therefore be that, at least since the advent of this framework, unions are tending to place less emphasis on the conclusion of 'top-down' recognition agreements with employers.

9 The relevance of this last point is to some extent highlighted by the fact that whereas in Britain trade unions have sought to improve the position of temporary workers via campaigning for better legal rights and encouraging negotiators to address their interests, in the Netherlands a central agreement was concluded in 1996 on 'Flexibility and Security': an agreement which apparently subsequently led to the overhaul of Dutch employment protection legislation (see Visser 1998).

10 It should be noted, however, that one British study, which utilized data from the British Household Survey, found no evidence of an increase in union coverage of various types of non-standard workers over the period 1991–97 (Booth and Francesconi 2000).

References

Aronsson, G. 1999. 'Contingent Workers and Health and Safety', *Work, Employment and Society*, 13: 3: 439–59.

Bain, G. 1970. *The Growth of White Collar Unionism*. Oxford: Oxford University Press.

Bain, G. and Elsheikh, F. 1979. 'An Inter-industry Analysis of Unionisation in Britain', *British Journal of Industrial Relations*, 27, 2: 137–157.

Bassett, P. and Cave, A. 1993. *All for One: The Future of the Unions*. London: Fabian Society.

Booth, A. and Francesconi, M. 2000. *Collectivism versus Individualism: Performance-related Pay and Union Coverage for Non-standard Workers in Britain*. Institute for Labour Research, Working Paper No. 61, University of Essex.

Boxall, P. and Haynes, P. 1997. 'Strategy and Trade Union Effectiveness in a Neo-Liberal Environment', *British Journal of Industrial Relations*, 35, 4: 567–92.

Bradley, H., Erickson, M., Stephenson, C. and Williams, S. 2000. *Myths at Work*, Cambridge: Polity.

Bronfenbrenner, K., Friedman, S., Hurd, R., Oswald, R. and Seeber, R. 1998. *Organizing to Win*. Ithaca: ILR Press.

Bureau of Labor Statistics 2001. *Contingent and Alternative Employment Arrangements*, Washington: US Department of Labor.

Carre, F. J., duRivage, V. L. and Tilly, C. 1994. 'Representing the Part-time and Contingent Workforce: Challenges for Unions and Public Policy', Friedman, S., Hurd, R. W., Oswald R. A. and Seeber, R. L. (eds.), *Restoring the Promise of American Labor Law*. Ithaca: ILR Press.

Carruth, A. and Disney, R. 1988. 'Where Have Two Million Trade Union Members Gone?', *Economica*, 55, 1: 1–19.

Cobble, D. 1997. 'Lost Ways of Organizing: Reviving the AFL's Direct Affiliate Strategy', *Industrial Relations*, 36, 3: 278–301.

Colgan, F. and Ledwith, S. 2002. 'Gender Diversity and Mobilization in UK Unions', in Colgan, F. and Ledwith, S. (eds.), *Gender, Diversity and Trade Unions: International Perspectives*, London: Routledge.

Commission on the Future of Worker–Management Relations. 1995. *Report and Recommendations*, Washington: Department of Labor.

Cully, M., Woodland, S., O'Reilly, A. and Dix, G. 1999. *Britain at Work: As Depicted by the 1998 Workplace Employee Relations Survey*. London: Routledge.

European Foundation for the Improvement of Living and Working Conditions. 1997. *Second European Survey of the Working Environment*. Luxembourg: Office for Official Publications of the European Communities.

Fairbrother, P. 2000. *Trade Unions at the Crossroads*. London: Mansell.

Fletcher, B. and Hurd, R. 1998. 'Beyond the Organizing Model: The Transformation Process in Local Unions', in Bromfenbrenner, K. Friedman, S. Hurd, R. Oswald, R. and Seeber R. (eds), *Organizing to Win*. Ithaca: IRL Press.

—— 1999. 'Political Will, Local Union Transformaton and the Organizing Imperative', in Nissen, B. (ed.), *Which Direction for Organized Labour: Essays on Organizing, Outreach and Internal Transformation*. Detroit: Wayne State University Press.

Frieze, J. 1987. *Part-time Workers: Conditions, Rights and Unions*. London: Workers Educational Association.

Gallie, D., Penn, R. and Rose, M. 1996. *Trade Unionism in Recession*. Oxford: Oxford University Press.

Gallie, D., White, M., Cheng, Y. and Tomlinson, M. 1998. *Restructuring the Employment Relationship*. Oxford: Oxford University Press.

General Accounting Office. 2000. *Contingent Workers: Incomes and Benefits Lag behind Rest of the Workforce*, Report to the Honorable Edward M. Kennedy and the Honorable Robert G. Torricelli, Washington, US Senate.

Heery, E. 1996. 'Campaigning for Part-time Workers', *Work, Employment and Society*, 12, 2: 351–366.

Heery, E., Simms, M., Delbridge, R., Salmon, J. and Simpson, D. 2000a. 'The TUC's Organizing Academy: An Assessment', *Industrial Relations Journal*, 31, 5: 400–415.

Heery, E., Simms, M., Conley, H., Delbridge, R. and Stewart, P. 2000b. *Beyond the Enterprise? Trade Unions and the Representation of Contingent Workers*, ESRC Future of Work Working Paper No. 7, University of Leeds.

—— 2002. *Trade Unions and the Flexible Workforce: A Survey Analysis of Union Policy and Practice*, ESRC Future of Work Working Paper No. 22, University of Leeds.

Hurd, R. W. 2002. 'Contesting the Dinosaur Image: The U.S. Labour Movement's Search for a Future', *Society in Transition*, 33, 2: 227–240.

Industrial Relations Services. 1997. 'Organizing the Unorganized', *IRS Employment Review*, 644, 4–10.

International Labour Organization. 1997. 'Part-time Work: Solution or Trap?', *International Labour Review*, 136, 4: 1–18.

Kelly, J. 1998. *Rethinking Industrial Relations: Mobilization, Collectivism and Long Waves*. London: Routledge.

Kelly, J. and Heery, E. 1989. 'Full-time Officers and Trade Union Recruitment', *British Journal of Industrial Relations*, 27, 2: 196–213.

Kelly, J. and Waddington, J. 1995. 'New Prospects for British Labour, *Organization* , 2, 3/4: 415–426.

Kjellberg, J. 1998. 'Sweden: Restoring the Model?', in Ferner, A. and Hyman, R. (eds.), *Changing Industrial Relations in Europe*. Oxford: Blackwell.

Lewis, R. 1990. 'Strike-free Deals and Pendulum Arbitration', *British Journal of Industrial Relations*, 28, 1: 32–56.

Mangan, J. 2000. *Workers without Traditional Employment Employment: An International Study of Non-standard Work*. Massachusetts: Edward Elgar.

Mason, B. and Bain, P. 1991. 'Trade Union Recruitment Strategies: Facing the 1990s', *Industrial Relations Journal*, 22, 1: 36–45.

Millward, N., Bryson, A. and Forth, J. 2000. *All Change at …* London: Routledge.

Nolan, P. and Slater, G. 2002. 'The Labour Market: History, Structure and Prospects', in Edwards, P. (ed.), *Industrial Relations: Theory and Practice*, 2nd edn. Oxford: Blackwell.

Organization for Economic Co-operation and Development. 2002. *Employment Outlook*. Paris: OECD.

Osterman, P. 1999. *Securing Prosperity. The American Labour Market: How It Has Changed and What to Do about It*. New Jersey: Princeton University Press.

Oxenbridge, S., Brown, W., Deakin, S. and Pratten, C. 2002. *Collective Employee Representation and the Impact of the Law: Initial Responses to the Employment Act 1999*, ESRC Future of Work Working Paper No. 23, University of Leeds.

Richardson, R. and Catlin, S. 1979. 'Trade Union Density and Collective Agreement Patterns in Britain', *British Journal of Industrial Relations*, 17, 3: 376–385.

Ross, P., Bamber, G. and Lansbury, R. 1998. 'Appendix: Employment, Economics,and Industrial Relations – Comparative Statistics', in Bamber, G. and Lansbury, R. (eds.), *International and Comprative Employment Relations*. London: Sage.

Sapper, S. 1991. 'Do Members' Services Packages Influence Trade Union Recruitment?'. *Industrial Relations Journal*, 22: 1, 63–78.

Sinclair, D. 1995. 'The Importance of Sex for the Propensity to Unionize', *British Journal of Industrial Relations*, 33, 2: 173–190.

Tailby, S. and Winchester, D. 2000. 'Management and Trade Unions, in Bach, S. and Sisson, K. (eds.), *Personnel Management in Britain*. Oxford: Blackwell.

Taylor, R. Undated. *Britain's World of Work: Myths and Realities*, ESRC Future of Work Seminar Series, Swindon, Economic and Social Research Council.

Tucker, D. 2002. *'Precarious' Non-standard Employment: A Review of the Literature*, Department of Labour, New Zealand.

Visser, J. 1998. 'The Netherlands: The Return of Responsive Corporatism', in Edwards, P. (ed.), *Industrial Relations: Theory and Practice*, 2nd edn. Oxford: Blackwell.

Waddington, J. 1992. 'Trade Union Membership in Britain, 1980–1987: Unemployment and Restructuring', *British Journal of Industrial Relations*, 30, 2: 287–322.

—— 2002. 'Trade Union Organization', in Edwards, P. (ed.), *Industrial Relations: Theory and Practice*, 2nd edn. Oxford: Blackwell.

Waddington, J. and Kerr, A. 1999. 'Membership Retention in the Public Sector', *Industrial Relations Journal*, 30, 2: 151–165.

Waddington, J. and Whitson, C. 1997. 'Why Do People Join Unions in a Period of Membership Decline?', *British Journal of Industrial Relations*, 35, 4: 515–546.

Walters, S. 2002. 'Female Part-time Workers' Attitudes to Trade Unions in Britain', *British Journal of Industrial Relations*, 40, 1: 49–68.

Weinbaum, E. 1999. 'Organizing Labor in an Era of Contingent Work and Globalisation', in Nissen, B. (ed.), *Which Direction for Organized Labour: Essays on Organizing, Outreach and Internal Transformation*. Detroit: Wayne State University Press.

Williams, S. 1997. 'The Nature of Some Recent Trade Union Modernization Policies in the UK', *British Journal of Industrial Relations*, 35, 4: 495–514.

Willman, P. 1989. 'The Logic of Market-share Trade Unionism: Is Membership Decline Inevitable?', *Industrial Relations Journal*, 20, 4: 260–270.

—— 2001. 'The Viability of Trade Union Organization', *British Journal of Industrial Relations*, 39, 1: 97–117.

Wood, G. and Brewster, C. 2002. 'Decline and Renewal in the British Labour Movement: Trends, Practices and Lessons for South Africa', *Society in Transition*, 33, 2: 241–257.

6

New forms of work and the representational gap: a Durban case study

EDDIE WEBSTER

The liberalization of the economy and the restructuring of work are having a profound but uneven impact on unemployment and the institutions that purport to represent the employed. It could be described as a process of 'connecting ' and 'disconnecting' to the global economy.

At one level, South Africa is at the beginning of a new manufacturing age. For the first time in South Africa's history, manufacturing is the country's highest export earner. This is illustrated by the highly successful export strategy of BMW. South Africa's economic success can also be seen through the rapid growth of South African multinationals in the region, such as the retail firm Shoprite Checkers throughout Africa.

On the other hand, the jobs that are being created are often precarious, lack benefits and the wages are low as our case studies on the retail and household appliance sectors demonstrate. Furthermore, the loss of formal sector employment has seen the rapid growth of informal work. I argue in this chapter that a 'crisis of representation' has developed as trade unions lose their capacity to provide a voice for the 'new poor'. For this new social group 'work' does not involve a regular income: in fact the research suggests that for many there is no income at all, but rather 'payment in kind'.

A 'citizenship gap' has opened up in South Africa where the expectations generated by the new democracy are not being fulfilled for many of the poor. The 'negotiated compromise' of the early 1990s has led to a successful management of political conflict but the social, economic and welfare legacy of apartheid has been only partially removed. The result is the emergence of social movements responding to the lack of basic needs such as clean water, electricity, housing, schooling, and access to health care.

This chapter develops a conceptual framework for examining the limits and possibilities of organizing informal work. It is based on a study of street vendors and homeworkers in Durban and develops a matrix to examine a grassroots attempt to empower self-employed women.

Welcome Happiness

Let me begin by introducing you to Happiness Jele. Happiness sells curry and rice in Durban's Warwick Avenue Triangle (Jele 2003). She works from 7:00am until 17:30 hrs every day of the week including public holidays. She makes between R10 and R50 per day. Happiness has many identities; she is black, she is Zulu speaking born and brought up in rural KwaZulu Natal, she is a woman, she is a widow, a member of the Shembe church, middle aged, a mother of six children and heads a household of seven dependants. However, the most important feature of her life is her lack of formal employment and the conditions she works in both on the street and at home. As Richard Brown suggests,

> The availability of opportunities for employment, and the conditions under which people are employed, still have more impact on most individuals' chances than many other more fashionable concerns. Work and employment structure our lives and shape inequalities of condition and opportunity to a greater extent than most if not all areas of social life. (Brown 1997: 1)

My point of departure, then, is that work is about those activities that are essential to our material and physical existence, to our place in the world, and, in fact, to every aspect of human life. But, as a point of departure, the life of Happiness Jele raises the question of whether Happiness is indeed 'a worker'. Most would describe her as self-employed. Others would describe her as an aspiring entrepreneur or even a member of the petty bourgeoise. This would, ofcourse, be absurd as Happiness is engaged in a survivalist strategy even though she does employ a helper to assist her make the curry and rice. Is she not a worker as she is dependent on her work as a street vendor to survive? She has limited formal education (three years of formal schooling) and started work as a domestic servant in Chatsworth at the age of 13. Since then she has worked as a cleaner in Point Road, as an assistant in a café in Jacobs, then she began selling fruit and vegetables on the street. She does, in other words, not have access to any productive resources or assets and is forced to sell her labour.

Happiness is not of course a traditional 'worker'; she does not earn a wage, nor is she an employee, and she has no employer as a counterpart to bargain with. But, then, the personification of 'the worker' is something relatively recent and arises in the nineteenth century with the establishment and rapid growth of labour in its 'pure' form, i.e. labour which was separated from other social activities and spheres. 'This process of differentiation', writes Claus Offe, 'made it possible for the first time ever in history to "personify" labour in the social category of "the worker'.This process includes the separation of the household and the sphere of production, the division between private property and wage labour, and the "freeing" of labouring activity from feudal ties' (Offe 1985).

Furthermore, Happiness is a widow brought up in rural KwaZulu where patriarchal values continue to shape the division of labour in the household. Her experience as a woman and, above all, as a widow, makes her experience of gender oppression a powerful tie of solidarity with women vendors on the streets of Durban. She is also deeply embedded in a tightly knit community of believers in the Shembe church, a network that provides her with emotional support and, at times, physical resources including finance.

The purpose of this chapter is to examine the impact of the changing nature of work on worker organization in Durban.[1] The aim is to provide a conceptual framework for identifying the areas of common interest as well as the barriers to organisation among informal workers. In particular, I am concerned to identify the bargaining leverage of those in informal work. It is argued that new forms of work have emerged that have created a representational gap. The chapter is concerned to identify the opportunities and barriers to overcome this gap.

The chapter is divided into three sections; the first examines the changing nature of work and how, throughout the history of capitalism, labour has struggled for a 'voice'. The recent change, the growing informalization of work, is identified and the threat this constitutes to the representation of workers is explored. In section two the innovative attempts in Durban to respond to these changes in the nature of work are examined. In section three an attempt is made to develop a conceptual framework for understanding the opportunities and barriers to organizing informal work. The chapter concludes by leaving open the possibility of a labour movement emerging that includes all workers, both formal and informal.

It is first necessary, however, to define the characteristics of informal work. Unni and Lund suggest that 'the defining characteristic of informal work is that it involves the lack of or unstable contracts and workers consequently do not obtain most of the benefits additional to the wage that is associated with formal employment' (Unni and Lund 2002: 7). They go on to classify informal work into three categories:

- *Self-employed*: independent self-employed persons, i.e. own-account workers – self employed persons who do not hire any paid workers on a regular basis.
- *Dependent producers*: producers who depend on others for the supply of work, raw materials or sale of finished goods, e.g. homeworkers.
- *Wage workers*: dependent wage workers who work as casual workers either irregularly for a single employer or who work on a regular basis for a single registered employer without, typically, a written contract, fixed wages or worker benefits.

This chapter focuses on two of the types of informal work identified above:

- street vendors;
- homeworkers.

The research has been designed in such a way as to identify the experience of informal work, the conditions under which they operate, and their attempts to find 'a voice' in the workplace. In order to capture these experiences the study adopted an ethnographic approach. Three researchers were employed part-time over a period of four months from December 2002 through to the end of March 2003. The researchers – Sipho Lushaba, Dudu Khumalo, Ntokozo Mthembu – are trade union organizers who are studying part-time at the Workers College on a degree programme at the University of Natal. The director of research at the College, Mike Koen, assisted with the supervision of the research.[2]

In order to capture the working lives of informal workers I decided to develop biographies of the workers. We met for a training session in December where we developed an open-ended biographical schedule covering basic demographic data, the nature of their work and working conditions, and the forms, if any, of representation. They were then asked to conduct interviews with key actors in the specific occupational group to provide a context for the biographies. Each researcher was asked to attempt to develop ten biographies and write up a report on the interviews with key actors. The respondents were selected through snowball sampling. We met five times during the research process to share information and guide the research.

In the last week of April I spent a week accompanying the organizer and regional secretary of the Self Employed Women's Union (SEWU), Thandiwe Xulu, on her visits to some of their branches in KwaZulu Natal. We visited four branches; homeworkers in the Emzinyathi branch, street vendors in Stanger, homeworkers in the Indwedwe branch, and homeworkers in the New Town branch of Kwa Mashu. I kept detailed notes during the visit while observing their meetings and interviewing selected members.

SEWU defines the women who work as street vendors and homeworkers as workers – not embryonic businesswomen – as they are dependent on their work in order to survive and do not have access to key productive resources. SEWU organizes along the lines of a trade union with a paid membership base and elected leaders accountable to its branches. They are quite insistent that they organize separately as 'women workers' as the 'men dominate' and women have specific issues to discuss. It is women-centred and has evolved a genuinely 'gendered' approach.

Importantly, this grassroots organization designed to empower women has developed close links with researchers at the University of Natal and, more recently, with a transnational organisation called WIEGO, Women in the Informal Economy Globalizing and Organizing. WIEGO was formed in 1997 to become an international research and advocacy platform for women in informal employment It aims to improve the status of women in informal employment through compiling better statistics, conducting research and developing enabling programmes and policies. Importantly, WIEGO is a partnership between relative equals – each brings to the engagement a different source of power, but that power is recognised and acknowledged by the other. There is little subordination, condescension, or patronage in these engagements. These partnerships with high calibre expertise, combined with a solid grassroots base, have enhanced their access to and impact on public policy (Batliwala 2002).

Labour worldwide at a turning point?

The transformation of work under capitalism is a contradictory process that closes down options as well as opening up new opportunities. The destruction of craft work by machine-based production undermined craft unionism, leading to dire predictions in the 1930s in the United States of the disappearance of the labour movement. These predictions were, Cobble (2001) reminds us, issued literally on the eve of the dramatic upsurge of labor organizing that began in 1933. Instead of labor disappearing, a new form of worker and work organization – industrial unionism – emerged, and grew in strength through much of the past century. Based on their strategic location in production, these relatively unskilled workers were able to take advantage of the interconnected nature of the assembly line to win recognition for militant shopfloor-based industrial unions and struggle for basic citizenship rights.

Table 6.1 illustrates the way in which the changing nature of work impacts on the bargaining leverage of workers and the forms of organization that emerge in response to these changes. Global informational capitalism has now created a similar crisis for industrial unionism, as the global restructuring of work leads to a multiplicity of precarious work arrangements threatening traditional union organization. This has led to a debate on how to reverse the problems of union decline and revitalize the union movement. A recent study identifies six major union revitalization strategies: organizing, which focuses on membership revitalization; organizational restructuring such as mergers and internal reorganization; coalition building with other social movements which helps unions acquire access to power resources; partnerships with employers at national, industrial or workplace level will allow unions to pursue new kinds of interests; political actions, and international links to facilitate the exchange of information and the mobilization of members in international campaigns (Frege and Kelly 2003: 2–24).

The authors provide a useful preliminary explanation of cross-national similarities and differences in union revitaliza-

Table 6.1 Nature of work, bargaining and community linkages

Bargaining leverage	Type of union in the workplace	Links with community
Skills	Craft	Ignore
Strategic location in production	Industrial	Citizenship

tion strategies. The identification of the strategy of coalition building is especially useful as it suggests ways in which unions can 'broaden their bases of legitimacy' as well as 'expand the sources from which they can draw support when they need to' (Casperz 2003: 4). However, because the study focuses only on labour in the developed world (Germany, Italy, Spain, the United Kingdom, and United States), the strategies identified assume that the task of 'revitalization' is to strengthen existing trade union organization rather than develop new forms of organization. In developing countries, where increasingly the majority of the workforce are not in formal employment, the need to think beyond existing organisation has become a necessity for the survival of organized labour (Gallin 2001: 228). In fact in many older industralized countries the informal sector is becoming increasingly significant, particularly for women.

A central reason for the growth of the informal sector is the changing nature of work in the modern enterprise. At the centre of the new work paradigm are two strategies, namely 'effective downsizing' and subcontracting all but the 'indispensable core' activities. By retrenching much of the core workforce and subcontracting activities to various forms of precarious labour, management not only reduces labour costs but shifts the responsibility for benefits onto the individual worker. 'The outer circle of this system', writes Gallin, 'is the informal sector: the virtual invisible world of microenterprises and home-based workers. The informal sector is an integral part of global production and marketing chains. What is particular to the informal sector is the absence of rights and social protection of the workers involved in it' (Gallin 2001: 231).

How has labour responded to this challenge? Munck detects a 'serious willingness' on the part of trade unions to engage with the informal sector, especially among women workers 'where ties of solidarity based on gender interests have been significant'

(Munck 2002. 116). The paradigmatic case is that of SEWA (Self Employed Women's Association) in India which evolved out of the Textile Labour Association.

The informal economy appears to have grown rapidly in South Africa under the impact of liberalization. Using the various October Household Surveys (OHS) and the more recent Labour Force Surveys (LFS) a recent report suggests that the informal economy has increased from 965,669 in 1997 to 1,873,000 in 2001 (Devey, Skinner, and Valodia 2002: 7).[3] How has organized labour in South Africa responded to this challenge? While the main trade union federation, Cosatu, has adopted recommendations to organize these 'flexible' workers, it has been less successful in implementing them. In 1998 the federation launched what they called the 'Autumn Offensive' to organize the unorganized, but it appears that the campaign did not target vulnerable workers but unorganized core workers. This points to a central problem, namely the limitations of industrial style unionism to deal with flexiworkers.

However innovative activists since the early 1990s have been responding 'on the ground' to the changing nature of work. Based on the model of SEWA in India, the Self-Employed Women's Union (SEWU) was formed in Durban in 1994 with the aim of representing the interests of self-employed and survivalist women engaged in the informal economy in the rural and urban areas.[4] There have been a number of informative accounts of the origins and nature of SEWU (Bennett 2003, Grest 2002; Horn 1995, 1997b, Lund and Skinner 1999; Motala 2002).

In section two of this chapter we will situate this latest innovation in union organizing in Durban in a historical context.

The city of Durban: crucible of innovation in the modern labour movement in South Africa

Durban provides an ideal case study for the examination of the impact of liberalization on work and worker organization for two reasons: firstly, because it is was the birthplace of the modern labour movement in South Africa, and, secondly, it was a pioneer in responding to the livelihood strategies of street vendors through imaginative urban planning. This facilitated the successful emergence of the first self-employed union in South Africa. Both cases are examples of innovative institutional responses to the changing nature of work.

In January and February 1973 over 100,000 black workers went out on strike over wages and working conditions in the industrial areas of Durban and Pinetown (IIE 1974).The transformation of the division of labour caused by the rise of mass production assembly line industries created an important base on which black workers could build industrial unions. Furthermore the racial division of labour provided additional sources of grievance for black workers, and possible bases of collective action. The intersection of brutal industrial conditions and direct racial oppression served as a source of deep discontent among workers facilitating mobilization.

The adoption by these emerging unions of a strategic use of power introduced a new way of operating.[5] Where possible, these unions sunk deep roots on the shopfloor, transformed as it was by the dramatic economic changes of the 1960s and 1970s. The introduction of the shop steward committee and the recognition agreement in factories in Durban at this time was the key institutional innovation through which shopfloor power was built. On the shopfloor, unions could develop a strong factory-based leadership, less prominent than head office activists, and closely tied to their members. With the strong backing of their members, factory leaders had the power to push concessions from management, which not only created space for further advances, but also won concrete improvements in workers' conditions, thereby reassuring them of the efficacy of direct action. Thus, the imperatives of organizing under authoritarian conditions coincided with the structural changes in the economy which had created a vast new semi-skilled workforce with potential leverage over production, leading to the creation of powerful shopfloor organization.

These fledgeling unions, in particular those affiliated to the Federation of South African Trade Unions (FOSATU), had made important strategic innovations which profoundly affected trade union development as well as the course of political transition. There were two important components to the union's approach to the strategic use of power: (1) democratic processes, to win voluntary consent from members for mobilization, and for restraint where necessary; and (2) tactical flexibility which included a capacity to distinguish principles from tactics, and to choose those tactics most likely to succeed, including negotiation and compromise.

By 1984 trade unions had consolidated a strong base in Natal industries (Bonnin *et al*. 1996) However 1985 was a turning point with the emergence of political violence between supporters of the traditional Inkatha Freedom Party (IFP) and the African National Congress (ANC) (Bonnin *et al*. 1996). Because of the instability in the rural areas many lost their livelihoods in the countryside and came to the towns. At the time Durban was considered the fastest growing city in the world leading to large numbers of street traders. The initial response of the city council was to try to prevent hawking. However the prohibition failed and there was a complete breakdown of the legal system from the 1980s, especially after the pass laws were abolished in 1986.

With the transition to a more open economy in the early 1990s most industries in Durban moved towards downsizing and retrenching labour especially in those sectors vulnerable to cheaper imports such as clothing, textile and leather (Sitas 2001: 13). The volume of trade through Durban harbour has increased by 400 per cent since 1993 and the city has been rejuvenated as a local and international tourism centre (Sitas 1998: 7). But what Sitas suggests is that three other types of economic activity have proliferated since 1994: firstly, 'new hunter-gatherer type societies' among the urban poor who survive by selling waste products and are often homeless; secondly, what he calls 'new forms of servitude' where individuals are forced to survive by being at the 'beck and call of individuals who demand chores, duties, sexual favours, etc.'; thirdly, the growth of street traders and hawkers who 'sell basic commodities to the black poor, memorabilia to tourists, and food to urban workers' (Sitas 2001: 13–14). In 1997 it was estimated that there were 19,000 street traders in the Durban metro area (Grest 2002: 6). These traders range from selling merchandise through to 'bovine head cookers', mainly women informal traders who occupy a stretch of pavement on the busy Warwick Avenue (Grest 2002: 19).[6] The characteristics of street worker and homeworkers are summarized in table 6.2.

Recently, there has been a rapid growth of a new form of social activism. Decentralized, multiform, network oriented and globally connected, these 'new social movements' constitute the beginnings of what some have described as an emerging global civil society (Cock 2003). Some of these movements, such as the Treatment Action Committee (TAC), are drawing on the rights based discourse of the new constitutional order to bring about a shift in power, with their appeal to the constitutional court for the provision of anti-retrovirals. Other examples are:

- the Soweto Electricity Crisis Committee;
- the Environmental Justice Networking Forum;
- the Landless Peoples Movement;
- the Anti-privatization Forum.

Ashwin Desai has eloquently captured the struggles of these movements in his highly acclaimed book (Desai 2002). He shows how a new wave of activism culminated in the establishment of the Durban Social Forum to coincide with the World Anti-Racism conference in August 2001. This new movement emerged out of the confrontation over rent evictions between the residents of Chatsworth, a township created for Indians during the apartheid period, and the ANC Durban Metro Council.

There is no doubt that these movements are tapping into real grievances among the poor. Put differently, there is a citizenship gap, between what people expect from the new democracy and what they are currently experiencing. At the core of Desai's argument is the notion of 'betrayal' by the ANC, a betrayal which he believes has come about because the new political elite are implementing policies that are deeply anti-poor.

The diversity of these social struggles, whether they can be defined as social movements, and what implications these struggles have for the consolidation of democracy, is currently being investigated (Ballard *et al.* 2003). An important question for our study is whether these movements will establish links with the labour movement in general, and the unions emerging among informal workers, in particular. Will we see the re-emergence of the kind of joint campaign action and alliances between unions and community groups that emerged in the mid-1980s in South Africa? (Webster 1988).

To answer this question it is necessary, firstly, to examine the nature of the organisations, such as SEWU, that are emerg-

Table 6.2 Informal sector workers; car guards, public phone operators and street vendors

	1	2	3	4	5	6	7	8
Born	Burundi	Congo	Pietersburg	Lusikisiki Transkei	Mandeni-KZN	Bizana Transkei	Umzimkhulu-KZN	Clermont
Age	44	40	35	40	42	42	28	27
Gender	Female	Male	Male	Female	Female	Female	Female	Female
Marital Status	Married 3 children	Unmarried no children	Unmarried 1 child	Unmarried, 3 dependants	Single, 7 dependants (incl. 2 of sister's children)	Married, dependants	Single, 1 dependant	Single
Education	Trained as a teacher	Trained as an accountant	Special standard 8 certificate – plus grade E security certificate	Standard 9	Standard 1	Standard 2	Matric – National Diploma in IT	Matric
Race	Black	Black	White	Black	Black	Black	Black	Black
Average Income per day (R)	33.00	28.00	40.00–50.00	100.00	10.00–50.00	100.00–150.00	200.00	80.00
Working hours	08h00–17h00	08h00–17h00	08h00–15h00	06h00–20h00 (7 days a week incl. public holidays)	06h30–17h30 (7 days a week)	08h00–18h30 (7 days a week)	06h00–19h30	07h00–19h30

'Employer'	Car Watch- pay R7 a day for a coat and a demarcated workplace	Car Watch- pay R7 a day for a coat and a demarcated workplace	Self-employed	Self-employed	Self-employed	Self-employed	Self-employed	Self-employed
Working conditions	No protection on streets, not provided with toilets or water	No protection, exposed to hooligans, toilets and water are far away	No access to toilets or water	Fair	Fair, but very poor	No water and toilets, no security	Animosity amongst vendors	
Job description	Car Guard	Car Guard	Car Guard	Sells fruit on the street	Sells curry and rice	Street trader	Street trader	Public phone provider
Previous employment	Teacher	Accountant	Security officer	Cashier	Age 13, worked as a domestic worker, then as a cleaner in a café	Domestic worker, age 18	Administrative Assistant	No previous employment
Membership of organization	None	None	None	None	None	None	Lapsed member of ACHIB	None
Capital Required	None R7 for coat	None R7 for coat	None	Rent, R35 per month	Need capital for ingredients	Start business with R800	R500 per month rental	R4750 to buy phones (R4500) and battery (R250)

ing among informal workers. Pat Horn, an ex COSATU trade unionist and the first general-secretary, began organising these workers into SEWU from 1994 onwards along the lines of a trade union (Horn, Interview, 18 December 2002). According to the SEWU constitution, membership is open to all women workers over the age of 18, who:

- are involved in any economic activity which is not covered by other trade unions;
- earn their living by their own effort (without regular or salaried employment);
- do not employ more than three other persons on a permanent basis (Bennett 2003: 34).

SEWU has members in three of South Africa's nine provinces. The majority – 1,600 – of its 2,300 paid-up members are located in KwaZulu-Natal, mainly in Durban although it does have membership in the more rural parts of the province (Bennett 2003: 34). In its early days, the SEWU targeted mainly street vendors but increasingly it is recruiting home-based members including home-based workers in rural areas.

Members pay R10 membership fee to join SEWU and then R5 per month. Because of fraud and embezzlement this money is now paid by debit order (Horn, Interview, 27 March, 2003). SEWU is built around a branch at the local level, with regional and national executives. Members elect trade leaders and trade leaders collectively form trade committees. The largest three branches are on the beachfront where members sell curios to tourists, Russel Street where there is a large concentration of traditional medicine sellers, and Stanger where they have a branch among the street vendors at the bus rank.

An important aim of SEWU is to empower homeworkers to improve their skills. Indeed an incentive for joining SEWU is that it gives members access to loans. They use their membership cards to apply for money from the Land Bank. The bank then transfers the money to their accounts. They do not need collateral and can obtain loans from R250 to R18,000. Members use these loans to buy vegetables or materials (Xulu, Interview, 23 April 2003). The branch meetings are used as training sessions. In fact in the branch meetings I attended, the organizer discussed how to tender successfully. She also discussed the concept of a joint venture, why they fail, how banks operate and to apply for grants from the Department of Welfare for projects (table 6.3).

Table 6.3 A breakdown of the activities of two of the branch meetings of homeworkers attended

Indwedwe branch		Emzinyathia branch	
Activity	Number	Activity	Number
Bead-working, gardening and block making	4	Dressmaking	8
Gardening and bead work	1	Dressmaking and crocheting	1
Gardening, bead work, dress making and chicken farming	3	Blockmaking, brickmaking and sewing	2
Gardening, making and selling traditional medicine	1	Gardening	2
Gardening, sewing, beadwork	1	Printing on cloth	4
Gardening and block making	4		
Total	15	Total	17

Through an effective campaign street vendors were able to win from the City Council in 1995 their demand for the introduction of infrastructure such as shelter, access to water, and clean toilets (Horn, Interview, 27 March, 2003). They were also able to negotiate for child care facilities for street vendors and for a special site for a new Muthi market in Warwick Avenue.[7] In addition to negotiation, SEWU engages in advocacy work. For example, they made a submission to the Minister of Labour to extend social security benefits such as maternity and sickness benefits to informal workers. They have also made submissions to government for a national system of child care and aim to introduce a funeral benefit system (Lund and Skinner 1999: 34–36). The impact on policy has been facilitated by their international linkages; in particular SEWU actively participates in Homenet, Streetnet and WIEGO –

Women in Informal Employment: Globalizing and Organizing. Training workshops to empower the members are an important part of their work.

SEWU feels that it has to remain non-aligned politically as an alignment with either the ANC or the IFP would divide their members. Their approach is to concentrate on the issues facing their members and party political preference is seen as a private matter (Xulu, Interview, 23 April, 2003).

I now turn to section three to develop a conceptual framework for identifying the opportunities and barriers to organizing.

Opportunites and barriers in building a sustainable grassroots voice among informal workers

In their research report on SEWU the authors suggest that 'in some respects organizing street traders is easier than organizing formal sector workers ... the streets are easier to access than factory floor workers ... (and) a street vendor's time can in principle be more flexible than that of a formal sector workers (Lund and Skinner 1999: 44). They then go on to identify six 'formidable barriers'. This section is also based on interviews with organizers:

- *Economic*. Their incomes are precarious and they do not have time to talk to an organizer.
- *The opportunity cost of time away from the trading site is clearly a major barrier*. As one organizer remarked: 'Since they are self-employed, they hesitate to join because they spend some time attending meetings and not earning income during that period' (Shezi, interview, 2003). Often street vendors live far away from their trading site. They often need to have their children with them at the trading site. They also need to face the extra risks of working at the trading site: time seeing/dodging officials, paying fines, being relocated, erecting plastic sheets against the weather and so on.
- *Previous experience of organizations*. Many street vendors are suspicious of recruiters because of experience with unscrupulous fly-by-night organizations. In the words of an organizer: 'The vendors do not trust organizations any more because they have been victims of bribery and exploitation' (Shezi, Interview, 2003). In some cases they have had negative expe-

riences of established unions in the formal economy who
have failed to provide them with support when they were
retrenched (Tshabalo, Interview, 2002).

- *Lack of resources to sustain organization and serve members.*
  The result is that they cannot develop enough resources to be
  self-sustainable.
- *Corrupt practices.* Perhaps because of the nature of the informal economy where corruption is rife a number of leaders of
  organizations have been discredited.
- *Political barriers.* Sharp political divisions remain in South
  Africa. In KwaZulu the IFP/ANC division is less of a barrier
  than in the past but remains a barrier.
- *Environmental barriers.* Working conditions for street traders
  are harsh such as heat, humidity and thunderstorms especially when there is nowhere to meet.
- *Psychological and cultural barriers.* Certain communities in
  South African society remain a strongly patriarchal culture.
  This is why SEWU believes women need to organize sepa-
  rately (Lund and Skinner 1999: 40–44).

Some of the barriers identified by the authors are similar to
problems facing organizers when approaching any workers (bad
experiences with organizations, corrupt practices and political
barriers); other barriers mentioned are peculiar to informal
work. However the key difference between a self-employed
workers union and a traditional union such as SEWU is that it
does not have an employer to negotiate with. Horn has quite
correctly proposed that to grasp the self-employed workers
'negotiating partner' one needs to 'identify the entity or authority responsible for the issues (you) wish to negotiate about – and
that entity must then be approached as the negotiating partner
for the demand(s) in question' (Horn 2002: 10)

In other words, the negotiating partner is usually an institution which has been identified as exerting one or more forms of
control over the workers who now approach it with demands for
negotiation. An attempt at reconceptualizing the form of control
from the perspective of informal workers who do not work in a
factory or a firm, for a single employer, or even for an employer
per se is reproduced in table 6.4. Although this matrix suggests
the need to reconceptualize the nature of control among informal workers, for Horn the organizational approach required is
much the same as that of any other trade union organizer
namely you:

Table 6.4 Forms of labour control

	Internal		External	
Occupation	Individual transactions	Economic system	Policies and regulations	Societal norms and institutions
Street vendors	Wholesale traders	Production/ distribution chain	Municipalities, police, zoning regulations, licensing policies	Gender division of labour and caste
Home workers	Subcontractors and lead firms	Subcontracting chain	Minimum wage policies, trade and investment policies	Gender division of labour; norms of seclusion

Source: Edited from Sudershan, R. and Cher, M. 2002. 'Reconceptualizing Control: Autonomy or Mutual Obligation?', Workshop on Reconceptualizing Work and Decent Work Indexes, ILO, Geneva: 12–13 December

- find out the needs/problems of the workers as this will determine the issues to take up;
- convert their needs into collective bargaining demands;
- identify who is the most appropriate authority to negotiate these demands with;
- initiate collective bargaining with that authority (or multiple authorities if appropriate);
- push for the establishment of regular, even statutory, collective bargaining structures (Horn 2003: 45).

However, Horn says, it is difficult to find people who have these skills and commitment. Initially she recruited ex-COSATU organizers but they were not able to adapt to the demands of organizing informal workers. Indeed many of them were subsequently dismissed for fraud and embezzlement (Horn, Interview, 27 March 2003; Xulu, Interview, 23 April, 2003). She realized that a different type of organizer from that being produced by established unions was required. Instead of an educated English-speaking career official, what was required, Horn decided, is a multi-skilled person with the following characteristics:[8]

- a person with creativity and initiative who can work independently and is willing and able to learn new things. Since self-employed workers cannot go on strike it is necessary to apply other strategies such as the media or be sensitive to the different contexts such as the need to cover your head when negotiating with the nkosi;

- a person who is committed to the vision of the organization and is not too concerned about their own working conditions. They must be willing to work overtime, use public transport, and, sometimes in the rural areas, to have to walk on foot, and not demand to stay in hotels but to stay in the homes of the members when travelling;
- a person who can speak the local languages. Most of the members have very little formal education and classes have to be conducted in a language that they understand (Horn, Interview, 27 March 2003).

This 'second generation' organizer is being recruited, Horn concluded, from the ranks of the self-employed. Thandiwe Xulu is an example of one (Xulu, Interview, 23 April 2003). She was married at a young age and has six children. She worked from home making dresses and was recruited into SEWU. She became a full-time organizer in 1995 and regional secretary in 2000. She feels she has been empowered as a woman. She attended a course on gender at the Workers College in Durban where she was able to improve her spoken and written English. She now uses the office computer to email donors and colleagues. She earns a salary of R3,500 per month. The job is hard work and she has to travel to the branches on public transport, sometimes walking by foot to the villages where their members stay. I asked her how her 'empowerment' had affected her relationship with her husband. She said he does not feel threatened by her. In fact, she says, he is very pleased with her as her acquisition of skills has led to an increase in their household income enabling her to pay for the schooling of their children.

A key part of their organizational strategy is the focus on women as a separate category of workers. 'We feel', argues Xulu, 'that men dominate and that we have to organize separately until we are "empowered"'. (Xulu, Interview, 23 April 2003). An imporant part of their activities are discussions on sexual abuse and harassment. They also run classes on how to treat AIDS sufferers.

What then is the bargaining leverage of informal workers? Sanyal has attempted to answer this question by identifying the various axes of commonality among self-employed workers. He begins by distinguishing between 'natural' factors (such as gender) and those that are 'socially created' (such as a steep rise in food prices) (Sanyal 1991: 45). Some, he argues, are inherently divisive in all contexts. These he labels axes of discord. This is a summary of the two axes.

Axes of commonality

Location and proximity

Self-employed workers who reside or work in the same area are more likely to be organized than those who are scattered. Physical proximity creates the conditions for shared experiences and it easier for organizers to reach large numbers of people if they are spatially concentrated.

Trade/occupation

Self-employed sector workers with similar business interests and constraints are likely to mobilize more frequently than others. Although these workers may also compete with each other for the same customers, particularly if they operate in the same area, they often have to deal with the same suppliers and middlemen and are affected similarly by certain regulations and macro-politics.

Sex roles

The emergence of a growing number of poor women's organisations in developing countries indicates that sex can be a unifying factor, particularly when socially determined sex roles restrict the access of women to economic opportunities in the formal sector.

Axes of discord

Competition for market share

Informal sector workers compete with each other, often fiercely, because commerce, unlike production, has an inherent potential for monopolies on desirable commodities and even more so on desirable locations. This gives rise to strong competition among informal sector workers and, particularly with the increasing number of new labour market entrants into such activities, adversely affects their mobilization as a single interest group.

Ethnicity, race and religious identity

Informal sector workers are often embedded in a set of exploitative relationships with family members, relatives and friends.

These identities may be more important to them than their 'class interests'.

Government policy of selective assistance

Government policies, and international donor agencies, may formalize a few small organized groups of informal workers who then become protective of their own group interests and try to restrict the entry of other informal sector workers to these groups.

Using this conceptual framework it is clear that street workers and homeworkers share a number of similarities but they also have some differences in their bargaining leverages.

Axes of commonality

Physical proximity

Both street workers and homeworkers operate largely alone, but they are concentrated in certain areas and this gives them opportunities for common action. Street vendors can mobilize around a rent boycott if they are dissatisfied with the shelter provided by the council as they are doing in the Stanger branch of SEWU. They can march in the streets and will be highly visible and can make an impact through disrupting traffic. Although homeworkers operate from separate homesteads they are concentrated in a specific geographical area, such as a neighbourhood or a village. This enables them to engage in common action but it is likely to be less visible.

Trade or ocupation

Both street workers and homeworkers cover a wide variety of economic activities and both can find common interests in negotiating with suppliers for lower prices or buyers of their goods. However homeworkers can be linked into a commodity chain and can use their bargaining leverage to put pressure on customers. This has been highly effective in the case of the production of sports goods, footwear and clothing. In a brand conscious world this can be a powerful bargaining lever (Klein 2001). The increasing internationalization of labour issues makes this a weapon that is being increasingly used by labour against sweatshop working conditions (Lambert and Webster, forthcoming).

Gender

Both types of workers have been able to find strong ties of gender solidarity. Organizing separately is proving an effective tool in building solidarity. For most of the women 'workplace' issues and 'household' issues are inseparable. They are able to engage in joint child-minding while they meet together and discuss common issues.

Axes of discord

Competition

Street traders face fierce competition between each other. A number of the street traders spoke of the shrinking of the market because of over trading and also the violence towards traders of different ethnic origins. Although producers, for example of dresses, can over produce, there is also greater opportunity to combine and benefit from economies of scale. In the Newtown branch of SEWU the members have built a church hall where they worship on Sundays and use it as a workshop during the week where they co-operatively make dresses.

Race and ethnicity

Tension between street traders on grounds of ethnicity or nationality are high; among homeworkers it is relatively low as they live in homogenous neighbourhoods.

Policies

During the apartheid period the state discriminated against people of colour and divided them along racial and ethnic grounds. This legacy of division continues especially where race groups find themselves in a situation of unequal bargaining power. The example experienced during my field work was one where black women street traders felt that the Indian wholesaler was acting as an intermediary and blocking their access to the supplier. They expressed their feelings in racially abusive terms. Both street traders and homeworkers are now attempting to develop policies that encourage and support the informal economy as an important and productive part of the economy.

Table 6.5 Street vendors and homeworkers compared

	Street vendors	Homeworkers
Axes of commonality		
Physical Proximity	Strong	Weak
Occupation	Strong	Strong
Gender	Strong	Strong
Axes of discord		
Competition	High	Low
Race and Ethnicity	High	Low
Policies	Low	Low

Source: Adapted version of Sudershan, R. and Chen, M. 2002, 'Reconceptualising Centrols: Autonomy or Mutual Obligation', Workshop or Reconceptualising Work and Decent Work Indexes, ILO, Geneva, 12–13 December

Table 6.5 compares the bargaining leverage of street vendors and homeworkers.

Conclusion

The chapter was introduced with an example of a street trader and we have ended it with developing a conceptual framework for identifying the opportunties and barriers to organizing informal work. Whether SEWU is sustainable on its own is unlikely. Unless it is able to form coalitions with other informal sector organizations and, above all, the labour movement, it is likely to stagnate and possibly disappear. Currently, it has reached a stalemate: in order to sustain itself it needs more resources, but if it wants access to resources without becoming dependent on donors, it has to increase its membership.

Clearly, the labour movement needs to build an alliance with these informal sector organizations. We have argued that organizing informal workers is different from organizing the formal sector. Pat Horn has suggested that there are a number of different ways in which infomal workers could be drawn into the labour movement:

- the scope of unions could be broadened to include informal sector workers;

- the existing union federations could initiate informal sector unions;
- an informal sector federation could be formed and form an alliance with existing federations;
- or established federations could start working with informal sector organizations.

Above all, labour needs to broaden its constituency and form alliances with groups outside of the traditional unions in the formal sector. It remains open as to whether such an alliance will emerge. The future of the labour movement and the organization of informal workers depends on such a coalition.

Notes

1 I started my research career in Durban in 1973. In this sense the research is an example of what Burawoy calls a 'revisit'; an opportunity to examine the changes in the object of knowledge, i.e. the world of work. 'The revisit involves a dialogue between successive experiences of the same world, experiences separated in time' (Burawoy, M., 'On the Shoulders of Giants: Bringing Theory and History to Ethnography', unpublished.

2 I would like to thank the researchers for the work they did on this project. It is difficult to balance work and study; adding a research project onto the workload was very demanding.

3 The authors are uncertain whether an almost doubling of the numbers in the informal economy over a period of four years is accurate. They suggest that part of the upward trend evident in the data is in fact a reflection of an improvement in the capturing of informal work rather than the growth in the phenomenon of informal work (Devey et al. 2002: 6).

4 It is not clear to what extent SEWU has been influenced by Gandhism. Although close links have been established between the two organizations at leadership level, SEWA has a much more spiritual approach than SEWU does. On the other hand the idea that collective empowerment is more important than the individual, and that means are as important as ends, is shared by both organizations and is influenced by Gandhi's philosophy.

5 I have drawn this section on organizational innovation in the emerging unions from a range of writing over a number of years best summarized in a co-authored article (Adler and Webster 1995).

6 They generally obtain their heads, Grest writes, fresh or frozen, from formal butcheries. Processing involves thawing, skinning, cutting up and boiling in vats large enough for two heads, each vat heated by four paraffin-fuelled primus stoves (Grest 2002: 19).

7 Umuthi translates as 'tree' in isiZulu and refers to herbal medicines.

8 Sakhela Buhlungu has suggested that during the anti-apartheid struggle

union officials were both organizers and activists, i.e. activist-organizers.With the decline of apartheid these roles have been separated resulting in three types of union officials: comrades, i.e. those who are ideologically driven and are committed to a broader vision of empowerment of workers; entrepreneurs, i.e. those who are using their positions as a stepping stone to government or the corporate sector; and career.

References

Adler, G. and Webster, E. 1995. 'Challenging Transition Theory: The Labor Movement, Radical Reform, and Transition to Democracy in South Africa', *Politics and Society*, 23,1: 1–39.

Ballard, R., Habib, A., Ngcobo, D. and Valodia, I. 2003. 'Globalization, Marginalization, and Contemporary Social Movements in South Africa', draft paper presented at the Globalisation, Marginalisation and Contemporary Social Movements Workshop, Centre for Civil Society, University of Natal.

Batliwala, S. 2002. "Grassroots Movements as Transnational Actors: Implications for Global Civil Society ', *Voluntas: International Journal of Voluntary and Nonprofit Organisations*, 13, 4: 393–409.

Bennett, M. 2003. 'Organizing in the Informal Economy: A Case Study of the Clothing Industry in South Africa', Small Enterprise Development (SEED) Working Paper No. 37, International Labour Office, Geneva.

Bonnin, D. Hamilton, G., Morrell, R. and Sitas, A. 1996. 'The Struggle for Natal and Kwazulu: Workers, Township Dwellers and Inkatha, 1972–1985', in Morrell, R. (ed.), *Political Economy and Identities in Kwazulu: Historical and Social Perspectives*. Durban: Indicator Press.

Brown, R. 1997. *The Changing Shape of Work*. London: Macmillan Press.

Caspersz, D. 2003. 'The Question of Union Revitalization and the Strategy of Coalition Building', *Labour Movements Research Committee Newsletter*, June, 2, 2: 4–5. International Sociological Association.

Cobble, D. 2001. 'Lost Ways of Unionism: Historical Perspectives on Reinventing the Labor Movement', in Turner, L., Katz, H. and Hurd, R. (eds.), *Rekindling the Movement: Labor's Quest for Relevance in the 21st Century*. Ithaca: ILR Press.

Cock, J. 2003. 'A Better or Worse World?', Report on the Third World Social Forum, Porto Alegre: Centre for Civil Society, University of Natal, Durban.

Desai, A., 2002. *We Are the Poors: Community Struggle in Post-Apartheid South Africa*. New York: Monthly Review Press.

Devey, R., Skinner, C. and Valodia, I., 2002. 'The Informal Economy: What is It, Who Works in It, and What Policies Are Appropriate?', School of Development Studies, University of Natal, Durban.

Frege, C. and Kelly, K., 2003. 'Union Revitalisation Strategies in Comparative Perspective', *European Journal of Industrial Relations*, 9, 1: 7–24.

Freund, B. and Padayachee, V. 2002. *(D)urban Vortex: South African City in Transition*. Scottsville: University of Natal.

Gallin, D. 2001. 'Propositions on Trade Unions and Informal Employment in Times of Globalisation', in Waterman, P. and Wills, J. (eds.), *Place, Space and the New Labour Internationalisms*. Oxford: Blackwell.

Grest, J. 2002. 'Urban Management, Urban Citizenship and the Informal Economy in the "New" South Africa: A Case Study from Central Durban', Political Science Programme, University of Natal, Durban.

Horn, P. 1995. 'Self-employed Women's Union: Tackling the Class-Gender Intersection', *South African Labour Bulletin*, 19, 9: 34–8.

—— 1997a. 'The Informal Sector: West African Women Organise', *South African Labour Bulletin*, 21, 1: 90–94.

—— 1997b. 'The Informal Sector: Building a Working Class Alliance', *South African Labour Bulletin*, 21, 5: 37–41.

—— 2002. 'Voice regulation and the Informal Economy', Workshop on Reconceptualising Work and Decent Work Indices, 12–13 December, Programme on Socio-Economic Security, International Labour Office, Geneva.

Horn, P. 2003. 'Organising in the Informal Economy', *South African Labour Bulletin*, 27, 2: 43–45.

Institute for Industrial Education. 1974. *The Durban Strikes 1973*. Durban: Institute for Industrial Education in association with Ravan Press.

International Labour Office (ILO). 1998. *The Asian Financial Crisis: The Challenge for Social Policy*. Geneva: International Labour Office.

—— 2000. *Your Voice at Work: Global Report under the Follow up to the ILO Declaration on Fundamental Principles and Rights at Work*. Geneva: International Labour Office.

Klein, N. 2001. *No Logo*. London: Flamingo.

Lambert, R. and Webster, E. 'What Is New in the New Labour Internationalism: A Southern Perspective', in Taylor, R. (ed.), *Global Civil Society*. Boston: Kumarian Press.

Lane, T. 1974. *The Union Makes Us Strong: The British Working Class, Its Politics and Trade Unionism*. London: Arrow Books.

Lund, F. and Skinner, C. 1999. 'Promoting the Interests of Women in the Informal Economy: An Analysis of Street Trader Organisations in South Africa', Research Report No 19. School of Development Studies, University of Natal, and Durban.

Maree, J. 1985. 'The Emergence, Struggles and Achievements of the Black Trade Unions in South Africa from 1973 to 1984', *Labour, Capital and Society*, 18, 2.

Morrell, R. 1996. 'The Struggle for Natal and KwaZulu: Workers, Township Dwellers and Inkatha, 1972–1985', in Morrell, R. (ed.), *Political Economy and Identities in Kwazulu-Natal: Historical and Social Perspectives*. Durban: Indicator Press.

Motala, S. 2002. 'Organizing in the Informal Economy: A Case Study of Street Trading in South Africa', Small Enterprise Development (SEED) Working Paper No. 36, International Labour Office: Geneva.

Munck, R. 2002. *Globalization and Labour: The New 'Great Transformation'*. London: Zed Books.

Offe, C. 1985. 'Work: The Key Sociological Category', in Offe, C. (ed.), *Disorganized Capitalism: Contemporary Transformation of Work and Politics*. Cambridge: Polity.

Sanyal, B. 1991. 'Organizing the Self-Employed: The Politics of the Urban Informal Sector', *International Labour Review*, 130, 1: 40–52.

Sitas, A. 1998. 'The New Poor and Social Movements in Durban', International Sociological Association, Montreal.

—— 2001. 'The Livelihoods Sector: Opportunities for Unions', *South African Labour Bulletin*, 25, 3: 12–16.

Sitas, A., Stanwix, J. and Shaw, C. 1984. 'Trade Unions: Monopoly Power and Poverty in Natal's Industries', Carnegie Conference Paper No. 108, Cape Town, 13–19 April.

Sudershan, R. and Chen, M. 2002. 'Reconceptualising Controls: Autonomy or Mutual Obligation?', Workshop on Reconceptualizing Work and Decent Work Indexes, ILO, Geneva, 12–13 December.

Unni, J. and Lund, F. 2002. 'Reconceptualizing Security', Workshop on Reconceptualizing Work and Decent Work Indexes, International Labour. Organisation, Geneva 12–13 December. Programme on Socio-Economic Security, International Labour Office, Geneva.

Webster, E. 1986. 'The Rise of Social-movement Unionism: The Two faces of the Black Trade Union Movement in South Africa', in Frankel, P., Pines, N. and Swilling, M., (eds.), *State, Resistance and Change in South Africa*. London: Croom Helm.

7

The changing impact and strength of the labour movement in advanced societies

MIKE RIGBY, ROGER SMITH
AND CHRIS BREWSTER

This chapter addresses the changing impact and strength of the labour movement in advanced societies. There are both evidential and conceptual difficulties involved here, but the task is an important one and worth the effort. Trade unions have been one of the bulwarks of a democratic society, in and beyond the workplace. We examine the pressures that the unions are facing; the evidence of the decline in their numbers and significance – exploring the meaning of power in this context, arguing that it may be both wider and more constrained than it appears. Finally, we conclude that there has been a decline in trade union power, that it is continuing, and that there is no evidence that this will be part of a cycle and union power will eventually be re-established to any former level. We also note, however, that the trade unions will remain embedded in the fabric of advanced societies and will continue to play an important role in democratic processes.

Our analysis is focused on the period since the late 1970s: but it is worth a note putting this discussion into historical perspective. We wish to make it clear that our analysis does not look back to any mythical 'golden age' of trade unionism. There was never a time when unions were able to achieve their objectives or had the power to change societies as they wished. Arguably, at certain points in time and at certain places, they were able to go beyond their classic role of preventing the worst excesses of those who would exploit the working classes in society, to achieving some of their substantive goals – in the Nordic countries during the third quarter of the twentieth century, for example. However, the unions have generally failed to change societies fundamentally, have failed to see wealth significantly redistributed and have failed to ensure justice for the weakest in the nation. This is not to argue that the union struggle has been without its victories, or has been in vain. Far from it: the unions have been vital to the development of the democracy that the advanced countries now enjoy. It is to argue that the unions have always been a countervailing force to the power of capitalism – and have never been in a position of 'being powerful'.

The challenges to the trade unions' power

Trade unions were created in the nineteenth century in most of the advanced societies. They grew and developed during the first three-quarters of the twentieth century but found it increasingly difficult to adapt to the demands of the last quarter of that century and the pressures of today. They have problems in three main areas: structural changes within society; socio-political-changes; and with the inadequacies of their own organizations. We deal with each in turn.

Structural changes

A significant *shift from primary and manufacturing industries to services* has occurred and, it is often argued (Clutterbuck 2000; Drucker 1994), now even a shift from services to a 'fourth age' of information technology. The number of manual workers in the advanced societies at the end of the century is well under half the numbers there were in the late 1970s. In place of giant 'manufactories' we now have small workshops, offices and retail stores. The problem for the unions is that they have tended to be strong in those industries that relied on natural resources and have found it difficult to attract members in the new employment sectors. Technological and economic changes, the growth of knowledge workers and the decline of manual workers, have moved employment away from the areas where the unions are strong to those where they are weak.

Globalisation and the growth of multinationals have created problems for nationally, or sometimes even locally, rooted trade unions. These giant multinational corporations (MNCs), with their ability to shift production and services from country to country, find it easier to out-manoeuvre the single-country focused unions. Despite the valiant attempts of a few individuals, the unions are poor at matching the MNCs international mobility and to handle corporations eager to transfer activities to the underdeveloped countries.

There has been a movement from public employment to private employment with, in all advanced countries, a rhetoric of privatization and, in many, significant changes in ownership. Traditionally, the public sector has attempted to be an exemplary employer and, even if that language has been replaced by that of 'business-like' employment, it remains a fertile ground for union membership. In the UK for example, union membership is almost 60 per cent of the public sector, but less than 20 per cent in the private sector (*Labour Market Trends* July 2002) In almost all of the advanced industrial countries, trade unionism increasingly is becoming a public sector phenomenon.

Employment sites are now much smaller. In most developed countries the trend is towards decentralisation: in government, in politics and in industry. Big business may dominate the planet, but it does so through small manufacturing and servicing units. The days when many thousands were employed on one site have, in the main, gone. In the 1960s one, or a small group of officials could deal with one issue at one workplace and help thousands of their members. Now they have to spend many hours travelling to different workplaces to service a fraction of the same number of members.

Collective bargaining has been decentralized. Decentralization of work has been directly involved with the decentralization of collective bargaining. The evidence from the USA and the UK is clear. Even in Australia and those European countries where centralized collective bargaining was the norm, this has now been dismantled, or is under pressure, with consequent pressures on the unions in general and local officers and staff in particular (Katz 1993; Niland *et al.* 1994; Traxler 1994).

The *growth of unemployment* in the advanced societies in the fourth quarter of the twentieth century meant the end of that unique period after the Second World War when, in broad international terms, the demand for and supply of labour in those countries was more or less in equilibrium. High levels of unemployment not only make it difficult for the unions (outside those countries, such as the Nordic states, where they administer unemployment schemes) to retain members, it also switches the

balance of power back to the more traditional employer dominant pattern.

Flexibility in work arrangements and practices has grown as
unemployment reasserted itself. Work has changed radically in
most of the advanced societies. The assumption that most
people have a full-time, long-term job that will involve them for
seven or eight hours most weekdays is now unsustainable.
Whilst the evidence is that employees in large firms with secure
jobs are just as likely to join unions, whatever their social background (Stoop 2003), this is a smaller and smaller proportion of
the workforce; already a minority pattern in many European
countries (Brewster *et al.* 2001; Brewster 1998). This growth in
what the British term 'flexibility', the Americans 'contingent
work', the European Union 'atypical work' and the unions
'vulnerable work' (all terms which are only partially accurate
and come laden with intellectual baggage) has had a major
impact on the trade unions. This is not the place to reprise the
debates that have taken place: see e.g. Atkinson 1984, 1987;
OECD 1986; Osterman *et al.* 2001; Pollert 1991, 1998; Treu
1992.

Here we are concerned with the impact of flexible working on
the trade unions. And the impact is clear: an ever greater need
for their services – and much greater difficulty and cost in
providing them. Part-timers in Britain are only half as likely to
be union members as full-timers, though in Scandinavia the
unions seem to have little difficulty in recruiting part-timers.
Similarly there has been growth in job-sharing; shift-working;
weekend working; there is an almost infinite variety of other
working patterns now available. And, again, the unions find
such workers harder to recruit. There has also been a growth in
contractual flexibility: a range of practices from temporary and
short-term contracts through to forms which actually avoid
employment altogether – self-employment, franchising, subcontracting the work out, use of agencies and consultants. They are
all increasing. Only one in five employees on short-term
contracts in the UK are union members; one in ten of those on
brief, less than one year, contracts. Other advanced societies
have a similar pattern. Self-employed people were a declining
proportion of those in the developed economies as fewer and
fewer worked in agriculture. But there has been a significant and
continuing upturn in the proportion of self-employed people
over the last few years as employers have moved away from

offering work in favour of offering contracts for services. There are now self-employed workers in every industry and occupation. Union membership levels amongst this group are even less than those for short-term employment. The place of work is also changing. The growth in home working and 'teleworking' from home has not reached anything like the levels that were being predicted a few years ago. However there is growth – and union membership amongst this group is perhaps the lowest of all.

There are other changes to the *type of worker* in the labour market. In all developed societies there are now more women – and unions have been criticized for not being women friendly. There are more ethnic minorities and, again, the unions have generally been poor at recruiting and retaining them as members. Most developed societies are having to cope with a declining birth rate, people retiring earlier and living longer – putting ever greater pressure on those who are involved in wealth creation and on the relevant government. At present, though, there are increasing numbers of young people coming into the workforce. But trade union membership amongst young people has crashed. Younger workers are far less likely to be union members. And the older people who are more likely to be unionized are also the ones most likely to lose their jobs. At the end of the 1980s, one in seven trade union members in the UK was under 25 years old: by the end of the century, the figure was less than half that. Union membership for those under 30 was less than 20 per cent, whilst for those in their 40s it was double the proportion (*Labour Market Trends July* 2002). In the Netherlands, membership density amongst the under 25s was 50 per cent in 1975, 46 per cent in 2000 (Stoop 2003). As the workforce gets younger, the union membership gets older. The unions seem to find it very difficult to recruit younger people who have no knowledge, or tradition, of unionization. Arguably, these workers are better educated, more consumer oriented and more demanding – and obviously less than impressed by what the unions have to offer.

Socio-political changes

There has been *a move away from collectivization* in society generally. Television has overtaken the theatre and cinema;

computer games hold greater sway than outdoor team sports; in most of the advanced societies even family networks are being weakened. Whilst there are suggestions here, there is little real evidence, but it may be no coincidence that the collectively based unions have struggled as collectivization in society has diminished.

Governments have not been favourable to the unions in the last quarter of the twentieth century, according to many of their defenders. The 'free labour market' philosophy espoused by Ronald Reagan in the USA, Margaret Thatcher in the UK and many other prime ministers and their followers throughout the advanced societies has involved key steps to weaken the unions. The unions can, fairly, point to unfavourable legislation and the antagonistic government approach to trade unions as part of the reason for their decline. However, there is little substance in the view that the trade unions' problems since the mid-1980s have been largely the result of attacks by unfriendly governments. The history of trade unionism around the world shows that the unions have rarely been able to, or in many countries ever expected to, rely on friendly political forces being in power. Many trade union movements have flourished directly in the face of unfriendly governments. There is indeed a serious argument that trade unions are one of the best bulwarks against and controls on otherwise undemocratic regimes. Union movements are the safeguards of democracy (see chapters 10 and 11). The fact that there were unfriendly political parties in power in many of the English speaking developed countries (the USA, the UK, Australia, and New Zealand) and in Japan and many of the European countries, at the turn of the millennium, is just one of the issues facing the unions. It has been the ability of these governments to exploit these other issues that has created the difficulties for the unions. The kind of sloppy thinking that attributed the unions' problems to government action (and, even more worryingly, assumed that the election of a friendly government would resolve the problems) has fallen into disrepute in the face of the evidence that even the election of Labour-linked governments has failed to solve the problems.

Having made these points, however, it is important to recognize that right-wing governments in many countries have taken advantage of the scenario in which they found themselves to make things difficult for the trade unions. They may not have done this very cleverly. (Arguably, the Thatcher government, for example, might have made things even more difficult for the unions if they had matched the withdrawal of legal rights for unions with the introduction of legal rights for individuals. And the imposition of balloting for some senior union officers has increased their legitimacy; and balloting on industrial action has given the unions another bargaining weapon.) Nevertheless, the general trend of such governments has been a problem for the unions: but one that could only have been so if the unions were already unpopular and lacking in support.

Changed managerial attitudes have also been noted by the trade unions. It is not true that unions have no role to play if management is able to avoid engaging with them: but it is clear that the role that they can play will be significantly reduced. In Europe, at least, there is little evidence to suggest that more than a minority of managements actively pursue an anti-union strategy and most organizations of any significant size continue to deal with the relevant trade unions (Morley *et al.* 1996). However, there is evidence from some countries – in particular the anglophone ones – that the value of establishing or maintaining collective relationships with the unions is increasingly being questioned by managers (Millward *et al.* 1992) and that some companies are taking increasingly tough anti-union stances. Many companies' 'industrial relations' old guard have retired; and been replaced by aggressive new HRM specialists. The notion of HRM, developed in the USA and imported into most other developed countries, is built around generating value for money from human resources as from others, with a strong focus, at least in the US version, on individuals and an antipathy to collective communication. Moreover, there is evidence that young workers may perceive progressive HRM policies in organizations as a substitute for union membership (Gomez *et al.* 2002). Again, the problem is real – but is limited in scope and anyway is hardly a new problem for trade unions to have to handle.

Inadequacies in union organization

The results of these pressures in their many and varied combinations are, as we will see below, that the unions are in decline.

Their influence on the public, on governments and on employers gets less and less. Their members feel disconnected from the union – and are unimpressed when they visit the unions' offices; these are often in tired, drab buildings with a distinctly unfriendly approach as far as most members are concerned. Membership, particularly the influx of new, younger members on which the future of any organization depends, has declined or stagnated.

Fewer and fewer members are prepared to put their head above the parapet and take up positions as local union representatives. In many cases it is more a case of finding someone who is prepared to do it, rather than of elections between candidates. Many of those who do take up such posts are enthusiastic, committed and capable; many are few or none of these things.

Those who do get involved with the union find that in many cases they are dealing with the depressing problems associated with steady decline: little interest, reducing memberships and poor support and facilities. In other cases they find themselves dealing with small groups of activists who have their own agendas, in which the continued existence of the union and its service to its members is secondary; groups that have taken advantage of the minimal involvement of others to capture significant committees within the union.

The lay executive committees of some unions consist of well-educated members who understand the management of organizations, who are familiar with concepts of strategy and who can understand balance sheets. But many others have lay executives who fall somewhat short of these capabilities.

And at the top of the involvement scale, at the level of the unions' decision-making bodies, the situation is little better. Trade union conferences are a tradition, a ritual – but do not have much to do with focussing and running an effective employee representative organization. Hundreds of people meeting on an annual or biennial basis in a traditional location costs the unions a fortune but has little effect on making the unions better run; or improving the terms and conditions of membership. Trade union leaders are rarely selected or elected for their managerial expertise and experience – though there are exceptions – and receive very little training for this complex and demanding task. So it is little wonder that many of them find the situation almost too much to grasp or to deal with.

The philosophy and structure of trade unions is rooted in the past: too many unions operate with a structure based on a social, commercial and industrial demography that no longer exists. In the last quarter of a century however, change has been dramatic: we are entering the era of the 'weightless economy' dominated by information and communications technology and the speed with which the lives of most people have changed, and continually change, is enormous. The unions have so far generally failed to adapt – even where they have thought of doing so. Unions are now faced with bargaining with a transnational company or a government body; negotiating from their national base with companies who are part of the new global division of labour. From their 'collective' orientation and structures they are trying to represent individual employees on a range of legal and quasi-legal matters in the courts or elsewhere; supporting workers who may be self-employed or only temporarily employed.

The structure is based on a demography that no longer exists; the operating methods of unions are based on a stable, male oriented, personal and social lifestyle that has gone – forever. There are obvious manifestation of this: loss of members; ageing memberships; loss of influence with governments and employers; the almost empty meeting rooms, with committees easily captured by ever smaller groups of people, some of which could be (and all too often are) unrepresentative minorities; and, for example, in the UK, more people are going to employment tribunals supported by the Citizens' Advice Bureaux than by the unions.

The evidence of decline

In the previous section a number of factors were discussed which have created an increasingly challenging environment for trade unions at the beginning of the twenty-first century. What evidence exists that this environment has contributed to a pattern of trade union decline in Europe? This question is considered by examining four indices of union strength: union membership density, role of representative bodies, collective bargaining coverage and industrial conflict.

Trade union membership density

In a global context, table 7.1 uses evidence from the European Industrial relations Observatory to indicate that membership density in the EU compares favourably with that of Japan and the USA.

The unweighted EU average (that is the mean of the individual density figures for each of the member countries) is more than double that of Japan; and more than three times that in the USA. Even when we compare the weighted EU average (which represents the proportion of the total EU labour force who are union members) density is still significantly higher in the EU than in the other countries. Europe is without doubt the most unionized region in the developed world.

Table 7.1 Membership density in Europe, USA and Japan, 2000 (per cent)

EU average unweighted	43.8
EU average weighted	30.4
Japan	21.5
USA	13.5

Source: EIRO. 2000. *Industrial relations in the EU, Japan and USA.* Dublin: Foundation for the Improvement of Living and Working Conditions.

Table 7.2 provides density levels for the EU in historical perspective. An examination of the evolution of density on a country by country basis emphasises the difficulty of identifying a consistent pattern of decline. There are a group of countries that experienced a decline in density well before the impact of factors such as globalisation became acute. In the case of Austria, France and the Netherlands, a decline in density can be traced back to the 1950s. There is another group of countries in which the beginning of decline can be traced to the 1970s and the early 1980s, more in line with expectations, given the earlier discussion about when the problems which the unions have faced began to intensify. Among this group figure Germany, the United Kingdom, Italy, Ireland and Portugal, the most dramatic declines being those of Portugal and the United Kingdom. A third group of countries does not fit into a pattern of decline. In three of the Nordic counties, Denmark, Sweden and Finland, density was maintained at a very high level throughout the 1980s and 1990s. Although there have been 'ups and downs' in the density for these countries during this period, they certainly do not represent a model of trade union decline. In Belgium the trade unions have generally improved membership density over the half-century, although they have not reached the levels of the Nordic countries.

These different patterns of evolution of membership density stress the difficulty of identifying convergent trends in national industrial relations systems. Different national political/institutional/ economic contexts inevitably have an impact upon the development of trade union movements, including their level of membership density. Hence, the association of the unions in the Nordic countries and Belgium with the management of unemployment benefit systems is part, but not all, of the explanation of their high density levels (Scheuer 1998) while the high level of deregulation and exposure to globalization in the United Kingdom helps, at least in part, to explain the collapse of union membership in that country in the 1980s and early 1990s.

In the case of two countries, Spain and France, membership density has been significantly lower than in other EU countries. In the case of France, this has been the case since the 1950s and in the case of Spain, once the initial surge of enthusiasm for

Table 7.2 Changes in trade union density since 1950 (per cent)

Country	1950	1955	1965	1970	1975	1980	1985	1990	1995	2000
Austria	61	64	63	62	56	58	58	48	43	40
Belgium	37	n/a	n/a	45	53	57	54	51	53	69
Germany[a]	36	38	38	38	37	41	39	33	30	30
Denmark	53	59	53	64	67	80	73	71	82	87
Spain	n/a	n/a	n/a	n/a	30	14	14	17	15	15
France	33	21	19	21	23	17	15	10	9	9
UK	44	45	43	49	52	55	49	39	39	32
Greece	n/a	n/a	n/a	36	n/a	37	37	34	n/a	32
Italy	45	43	29	38	43	54	51	39	39	35
Ireland	37	n/a	n/a	53	55	57	56	50	38	44
Netherlands	43	41	40	40	38	35	29	25	26	27
Portugal	n/a	n/a	n/a	59	52	59	52	32	32	30
Sweden	67	71	68	73	75	88	92	82	83	79
Finland	34	33	42	51	67	70	69	72	81	79

Note: [a] West Germany until 1990.
Source: EIRO 2002. *Industrial Relations in the EU Member States and Candidate Countries.* Dublin: Foundation for the Improvement of Living and Working Conditions.

membership at the end of the Franco dictatorship had subsided, since the beginning of the 1980s. Again, institutional factors form an important part of the explanation. In both countries there are strong systems of worker representation via enterprise level works councils that tend to be dominated by trade union candidates. Workers in France and Spain therefore have a vehicle for showing their support for the unions without joining them. They vote for union candidates in elections and support them as their works council delegates. This does display the difficulty of taking one index such as membership density and assuming it is measuring the same phenomenon across national boundaries. For the reasons given above, membership is not as important to the trade union movements in France and Spain as in other countries, and therefore low density figures in these countries are not necessarily strong evidence of decline.

This discussion suggests a complex panorama when union membership density is considered as an index of union strength with different patterns of decline, some countries able to at least maintain density levels and, in two cases, density being less significant for institutional reasons. However when the five largest economies in the EU (Germany, France, Italy, the United Kingdom and Spain) are considered, the picture as far as membership density is concerned is less than encouraging for the trade unions. In the case of Germany, Italy and the United Kingdom, major declines in density have been experienced which, whilst they may have been slowed, show no signs of being reversed. In the case of Spain and France, while accepting the difficulty of comparing their membership density with a country such as the United Kingdom where recognition for bargaining purposes largely depends upon membership strength, their low level of density severely constrains enterprise-level activity because of a lack of activists, and constrains national-level activity because of a lack of funds. Thus, when the weight of these 'big five' economies is taken into account, the evidence for trade union decline in terms of membership density does seem to be stronger.

The membership densities of the countries of Central and Eastern Europe have not been included in the above discussion. The lack of a sufficiently long historical profile and difficulties in obtaining trustworthy data determined this decision. Table 7.3 indicates the density of the ten candidate countries to EU membership. The weighted EU average (30.4 per cent) is nearly half as high again as the candidate countries figure, with particularly low density levels in the three biggest countries, Poland, the Czech Republic and Hungary. The entry of the new members will not therefore strengthen the pattern of membership density in the EU.

Table 7.3 Union membership density in candidate countries (per cent)

Cyprus	70
Malta	65
Slovenia	41
Slovakia	40
Czech Republic	30
Latvia	30
Hungary	20
Lithuania	15
Poland	15
Estonia	14
Unweighted average	34
Weighted average	21

Source: EIRO 2002. *Industrial Relations in the EU Member States and Candidate Countries*. Dublin: Foundation for the Improvement of Living and Working Conditions.

The trade union role on representative bodies

We have already noted that any assessment of the representative strength of the trade unions which concentrates on union membership and density levels ignores the importance of other forms of representation. All EU countries, with the exception of the UK and Ireland (an exception which is about to be terminated with the EU national works council directive coming into effect), have some form of statutory provision for a system of worker committees or works councils at enterprise level. These are bodies to which workers elect delegates and/or a system of employee representation on the board of directors or supervisory board of enterprises. Works council-type bodies existed also in the past in most Central and Eastern European countries although the present situation varies considerably. Currently they exist only in the Czech Republic, Hungary, Poland,

Slovakia and Slovenia and only in Hungary and Slovenia are the bodies comparable with the EU model (EIRO 2002). Whilst sometimes elaborate participation systems exist in organizations in Japan and the US, these are of an essentially different kind from the works council model which pertains in Europe. They lack a statutory basis, and the rights of employees to information and consultation are left for management to decide (Eaton 2000).

Works councils in Europe often play an important role in collective bargaining at enterprise level and, therefore, elections to them can determine the bargaining agent(s). In some countries, like Germany and the Netherlands, the powers of these councils extend well beyond the collective bargaining arena into significant other areas of management of the organization such as employee resourcing. In addition, works council election results are often used as the basis for determining membership of representative bodies outside the enterprise such as the bargaining agents in sectoral and/or regional negotiating structures or the membership of national bi- and tri-partite consultative bodies. In some cases e.g. Spain, the election results are also used as the basis for the allocation of a public subsidy to the unions.

It is therefore significant that trade unions dominate works councils elections in countries like Germany where membership density has declined and in France and Spain where density is at a low level. Table 7.4 summarizes the results of recent works council elections in these three countries.

Table 7.4 Performance of trade unions in works council elections

Country	Percentage of elected works council delegates sponsored by trade unions
France	74 (1999)[a]
Germany	80 (2002)[b]
Spain	92 (2001)[c]

Source: [a] French Ministere du Travail; [b] WSI Hans-Boeckler-Stiftung; [c] Ministerio de Trabajo Asuntos Sociales.

The dominance which the trade unions enjoy in works council elections (and therefore in enterprise level bargaining) taken together with the relatively high election turnout (from 80 per cent in Germany to 66 per cent in France), tends to suggest that any conclusions about the decline of trade unions are premature. Through this system of 'voters' trade unionism' the trade unions would appear to remain a strong vehicle for articulating worker interests at all levels of the economy. A similar trade union dominance of representative channels exists in the case of European Works Councils. In addition the recently adopted European Directive on Employee Consultation is likely to extend enterprise-level representative structures dominated by trade unions to candidate countries. It will also, as we have noted, extend the system to Ireland and the United Kingdom, the two member states currently without established statutory systems of employee consultation and representation. There are, as we write, debates going on in both countries in which the underlying motif is the extent to which the domination of trade unions of such bodies is inevitable and whether the legislation can be introduced in such a way as to restrict it.

It is important to record that the representative systems do face pressures. Their coverage tends to be much less in the case of the private service sector and small firms and therefore, given structural changes in this direction, the proportion of the labour force which has the opportunity to vote in works council elections is likely to decline. Thus, in the case of Germany, the proportion of private sector workers covered by works councils declined from 52 per cent in 1981 to 42 per cent in 1994, although union problems of organization in East Germany also played a role in this decline (Hassel 1999). In France, works councils covered only 5.5 million of the 14 million private sector employees in 1998 (French Ministere du Travail 2000). Trade unions have sought to address this problem by allocating more resources to the organization of elections in smaller firms and by supporting the streamlining of election procedures, e.g. through the Works Constitution Act 2001, in Germany.

Bargaining influence

Perhaps the most significant indication of the strength of trade unions is the extent to which they are able directly to influence the working conditions of employees (and potential employees). It is important to understand that this influence can operate at two levels. The most commonly recognized level is that of the collective agreement which regulates the terms and conditions of employees. However, trade unions are also able to exercise influence over terms and conditions through their involvement as social partners in national tri-partite machinery: any assessment of the contemporary trade union role needs to take this into account.

Table 7.5 indicates the proportion of employees covered by collective agreements in EU countries. Trade unions, in their collective bargaining role, would still seem to exert a strong influence over the terms and conditions of employees. In countries such as France and the Netherlands systems of extending sectoral agreements to employers and employees that are not members of signatory organizations contribute to high coverage levels. In other countries many companies not covered by collective agreements still use the standards set by collective bargaining as a point of reference (in the case of Western Germany this has been estimated at 39 per cent of companies not covered by agreements (Kohaut and Schnabel 2001). The exception to this picture of high coverage is the United Kingdom where the high level of decentralization of bargaining and the decline of multi-employer bargaining have resulted in only a minority of the labour force being covered by collective agreements. In the other countries represented in table 7.5, multi-employer sectoral bargaining, whether at regional or national level, remains the most important source of collective agreements. However, notwithstanding the high level of coverage indicated in table 7.5, there are a number of reasons for suggesting that bargaining coverage may be coming under pressure on a wider basis than just the United Kingdom.

In the case of Germany the proportion of employees covered by regional agreements in the western part of the country declined from 72 per cent to 62 per cent between 1995 and 2000, while only 45 per cent of employees are covered by regional agreements in the eastern part. Although there has been an increase in the number of company-level agreements, the proportion of employees covered by such agreements has remained relatively static and has not compensated for the declining role of regional agreements (Kohaut and Schnabel 2001). Another recent feature of collective bargaining in Germany has been the 'opening up' of regional agreements to make them less prescriptive and to facilitate plant-level negotiations. There is some evidence to suggest that this flexibility has

Table 7.5 % of workers in EU countries covered by collective bargaining

Belgium	100
Austria	98
Sweden	94
Finland	90
France	90
Denmark	85
Spain	81
Netherlands	78
Germany	67
Portugal	62
Luxembourg	60
UK	36

Source: EIRO. 2002. *Industrial Relations in EU Member States and Candidate Countries.* Dublin: Foundation for the Improvement of Living and Working conditions.

been used by companies to undermine regional agreements, sometimes in alliance with their works councils.

In Spain, it has been suggested that an increasing number of employees in companies nominally covered by collective bargaining are *de facto* employed on terms and conditions outside the provisions of agreements. Just under one-third of the Spanish labour force is employed on temporary contracts and often does not enjoy the terms established in collective agreements (Rigby and Lawlor 2001). The organizational weakness of the Spanish unions at enterprise level makes it difficult for them to monitor the implementation of agreements (Martinez and Lucio 1998). Increasing numbers of management and non-manual employees are employed on terms outside those of collective agreements, either as a result of management decision or through informal agreements.

In all of the countries represented in table 7.5, the two groups of employees least likely to be covered by collective agreements – non-manual salaried employees and workers in small firms – are growing steadily as a proportion of the labour force. In the case of Denmark, Scheuer (1997) points out that only 39 per cent of private sector salaried employees are covered by collective bargaining. In Germany, small and medium sized firms are less likely to be party to a collective agreement and tend to determine terms and conditions through different mechanisms (Kohaut and Schnabel 2001). Small firms in Spain will often be party to collective agreements through an extension mechanism in their sector but are less likely to implement the terms of sectoral agreements.

In the case of candidate countries to the EU, bargaining coverage is lower than in the current EU countries, reflecting the decentralized bargaining pattern and lower union density that table 7.6 indicates. Significantly, the major exception, Slovenia, has a system of centralized bargaining. Trade unions are also able to influence the terms and conditions of employees through their impact upon national government policies: either via informal lobbying or membership of formal tri-partite machinery. Clearly it is difficult to measure this influence quantitatively. Nonetheless, trade unions would still seem to maintain considerable influence over the social and economic agenda of European national governments. Despite the views of writers such as Leijense (1996) that the neo-corporatist model was a transitory phase in the 1960s and 1970s when governments were seeking to curb excessive wage demands, in the 1990s there has been a revival of central co-ordination and concertation. Examples since the 1990s of the trade union impact in areas like social security coverage, pensions, labour market flexibility, working hours, and lifelong learning, and occupational health and safety are frequent. Nor has trade union influence depended upon collaboration with left leaning social democrat governments. Both in Italy and Spain, there have been notable union successes in opposing increased labour market flexibility and cuts in social security benefits. Again, the United Kingdom tends to be the major exception to this trend with the trade unions largely being kept at arm's length from national policy development.

Table 7.6 Collective bargaining coverage in selected candidate countries

	per cent coverage
Slovenia	100
Slovakia	48
Poland	40
Hungary	34
Czech Republic	25–30
Estonia	29
Latvia	under 20
Lithuania	10–15

Source: EIRO. 2002. Industrial Relations in the EU Members States and Candidate Countries. Dublin: Foundation for the Improvement of Living and Working Conditons.

Observers have, however, suggested that the corporatism of the 1990s has been different from the 1970s vintage. Regini (1992) argues that recent concertation tendencies are less stable than those of the 1970s – rather than a set of exchanges of benefits as before, which often could not be delivered, recent concertation tends to be structured round the devolution of competences for policy making to organized interests. Thus, it is regulative rather than distributive.

Industrial conflict

The ability of trade unions to engage in industrial conflict is a problematic measure of trade union strength. In the first instance this is because it tends to depend upon comparisons of strike rates. Strike statistics are notoriously difficult to compare because of the different measures employed at national level while, as Blyton and Turnbull (1998) point out, strikes are only one manifestation of industrial conflict. In addition, strike rates are very conditioned by the structure of collective bargaining and miss out, for example, Japanese 'days of action' designed partly to shame employers whilst employees continue working. An employment relations system characterized by sectoral bargaining often exhibits a high strike rate because of the large numbers of workers involved in sectoral disputes. Last but not least, for some commentators (Ross and Hartman 1960), a low strike rate has been interpreted as a sign of union consolidation and maturity rather than weakness. Notwithstanding these reservations, commentators have argued that declining levels of strike activity indicate the increasing inability of trade unions to mobilize their members in industrial action and of union power being curbed (Kessler and Bayliss 1998).

Table 7.7 indicates the average annual working days lost through strike action in EU countries. In nine of the fourteen countries, the rate of strike activity declined steadily in the period covered. In the case of Austria, Germany, Luxembourg and the Netherlands, the level of strike activity was already so low at the beginning of the period examined that further significant decline was difficult. Perhaps the major exception is Denmark, the statistics for which in the final period were very much influenced by a major national-level pay dispute in 1998.

There is therefore some evidence to support the view that trade unions are now less able, or less willing, to opt for industrial action in spite of the considerable variations in level of strike activity to be found in different EU countries. The developments that have impacted upon the other indices of trade union decline, such as the contraction of the manufacturing sector and the reduction in size of enterprise, would also appear to be affecting the mobilizing capacity of the unions.

Table 7.7 Average annual working days lost per 1000 employees in all industries and services, 1987–99

	1987–91	1992–96	1997–1999
United Kingdom	126	29	11
Austria	6	2	2
Belgium	41	38	16
Denmark	39	46	466
Finland	186	171	45
France	98	97	56
Germany	5	17	2
Ireland	186	111	90
Italy	276	172	62
Luxemburg	0	13	0
Netherland	15	30	6
Portugal	62	30	25
Spain	630	400	152
Sweden	101	54	10
EU average	126	86	67

Sources: Labour Market Trends. 1998. 'International Comparisons of Labour Disputes in 1996', 189–194. Labour Market Trends 2000. 'International Comparisons of Labour Disputes in 1998', April: 147–155
Note: Greece is excluded because it no longer collects data on labour disputes.

Conclusions

It is clear that it is unwise to rely on any particular set of statistics – and that there is anyway considerable diversity amongst the advanced countries in the position of their trade unions and the trends in their influence. It is also a fact, as we have noted above, that there never was a 'golden age' when the unions were able to exert power in any dominant sense. However, there seems little doubt that overall the unions have suffered a significant decline in their power and influence.

The editors of a recent authoritative review of union power and influence introduce their overview with the statement, 'Trade union decline is a world-wide phenomenon' (Verma, Kochan and Wood 2002). The pressures exerted on national labour markets resulting from globalization, and the associated shifts in the sectoral and occupational structures of the advanced industrial countries, are among the primary causes of the continuing difficulties that unions in the vast majority of those countries are experiencing. Whilst unionization rates remain relatively high in traditional sectors, including public services, unions have largely failed to organize amongst emergent groups of service sector and 'knowledge' workers, in SMEs, and, critically, amongst young workers (Gomez et al. 2002; Visser 2002; Waddington 2001). Whilst raw membership numbers are not the only basis for power, membership subscription income is critical in the long term for organizational survival. Moreover, maintaining social relevance and political influence in the absence of visible capacity to attract members can only be guaranteed by the continuing willingness of governments to legitimize union claims to represent the interests of the workforce as a whole.

The evidence for union decline is incontrovertible, and, indeed, accepted by union organizations themselves (Waddington and Hoffman 2000). The question then becomes, not whether union decline is taking place, but whether the unions and other social actors sympathetic to their general aims can do anything to halt or reverse the decline.

It is against this general backdrop that the evidence we have presented in this chapter regarding the position of unions within the EU must be seen. Unions have enjoyed a relatively privileged status in the European Union in recent years. As we have seen, in part this has been due to the fact that, overall, higher density levels have been maintained than in other economic regions of the world. However, the high power visibility of unions in Europe has largely rested on the willingness of political interests in the EU to involve union organizations at strategic levels in policy-formulation bodies dealing with social and economic issues. This has extended the approach, which has existed at national state level in many of the countries in northern Europe, of granting social partner status to unions. It has also been seen as a policy to 'roll out' and institutionalize that approach across member states where unions have not previously enjoyed this secure status.

Many analyses of the position and prospects for unions in Europe since the early 1990s, when institutional decline became a commonly discussed theme, have laid great emphasis on the capacity of EU institutions to defend and indeed promote trade union interests (Bridgford and Stirling 1994; Leisink *et al.* 1996; Rigby *et al.* 1999; Teague and Grahl 1992). Attempts to produce labour market convergence through, *inter alia*, training policies, social dialogue, and the development of a Europe-wide framework of employment rights, have all involved the strategic participation of unions. This has not only given them ready access to a wide range of power-brokers in employer organizations, and national and EU governmental organizations, but has granted them political legitimation. There have clearly been considerable gains from this process in terms of improving the representation of union interests. There have also been gains in terms of the improvement of individual and collective employment rights.

However, what this political sponsorship has not generally provided has been increased capacity to persuade individual non-union employees at the workplace that it is in *their* interests to take up union membership. The development of new recruitment strategies, the widening and improvement of services to members, and internal structural reforms both to improve internal representativeness and to provide financial efficiencies (see chapter 12), have mainly contributed to maintaining the membership in traditionally strong areas. They have not generally translated into increased capacity to attract new customers, either in terms of employers, or employees. This remains the most critical issue for unions to address, if they are to preserve their claim to political representativeness.

There are two serious potential threats that face unions in the EU region in the near future. The first is that developments in legal protection, consultation rights via works councils,and in progressive management practice may be perceived by sections of the workforce as substituting for trade union membership. The second is a concentration by sections of union leaderships on maintaining their participation in dialogue bodies at European level at the expense of other areas of activity. Both are related to the danger of pinning too many hopes on the capability, and indeed continuing willingness, of EU political elites to sponsor and protect union interests. This is particularly important given the change of emphasis in employment policy after the Amsterdam Treaty of 1997, away from a process of pacifying union interests by developing elaborate employment protections, and instead concentrating much more directly on employment policies designed to remove labour market rigidities and improve regional competitiveness. Moreover, there are strong signs that the candidate states for enlargement have little enthusiasm for employment protection regulation which will add to their labour costs (Keller 2001).

A weakening membership presence among young workers, and in new sectors, reduces the visibility of the distinctive employment gains which unions provide, and carries with it the risk that these employees may see other bodies appearing to provide functional alternatives to union protection. There is evidence that young workers in particular see progressive employer policies of Human Resource Management as *substituting for* the protections their parents would have expected from union organization (Gomez *et al.* 2002). There is a danger that apparently comprehensive systems of employment protection legislation might have the same effect for employees unused to the benefits of union protection. General tendencies for the decentralization of collective bargaining, and the resultant stronger focus on company and workplace issues, have tended to enhance the role of works councils. Unions have long been aware of the union substitution potential of such bodies. However, though unions might have been successful in maintaining, or even extending, the electoral successes of union candidates to works councils, they have not, as our evidence has shown, been able to convert this into increased membership.

The mobilization of union influence to help create a political consensus in favour of the development of the Single European Market was politically convenient, and indeed highly effective, in the 1980s and early 1990s. Union leaderships and national union organizations became progressively involved in a wide range of tri-partite bodies responsible for creating strategic social and economic policy. The centre of gravity of political lobbying has as a result moved towards Brussels and Strasburg, and away from a mainly national government focus. Moreover, the development of more elaborate arrangements for European-level sectoral social dialogue since 1998 have established many new bodies, and resulted in increased opportunities for union representative participation. This enhanced role for union representatives at supranational level has also facilitated strategic participation within national state structures, in the form of social pacts at inter-professional level, and sectoral pacts on employment and competitiveness (PECs). However, whilst these bodies have provided a platform for the articulation of union interests, union strategy has been largely defensive, and resulted in major concessions being made without notable gain: 'initiatives associated with social pacts have allowed unions to achieve a wider range of institutional security, albeit at the cost of concessions on wages and social security provisions' (Waddington 2001). This echoes earlier disenchantment with the limited role of the social partners envisaged in the 1994 White Paper on Employment by the European Commission (Leisink *et al.* 1996). And at that stage, also, the strategy of 'institutional security' was adopted by the European Trade Union Congress, in the hopes of longer-term payoff (Goetschy 1996).

The danger exists that the pursuit of institutional security, whilst important in terms of creating a long-term base for the articulation of trade union interests, becomes an end in itself, with no clear beneficial result for employees in the workplace. In that sense, the strategic consultation bodies may turn out to be an 'empty shell' of bureaucratic and ritual institutional survival, but within which the power balance is such that little is achieved for employees as a whole. To maintain these bodies as arenas within which trade union *power*, or influence, can be exercised, the capacity to develop articulation between that level and a vibrant and organized membership base at workplace level becomes critical. Whilst membership is not the only source of power available to unions, the absence of credible levels of membership exposes the unions increasingly to managerial and political challenge as to the legitimacy of their claims as official representatives of workforce interests.

Unions in Europe, perhaps especially, have been important social actors involved in progressive developments like the establishment of liberal democratic political systems, and the development of welfare states. Latterly, they have participated positively in the process of labour market modernization. In some countries, they are deeply embedded in other state-sponsored institutions. Union influence is, in these circumstances of strong political legitimation, unlikely to disappear in the short or even medium term. In Europe, at least, the unions are embedded in social structures and institutions. This is not the case in other advanced economies. A likely scenario seems to be that union power will become increasingly differentiated, strong in some countries and sectors, weak or non-existent in others. However, in Europe, the twin threats of continuing failure to attract new members in growth areas of the economy, and the potential weakening of the willingness of EU institutions to sponsor the strategic participation of unions (especially with the imminent accession of many former Communist states with very different union traditions to the European mainstream), could prove extremely damaging in the long term.

References

Atkinson, J. 1984. 'Manpower Strategies for Flexible Organizations', *Personnel Management*, August: www.umi.com

—— 1987. 'Flexibility or Fragmentation? The UK Labour Market in the Eighties', *Labour and Society*, 12, 1: 87–105.

Blyton, P. and Turnbull, P. 1998. *The Dynamics of Employee Relations*, 2nd edn. London: Macmillan.

Brewster, C. 1998. 'Flexible Working in Europe: Extent, Growth and Challenge for HRM', in Sparrow, P. and Marchington, M. (eds.), *HRM: The New Agenda*. London: Pitman.

Brewster, C., Communal, C., Farndale, E., Hegewisch, A., Johnson, G. and van Ommeren, J. 2001. *HR Healthcheck: Benchmarking HRM Practice across the UK and Europe – Management Research in Practice Series*. London: Financial Times/Prentice Hall.

Bridgford, J. and Stirling, J. 1994. *Employee Relations in Europe*, Oxford: Blackwell.

Clutterbuck, C. 2000. *Living on Thin Air*. London: Penguin.

Drucker, P. 1994. ' The Age of Social Transformation', *Atlantic Monthly*, 274, 5: 53–80.

Eaton, J. 2000. *Comparative Employment Relations*. Cambridge: Polity.

EIRO. 2000. *Industrial Relations in the EU, Japan and the USA*. Dublin: Foundation for the Improvement of Living and Working Conditions.

—— 2002. *Industrial Relations in the EU Member States and Candidate Countries*. Dublin: Foundation for the Improvement of Living and Working Conditions.

Goetschy, J. 1996. 'The European Trade Union Confederation and the Construction of the European Union', in Leisink, P., Van Leemput, J. and Vilrokx, J. (eds.), *The Challenges to Trade Unions in Europe*. Cheltenham: Edward Elgar.

Gomez, R., Gunderson, M., and Metz, M. 2002. 'Comparing Youth and Adult Desire for Unionization in Canada', *British Journal of Industrial Relations*, 40, 3: 521–542.

Hassel, A. 1999. 'The Erosion of the German System of Industrial Relations', *British Journal of Industrial Relations*, 37, 3: 483–505.

ILO. 1997. *World Labour Report 1997–1998: Industrial Relations, Democracy and Social Stability.* Geneva: International Labour Office.

Katz, H. 1993. 'The Decentralization of Collective Bargaining: A Literature Review and Comparative Analysis', *Industrial and Labor Relations Review*, 47, 1: 3–22.

Keller, B. 2001. 'The Emergence of Regional Systems of Employment Relations: The Case of the European Union', *Journal of Industrial Relations*, 43, 1: 3–26.

Kessler, S. amd Bayliss, F. 1998. *Contemporary British Industrial Relations*, 3rd edn. Basingstoke: Macmillan.

Kohaut, S. and Schnabel, C. 2001. *Tarifvertrage-nein dankel? Einflussfaktoren der Tarifbindung west- und ostdeutscher.* Nuremburg: Friedrich Alexander Universitat.

Labour Market Trends. 1998. 'International Comparisons of Labour Disputes in 1996', April: 189–194.

—— 2000. 'International Comparisons of Labour Disputes in 1998', April: 147–155.

—— 2002. 'Trade Union Membership: An Analysis of Data from the Autumn 2001 LFS', July: 343–355.

Leijense, F. 1996. 'The Role of the State in Shaping Trade Union Policies', in Leisink, P., Van Leemput, J. and Vilrokx, J. (eds.), *The Challenges to Trade Unions in Europe.* Cheltenham: Edward Elgar.

Leisink, P., Van Leemput, J. and Vilrokx, J. (eds.). 1996. *The Challenges to Trade Unions in Europe.* Cheltenham: Edward Elgar.

Martinez Lucio, M. 1998. 'Spain: Regulating Employment and Social Fragmentation', in Ferner, A. and Hyman, R. (eds.), *Changing Industrial Relations in Europe.* Oxford: Blackwell.

Millward, N., Stevens, M., Smart, D. and Hawes, W. R. 1992. *Workplace Industrial Relations in Transition.* Aldershot: Dartmouth.

Morley, M., Brewster, C., Gunnigle, P. and Mayrhofer, W. 1996. 'Evaluating Change in European Industrial Relations: Research Evidence on Trends at Organizational Level', *International Journal of Human Resource Management*, 7, 3: 640–656.

Niland, J., Lansbury, R. and Verevis, C. 1994. *The Future of Industrial Relations.* London: Sage.

OECD. 1986. *Labour Market Flexibility.* Paris: Organization for Economic Cooperation and Development.

Osterman, P., Kochan, T., Locke, R. and Piore, M. 2001. *Working in America: A Blueprint for the New Labor Market.* Cambridge, Mass.: MIT Press.

Pollert, A. 1991. *Farewell to Flexibility.* Oxford: Blackwell.

—— 1998. 'Dismantling Flexibility', *Capital and Class*, 34: 3–31

Regini, M. 1992. *The Future of Labour Movements.* London: Sage.

Rigby, M., Smith, R. and Lawlor, T. 1999. *European Trade Unions: Change and Response* London: Routledge.

Rigby, M. and Lawlor, T. 2001. 'The Spanish Labour Movement. The Quest for Flexibility', *International Journal of Iberian Studies*, 14, 3: 168–178.

Ross, A. H. and Hartman, P. T. 1960. *Changing Patterns of Industrial Conflict*. New York: Wiley.

Scheuer, S. 1997. 'Collective Bargaining Coverage and the Status Divide: Denmark, Norway, and the United Kingdom Compared', *European Journal of Industrial Relations*, 3, 1: 39–57.

—— 1998. 'Denmark: Return to Decentralisation', in Ferner, A. and Hyman, R. (eds.), *Industrial Relations in the New Europe*. Oxford: Blackwell.

Stoop, S. 2003. *FNV Working Paper on Union Membership*. Amsterdam: FNV.

Teague, P. and Grahl, J. 1992. *Industrial Relations and European Integration*, London: Lawrence and Wishart.

Traxler, F. 1994. *Collective Bargaining: Levels and Coverage – Employment Outlook*, Paris: OECD.

Treu, T. 1992. 'Labour Market Flexibility in Europe', *International Labour Review*, 131, 4: 497–512

Verma, A., Kochan, T. and Wood, S. 2002. 'Union Decline and Prospects for Revival: Editors' Introduction', *British Journal of Industrial Relations*, 40, 3: 373–384.

Visser, J. 2002. 'Why Fewer Workers Join Unions in Europe: a Social Custom Explanation of Membership Trends', *British Journal of Industrial Relations*, 40, 3: 403–430.

Waddington, J. 2001. 'Articulating Trade Union Organization for the New Europe?', *Industrial Relations Journal*, 32, 5: 449–463.

Waddington, J. and Hoffman, R. 2000. *Trade Unions in Europe*. Brussels: ETUI.

Waddington, J. and Kerr, A. 2002. 'Unions Fit For Young Workers?', *Industrial Relations Journal*, 33: 298–315.

8

The US and Canadian labour movements: markets vs. states and societies

JOHN GODARD

Since the late 1970s, many have come to believe that unions are facing an almost inevitable membership decline. Forces commonly associated with 'globalization', including increased international competition, new technologies, greater capital mobility, often harsh labour market conditions, and the spread of neo-liberal ideologies are in combination thought to have undermined both the ability of unions to serve their members and the demand for union representation. This belief has been especially prevalent in liberal market economies such as Canada and the US, where the institutional strength of labour unions has been comparatively weak.

This chapter explores the extent to which such a view can be supported. I begin by briefly outlining the institutional context and history of unions in the US and Canada. I then examine the extent to which market explanations associated with a crude version of the globalization thesis can account for union density trends in either country, juxtaposing these explanations against alternative, state and societal based explanations. Finally, I discuss the limits to union growth in both countries and the conditions necessary for them to grow in future. I argue that there may be a meaningful future for the US and Canadian labour movements, but that it will likely require the development and promotion of a new paradigm or ideology, one that is directed not only at improving the ability of labour unions to organize and represent workers, but also at changing perceptions of what unions can do.

Throughout, I focus on union density trends, defined as the percentage of the non-agricultural paid labour force that are union members. Although union density cannot be viewed as the only measure of the health of a labour movement (Godard 2003c), the primary role of unions in the US and Canada is the negotiation and administration of collective agreements at the workplace level, and the likelihood of coverage by a collective agreement is exceedingly low (about 3 per cent) if one is not a union member. As such, density is the primary and most concrete indicator of labour movement health in these two nations, and understanding union density trends is central to understanding what has happened to labour unions and what their futures are likely to be in both.

Figure 8.1 charts overall density levels in both countries. US data are from the US Current Population Survey after 1973, and from various sources prior to that, as reported by Farber and Western (2001) and Freeman (1998). Canadian data are drawn from three series. The first is based on union membership reports dating from 1921 and collected by Human Resources Development Canada (HRDC).[1] The second is based on union financial statements, as collected under the Corporations and

Figure 8.1 Union density, the US and Canada, 1911–2001

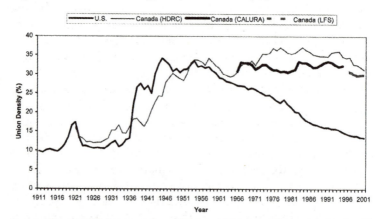

Source: For the US for years from 1911 to 1981, I use the series developed by Freeman (1998); for 1983 to 2000 (there are no data for 1982), I use calculations provided by Larry Hirsh, based on the Current Population Survey Outgoing Rotation Group (see www.trinity.edu/bhirsch); for 2001, I use estimates obtained from the BLS website. In the early 1980s, the Hirsch estimates parallel those of the Freeman series, but the latter estimates somewhat lower density levels as of the 1990s (e.g., 14.0 in 1995). I use the Hirsch series because it matches up with the official BLS estimates for 1999–2001, and it is these estimates that tend to be most referred to in discussions of current union density. For Canada, the HRDC series is from the *Directory of Labour Organizations*, various years, prior to 1988, and after that, from the *Workplace Gazette*, 2001: 36; the CALURA data is from Mainville and Olineck 1999; the LFS data were obtained directly from Statistics Canada.

Table 8.1 Private-sector density estimates, US and Canada

Year	United States	Canada		
		Bergeron	Meltz and Verma	Labour Force Survey
1961	31.9	30.0		
1966	30.8	28.6		
1970	29.1	29.3		
1974	23.8	28.3		
1975	21.9			
1980	20.4	26.0		
1984	15.5		20.6	
1985	14.6			
1986	14.0	21.0		
1989	12.4	21.5	20.5	
1990	12.1		20.5	
1991	11.9		20.4	
1992	11.5		20.2	
1993	11.2		18.4	
1994	10.9		18.0	
1995	10.4		18.2	
1996	10.2			
1997	9.8			19.0
1998	9.6			18.8
1999	9.5			18.1
2000	9.0			18.4
2001	9.0			18.3

Source: US data to 1970 are from Troy and Sheflin (1985); for 1974–80 they are from the May Current Population Survey (CPS), as provided by Larry Hirsch (www.trinity.edu/bhirsch); for 1984–1999, they are from CPS Outgoing Rotation Group Earnings Files, also as provided by Larry Hirsch; for 2000–1, they are from the BLS website. For Canada, the Bergeron estimates are from various sources (see Bergeron 1993), the Meltz and Verma estimates from the CALURA series, and are based on the Meltz and Verma (1995) method, which includes agriculture, forestry, fishing, mining, manufacturing, construction, trade, finance, bus. services, accommodation, and 'other' services as in the private sector; the LFS estimates were obtained directly from Statistics Canada. Note that the CALURA breakdowns required for the Meltz and Verma calculations are not available prior to 1989.

Labour Unions Reporting Act (CALURA) (see Mainville and Olineck 1999). It is considered to be more accurate, but is only available for the years 1965 to 1995. The third is based on the Statistics Canada Labour Force Survey (LFS), which although considered to be even more accurate, only began to collect density data in 1997 (Godard 2003a). Throughout this chapter, I will refer to the HRDC series unless otherwise noted.

Table 8.1 in turn reports private sector density data from 1960 to present. The US data are from the same sources as in figure 8.1. The Canadian data from 1997 to 2001 are from the Statistics Canada LFS series. There are no series from before 1997 that provide a clear public/private sector breakdown. However, a number of scholars have estimated private sector density for select years, based on various data sources. In this chapter, I rely on estimates compiled by Bergeron (1993) for various years from 1961 to 1989 and by Meltz and Verma (1995) for 1984 and 1990. I have also extended the latter estimates to cover the years from 1989 to 1995, using the same method.

Institutional and historical contexts: similar, but with divergent outcomes

Labour unions date back to the late eighteenth century in both the US and Canada, although it was not until the late nineteenth century that the 'modern' labour movement was born in each country. In both countries, a variant of 'business unionism' came to predominate and, by the middle of the twentieth century, both had highly similar industrial relations systems. However, the subsequent fortunes of the labour movements in each country have been substantially different, raising important questions as to the significance of states and societies relative to market forces in shaping their respective futures.

The United States

In the US, a lack of working-class radicalism, coupled with a weak state and strong employer resistance to pro-labour reforms, meant that 'business' or 'bread and butter' unionism had come to predominate by the late nineteenth century (see Jacoby 1991), and was to continue to do so throughout the twentieth. Although this model was not to go unchallenged, labour unions in the United States came to view their primary purpose as the maximization of membership gains through collective bargaining. They organized primarily at the level of the workplace, and it was at this or the employer level that their main activities took place, although they sought to co-ordinate settlements across workplaces and employers and hence to 'take wages out of competition'. Unions also engaged in political activities, but these tended to be secondary in importance and to be narrowly drawn, focused on winning improvements in labour and employment laws and seeking economic policies favourable to collective bargaining.

In the absence of effective state protections, unions were able to gain employer recognition and engage in meaningful collective bargaining only where their members had skill levels sufficient to be able to effectively shut down their employer without fear of being fired or replaced. Thus, labour's initial stronghold was in the skilled trades, and it was skilled trades or craft unions that had come to dominate the US labour movement by the early 1900s. But, partly as a result, density remained stalled, at around 10 per cent, until after the passage of the National Labor Relations Act (NLRA) and the establishment of the National Labor Relations Board (NLRB) to administer it. Enacted in 1935 as part of President Franklin Delano Roosevelt's 'New Deal' legislation to revive the US economy, the NLRA embodied what has come to be referred to as the 'Wagner model', after the senator who sponsored it through Congress. It was to provide what continues to be the basic framework for the regulation of industrial relations in the US.

The NLRA was designed to establish and protect the right of private sector workers to organize and bargain collectively with their employer. Under the NLRA, employers are not required to recognize and bargain with a union until that union has been legally certified as the bargaining agent for their employees in a given workplace. To do so, it must have the demonstrated support of a majority of eligible workers, as determined by the NLRB. Once certified, it becomes the designated legal agent of all workers eligible for coverage, even if they do not join the union. Management has a legal duty to bargain in 'good faith' with it over virtually all terms and conditions of employment, but not over issues pertaining to the management of the workplace (e.g., technological change). Attempts by employers to undermine a union organizing drive through dismissals, threats or intimidation, and failure to bargain in good faith are designated under the law as unfair labour practices, and employers found guilty of these practices are subject to a 'make whole' remedy (e.g., reinstatement with back pay if dismissed for union activities).

The NLRA was to be weakened before the 1930s were even out (see Logan 2001). However, union density grew substantially subsequent to its passage, especially after the Supreme Court upheld its constitutionality in April 1937. Union density subsequently increased from 13 per cent the year before to 28 per cent by 1939, then to 34 per cent by 1945. Although aided by the labour friendly policies of the War Labor Board during the Second World War, and by worker discontent emergent in the 1930s (Freeman 1998), there can be little question that the passage of the NLRA played a major role in spurring union organization.[2]

During the post-Second World War era (1946 to the mid-1970s), it was widely believed that labour and capital had reached an accord satisfactory to both sides. To the extent that discord occurred, it was typically attributed to immature, corrupt or undemocratic unions, not recalcitrant employers, and so the primary concern became one of how to improve union professionalism and democracy. A closer look, however, suggests that things were not as they seemed. Employer hostility and political power, combined with weaknesses in the NLRA, meant that worker rights and protections under the Act were to be gradually weakened by legal reforms, NLRB decisions, and court rulings throughout the post-war era (Logan 2001). Collective bargaining came to be largely contained in large 'core sector' firms, and even a number of these firms opted for a union free welfare capitalist approach (Jacoby 1997). Union density ceased to grow after 1954, peaking at only 34 per cent. By the late 1950s, it had begun what was to be a steady long-term decline, with employer efforts to undermine unions becoming increasingly brazen (see Logan 2001). By 2001, density had dropped to only 13.4 per cent overall, and was only 9 per cent in the private sector.

Canada

The Canadian labour movement's development was significantly linked to that of its US counterpart. This was especially true after the 1890s, when US based 'international' unions began to organize in Canada in an attempt to take the wages of US workers out of competition with those of their Canadian counterparts. By 1905, these unions accounted for 95 per cent of all union members in Canada. Although it was to subsequently decline, this figure remained as high as 70 per cent a quarter of a century later (Labour Canada 1970). Thus, despite a number of differences in working-class development and in state orientations (see below), a variant of business unionism also came initially to predominate. Yet in Canada, labour and employment legislation were (and still are) primarily the jurisdiction of the ten provinces, with the federal government having jurisdiction over only its own employees and those working in a handful of selected industries (presently about 10 per cent of the labour force). Partly as a result, meaningful protections for unions were not established until 1944, when the federal government invoked special war-time powers and issued an order-in-council imposing a Canadian version of the Wagner model on all jurisdictions. Although this order was revoked after the war, it established the basic model for Canadian labour law, and, by the end of the 1940s, all Canadian jurisdictions had adopted a variant of it.

In part because of the later adoption of collective bargaining legislation, union growth was to be slower in Canada than in the US, with density fluctuating between 13 and 18 per cent throughout the 1930s, increasing to only 24 per cent by the end of the war, and not reaching 30 per cent until 1948, when it came to equal that in the US. The Canadian labour movement was to increasingly diverge from its US counterpart as the post-Second World War era progressed. But throughout the 1950s and the early 1960s the Canadian industrial relations 'system' appeared to be little different from its US counterpart. Density levels remained within 2 per cent of US levels during this period, and US based international unions, after a decline in the 1940s, again accounted for slightly over 70 per cent of all union members in Canada (Labour Canada 1970).

As in the US, employer acceptance of unions was to be limited. But in contrast to the US, overall density decline since the mid-twentieth century appears to have been relatively small. The HRDC series suggests that density peaked at 37.2 per cent, in 1984, and was as high as 36.1 per cent a decade later. This series also suggests a 5 percentage point decline from 1994 to present, but as much as 1.4 percentage points of this decline may reflect a change in data collection methods (Godard 2003a: fn 4), and another 1.5 percentage points may reflect a decline in public sector employment as a percentage of all employees, in reflection of a 3 percentage point decline in government employment as a proportion of the labour force in the mid-1990s. Consistent with these arguments, both the CALURA and LFS series suggest greater stability, with the former showing density as fluctuating between 30 and 33 per cent from 1965 to 1995 (when the series was discontinued) and the latter showing it to have declined only marginally since 1997 (when it began), from 30.8 to 30.0 per cent.

Leo Troy (2000) has argued that this apparent stability in part reflects public sector density growth, thus masking private sector density decline. Yet the estimates in table 8.2 suggest that this decline has been less dramatic than in the US (table 8.1). As in the US, a large portion of the decline appears to have occurred from the mid-1970s to the mid-1980s, especially the early 1980s. Yet even during this period, the rate of decline was smaller than in the US (Godard 2003a: 466–467). Moreover, while the US faced continuous decline for the remainder of the century, subsequent Canadian declines were concentrated in two years, from 1992 to 1993 and from 1997 to 1998, and remained smaller than in the US in both absolute and relative terms. As a result, Canadian private sector density was double that of the US by the early 1990s, and remained so a decade later, standing at 18 per cent as of 2003. The LFS series (Statistics Canada 2003: 50) reveals that public sector density is also now double, at 73 per cent compared to 37 per cent.

In short, the Canadian and US systems are on the surface very similar, based in effect on the same regulatory model and characterized by similar industrial relations traditions. Yet the outcomes associated with them, especially as measured by union density, appear to have been quite different. In contrast to the substantial decline in the US, overall density in Canada has remained relatively stable (despite some possible decline in the late 1990s), and there has been only limited private sector decline since the mid-1980s.

Accounting for union decline: markets vs. states and societies[3]

There has been much debate over the reasons for union decline in the US and why it has been more severe than in Canada. This debate is critical to understanding the future of labour unions in both countries, because it addresses the extent to which decline is inevitable in a global economy. Essentially three sets of explanations can be identified: market explanations, state explanations and societal explanations.

Market explanations

It is possible to identify three market explanations for union decline. First, as markets become more highly integrated and competitive forces gain greater momentum, employers are increasingly unable to bear the costs associated with collective bargaining. As a result, union employers either lose market share and eventually fail, or they take steps to weaken and eventually eliminate their union, either through direct union-breaking practices or through relocation to a non-union, 'greenfield' location. Second, as nations industrialize, there is a job shift away from the blue-collar sectors and occupations that have traditionally formed the core basis for union support and towards service sectors and occupations that are more difficult to organize. This occurs not just because the service sector comes to account for an increasing percentage of GDP, but also because new technologies increasingly displace traditional blue-collar work, shrinking the membership base of unions in even their traditional strongholds. Third, it is generally assumed that pressures for flexibility lead to a substantial shift towards temporary and part-time jobs, and that workers in these jobs are also more difficult to organize.

On the surface, the US case does suggest some support for these explanations. Employer anti-unionism is generally considered to have increased substantially beginning in the late 1970s and early 1980s, when it is generally believed that the forces of globalization began to take hold. Although the decline in union density was well under way prior to this period, private sector decline was especially dramatic in the early 1980s. There was also a substantial decline in union certification elections at this time (Farber and Western 2001: 471). It is plausible to argue that this reflected increases both in competitive pressures and hence in employer hostility and in the rate of job shift away from traditional union sectors. Moreover, the employment growth rate in the union sector substantially lagged the non-union sector growth rate after 1975, especially during the early 1980s (Farber and Western 2001: 471).

On the other hand, there is little evidence of a decline in the likelihood of unions winning a certification election after 1975 (Farber and Western 2001: 467), which one might expect to observe if the problem was increased employer resistance. It may be that the decline in union organization simply reflected a lower demand for unions due to a more coercive economic environment, coupled with lower union organizing resources following devastating membership losses in the early 1980s. More important, if the US can be viewed as a paradigm case, Canada should not be far behind. Not only are the Canadian and US IR systems similar, Canada has become increasingly integrated with its US counterpart, so much so that trade with the latter now amounts to roughly two-fifths of Canadian GNP. Yet as discussed above, Canadian unions appear to have fared much better than their US counterparts and declines in the private sector appear to have been less dramatic and more sporadic than in the US.

It is possible that Canada is simply lagging the US, and that it is a matter of time before private sector density drops to US levels. According to the main exponent of this argument, Leo Troy (1999, 2000, 2001), such a lag existed in the 1950s, reflecting a slower rate of job shift to service occupations. Troy also argues that Canada's private sector membership peaked in 1979, nine years later than in the US, again demonstrating a lag. But there is little evidence that Canada continues to lag the US in the shift to service industries, and union density in any case remains at least double that of the US in most sectors for which there are comparable data (Godard 2003a: 469), so any compositional differences between the two countries cannot explain differences in overall density levels.

It is also possible that increased integration with the US has not yet had enough time to work its way through the Canadian economy, especially because the Canadian dollar has in recent years been undervalued by 10 to 20 per cent against its US counterpart. Yet the US–Canada free trade era began in 1989, and the two economies were already closely linked at that time, with the US exports accounting for a fifth of Canada's GNP. Moreover, even if one assumed that only market explanations mattered, and hence that density could be expected to decline to US levels in the two industries likely to be most affected (manufacturing and natural resources), overall private sector density would still drop by only 3.7 percentage points, or only 40 per cent of the current Canada–US private sector density difference (Godard 2003a: 472).

In addition, the private sector declines that have occurred in Canada do not seem to reflect the gradual erosion that one might expect from market explanations. Rather, they have occurred largely during economic downturns, which have long been believed to cause union stagnation and decline (e.g., Bain and Elsheikh 1976; Western 1997). They are also difficult to disentangle from the effects of government policies, including anti-labour policies adopted in the largest jurisdiction (Ontario) during the late 1990s and federal government economic policies during the 1980s and 1990s.[4] But even if politics did not matter, private sector decline has still been substantially lower in Canada than in the US.

The Canadian case would thus appear to show that union decline in the US cannot be accounted for solely or even primarily by market explanations. Critical scrutiny of these explanations may explain why. First, the assumption that unions necessarily engender prohibitively high costs and hence undermine competitiveness is unduly deterministic, especially as it underestimates their non-economic roles (e.g., fairness and voice), and hence the ability of unions to moderate their economic demands without necessarily undermining member support. For example, the available research shows that, since the 1970s, the union wage effect has dropped from approximately 22 to 13 per cent in the US (Bratsberg and Ragan 2002) and from 25 to 8 percent in Canada (Gunderson and Hyatt 2001: 393; Statistics Canada 2002). There is some research suggesting that union presence is associated with lower profits and investment in manufacturing (e.g., Becker and Olson 1992), but most or all of this research is based on data from the early 1980s and before and hence may be badly out of date in view of the decline in wage effects. Indeed, evidence based on US data from the mid-1990s shows no association between union presence and the likelihood of insolvency (Freeman and Kleiner 1999).

Second, the extent to which 'non-traditional' sectors are inherently antithetical to union organising is not clear. The substantially higher Canadian density levels in these sectors (noted earlier) provide strong reason to believe that the potential for growth in traditionally non-union sectors is much higher than US density data suggest. Even in Canada, it is likely that density levels would be significantly higher in these sectors if, for example, sectoral bargaining was to be established. Third, the belief that a growth of part-time and temporary jobs helps to account for union decline suggests that there has been a major shift to these types of jobs and that workers in these jobs are substantially more difficult to organize than their more traditional counterparts. Yet such jobs have grown only marginally as a percentage of the US labour force since the late 1970s (see Ellwood *et al.* 2000: 53; Jacoby 2000). Moreover, in Canada, union density is 24 per cent among part-time workers, and 27 per cent among temporary workers (Statistics Canada 2003: 50–51).

In short, market explanations for the US decline are not only undermined by the absence of a similar decline in Canada, but also by faulty assumptions. Either way, they would seem to fall far short as primary or even major explanations for the fate of unions in Canada and the US. As shall become apparent, there is much greater support for state explanations.

State explanations

Within the North American context, states can be seen to have affected union fortunes in a number of ways (Godard 2002). For example, government economic policies, though no doubt an effect as well as a cause of economic conditions, may explain some or even all of the decline in Canadian private sector density in the early 1980s and 1990s – as suggested earlier. But labour laws and their administration have served as the primary state-based explanation for union density trends in North America, with labour law scholars, union officials, and human rights advocates blaming the US decline on labour law weaknesses and often arguing that higher density levels in Canada reflect legal differences (e.g., Block *et al.* 1996; Gould 1993; Human Rights Watch 2000; Weiler 1983; Wood and Godard 1999). Thus, I focus on these arguments. I begin by outlining problems that have been identified with the US system (e.g., Human Rights Watch 2001).

It is generally agreed that the US system allows employers substantial opportunity to interfere with a union organizing drive, an opportunity which is all too often taken advantage of given employer opposition to unions. In particular, subsequent to the Taft-Hartley Act of 1947, a ballot must be held for all certification applications. In addition, the labour board must hold a hearing to establish the appropriate election unit prior to holding a ballot, thus introducing potentially lengthy delays. This creates a circumstance under which employers have ample opportunity to intimidate employees. Although overt intimidation tactics constitute unfair labour practices, charges to this effect are difficult to prove and subject to lengthy appeal processes, and the 'make whole' remedies at the labour board's disposal mean that employers often suffer minimal penalties once guilt has been established and the appeal process exhausted. In addition, the employer may hold captive audience meetings and resort to anti-union lies and propaganda in an attempt to dissuade union workers from voting for the union. Yet union organizers have no corresponding right, and workers can be fired if they engage in any pro-union speech or activities on employer time, even if this is simply to counter employer propaganda.

State level 'right-to-work' laws are also now prevalent in 22 states, and both the federal government and most states require open shops for most of their employees. In effect, these laws mean that, although unions must represent all workers eligible for union membership, workers are not required to join a union or pay dues. Thus, these laws allow 'freeriding'. They also mean that the majority principle underlying the Wagner model is one-sided. Even if a union wins a certification vote, the employer can continue to undermine support for it by discouraging workers from joining or even paying dues.

Once a union is certified, there is still no guarantee that it will succeed in negotiating a collective agreement. Although employers are required by law to negotiate in 'good faith' over virtually all issues pertaining to the terms and conditions of employment, there are a number of ways in which they can prevent a contract from ever being reached. First, there are broad grounds for employer appeals of certification decisions, and no requirement that the employer engage in collective bargaining until such appeals have been settled. Appeals can take a year or more, thus significantly delaying negotiations and dampening member support. Second, a failure of an employer to bargain in 'good faith' is difficult to prove and to enforce, making it possible for employers to frustrate the bargaining process once it has begun, and to ultimately push the union into a lengthy strike. Third, once a strike (or lockout) has been called, employers may hire replacement workers on a permanent basis, provided only that strikers be given priority for any new positions that open up after the strike.

A further problem often identified is the limited coverage of the NLRA. Workers who perform any managerial duties whatsoever, including simple supervisory ones, are excluded from coverage under the Act, a problem that has become of growing importance in recent years given the 'empowerment' of workers in a number of occupations (Clark *et al.* 2002). For example, charge nurses (those in charge of a nursing team or unit) have been excluded from coverage on these grounds. Public sector workers are also not covered under the Wagner Act, and although they may be covered by public sector bargaining laws at the state level, these laws often provide very limited rights. For example, only 23 states had laws mandating bargaining rights for state employees as of the mid-1990s, and only 14 of these provided a right to either strike or go to arbitration (Lund and Maranto 1996: 52–54).

There is some direct evidence that these limitations matter. For example, studies have found that employers illegally discharge one or more employees for union activities in almost one-third of NLRB elections, and that the odds of an employee being fired for exercising the right to join a union are about one in ten (Logan 2001). As high as one-third of all newly certified unions are unable to negotiate a first agreement with their employer (Commission on the Future of Labor–Management Relations 1994), which in the US (and Canada) effectively means its demise. Moreover, close to a third of the US private sector labour force is now thought to be excluded from coverage under the NLRA (Strauss 1995).

It is also noteworthy that US union density decline began in the late 1950s, following changes in labour laws and their administration, not in markets. Under the Taft-Hartley Act of 1947, the right of workers to gain certification through the signing of membership cards was withdrawn, employers were given the right to use anti-union propaganda, and states were given jurisdiction to enact right-to-work laws. The full effect of these changes was not, however, to be realized until after 1953, when the Eisenhower administration appointed three pro-management representatives to the five-member National Labour Relations Board (NLRB), charged with administering the NLRA (Logan 2001). It may thus be no coincidence that density ceased to grow after the following year.

The strongest evidence, however, once again comes from a comparison with the Canadian case. Although based on the same model, and despite some weakening in a number of juris-dictions since the 1990s, labour law in Canada was if anything strengthened throughout most of the post-Second World War era and in most jurisdictions contains a number of provisions that address the limitations in the US system.

In Canada, a majority of jurisdictions allow for automatic card certification, although the percentage of eligible workers required ranges from a bare majority (the federal jurisdiction) to 65 per cent (the Province of Manitoba). Even in those jurisdictions without card certification, the labour board typically has tight time constraints, ranging from a maximum of 5 days (in 3 jurisdictions) to 10 (in 1 jurisdiction), within which a ballot is to be held subsequent to a union's application. As in the US, it is difficult to prove employer intimidation. But it is also difficult to appeal board decisions, and the board has stronger remedies at its disposal than in the US. These include punitive fines and, in six jurisdictions, the ability to order automatic certification if it believes an employer has tainted the process, even where there is no evidence that a majority of workers was ever in favour of union representation. There is also no requirement that the board hold a hearing to determine the appropriate election unit, and if the board has reason to believe that the employer is engaging in illegal tactics or is likely to do so it may in some jurisdictions hold a 'prehearing vote' as early as two to three days after a union has applied for certification. As in the US, employers may hold captive audience meetings, unions have no corresponding rights, and workers may be fired for union-related speech or activities if on company time. However, employers cannot engage in propaganda. Rather, they may only present factual information, and must not do so in a way that can be construed as an attempt to intimidate. Finally, there are no right-to-work laws and, indeed, virtually all jurisdictions contain laws to discourage or even ban open-shop arrangements, effectively requiring that all workers in a bargaining unit at minimum pay the equivalent of union dues.

Once a union has been certified, there is again very little ground for appeal, and the employer must engage in collective bargaining regardless of whether an appeal is in process, until and unless the labour board's initial decision is overturned. There are no formal legal restrictions on the issues that a union may ask the employer to bargain over, although unions in Canada have typically not attempted to bargain far beyond the scope of their US counterparts and labour boards typically do not rule against employers that refuse to do so. As in the US, a failure to engage in good faith bargaining is difficult to prove. But most jurisdictions allow for mandatory first contract arbitration if the parties are unable to reach an agreement on their own, thus reducing the ability of employers to push a newly certified union into a lengthy strike.

A further important difference is the right of strikers to return to their job once a strike has ended. Not only is the use of permanent replacement workers illegal in all jurisdictions, in two of the three largest provincial jurisdictions employers cannot even use temporary replacements. In one other jurisdiction (the federal), it is an unfair labour practice for employers to hire replacements if the purpose appears to be to break a union. In yet another, arbitration may be ordered once a strike has lasted 60 days, thus reducing the incentive to hire replacements with the intention of breaking a union through a strike of indefinite duration.

Finally, coverage is much broader in Canada. For example, workers who perform low-level supervisory jobs or limited managerial duties are typically eligible for coverage as long as they are not in confidential or predominantly managerial positions. Public sector workers are often covered by separate legislation, but are subject to far fewer restrictions than is typical in the US. In particular, although most jurisdictions restrict or outlaw the right to strike for occupations deemed essential to public health and safety, all at minimum allow for independent arbitration in the event of an impasse.

These differences do not suggest that Canadian labour law provides workers with appreciably more rights than in the US. Rather, they suggest that Canadian laws are designed so that these rights are more likely to be effectively exercised and upheld. The available evidence overwhelmingly suggests that this is indeed the case.[5] For example, from 1980 to 1995 (before the election of a hostile government in Ontario, which accounts for a third of all Canadian workers), the likelihood of a union winning certification after having applied to a labour board was 69 per cent in Canada, compared to 48 per cent in the US (Rose and Chaison 1996: 83). Charges of illegal employer activity in Canadian jurisdictions were only one-quarter to one-tenth (depending on the jurisdiction) as high as in the US, even though they are easier to file and win in Canada (Bruce 1993 1994). Finally, there is also indirect evidence from labour force surveys to indicate that demand for unions is the same in the

US as in Canada, and that density levels would likely be equivalent if workers faced the same organizing conditions (Godard 2003a: 477–478; Gomez *et al.* 2001).

Multivariate research suggests that card certification has made an especially important difference, with one estimating it to account for 17–26 per cent of the US–Canada density gap as of 1995 (Johnson 2002). However, a number of studies (e.g., Martinello 1996; Taras and Ponak 2001; Thomason 1994) have found other labour law differences to matter as well, with implications for the divergence in US–Canadian density levels. Finally, US studies (e.g., Bronfenbrenner 1997; Cooke 1983, 1985) have found union organizing success to be significantly lower where the time delay for a ballot is longer, where employers commit unfair labour practices, and where employers engage in activities (e.g., anti-union propaganda) that, although legal in the US, are not in Canada.

There is thus strong empirical as well as intuitive evidence that state policies, especially labour laws, have made an important difference to the fate of the Canadian and US labour movements. Yet it is possible that broader, more societal differences have also mattered, either independently of or in conjunction with labour laws. At minimum, labour laws cannot be fully understood apart from societal factors.

Societal explanations

For present purposes, societal explanations include not just broad cultural or normative differences, but also differences in labour and management ideologies and strategies within a given national context. Little attempt has been made to argue that changes in the former explain the decline in US union density. Particularly notable has been the lack of attention to individualization processes often identified as a problem for European labour unions (e.g., Beck 1992). This is likely because the US has always tended to be relatively individualistic and, consistent with this, labour unions have tended to have a narrow focus, concentrating on achieving gains in individual terms and conditions of employment. Thus, Canada–US differences rather than societal changes have, once again, been most often invoked to account for differences in the fates of their respective labour movements. It is possible to identify four such explanations.

First, and most fundamentally, Canada never had a US-style

revolution, and, in contrast to the individualist development of the US 'frontier', Canada's early development was driven by large fur trading companies and by the North West Mounted Police. As a result, Canadians have tended to have greater trust in and respect for authority and a more collectivist, social democratic orientation than have their US counterparts. These broad cultural differences are in turn argued to translate into greater support for labour unions (Lipset 1989).

Second, and partly as a result, it is argued that the Canadian labour movement had begun to adopt more of a social unionist philosophy by the early 1960s, coinciding with the formation of Canada's equivalent of the British Labour Party, the New Democratic Party (NDP), and accompanied by a growing independence from US-based international unions since then.[6] In theory, this has ensured the Canadian labour movement a broader legitimacy and appeal than its US counterpart, which continued with its narrow, business unionism philosophy and as such came to be viewed more as an interest group than a movement (Robinson 1992).

Third, it is sometimes argued that Canadian labour unions have invested more resources in organizing, and that this also helps to explain why they have done better (Rose and Chaison 1996). This may be seen as simply a matter of strategic choice. But it would seem difficult to separate it out from the social unionism and ultimately the cultural differences explanations. Specifically, one could argue that any decision by Canadian labour unions to invest more in organizing reflects a lesser concern with simply maximizing the short-term returns to their members than with ensuring bargaining rights for as many Canadian workers as possible (Rose and Chaison 1996: 86).

Finally, it has been argued that employers have been less hostile to unions in Canada (Thompson 1995). There is reason to argue that the exceptional antagonism of US employers towards unions reflects their history of relative power and dominance within the US political system (Jacoby 1991). But a further argument is simply that cultural differences have meant that employers operate within a different normative environment, one that is less tolerant of anti-union behaviour.

These arguments can be used not just to explain Canada–US differences, but also to explain why US unions have fared so poorly in comparison with labour movements in most developed nations. In particular, worker individualism and virulent employer anti-unionism, coupled with narrow union goals and a lack of resources devoted to organizing, may essentially explain why union density is so low in the US. Yet there is little evidence to corroborate them. As noted earlier, support for unions is as high in the US as in Canada, which would appear to be contrary to both the cultural difference and the social unionism explanations. Moreover, although Canadian unions were involved in a higher number of certification applications per capita in the 1980s and 1990s (Rose and Chaison 1996: 83–86; Yates 2000), this may be an artefact of more favourable organizing laws, laws that have yielded much higher success rates and so offer greater inducements for unions to engage in organizing. A similar argument can be made with regard to the apparently higher levels of employer resistance in the US. As suggested earlier, it is likely that Canadian labour laws have created an environment in which virulent anti-unionism is less likely to pay, and that employers have as a consequence developed values that are consistent with such behaviour. But the limited evidence that exists in any case suggests that, at least in Canada, employer values and beliefs about unions may be of limited use for predicting anti-union behaviour (Godard 1997: 220). There is also little convincing evidence of differences in employer values between the two countries (see Godard 2003a: 481).

Where societal factors may have mattered, however, is indirectly, through their implications for politics and the law. First, there is a general consensus that advances for labour unions tend to be linked to the presence of a distinctive social democratic political party with close ties to labour (see Western 1997). In Canada, the NDP has played a significant role in the promotion and, where elected, adoption of more favourable labour laws than in the US. Second, there is some evidence that Canadians are more sympathetic than are their US counterparts to state intervention in the economy generally, and the enactment of stronger labour laws, more specifically (Lipset and Meltz 1998: 17). Third, and perhaps reflecting this greater sympathy for government intervention, Canada has a much stronger tradition of administrative law and a legal system that renders administrative law decisions much less susceptible to appeal (Taras 1997). Fourth, Canadian governments have, especially (but not only) at the federal level, a much stronger tradition of 'Tory paternalism', one that emphasizes order and stability and hence laws that effectively regulate conflict.

In short, although societal factors may provide some a priori explanation for differences in the fates of the Canadian and US labour movements, it may be that their role has been either secondary, reflecting labour law differences, or indirect, through their implications for politics and hence labour law.

The future of the US and Canadian labour movements

The analysis so far suggests that the market forces that have come to be associated with globalization do not appear to provide a very good explanation for what has happened to the US labour movement or for why its Canadian counterpart appears to have done so much better. Rather, the most convincing explanation would appear to be differences in the law, although societal factors that ultimately derive from the early development of the two nations may have played an important role in accounting for these differences and their effects. By implication, the adoption of Canadian-style labour law reforms in the US could create the conditions for substantial growth, although societal factors unique to the US could also serve as barriers to both the adoption and effectiveness of such reforms unless adapted to the US context.

Such a conclusion would be consistent with so-called historical institutionalism, suggesting an extension of what has come to be referred to as the 'varieties of capitalism' thesis (Hall and Soskice 2001) to account more carefully for differences across 'liberal market' economies and how they matter instead of simply contrasting these economies in general with 'co-ordinated' market economies (e.g., Germany). But there are at least two possible problems with it. First, while this analysis explains differences between the US and Canada, and suggests that the key problem has been one of labour law in the US, it does not explain why the Canadian labour movement has not continued to grow and, indeed, has been unable to even recapture lost ground in the private sector after the declines of the early 1980s and then the early 1990s. Second, the Canadian labour movement represents only one in three workers overall, and only one in five in the private sector. This constitutes a success in comparison to the US. But by any meaningful standard of democracy, it constitutes a failure.

It is plausible to argue that, even if market forces have not caused significant decline in Canada, they represent the primary reason for the Canadian labour movement's failures. In this regard, we can argue that market forces may well matter, with Canadian labour law serving to blunt but not negate their implications for union density. If so, the converse may also be true. That is, market forces may have blunted any positive effects that labour law might otherwise have had on union growth over the past few decades. We might view this as a 'Mexican standoff' between markets and states, except that the inability of the Canadian labour movement to regain its lost ground after economic downturns suggests that market forces may be winning out over the long run, even if it may be taking them longer than in the US to have their way with labour. Yet any such explanation would be too limited. It would appear that the real problem faced by the Canadian labour movement has, paradoxically, been its main benefactor, the state.

First, throughout the 1980s and early to mid-1990s, unduly harsh monetary policies, an over-inflated Canadian dollar, and massive cutbacks in government spending helped to create unduly hostile economic conditions for unions, and that, in the absence of such policies, labour unions would have been able to at least regain lost ground. These policies eased somewhat in the latter half of the 1990s, but by then the Canadian labour movement had come to face more coercive federal labour market policies, especially as engendered in massive cuts to unemployment benefits. In addition, an anti-labour government in Ontario, elected in 1995, substantially weakened labour law, eliminating automatic card certification and restoring the right of employers to use temporary replacement workers during a strike (Martinello 2000). Although a few Canadian jurisdictions already had similar provisions, the Ontario jurisdiction accounts for roughly a third of all employed Canadians.

If state policies can be argued to provide an important explanation for union stagnation, then it might also be argued that the fortunes of the Canadian labour movement could be substantially improved if Canadian public policy was to swing in the opposite direction. Such a swing would include more generous labour market policies and a strengthening of labour laws so that not only Ontario, but all jurisdictions had all of the characteristics that have come to be identified with the Canadian system. The problem is that, even if such a swing was to occur, it is likely that the Canadian labour movement would still represent only a minority of Canadian workers. For example, even in Canadian jurisdictions with most or all of the laws associated with the Canadian system (e.g., Quebec), unions represent only one in four private sector workers. This represents a significant improvement over current density levels in the US and so should not be disregarded. But it suggests that more conventional policy reforms will not be sufficient to place labour unions on a long-term growth trajectory.

The problem is arguably more fundamental than this, arising from the Wagner model itself. Specifically, it may be argued that, although this model (if properly implemented and enforced) can provide important rights and protections for labour unions, it also substantially limits the prospects for union growth and effectiveness. It is possible to identify at least four ways in which this is so.

First, the general assumption underlying the Wagner model is that, with the exception of discipline and dismissal, anything not covered in the collective agreement is subject to management authority. Unions have few if any a priori consultation or co-decision rights if employers should seek to exercise their authority in ways that harm union members. As a result, unions are required to negotiate restrictions on the exercise of employer authority and then ensure that these restrictions are adhered to. This places them in reactive positions and substantially limits their ability to effectively represent their members. It also promotes an adversarial and narrow form of unionism. Both may limit the appeal of unions among significant segments of the labour force and heighten employer resistance.

Second, the Wagner model has led to highly decentralized bargaining, largely because bargaining rights are granted at the workplace level. In the 'golden era' of the 1950s and 1960s, employers in more concentrated, core sector industries generally found it to their advantage to follow industry patterns, and unions typically possessed sufficient power to impose these patterns if need be. Thus, decentralized bargaining may have seemed to be of little consequence. But bargaining patterns began to break down in the 1980s, as employers found themselves subject to increased competitive pressures and as economic conditions substantially undermined union power. More important, it has been virtually impossible for unions to enforce patterns across employers in more competitive sectors. As a result, union organization has been seen by employers in these sectors to be a much greater threat than otherwise, and unions have been much less successful in negotiating meaningful improvements for their members where they have succeeded in becoming organized. This is probably a key reason why union density has always tended to be lower in so-called 'non-traditional' sectors such as trade, accommodation and food services

A third problem is the majority requirement. This denies legal union representation rights to workers who would like to have such rights, but are in the minority in their workplace. One poll suggests that, among non-union workers, this proportion is one in two in the US, and one in three in Canada (Lipset and Meltz 1998). By refusing meaningful union representation to these workers, the law essentially places a large portion of the labour force out of the reach of the labour movement.

Finally, as Roy Adams (1993, 1995) has forcefully argued, the certification process associated with the Wagner model may create an unduly adversarial and hence hostile environment. According to Adams, a union organizing attempt tends to be seen as an attack on management, inducing a hostile response. A culture has thus developed in which employers are more hostile to union organisation than otherwise, and in which signing up for a union is viewed as an act of disloyalty. Workers not only have reason to fear retribution from their employer, they also come to view the exercise of a basic democratic right (i.e., to union representation) as an act of disloyalty. Not only does this reduce the likelihood of a union becoming organized, it also means that organizing drives are likely to be successful only where there are high levels of worker distrust and resentment. The result is that, once a union does become established, its relationship with management is likely to be unduly adversarial, reinforcing the view that unions are essentially negative forces in the economy and limiting their appeal to significant segments of the labour force.

If the Wagner model is a major barrier to a long-term union growth trajectory, as these arguments suggest to be the case, then the future of the Canadian and US labour movements can be argued to depend on reforms that in effect go beyond this model. For example, it might be possible to establish universal 'agency' rights that fall short of those associated with traditional collective bargaining but which include the right for union representatives to serve as agents of individual members or groups thereof on matters involving the terms and conditions of their employment, fair treatment and due process, and workplace change decisions, with mandatory information sharing, consultation, and even co-decision rights in these areas. Unions might also serve as agents for their members with regard to employment standards implementation and enforcement, and possibly even help to establish minimum terms and conditions of employment in specific industries, much as British wages councils used to do.

If properly designed and implemented, such reforms might significantly reverse the fortunes of labour unions in both countries and in so doing increase workplace representation levels. Such reforms would likely be especially effective if complemented by the changes to labour market programmes and traditional labour laws suggested earlier, and perhaps by a more active attempts by the state to create a more favourable normative environment for unions, one characterized by less employer antagonism (see Godard 2002).

The problem with this argument may, however, be not with whether such reforms could be expected to work but rather with whether they are at all realistic. In this respect, to suggest that either legal or broader policy reforms can provide the basis for meaningful growth may be seen as simply missing the point. In the US, hopes for even modest reforms appear to have been crushed in the early 1990s during the so-called 'Republican Revolution', as symbolized by the tepid and widely ignored recommendations of President Clinton's Commission on the Future of Worker–Management Relations (1994). In Canada, the prospects would also appear to be dim at present (see Godard 2003c). Labour appears to have become increasingly marginalized politically, and there appears to be little support for stronger labour laws. There is now only one jurisdiction with a majority NDP government, and this government appears to have little stomach for progressive reforms (Godard 2003c).

These conditions have led some to believe that, although the state, and the Wagner model in particular, may be the problem, the route to union growth lies not in policy reforms but rather in union self-help strategies that by-pass the state (e.g., Arthurs 1996). In particular, these people argue that there is a need for unions to seek out new organizing strategies, largely 'outside of' the Wagner model. A number of strategies have been identified, including the 'network' model used to organize janitorial workers in California (Erikson *et al.* 2002), the 'organizing' model associated with the Service Employees International Union in both Canada and the US, and the 'bargaining to grow' model employed by a number of unions in 'traditional' sectors such as automobiles and steel (Bank 2002). Yet in the US in particular, such strategies have been attempted with little positive effect. Thus, although such strategies could prove necessary and even critical for unions to take advantage of opportunities provided by the sorts of labour law and policy reforms suggested above, they do not appear to be sufficient in the absence of such reforms.

It would thus appear to be critical to alter the political environment in a way that is more conducive to labour policy reforms. Although this may be made difficult by the economic 'realities' of the past few decades, states would still appear able to make meaningful choices (e.g., Garrett 1998; Fligstein 2001, 213–220). Much of the problem may thus lie not with economic realities but rather with political will and, ultimately, on societal forces. But although there is evidence of widespread general support for unions in both the US and Canada, this support does not appear to have translated into widespread support for legal reforms, especially of the kind suggested above. The future of the labour movements in both countries may thus ultimately depend on their ability to generate such support.

One strategy may be to promote the human rights perspective advocated in some circles and most exemplified by the recent Human Rights Watch report, *Unfair Advantage* (2000; also see Friedman and Wood 2001). Yet this strategy has typically entailed advocacy of traditional, Canadian-style labour law reforms in the US. It is not clear that international human rights principles would be sufficient to provide justification for broader reforms of the kind suggested in the present analysis. A further problem is that such a strategy runs the risk of being dismissed on the grounds that human rights are being invoked for cynical reasons, to serve the vested interests of 'big labour', rather than as ends in themselves.

An alternative developed more fully elsewhere (Godard 2003c) is to couch such reforms under the rubric of a 'good practice' paradigm. The kinds of reforms suggested above are consistent with what has always been advocated as good practice in management circles, and they address a myriad of more concrete problems faced by workers, particularly as they pertain to insecurity and coercion in the workplace. They might thus be promoted as a sort of a third way, similar to (but going beyond) the approach of the Blair government in the UK. But they would be promoted not on the basis of their implications for the labour movement or in terms of universal human rights, but rather on the grounds that they are simply consistent with basic principles of dignity, fairness, and voice that one would expect to be realized in any advanced civilization. Unions would be seen to provide a source of 'institutional backup' necessary for the effective implementation of such reforms. Thus, increased union density would be viewed as instrumental to their effectiveness, not as an end in itself.

How optimistic can one be about the prospects for such a strategy? Probably not very. In the US, any such strategy would be more likely to work if it focused on the promotion of individual rather than collective rights, because this is more consistent with American values and traditions (Lipset 1989). But it would still face the traditional anti-statism of the US and competing claims to property rights (Hutton 2002). More important, the extant power structure within the US political system represents a formidable barrier to meaningful reforms regardless of the level of societal support that might be achieved, while corporate control over the popular media represents a formidable barrier to achieving such a level in the first place.

In Canada, there may be somewhat more room for optimism in view of the societal differences identified earlier (i.e., more collectivist values). The Canadian political structure may also be more conducive to such a strategy, especially as the existence of eleven jurisdictions allows more opportunity for experimentation. Moreover, Canada still has a state-owned, arm's-length national broadcasting system and a social democratic party that could assist in the promotion of such a paradigm. Although the latter is currently in a weakened state, the adoption of such a strategy could serve as part of a 'new paradigm' designed to reverse its fortunes as well.

In both countries, however, some sort of societal mobilization may be needed if labour unions, and, more generally, workplace representation, are to enjoy anything approaching a renaissance. The likelihood of such mobilization may depend on a variety of factors (e.g., Kelly 1998). But it is especially likely to depend on the development of an effective strategy and ultimately paradigm for enhancing employment rights and the quality of the work experience in general. Indeed, in the absence of such a paradigm, it is likely that labour movements in both nations will find themselves increasingly marginalized. The development of a 'good practice' paradigm in some form could be critical not only to the futures of these labour movements, but to the future of workplace rights and standards in general and, ultimately, to the extent to which basic democratic principles are likely to be realized at work.

Notes

1 For 1921 to 1973, I rely on density estimates reported in Eaton 1975. These differ somewhat from those calculated by Bain and Price (1980) and used in work by Freeman (1998). I use them because they were computed by an employee of the Canadian federal government and appeared in an official publication. From 1973 to 2001, I rely on reported density figures supplied in Labour Canada's *Directory of Labour Organizations*, as subsequently adjusted by the Workplace Information Directorate of HRDC and appearing in the *Workplace Gazette* 2001, 3–4: 36.

2 As Richard Freeman (1998: 282) points out, three-quarters of the new recognitions in 1937 followed recognition strikes. He concludes that this is evidence that 'bottom-up' factors (worker militancy) were more important than the NLRA. But it is just as likely that the NLRA, coupled with the Supreme Court ruling, served as spurs to worker organization and to employer recognition, especially given the limited resources and hence capacity of the NLRB to process certification requests in a timely fashion. In essence, workers were asserting their legal rights even if the administrative process for realizing these rights was not yet fully in place, and employers were more willing to concede these rights after support had been demonstrated through a recognition strike, in the belief that the union would in any case win certification through the board.

3 This section draws extensively from Godard 2003a.

4 In the early 1980s, both government imposed wage restraints and a decision to shift to monetarism at minimum aggravated the effects of already harsh conditions. Moreover, beginning in the late 1980s, the Bank of Canada adopted a 'zero inflation' policy that greatly aggravated the 1992–93 economic downturn and hence the effects of this downturn on private sector density.

5 For a more thorough review, see Godard 2003a, 2003b.

6 As of 2001, only 30 per cent of Canadian union members were in international unions, compared to 71 per cent in the early 1960s. This drop largely reflects the growth in public-sector unionism, which is almost entirely Canadian based and now accounts for roughly half of the Canadian labour movement. However, there have also been some noteworthy breakaways (the Canadian region of the United Auto Workers in the early 1980s) and numerous cases where US parent unions have granted increased autonomy to their Canadian affiliates.

References

Adams, R. 1993. 'The North American Model of Employee Representational Participation: 'A Hollow Mockery', *Comparative Labor Law Journal*, 15, 4: 4–14.

—— 1995. *Industrial Relations under Liberal Democracy*. Columbia, S.C.: University of South Carolina Press.

Arthurs, H. 1996. 'Labour Law Without the State', *University of Toronto Law Journal*, 46,1: 1–45.

Bain, G. and Elsheikh, F. 1976. *Union Growth and the Business Cycle*. Oxford: Basil Blackwell.

Bain, G. and Price, R. 1980. *Profiles of Union Growth*. Oxford: Basil Blackwell.

Bank, R. 2002. 'Practitioner Commentary', in Clark, P., Delaney, J. and Frost, A. (eds.), *Collective Bargaining in the Private Sector*. Urbana-Champaign, Ill: Industrial Relations Research Association.

Beck, U. 1992. *Risk Society: Towards a New Modernity*. London: Sage.

Becker, B. and Olson, C. 1992. 'Unions and Firm Profits', *Industrial Relations*, 31, 3: 395–416.

Bentham, K. 1999. 'The Determinants and Impacts of Employer Resistance to Union Certification in Canada'. PhD diss., University of Toronto, Toronto.

Bergeron, J. 1993. 'Unionization in the Private Service Sector'. Ph.D. diss. University of Toronto, Toronto.

Block, R., Beck, J. and Krueger, D. 1996. *Labor Law, Industrial Relations, and Employee Choice*. Kalamazoo, Mich.: W. E. Upjohn Institute.

Bratsberg, B. and Ragan, J. F. Jr. 2002. 'Changes in Union Wage Premium by Industry', *Industrial and Labor Relations Review*, 56, 1: 65–83.

Brody, D. 2001. 'Labour Rights as Human Rights: A Reality Check', *British Journal of Industrial Relations*, 39, 4: 596–600.

Bronfenbrenner, K. 1997 'The Role of Union Strategies in NLRB Certification Elections', *Industrial and Labor Relations Review*, 50, 2: 195–212.

Bruce, P. 1993. 'State Strategies and the Processing of Unfair Labor Practice Cases in the US and Canada', in Jenson, J. and Mahon, R. (eds.), *In the Challenge of Restructuring: North American Labor Movements Respond*. Philadelphia: Temple University Press.

—— 1994. 'On the Status of Workers Rights to Organize in the United States and Canada', in Bronfenbrenner, K., Friedman, S., Hurd, R. W., Oswald, R. and Seeber, R. (eds.), *Restoring the Promise of American Labor Law*. Ithaca: Cornell University Press.

Clark, P., Delaney, J. and Frost, A. 2002. 'Private Sector Collective Bargaining: Is This the End or a New Beginning?', in Clark, P., Delaney, J. and Frost, A. (eds.), *Collective Bargaining in the Private Sector*. Urbana-Champaign, Ill.: Industrial Relations Research Association.

Commission on the Future of Worker–Management Relations. 1994. 'Report and Recommendations'. Washington: US Department of Labor and Department of Commerce.

Cooke, W. 1983. 'Determinants of the Outcomes of Union Certification Elections', *Industrial and Labor Relations Review*, 36, 3: 402–414.

—— 1985. 'The Failure to Negotiate First Contracts: Determinants and Policy Implications', *Industrial and Labor Relations Review*, 38, 2: 163–178.

Dunlop, J. T. 1949. 'The Development of Labor Organization: a Theoretical Framework', in Lester, R. and Shister, J. (eds.), *Insights into Labor Issues*. New York: Macmillan.

Ellwood, D., Blank, R., Blasi, J., Kruse, D., Niskanen, W. and Lynn-Dyson, K. 2000. *A Working Nation*. New York: Russell Sage Foundation.

Erikson, C. L., Fisk, C., Milkman, R., Mitchell, D. and Wong, K. 2002. 'Justice for Janitors in California: Lessons from Three Rounds of Negotiations', *British Journal of Industrial Relations*, 40, 3: 543–568.

Ewing, K. 2002. 'Human Rights and Industrial Relations: Possibilities and Pitfalls', *British Journal of Industrial Relations*, 40, 1: 138–149.

Farber, H. and Western, B. 2001. 'Accounting for the Decline of Unions in the Private Sector 1973–1998', *Journal of Labor Research*, 22, 3: 459–486.

Fligstein, N. 2001. *The Architecture of Markets*. Princeton, NJ: Princeton University Press.

Freeman, R. 1998. 'Spurts in Union Growth: Defining Moments and Social Processes', in Bordo, M., Goldin, C. and White, E. (eds.), *The Defining Moment: The Great Depression and the American Economy in the Twentieth Century*. Chicago: University of Chicago Press.

Freeman, R. and Kleiner, M. 1999. 'Do Unions Make Enterprises Insolvent?', *Industrial and Labor Relations Review*, 52, 4: 510–527.

Freeman, R. and Rogers, J. 1999. *What Workers Want*. Ithaca: Cornell University Press.

Friedman, S. and Wood, S. 2001. 'Employers' Unfair Advantage in the United States of America', *British Journal of Industrial Relations*, 39, 4: 586–590.

Garrett, G. 1998. 'Global Markets and National Politics: Collision Course or Virtuous Circle?', *International Organization*, 52, 4: 787–825.

Godard, J. 1997. 'Whither Strategic Choice: Do Managerial IR Ideologies Matter?', *Industrial Relations*, 36, 2: 206–229.

—— 2000. *Industrial Relations, the Economy, and Society*, 2nd edn. Toronto: Captus Press.

—— 2002. 'Institutional Environments, Employer Practices, and the State in Liberal Market Economies', *Industrial Relations*, 41, 2: 249–286.

—— 2003a. 'Do Labor Laws Matter? The Density Decline and Convergence Thesis Revisited', *Industrial Relations*, 41, 3: 458–492.

—— 2003b. 'U.S. and Canadian Statutory Regimes for Regulating Unfair Labour Practices as They Pertain to Union Organizing'. Report to the Department of Trade and Industry, Government of Great Britain, forthcoming.

—— 2003c. 'Labour Unions, Workplace Rights, and Canadian Public Policy', *Canadian Public Policy*, 29, 4: 1–19.

Gomez, R. Lipset, S. and Meltz, N. 2001. 'Frustrated Demand for Unionization: The Case of the United States and Canada Revisited', *Proceedings of the 53rd Annual Meeting*. Champaign, Ill.: Industrial

Relations Research Association.

Gould, W. B., IV. 1993. *Agenda for Reform: the Future of Employment Relations and the Law*. Cambridge, Mass.: MIT Press.

Gunderson, M. and Hyatt, D. 2001. 'Union Impact on Compensation, Productivity, and Management of the Organization', in Gunderson, M, Ponak, A. and Taras, D. (eds.), *Union–Management Relations in Canada*, 4th edn. Toronto: Addison Wesley Longman.

Hall, P. and Soskice, D. 2001. 'An Introduction to Varieties of Capitalism', in Hall, P. and Soskice, D. (eds.), *Varieties of Capitalism: the Institutional Foundations of Comparative Advantage*. Oxford: Oxford University Press.

Human Rights Watch. 2000. *Unfair Advantage: Workers Freedom of Association in the United States and International Human Rights Standards*. Washington, D.C.: Human Rights Watch.

Hutton, W. 2002. *The World We're In*. London: Little Brown

Jacoby, S. 1991. 'American Exceptionalism Revisited: the Importance of Management', in Jacoby, S. (ed.), *Masters to Managers*. New York: Columbia University Press.

—— 1997. *Modern Manors: Welfare Capitalism Since the New Deal*. Princeton, NJ: Princeton University Press.

—— 'Melting into Air? Downsizing, Job Stability and the Future of Work,' *Chicago-Kent Law Review*, 76: 1195–1234.

Johnson, S. 2002. 'Card Check or Mandatory Representation Votes? How the Choice of Union Recognition Procedure Affects Union Certification Success', *Economic Journal*.

Kelly, J. 1998. *Rethinking Industrial Relations: Mobilization, Collectivism, and Long Waves*. London: Routledge and the London School of Economics.

Labour Canada. 1970. *Union Growth in Canada 1921–1967*. Ottawa: Information Canada.

Lipset, S. 1989. *Continental Divide: The Values and Institutions of the United States and Canada*. Toronto and Washington, D.C.: C.D. Howe Institute and National Planning Association.

Lipset, S. and Meltz, N. 1998. 'Canadian and American Attitudes Toward Work and Institutions', *Perspectives on Work*, 1, 3:14–19.

Logan, J. 2001. 'Is Statutory Recognition Bad News for British Unions? Evidence from the History of North American Industrial Relations', *Historical Studies in Industrial Relations*, Sept.: 63–108.

Lund, J. and Maranto, C. 1996. 'Public Sector Law: An Update', in Belman, D., Gunderson, M. and Hyatt, D. (eds.), *Public Sector Employment in a Time of Transition*. Madison: Industrial Relations Research Association.

Mainville, D. and Olineck, C. 1999. 'Unionization in Canada: A Retrospective', *Perspectives on Work and Employment*, 11, 2: supplement (cat. no. 75–001–SPE).

Martinello, F. 2000. 'Mr. Harris, Mr. Rae and Union Activity in Ontario', *Canadian Public Policy*, 26–1: 17–33.

Meltz, N. and Verma. A. 1995. 'Developments in Industrial Relations and Human Resource Management in Canada: An Update from the 1980s', in Locke, R., Kochan, T. and Piore, M. (eds.), *Employment Relations in a*

Changing World Economy. Cambridge, Mass.: the MIT Press.

Robinson, I. 1992. 'Organizing Labour: The Moral Economy of Canadian–American Union Density Divergence 1963–1986', *Queen's Papers in Industrial Relations 1992*. Kingston, Ont.: Queen's University.

—— 1994. 'NAFTA, Social Unionism, and Labour Movement Power in Canada and the United States', *Relations Industrielles/Industrial Relations*, 49, 4: 657–693.

Rose, J. and Chaison. G. 1996. 'Linking Union Density and Union Effectiveness: The North American Experience', *Industrial Relations*, 35: 78–105.

—— 2001. 'Unionism in Canada and the US in the 21st Century: The Prospects for Revival', *Relations Industrielles/Industrial Relations*, 56, 1: 34–65.

Slinn, S. 2003. 'Union Certification Procedures'. Paper presented at the annual meetings of the Canadian Industrial Relations Association, Halifax, 30 June–2 July.

Statistics Canada. 2002. 'Statistics Canada Daily for Sept. 26 2002'. Ottawa: Statistics Canada.

—— 2003. 'Unionization', *Perspectives on Work and Income*, 15, 3: 48–55.

Strauss, George. 1995. 'Is the New Deal System Collapsing? With What Might It Be Replaced?', *Industrial Relations*, 34, 3: 329–349.

Taras, D. 1997. 'Collective Bargaining Regulation in Canada and the United States: Divergent Cultures, Divergent Outcomes', in Kaufman, B. (ed.), *Government Regulation of the Employment Relationship*. Madison, Wis.: IRRA.

Taras, D. and Ponak, A. 2001. 'Manadatory Agency Shop Laws as an Explanation of Canada–U.S. Union Density Differences', *Journal of Labor Research*, 22, 3: 541–568.

Thomason, T. 1994. 'The Effect of Accelerated Certification Procedures on Union Organizing Success in Ontario', *Industrial and Labor Relations Review*, 47, 2: 207–226.

Thompson, M. 1995. 'The Management of Industrial Relations', Anderson, J., Gunderson, M. and Ponak, A. (eds.), *Union–Management Relations in Canada*. Don Mills: Addison Wesley.

Troy, L. 1990. 'Is the US Unique in the Decline of Private Sector Unionism?', *Journal of Labor Research*, 11, 2: 111–144.

—— 1992. 'Convergence in International Unionism, etc.: The Case of Canada and the USA.', *British Journal of Industrial Relations*, 30, 1: 1–43.

—— 1999. *Beyond Unions and Collective Bargaining*. Armonk, N.Y.: M.E. Sharpe.

—— 2000. 'US and Canadian Industrial Relations: Convergent or Divergent?', *Industrial Relations*, 39, 4: 695–713.

—— 2001. 'Twilight for Organized Labor', *Journal of Labor Research*, 12, 2: 245–260.

Troy, L. and Neil Sheflin, N. 1985. *Union Sourcebook: Membership, Structure, Finance, Directory*. West Orange, NJ:IRDIS.

Weiler, P. 1983. 'Promises to Keep: Securing Workers' Rights to Self-Organization Under the NLRA', *Harvard Law Review*, 96:1769–1827.

Western, B. 1997. *Between Class and Market*. Princeton: Princeton University Press.

Wood, S. and Godard, J. 1999. 'The Statutory Recognition Procedure in the Employee Relations Bill: A Comparative Perspective', *British Journal of Industrial Relations*, 37, 2: 203–245.

Workplace Gazette. 2002. 'Union Membership in Canada – 2001', *Workplace Gazette*, 4, 3: 35–42.

Yates, C. 2000. 'Staying the Decline in Union Membership: Union Organizing in Ontario 1985–1999', *Relations Industrielles/Industrial Relations*, 55, 4: 640–674.

9

The rise and fall of the organizing model in the US

RICHARD W. HURD

> With union representation at an all-time low
> and public support for unions the highest it's
> been in years, there's never been a better time
> for changing to organize. (*AFL-CIO, 1996: 8*)

Organizing has been at the centre of union strategy discussions
in the US since the late 1970s, and since 1995 new member
recruitment has been the top priority of the American
Federation of Labor–Congress of Industrial Organizations (AFL-
CIO) and of many individual national unions. Prompted
originally by a steep drop in membership during the Ronald
Reagan era, attention to organizing increased over time as it
became clear that modest adjustments in practice were not
halting decline. During the late 1980s an important step was
taken with the founding of the Organizing Institute (OI), ostensibly a training school for organizers but symbolizing dreams for
union revitalization.

   In the 1990s impatience with continued stagnation grew
among national union leaders, and John Sweeney was elected as
President of the AFL-CIO on a platform that emphasized organizing. Sweeney had constructed labour's most successful
recruitment programme as the President of the Service
Employees International Union (SEIU), and the hope was that
he would be able to apply his magic touch to the labour movement as a whole. The enthusiasm and sense of movement
inspired by Sweeney's election in 1995 served to magnify interest from abroad in the now clearly established organizing
priority, especially among labour leaders and sympathetic
academics in Great Britain, Australia, New Zealand and
Germany where union fortunes were also in decline. The OI

served as a prototype for Australia's Organizing Works and Britain's Organizing Academy.

Much of the strategic debate in the US has revolved around the *organizing model*, which is associated with more activist, grassroots methods of organizing and member mobilization. In spite of widespread endorsement of this model, the reality is that rhetoric has far outpaced action and mobilization is still a relatively isolated phenomenon. Furthermore, with only occasional pauses union density has continued its downward trend, especially in the private sector. This chapter reviews the evolution of recent union strategy in the US, with particular attention to organizational change initiated to promote the organizing priority. It also assesses the failure of organizing to halt contraction in spite of isolated successes, and evaluates future prospects.

Historical background

Increased attention to organizing began in the 1970s in the context of political defeat and economic dislocation. In 1978 a concerted labor law reform effort designed to facilitate recruitment failed in spite of Democratic Party control of both houses of Congress and support from President Jimmy Carter. The proposal was modest, increasing penalties for employer violations of the law and providing union staff with limited access to the workplace during recruitment campaigns. Nonetheless, passage would have facilitated growth without the need for organizational change; union organizers could have maintained their insurance agent posture and increased their sales activity, assured of adding new member-customers fully within the context of the (as yet unnamed) *servicing model*. Two years later President Carter's bid for re-election failed and the anti-union reign of Ronald Reagan began.

The labour movement lost more than one-fifth of its private sector members during the first half of the 1980s. Although the president's appointees to the National Labor Relations Board issued a steady stream of adverse legal decisions, economic change proved far more devastating. Twin recessions in 1981 and 1983 were bad enough alone, but unions also faced the combined forces of globalization, deregulation (which started in the Carter years) and technological change. Manufacturing was hit particularly hard and leading unions like the United Steelworkers of America (USWA) and the United Automobile Workers (UAW) experienced sharp membership losses and dwindling resources. Concessionary bargaining began in manufacturing but quickly spread to other sectors. Unionized companies throughout the private economy began to turn to non-union contractors to perform work formerly assigned to their own employees.

It was in the context of this crisis that national union leaders confronted the deficiencies in prevailing union practice. The AFL-CIO Executive Council initiated strategic planning under the auspices of the newly created Evolution of Work Committee in 1983, with the presidents of the UAW, the USWA and most other top unions participating in the process. Initial consideration of dramatic restructuring of the labor movement through mega-mergers to consolidate around 'cones of influence' with clearly defined jurisdictions proved too threatening to some unions and the idea was abandoned.[1] Instead, a blueprint for change was adopted in 1985 that included reorientation of the AFL-CIO as well as suggested courses of action for affiliated unions.

The strategic plan was summarized in *The Changing Situation of Workers and Their Unions* (AFL-CIO 1985). Five sets of modest recommendations were included:

- new methods of advancing interests of workers (including associate membership programmes and union sponsored credit cards);
- increasing members' participation in their union;
- improving the labor movement's communications;
- improving organizing activity;
- structural changes to enhance the labor movement's overall effectiveness (including merger guidelines, a shadow of the cones of influence proposal).

The AFL-CIO's first major effort to promote organizing under the new plan was a co-ordinated campaign by nine different unions to recruit members at Blue Cross–Blue Shield, the largest provider of health insurance in the country. The experiment got off to an inauspicious start with a year's delay while the AFL-CIO first set up bureaucratic oversight of the effort then mediated competing union jurisdictional claims for different sub-units of the targeted company. By the time recruiting actually began, Blue Cross–Blue Shield had implemented a union avoidance programme and the response of workers was predictably cautious. There were a few isolated victories in small units, but the initiative ultimately failed and was abandoned (Northrup 1990).

Although the AFL-CIO's attempt to broker a major organizing campaign was a disappointment, a small number of national unions took to heart the recommendations of *The Changing Situation* and implemented innovations in their own recruitment efforts. A theme issue of *Labor Research Review* (1986), aptly titled 'Organize!', highlighted campaigns by SEIU, the Hotel Employees and Restaurant Employees (HERE), the Communications Workers of America (CWA), the International Brotherhood of Electrical Workers (IBEW), the American Federation of State, County and Municipal Employees (AFSCME), and the Amalgamated Clothing and Textile Workers (ACTWU, now part of UNITE, the Union of Needletrades and Industrial Textile Employees). These six national unions along with a few others subsequently have continued to lead the effort to establish an organizing priority. Given the decentralized structure of the US labour movement, it is no accident that the AFL-CIO backed away from direct involvement in organizing after the Blue Cross–Blue Shield debacle and assumed a more supportive role. Supportive does not mean irrelevant, however, and the *organizing model* concept itself originated in two distinct initiatives sponsored by the federation.

Emergence of the organizing model

The original specification of the *organizing model* can be traced to a massive teleconference on 'internal organizing' sponsored on 29 February and 1 March 1988, by the AFL-CIO and broadcast by satellite to multiple locations across the country with hundreds of elected leaders and union staff participating. In the US internal organizing is used to refer to activity within unionized workplaces, and though some recruiting of non-members may result, the focus is on mobilizing current members for union action. The labor educators and organizers planning the conference decided to contrast the typical union workplace with an activist one using the terms *servicing model* and *organizing model*. As defined in *Numbers That Count* (Diamond 1988), a training manual developed based on the teleconference, the *servicing model* is 'trying to help people by solving problems for them', while the *organizing model* is 'involving members in solutions'. The idea is that unions can be more effective at representing workers if they use the same mobilizing techniques with current members that are most effective when recruiting new members.

Throughout the late 1980s the *organizing model* was used almost exclusively to apply to internal organizing. The concept was refined based on practice as summarized in union oriented publications like the *Labor Research Review*. In an issue devoted to 'Participating in Management,' most of the discussion stressed strengthening the union by pushing joint labor management decisions down to the rank-and-file level. Internal organizing was emphasized (Banks and Metzgar 1989:49):

> The key component of the organizing model is its emphasis on mobilization of the rank and file to do the work of the union . . . [which] gives members a sense of power as a group. When the members share in the decisions and all the activities of the union, they will also be sharing in the victories.

The concept was further refined, again based on practice, in another issue devoted exclusively to the topic, 'An Organizing Model of Unionism' (*Labor Research Review* 1991). Two of the articles reflect the theme: 'Organizing Never Stops' (Muehlenkamp 1991), and 'Contract Servicing from an Organizing Model' (Conrow 1991). Throughout this period, the discussion, writing and training on the *organizing model* concentrated on mobilization within existing units. There were reminders, though, of the close connection to recruitment, or 'external organizing' as it is often called in the US. Morton Bahr, President of CWA, in a response to the discussion of participation in management, noted for example, 'the mobilization model of participation is also the basis of CWA external organizing' (Bahr 1989: 64).

The AFL-CIO's most influential recruitment initiative during this period was the formation in 1989 of the Organizing Institute (OI) to train union organizers. Headed by former ACTWU star organizer Richard Bensinger, the OI was established by the AFL-CIO as an independent entity insulated from the bureaucratic culture of the tradition bound federation. It promoted an activist grassroots approach, and became something of an oasis for militant organizers from the dozen AFL-CIO affiliated unions with active recruitment programmes. The OI developed a systematic process to train and place organizers that it still follows today. Potential organizers are identified in local unions, on college campuses, and at social action organizations and invited to apply to the OI. Those who are accepted go through a three day training programme on organizing methods, then are placed in three-week internships with large-scale organizing campaigns. If they perform well as interns they are offered six to twelve week apprenticeships sponsored by participating unions, then often move into staff jobs as organizers (Foerster 2001: 161–162).

By the mid-1990s the OI had trained and placed hundreds of organizers, and the style of member recruitment it promoted was accepted as the prevailing 'model' of organizing. Perhaps because of the parallels to the mobilization approach to internal organizing outlined in *Numbers That Count*, it became commonplace for those in union circles to refer to the OI approach as the *organizing model*. Although the OI did not advocate this terminology, by 1995 the *organizing model* concept was indiscriminately used to refer to both internal organizing to mobilize members, and external organizing that promotes grassroots activism as a way to build support for union representation.

It is this merged conceptualization of the *organizing model* that has been exported from the US to other labour movements (see for example: Carter and Cooper 2002; Gall 2003; Heery 2001). The concept has been refined to incorporate academic research that lends credence to the effectiveness of recruitment strategies based on grassroots activism (e.g., Bronfenbrenner *et. al.*, 1998). As summarized by Heery *et al.* (2000: 996):

> The 'organizing model . . . tends to be used in two overlapping senses. First, it can refer to a model of good practice which contributes to membership growth . . . Elements of this good practice include: reliance on targeted and planned organizing campaigns; . . . identification of issues around which workers can be mobilized and the use of mobilizing tactics in the workplace . . .; the use of rank-and-file organizing committees to plan and conduct campaigns . . . Second, it represents an attempt to rediscover the 'social movement' origins of labour, essentially by redefining the union as a mobilizing structure which seeks to stimulate activism among its members.

Changing to organize, organizing for change

In spite of laudable efforts to promote mobilization and organizing, the US labour movement continued to decline through the late 1980s and early 1990s. The pace of decline slowed as the economy recovered and the strategic response of labor took root, but there were no indications that widespread revitalization was close at hand. When the Republican right seized control of Congress in the November 1994 elections, a group of progressive national union leaders was spurred to action. It was their conviction that the AFL-CIO needed to adopt a more aggressive posture, and they turned to John Sweeney of SEIU as their standard bearer. Sweeney announced his candidacy for president of the AFL-CIO in the spring of 1995; his 'New Voice' slate also included Richard Trumka of the United Mine Workers and Linda Chavez-Thompson of AFSCME. Most of the national unions with active organizing programmes supported Sweeney. The New Voice campaign was based on a series of proposals for change founded on the premise that 'the most critical challenge facing unions today is organizing', and they included a call to 'organize at a pace and scale that is unprecedented' (Sweeney *et al.* 1995: 2,3). With organizing at the top of the agenda, the subsequent victory of Sweeney's slate was widely interpreted as an endorsement of this priority.

Once in office, the Sweeney team adopted a mission statement that specified four goals (AFL-CIO 1997: 1):
- building a broad movement of America's workers through organizing;
- making government work for working families;
- providing a new voice for workers in a changing global economy;
- providing a new voice for workers in our communities.

The emphasis on recruitment was obvious as the new officers criss-crossed the country promoting the organizing priority. An organizing department was created (formerly recruitment was assigned to the Department of Field Services), and Richard Bensinger was appointed director. The OI was moved into the organizing department, its budget was increased sharply, and a new fund was established to subsidize strategic organizing campaigns.

In addition to overseeing the expansion of the OI and developing a process to select organizing campaigns worthy of subsidy, Bensinger was charged with redefining the federation's role in organizing. This was a daunting task because there was no tradition of leadership from the centre in this arena. Apart from the Blue Cross–blue Shield experiment, the AFL-CIO had restricted itself to supporting the recruitment efforts of affiliated unions, typically only in response to requests for assistance. The OI training program was far and away the most extensive undertaking in this field to date under the sponsorship of the federation.

With the endorsement of Sweeney and the other officers, Bensinger's organizing department set out to convince union leaders at the national and local level to embrace the organizing priority and to initiate institutional change to sustain increased organizing efforts. Bensinger worked closely with a group of union officials who had embraced the OI as participants in its elected leader task force. Bensinger kept the original OI group intact and added a few new members to form the AFL-CIO Elected Leader Task Force on Organizing, chaired by Bruce Raynor who at the time was Executive Vice President of UNITE (he has since been elected national President).

The Elected Leader Task Force held a series of retreats for union officials who expressed an interest in organizing, then late in 1996 released a blueprint titled, 'Organizing for Change, Changing to Organize'. The report called upon union leaders to take risks and make the dramatic changes necessary to succeed at organizing. It identified four keys to winning (Raynor 1996: 13):

• devote more resources to organizing;
• develop a strong organizing staff;
• devise and implement a strategic plan;
• mobilize your membership around organizing.

This simple agenda but complex task dominated the work of the organizing department.

The AFL-CIO officers were fully engaged, and shifting resources to support recruitment efforts quickly became the focal point of both their speeches and the Organizing Department's campaign. In consultation with Bensinger, Sweeney decided to operationalize the call to shift resources by asking all unions to move toward a goal of devoting 30 per cent of their budgets to recruitment. To promote acceptance of the challenges associated with 'Changing to Organize' the organizing department set as an objective for 1998 to: 'lead an expanded

Changing to Organize program and provide technical assistance to unions on crafting strategic plans to support a greatly increased organizing focus', and to 'help unions move the Changing to Organize message deeper and broader among local union leaders' (AFL-CIO 1998:7).

Although the expanded OI training programme continued to promote an activist approach tied to mobilization, it was in the late 1990s that strategic debates about recruitment moved away from the *organizing model* and began to concentrate on institutional structure and budgetary decisions. In order to understand the shift it is important to look at the barriers to organizational change that had stalled progress.

Impediments to the organizing model and organizational change

Back in the late 1980s and early 1990s the *organizing model* as originally conceived had attracted great attention throughout the US labour movement. *Numbers that Count* was the most requested publication of the AFL-CIO. Many unions developed internal organizing initiatives. The CWA and SEIU, for example, had extensive union-wide efforts, with the SEIU programme stressing the connection between member mobilization and external organizing. However, implementation of the *organizing model* proved to be difficult except during the period immediately preceding the expiration of collective bargaining agreements (a time when member interest in local union affairs typically is at a peak no matter what model of unionism is practised). It seems that at least in the US members do not have a taste for continual warfare, preferring stability rather than ongoing class struggle. Furthermore, mobilization does not free time for other pursuits; to the contrary, it requires careful planning and intense effort by staff and elected leaders in order to succeed. True, locals with effective internal organizing programs are vibrant, members are engaged, and effectiveness in the workplace improves. But this does not translate into growth because it concentrates attention on practice within existing units rather than outreach to potential new members (Fletcher and Hurd 1998).

This reality led labor leaders who embrace the organizing

priority to refocus their efforts towards mobilization designed to support external organizing. As one unionist explains it (not coincidentally this individual is now the organizing director of a major union and a member of the AFL-CIO Elected Leader Task Force on Organizing): 'The organizing model . . .points us in the most narrow way. The better job you do with fifteen per cent of the market, the more it motivates the boss to wipe you out. We have to direct our energy outside' (Fletcher and Hurd 1998: 45). It is this perspective that lies behind the AFL-CIO led campaign to persuade unions to shift resources away from representation and to concentrate instead on recruitment.

But adoption of the organizing priority is itself fraught with problems. Although mobilizing members in support of organizing is ostensibly an integral part of Changing to Organize, this component of the framework has been overshadowed with attention centred on building support among union leaders for a shift in resources. However, union members continue to demand representation. They are mostly pragmatists and it is difficult for them to accept the argument that devoting substantial resources to organizing will pay off eventually in the form of increased bargaining power and better contracts. Although those in the activist core often comprehend the basis for the emphasis devoted to recruitment, they nonetheless give most of their attention to representational functions.

In this context, union leaders at all levels are cautious. Even if they agree that recruitment is important they will pull back if they sense resistance from union members. This is especially a problem at the local level and in those instances where the leader has no personal expertise in organizing. Union staff also may be recalcitrant; though few will openly challenge leaders that promote organizing, those assigned to representation express pessimism and resent the increased workload that typically accompanies resource reallocation (Fletcher and Hurd 2001).

The push for unions to reallocate resources to recruitment is far removed from the *organizing model* ideal of engaging workers in the life of the union. It appears that in many corners of the US labor movement the objective of achieving grassroots activism and member mobilization as the key to injecting social movement zeal has been abandoned at the alter of quantitative recruitment goals. The ultimate limitation in the AFL-CIO's Changing to Organize is that it does not require organizational change beyond resource reallocation, but rather implies that union revitalization is simply a matter of adding members and spreading the labor movement as it exists. On the one hand this approach is pragmatic given the difficulty encountered in sustaining the *organizing model* and the need for resources to construct an extensive recruitment effort. On the other hand it seems likely that without more substantive organizational change even the narrow goal of sustained membership growth will be difficult to achieve.

Is organizing enough?

In the summer of 1998 Richard Bensinger was asked by John Sweeney to step down as organizing director. His commitment to the organizing priority was unquestioned, but his frank criticism of national union leaders who did not demonstrate sufficient enthusiasm for the Changing to Organize agenda won few friends, and pressure mounted from members of the AFL-CIO Executive Council to have him replaced (Meyerson 1998). In reality though the problem was not only with Bensinger, who had done a great deal to further the Sweeney goal of establishing organizing as the most important challenge facing unions. What Sweeney and his advisors had envisioned was re-positioning the federation so that it could assume a leadership role in organizing and other aspects of union strategy. But this dream of a stronger centre building consensus around a common set of objectives was resisted on all sides by national union leaders with their own priorities.

After Bensinger's departure the AFL-CIO struggled to capture some semblance of authority in the organizing arena. In 2000 Sweeney was able to persuade the Executive Council to endorse a specific goal of organizing one million workers a year, and the federation's organizing programme embraced a three-point process to achieve the objective (AFL-CIO 2001: 8):
- Encourage national affiliates to set and achieve higher numeric organizing goals.
- Assess how the federation's resources can best be used to help achieve these increased goals.
- Track and share information about organizing campaigns.

The one million goal was never taken seriously by affiliates, and the organizing department eventually retreated to a more modest role comparable to the AFL-CIO's stance prior to Sweeney's election. The current practice is to provide assistance to national union organizing campaigns where possible, to continue to offer guidance to unions that agree to invest more resources into organizing, and to design a long-term campaign to amend labor law to establish an enforceable right to organize unions (AFL-CIO 2002). Labor law reform is the most public part of the current effort and is referred to as the Voice @ Work campaign.

The reality is that individual national unions determine their own resource allocations and develop their own organizing programmes. In response to Sweeney's prodding the leaders of the national unions have indeed accorded more importance to the recruitment priority, and virtually all lend at least rhetorical support. Most unions have increased the funding of their organizing departments, and many have devoted substantial resources to the effort. However, the individual unions jealously guard their authority over organizing strategy, staffing, target selection and all decisions related to co-ordination with other unions. The federation's role as arbiter of disputes where there is competition between unions in specific recruitment campaigns is accepted, but efforts by the AFL-CIO to broker broader agreements regarding organizing jurisdiction have been rejected.

National unions have followed the AFL-CIO's lead in establishing specific targets for budget reallocation and recruitment, though few have embraced the 30 per cent guideline for budgets or the recruitment objectives implied by the one million new members a year benchmark. The individual unions' adoption of the practice of setting quantitative goals has forced them to act pragmatically, looking for organizing opportunities with the best chance of success. Although this often has meant seeking out workers who fit the culture and traditional industrial and/or occupational base of the union, many have seized the moment and taken steps to extend their jurisdictional boundaries. It is not unusual for them to conduct recruitment campaigns among workers in totally unrelated industries simply because there is a good chance of success. For example the UAW now has a very active program to recruit teaching assistants, research assistants and adjunct faculty on college campuses, and the USWA is organizing healthcare workers. In fact, there are at least a dozen unions organizing in healthcare, some with a long history in the industry but others like USWA with only indirect connections or no rationale other than capitalizing on the opportunity to add members.

A number of unions have implemented extensive and strategically focused programmes, most notably the SEIU and the United Brotherhood of Carpenters (UBC) both of whom now allocate 50 per cent of their national budgets to organizing. UNITE and HERE have comparable levels of commitment to the priority, and all four of these unions have accomplished the transition to organizing by strengthening the role of the national union and mandating change at the local level. Other unions (for example, CWA and IBEW) have adopted a different approach with some success, with the national union supporting and facilitating change at the local level but with less centralized control of the mechanics of the organizing itself (Hurd 2001). Variation in the locus of control is only one of many differences in approach to organizing. With national unions operating independently and making pragmatic decisions about recruitment, it is not surprising that there is a wide range of opinions. As activity has increased these differences have spawned open debate about all aspects of organizing. The earlier apparent consensus regarding the *organizing model* and the grassroots approach to recruitment has long since dissolved. In the context of quantitative goals, the ideal of organizing as a method of engaging members and building commitment has given way to debates about how to be cost effective and manage recruitment programmes efficiently.

The lack of consensus about organizing strategy has come to the surface because union density has continued to decline in the US. This is in spite of a long term under the leadership of John Sweeney and in spite of broad endorsement for the organizing priority. Tables 9.1 and 9.2 summarize the grim reality. Table 1 compares three contiguous seven year periods – the first seven years of Sweeney's presidency (1995–2002), the last seven years under his predecessor Lane Kirkland (1988–95), and the Reagan years (1981–98). Clearly union density declined most rapidly during the Reagan years, but the results for the Kirkland years after the release of *The Changing Situation* and the Sweeney years are almost identical.

Table 9.2 looks at comparative trends for the ten industry groups with the most union members (accounting for approximately 90 per cent of total membership). The story is the same;

Table 9.1 Relative change in union density, by sector

	1981–88	1988–95	1995–2002
Total	–21.5	–11.3	–10.7
Private	–32.1	–18.9	–16.5
Public	+6.7	+3.0	+0.3

Sources: Hirsch, B. T. and Macpherson, D. 2003. *Union Membership and Earnings Data Book*, 2003 edition, pp. 11, 12, 16.

although the pace of decline has slowed a bit for some industry groups (and even turned around for the hospital industry), contraction has accelerated for others. Even in those industries and occupations where recruitment efforts have been most obvious and where there have been notable major victories, the results are extraordinarily disappointing. Clearly the heightened level of organizing activity has not been sufficient to overcome either the difficult environment for unions in the US, or the institutional inertia inherent in the labor movement.

Table 9.2 Relative change in union density, by industry group

	1988–95	1995–2002
Construction	–13.7	–0.5
Durable goods manufacturing	–20.3	–17.5
Non-durable goods manufacturing	–20.1	–20.8
Transportation	–11.9	–10.8
Communication	–23.6	–23.7
Utilities	–6.4	–9.3
Retail trade	–9.1	–25.0
Hospitals	–5.4	+1.4
Education	+1.4	–1.4
Public administration	+6.0	+1.6

Sources: Hirsch, B. T. and Macpherson, D. 1996, 1999, 2003. *Union Membership and Earnings Data Book*, 2003 edition, pp. 48–55.

The future of organizing[2]

Strategic discussions in US labour circles about what needs to be done at this juncture to reverse the slide in density start from the premise that recruitment is the key. The debate revolves around not what else may need attention to promote revitalization, but instead on how to increase the effectiveness of organizing campaigns. One prominent view advises patience, arguing that progress is modest because members and local leaders are still wed to the *servicing model*. With time and experimentation, the organizing priority will spread more widely and deeply and density will begin to rebound.

The strongest proponents of the Changing to Organize framework concur that the *servicing model* still prevails, but go on to argue that this is unacceptable. They stress the urgency of the situation and criticize national union officers' lack of deep commitment to recruitment as reflected in an insufficient shift of resources. A related issue is also raised with a call for more attention to training and retaining organizing staff, and especially to redressing the serious shortage of experienced organizers capable of leading campaigns.

Another viewpoint is that in spite of increased activity, not enough unions are using the appropriate organizing tactics. According to this argument unions are not developing momentum because they are using ill advised, partial or outmoded recruitment methods rather than following the comprehensive union building strategy associated with the *organizing model*. A variation of this critique is that top down approaches to organizing and centralized control of recruitment are failing, largely because they are undemocratic and eschew rank-and-file empowerment.

Having retrenched from its aspirations to exercise strategic leadership in organizing, the AFL-CIO has not engaged openly in the debate about the most effective strategy. It has continued to promote resource reallocation, and has focused much of its attention on the Voice@Work campaign to amend labor law. John Sweeney has held steadfastly to the position that aggressive organizing is the key to revitalization: 'the first and foremost challenge for the American union movement [is] helping the tens of millions of workers in this nation who want to form a union to have that chance' (AFL-CIO 2003).

Early in 2003 the SEIU fuelled the flames of debate by publishing a position paper calling for dramatic restructuring to consolidate resources and promote expansion. The SEIU framework is presented as an antidote to creeping general unionism. The premise captures the widely shared frustration with the lack of progress: 'despite many victories and reasons for hope within

... the broader labor movement in recent years, the strength of ... unions in the United States continues to decline' (SEIU 2003:2). The SEIU argues that simply increasing the pace and scale of recruitment will not be enough, that simply adopting the correct organizing methods will not be enough, that simply being militant will not be enough. The conclusion is that there is a fundamental weakness in the movement's structure that must be addressed. The SEIU explicitly calls for realignment so that there is a smaller number of large unions that are 'industry focused ... not general' (SEIU 2003:21). Such a realignment will enable unions to demonstrate market power, giving non-union workers more incentive to join. The paper closes with a call for open debate about how to establish the rules and culture necessary to facilitate restructuring.

The direction proposed by the SEIU offers an intriguing alternative to the creeping malaise that hangs over the US labour movement. The explicit recognition that simply doing more will not be sufficient is clearly on target. Although the shift in resources to organizing may have fallen short of expectations, there is little to show for the obviously much higher level of recruitment activity. And with a political-economic environment that is decidedly less friendly to unions than when the shift to an organizing agenda began in earnest, it is hard to see how resources alone will be sufficient to turn the tide.

But does the structural proposal of the SEIU offer any more promise? The Sweeney-led AFL-CIO's modest attempt to strengthen the role of the centre in organizing was halted unceremoniously by a broad consensus of national union leaders, determined to retain their strategic independence. The much more dramatic reorganization proposed by the SEIU seems to be unrealistic, and in fact has won little support in the other national unions. Furthermore, it is not clear that structural change alone would do anything to invigorate unions, and indeed the administrative complexity of implementing such realignment would draw attention away from strategic challenges.

The AFL-CIO's Voice@Work campaign is no more realistic. What are the chances for favourable labour law reform with union density and influence clearly on the wane? Shifting resources, restructuring and labour law reform all share a common flaw; they are top down solutions that do not confront weaknesses inherent in the labour movement as it exists. None address the critical challenge of redefining the movement so that it appeals to the mass of unrepresented workers. None offer an alternative to pragmatic, job oriented business unionism that is so weakened that it struggles to deliver its narrow promise of improved wages and working conditions.

The *organizing model* does suggest hope for an activist revival, but there is little evidence that mobilization has created any momentum for growth. It is widely accepted that recruitment campaigns utilizing tactics consistent with the *organizing model* have the best chance for success. But as the SEIU paper implies, effective recruitment strategy without more substantive institutional change will do no more than stir excitement. External forces will continue to overwhelm individual campaign victories. And though the proponents of union democracy have a valid complaint that top down change does little to motivate the rank and file, there is no evidence that union members are any more willing than leaders to promote radical transformation.

The inherent weakness in both the *organizing model* and the AFL-CIO's Changing to Organize is the implication that mobilization and effective recruitment will be sufficient to stimulate union renewal. Effective organizing devoid of attention to the complexities of organizational change is self-limiting. True transformation requires greatly expanded member education, co-ordinated efforts to address resistance from staff and elected leaders, balanced attention to representation and organizing, and comprehensive strategic planning (Fletcher and Hurd 2001). But it also requires a willingness to redefine the role of unions.

Traditional union approaches have not inspired the new workforce, and no level of organizing activity no matter how well conceived can overcome this deficiency. At least in the US, the future of labor requires adaptation and experimentation with diverse forms of representation that respond to the concerns of the expanding professional and technical workforce, that address the instability experienced by part-time and contingent workers, and that create a culture that engages low wage service workers most of whom are immigrants, people of colour and women.

But radical transformation is unlikely. Paul Booth, organizing director for AFSCME, has composed a thoughtful response to the SEIU restructuring proposal. He points out that the SEIU conceptualization is only one of several approaches stimulated by 'frustration that the change to organize movement hasn't yielded an overall gain in union density' (Booth 2003:1). He argues that no one strategy for growth is likely to generate consensus at this juncture and posits that a variety of strategies may be required to deal with the range of challenges faced by unions in different sectors of the economy. He calls for open dialogue, experimentation and careful assessment of results from implementation of nine separate strategic approaches that he identifies. His point is that experimentation is better than retrenchment, and that organizing is still central to hope for survival (Booth 2003).

Realistically, the US labour movement can do little more than continue to pursue revitalization on as many fronts as possible. But the failure to date of the *organizing model* and the organizing priority should be a lesson to leaders and allies of labour movements in other countries who have been impressed by the promise of narrowly conceived revitalization. Organizing alone is not enough in the US and is unlikely to drive labour movement renewal elsewhere.

Notes

1 Interestingly, this concept has resurfaced in the form of a framework proposed by the SEIU, as discussed in the final section of this chapter.

2 This section is based in part on presentations at a meeting of the Organizing Research Network held at Harvard University on 23 and 24 June 2003. Especially relevant were the formal comments of Steven Lerner of SEIU, Paul Booth of AFSCME, Phil Kugler of the American Federation of Teachers, Kim Moody of *Labor Notes*, and Sheldon Friedman of the AFL-CIO. The conclusions reached reflect the author's long-term collaborative work with Bill Fletcher, Jr., of the TransAfrica Forum.

References

American Federation of Labor–Congress of Industrial Organizations. 1985. *The Changing Situation of Workers and Their Unions*.

—— 1996. 'Bold Moves', America@Work, November–December, 7–9.

—— 1997. *'Program Summary'*, February.

—— 1998. 'Program Summary and Budget Proposal', January.

—— 2001. *America@Work*, January.

—— 2002. 'FY2002–2003 Program Summary', February.

—— 2003. 'Remarks by AFL-CIO President John Sweeney, Organizing Press Conference', press release, 26 February.

Bahr, M. 1989. 'Mobilizing for the '90s', *Labor Research Review*, 14: 59–65.

Banks, A. and Metzgar, J. 1989. 'Participating in Management: Union Organizing on a New Terrain', *Labor Research Review*, 14: 1–55.

Bensinger, J. 1998. 'When We Try More, We Win More: Organizing the New Workforce', in Mort, J. (ed.), *Not Your Father's Labor Movement*.

Booth, Paul. 2003. 'Nine Theories in Search of Evidence', Presented to the Organizing Research Network, Cambridge, Mass. 23 June.

Bronfenbrenner, K., Friedman, S., Hurd, R. W., Oswald, R. A. and Seeber, R. L. 1998. *Organizing to Win*. Ithaca: Cornell University Press.

Bronfenbrenner, K. and Hickey, R. 2004. 'Changing to Organize: A National Assessment of Union Strategie', in Milkman, R. and Voss, K. (eds.), *Organize or Die: Labor's Prospects in Neoliberal America*. Ithaca, N. J.: Cornell University Press.

Carter, B. and Cooper, R. 2002. 'The Organizing Model and the Management of Change: a Comparative Study of Unions in Australia and Britain', *Relations Industrielles*, 57, 4: 712–742.

Conrow, T. 1991. 'Contract Servicing From an Organizing Model', *Labor Research Review*:17, 45–59.

Diamond, V. 1988. *Numbers That Count*. AFL-CIO.

Fletcher, B. and Hurd, R. 1998. 'Beyond the Organizing Model: The Transformation Process in Local Unions', in Bronfenbrenner, K. *et al.*, *Organizing to Win*.

—— 2000. 'Is Organizing Enough? Race, Gender and Union Culture', *New Labor Forum*, 6: 59–69.

—— 2001. 'Overcoming Obstacles to Transformation: Challenges on the Way to a New Unionism', in Turner, L. *et al.* (eds.), *Rekindling the Movement*.

Foerster, A. 2001. 'Confronting the Dilemmas of Organizing: Obstacles and Innovations at the AFL-CIO Organizing Institute', in Turner, *et al.* (eds.), *Rekindling the Movement*.

Frazer, S. 1998. 'Is Democracy Good for Unions', *New Labor Forum*, 3: 74–93.

Gall, G. 2003. *Union Organizing: Campaigning for Trade Union Recognition*. London: Routledge.

Heery, E. 2001. 'Learning from Each Other: A European Perspective on American Labor', *Journal of Labor Research*, 22, 2: 307–319.

Heery, E., Simms, M., Delbridge, R., Salmon, J. and Simpson, D. 2000. 'Union Organizing in Britain: Survey of Policy and Practice', *International Journal of Human Resource Mangement*, 11, 5: 986–1007.

—— 2003. 'Trade Union Recruitment Policy in Britain: Form and Effects', in Gall, G. (ed.), *Union Organizing*.

Hurd, R. 2001. 'Contesting the Dinosaur Image: the U.S. Labour Movement's Search for a Future', *Transfer: The European Review of Labour and Research*, 7, 3: 451–465.

Hurd, R., Milkman, R. and Turner, L. 2003. 'Reviving the American Labor

Movement: Institutions and Mobilization', *European Journal of Industrial Relations*, 9, 1: 99–117.

Labor Research Review. 1986. 'Organize', no. 8.

—— 1989. 'Participating in Management', no. 14.

—— 1991. 'An Organizing Model of Unionism', no. 17.

Meyerson, H. 1998. 'A Second Chance: The New AFL-CIO and the Prospective Revival of American Labor', in Mort, J. (ed.), *Not Your Father's Labor Movement*.

Mort, J. 1998. *Not Your Father's Labor Movement*. New York: Verso/New Left Books.

Muehlenkamp, R. 1991. 'Organizing Never Stops', *Labor Research Review*, 17: 1–6.

Northrup, H. R. 1990. 'The AFL-CIO Blue Cross–Blue Shield Campaign', *Industrial and Labor Relations Review*, 43, 5: 525–541.

Raynor, B. 1996. *Organizing for Change, Changing to Organize*. AFL-CIO.

Service Employees International Union. 2003. 'United We Win: A Discussion of the Crisis Facing Workers and the Labor Movement'. February: www.newcitizen.org/english/p_publication

Sweeney, J., Trumka, R., and Chavez-Thompson, L.C. 1995. 'A New Voice for American Workers', June 28 (Mimeo).

Turner, L., Katz, H. C. and Hurd, R. 2001. *Rekindling the Movement: Labor's Quest for Relevance in the 21st Century*. Ithaca: Cornell University Press.

10

Union growth and reversal in newly industrialized countries: the case of South Korea and peripheral workers

DAVID PEETZ AND NEAL OLLETT

In Western industrialized countries, the rise of trade unions took place during a phase of capitalist expansion which was characterized by employment patterns that were dominated by the standard, full-time employment model comprising long hours worked by employees over the great majority of the calendar week. Unions emerged as bodies representing the interests of those workers and fought, amongst other things, to reduce the standard working week from 48 hours per week to 44 hours, 40 hours (Hagan 1983:42) and, in many countries, even less. In recent years, union membership has been threatened by, amongst other things, the growth of non-standard or peripheral forms of employment, characterized by part-time working hours, temporary or 'casual' forms of engagement, and low union density. The relative growth of peripheral employment has been a significant factor in union decline in a number of Western countries.

Industrialization and the emergence of trade unions in non-Western countries have followed different patterns. On the one hand, capitalist production has sought to make much greater use of peripheral forms of employment, in many cases even denying the existence of an 'employment' relationship. On the other hand, such transient relationships have not always matched local values, and in adapting to national circumstances capitalism has taken many different guises. In East Asian countries such as Japan, South Korea (hereafter 'Korea') and early capitalist China, a 'lifetime' employment model persisted in which many (mostly male) workers held jobs virtually for life if they wished and it was difficult or impossible for employers to dismiss them (Koo 2001: 207). Such models were often more prominent in rhetoric than practice – for example, the core of the Japanese workforce that benefited from 'lifetime employ-ment' was supported by a highly flexible periphery of smaller, contracted firms where employment conditions were inferior and employment was insecure. Nonetheless, for those in the core, lifetime employment brought real benefits in terms of security, pay and benefits.

In China and Korea, the key capitalist challenges to the life-time employment model took root in the 1980s and gained full momentum in the 1990s, albeit in quite different circum-stances. In China, the 'iron rice bowl' was seen by policy makers as inconsistent with the need for labour flexibility as capitalist firms established sole or joint venture operations in the country and former state-owned enterprises were subjected to competi-tion and expected to close down if unprofitable. In Korea, policy makers played a key role – but so too did unions themselves. In this chapter we will examine the relationship between unions, the state and the growth of peripheral employment in Korea, and consider the impact it is having on Korean unions. The ques-tions we will ask are: first, why has peripheral employment reached such substantial proportions in Korea; second, how have unions responded; and third, what can they do from here?

Our research is based on published and unpublished materi-als, and 35 interviews we conducted with union officials from the peak, industry, enterprise and workplace levels as well as employers, employer organizations and government officials, mostly in 2000, updated by further desk-based research since then. We looked at the Korean labour market generally as well as interviewing unions and employers in four industries in particular: banking and insurance; electrical goods and electron-ics manufacturing; automobiles manufacturing; and heavy industry. We interviewed officials from the two peak federa-tions: to use their English names, the Federation of Korean Trade Unions (FKTU) and the Korean Conferedation of Trade Unions (KCTU). At the industry level we interviewed two FKTU affiliated federations, in metals manufacturing (which covers the three manufacturing industries encompassed by our interviews) and finance, and the corresponding KCTU industry federations, as well as two women's unions. These are listed in table 10.1 below. We followed a semi-structured interview protocol, which varied according to the level of the organization and official as well as the time the respondent had available. Because of the importance of identifying the affiliation of particular unions, the plethora of acronyms involved, and the unwieldiness of saying 'a KCTU-affiliated union' after each reference to it, we adopt an unusual convention to make life easier for the reader: we mark all FKTU-affiliated unions and federations with the superscript [f] and all KCTU-affiliated unions and federations with the superscript [c].

Table 10.1 Unions and federations interviewed (to November 2000)

KCTU-affiliated	FKTU-affiliated
KCTU, Korean Confederation of Trade Unions	FKTU, Federation of Korean Trade Unions
Industry federations	
KFCFLU,[c] Korean Federation of Clerical and Financial Labour Unions	KFBFU[f], Korean Federation of Bank and Financial Unions, soon to be the Korean Financial Industry Union (KFIU[f])
KMWF,[c] Korean Metal Workers Federation	FKMWTU,[f] Federation of Korean Metal Workers Trade Unions
Enterprise unions	
Electronics (E4[c]) Auto (A1[c]–A3[c]) Banking (B1[c])–B2 Heavy Industry (H1[c],H2[c])	Electronics (E1[f]-E3[f]). B3–B5
Women's unions	
KWCTU[c], Korean Womens Confederation of Trade Unions	KWTU, Korean Womens Trade Union (unaffiliated)

The structure of our chapter is as follows. We commence by briefly outlining a theoretical framework through which we shall analyse the situation of Korean unions vis-a-vis peripheral workers, a model we refer to as the Murray/Pocock model. We then move to a very short summary of the institutional background to the development of Korean unionism, in particular the role of the state, and locate the growth and decline of Korean unions in recent decades within this context. As in many developing and newly industrializing countries, the state at various times has had a crucial role in suppressing the development of effective unionism and shaping the unions that do emerge. Korean union members continue to face persecution at the hands of their employers and government. An instance of employer initiated persecution is the self-immolation of a construction worker in protest at company tactics in 2003 (Labourstart 26 February 2003). And, despite 'democratization', as recently as 1999 some 17 union leaders were in gaol and a further 86 had arrest warrants current (KCTU, 1999). The role of the state has been so pervasive that it would be easy to write a chapter solely about the impact of state repression on trade unions, as others have already done (Deyo 1989; Koo 2001; Lee 1993; Leggett and Kwon 1998; You 1994). However, our aim is to go beyond this and look at the specific interactions around the issue of peripheral employment. Accordingly, while we recognize the importance of state repression in explaining Korean unionism, we summarize rather than elucidate this impact and subsequently deal with the state's role in the context of the issue of peripheral workers and associated concerns. Next, we describe the situation of peripheral workers in Korea. In subsequent sections we then undertake the analysis of Korean unionism and peripheral workers in the context of the Murray/Pocock model, before making some concluding observations.

Union power resources: a framework

Before proceeding to discuss the specifics of the Korean case, we first outline a theoretical framework within which our analysis is located. Our emphasis is in conceptualizing the Korean unions' experience in terms of their capacity or power resources, and in this regard two recent sets of authors are particularly relevant. Murray (1998) identified six aspects of union power resources that were critical for union success: unions' mobilizing capacity (density, membership support); coordinating capacity (including internal, external and international structure and coordination); material capacity (dues, property, etc.); discursive capacity (articulation of a discourse and the internal and external communication of a discourse); political capacity (lobbying, role of union confederations, links with political parties, coalition with other groups); and strategic capcity (existence of specialist resources, access to strategic analysis and role of strategic analysis within the union). In a subsequent refinement Levesque and Murray (2002) collapse these into three key features of local union power resources: unions' internal solidarity (in particular, the strength of internal union democracy); their discursive capacity, by which they set an agenda both within the union and to the outside world; and their external alliances, being the extent to which they are able to build and make effective use of alliances with other unions and community, political and other organizations, and the degree of articulation with other levels of the union movement. Although their model is situated within the North American context, it has broad applicability.

Pocock (2001) builds upon this conceptualization to define six dimensions to a model explaining the degree of union power: mobilizing and organizing power; structural capacity (these first two dimensions are an 'unbraiding' of Levesque and Murray's 'internal solidarity'); external solidarity; discursive power; culture and competence – ' the union's capacity to recognise its situation ... and its capacity for institutional agency [that is] its capacity to act, to change its course, its culture, to control its resources, structure and remake its institutional character and renew its power in the context of changing circumstances' (Pocock 2001: 16–17); and finally, the external environment within which the union operates. The first four of these are directly derived from the Levesque and Murray (2002) model, while the fifth is built from the work of Hyman (1997), Allen (2000) and writers on organizational and union culture including herself (e.g. Pocock 1998; Schein 1996). Unions that have high capacity in each of these areas, and have a favourable environment, will have high power. These are concepts that can be applied to help us understand the successes and failures of the Korean union movement, particularly in relation to peripheral workers and the decline in union density. But first, a word from the past.

The state and Korean unionism in decline

Trade unions emerged in Korea among waterside workers and miners in the late nineteenth century (Kim Hwang-joe 1993: 134). During the Japanese colonial period unions were an important part of the anti-Japanese movement. In the post-Second World War era left-wing leaders captured the movement but were then crushed by the US military government and replaced with business oriented trade unions formed on a craft or enterprise basis (Choi Jang Jip 1989: 28–29). The Federation of Korean Trade Unions (FKTU) was formed in 1946 and until 1999 was the only legal peak union body. It traditionally has had a close relationship with government and business (Lee 1993: 255). In 1961 Park Chung-hee led a military coup and dissolved all political and social institutions, including trade unions. After consolidating power, Park ordered the union movement be re-established on industry lines with a single national centre, the FKTU (Lee 1993: 255). In 1979, during another period of political and economic unrest, Chun Doo-hwan staged a successful coup (Moon and Kang 1995: 175). In 1980, to reduce organized labour's bargaining power, the new regime again changed the structure of trade unions from industry unions to enterprise unions and established Labour–Management Councils (Kim Hwang-joe 1993: 137). Thus for a long period unions were controlled, labour dissent was violently suppressed and trade union leaders imprisoned (Deyo 1989: 1–2; Park and Leggett, 1998: 291).

As shown in table 10.2, in absolute terms in the ten years from 1961 until 1970 the number of workers in recognized trade unions and the number of trade unions increased relatively slowly compared to the period from 1970 to 1980. This acceleration in the 1970s occurred because of growing employment in the heavy industry sector and a tightening labour market that made unions more attractive. In the 1980s, Chun's efforts to establish LMCs as alternatives to unions may have been partially successful in that the number of trade unions and union density fell, but the trend of increased union power in enterprise level bargaining continued.

While the independent trade union movement and non-organized workers took a major role in the protests that led to the Democracy Declaration, the FKTU supported the Chun regime's decision to suspend discussions on constitutional reform. It was this decision by the regime that led to the intensification of civil disorder in early 1987 (Park 1994: 157–159). In that year democratization began with the fall of Chun Doo-hwan. Workers established unions in enterprises where repression had previously made this impossible and in a few of the larger *chaebol* (large, family owned conglomerates that have dominated the Korean economy since the late 1950s) enterprise

Table 10.2   Legally recognized trade unions, workers, and density, 1963–97

Year	Total trade unions	Industry unions	Trade union units	Number of unionized workers	Density Total	Male	Female
1963	2,150	16	1,820	224,420	20.3	20.8	18.5
1965	2,634	16	2,255	301,522	22.4	23.5	19.1
1970	3,500	17	3,063	473,259	20.0	20.1	19.7
1975	4,091	17	3,585	750,235	23.0	21.4	27.4
1980	2,635	16	2,618	948,134	20.1	18.5	23.5
1985	2,551	16	2,534	1,004,398	15.7	15.9	15.2
1986	2,675	16	2,658	1,035,890	15.1	16.2	14.2
1987							
30 June	2,742	16	2,725	1,050,201	14.7	15.6	12.9
31 Dec	4,103	16	4,086	1,267,457	17.3	18.5	15.0
1988	6,164	21	6,142	1,707,456	22.0	23.9	18.1
1989	7,883	21	7,861	1,932,415	23.3	25.8	18.5
1990	7,698	21	7,676	1,886,884	21.5	24.4	16.3
1991	7,656	21	7,634	1,803,408	19.6	22.7	14.1
1992	7,527	21	7,505	1,734,598	18.3	21.8	12.1
1993	7,147	26	7,120	1,667,373	17.2	20.5	11.3
1994	7,025	26	6,998	1,659,011	16.3	19.9	10.0
1995	6,606	26	6,579	1,614,800	15.2	18.7	9.3
1996	6,424	26	6,397	1,508,558	14.7	18.4	8.4
1997	5,733	40	5,692	1,484,194	13.5	17.5	7.0
1998	5,560	42	5,517	1,401,940	13.8	17.8	6.9
1999	5,673	43	5,592	1,480,666	14.9	18.7	8.4
2000	5,698	44	5,652	1,526,995	14.6	18.6	7.8
2001	6,150	45	6,150	1,568,723	14.5	19.0	7.4

Source: Korean Labor Institute. 2003. *Monthly Labor Bulletin*, February, Seoul.
Note: Estimated number of union organizations excludes the peak union organization(s).

unions were formed in tandem with *chaebol* unions (Kim Hwang-joe, 1993: 145). The fall of the Chun regime and the Democracy Declaration of 1987 created massive change in the number and density of trade unions. In the period from the last six months of 1987 until 1989, the number of enterprise unions increased by over 5,000, the number of organized workers climbed by more than 880,000, and union density surged from 14.7 per cent to 23.3 per cent.

During the post-democratization period there was a plethora of industry trade unions and federations, *chaebol* trade unions, and peak unions established by workers who wanted fairer representation. These new unions included the Union Federation by Trade (UFT) which represented trade unions of teachers, clerical workers, etc. The UFT was an illegal union as it had the Korean Teachers and Educational Workers Union (KTEWU, *Chunkyojo*), an illegal union, as an affiliate. The *Yondeahoei* was established to represent unions in *chaebol* such as Hyundai Heavy Industry, Hyundai Motors and Daewoo heavy industry and Daewoo Motors (Lee 1993: 258). These trade unions and trade unions in the subway transportation and telecommunication industries were strategically located so as to have the potential to cause maximum damage to the economy if they choose to do so. The Council of Representatives of Public Sector Unions (CRPSU, *Kongdodae*) was formed in the early 1990s (Park and Leggett, 1998: 289). None of these federations or representative bodies affiliated with the FKTU and only the CRPSU was officially recognised (Lee 1993: 258; Park and Leggett 1998: 289). As of December 1990 the FKTU represented 21 industrial federations, the largest of which was the Korean Metal Workers Trade Union Federation (KMWTUF), 7,676 enterprise unions and 1,886,884 members (Lee 1993: 258).

In 1990 workers and trade unionists created the Korean Trade Union Congress (KTUC, Cheonnohyeob) as an alternative to the FKTU (Park and Leggett, 1998: 278). In 1990 the KTUC had 600 affiliated trade unions and 190,000 members (Lee 1993: 257), but was not recognized by government as a legal peak union body. Notionally, this also meant that all affiliated trade unions were also illegal, even if they otherwise met all the conditions for legality. In 1995 the KTUC joined with other non-recognized representative trade union organizations to form the KCTU. In 1997 the KCTU had 907 affiliated unions and 400,000 members. In 1996 the KCTU received legal recognition, albeit deferred until 1999 (Park and Leggett 1998: 278–279). The competition between the two peak bodies for members has seen many trade unions formerly affiliated with the FKTU joining the KCTU (Interview, FKMTU official, 12 June 2000).

During the post-democratization period, measured union density fell, from a peak of 23.3 per cent in 1989 to just 13.5 per cent in 1997. Unfortunately, union density estimates are not fully reliable, as they purportedly only account for legal unions. However, the inclusion of the KCTU in 1999 seems to have had a relatively small impact on the figures, with that year seeing a recorded growth of just 79,000 in the number of union members or an increase of 1.1 percentage points in union density. It would appear that many of the major KCTU-affiliated unions, probably including those affiliated via an industry union, may have been counted since around the time they were formed. Still, it suggests that the official statistics, if anything, understate the decline in density between the early 1990s and 1999 or later.

The Korean financial crisis began in mid-1997 and represented a major reversal to the sustained economic growth experienced over the preceding three decades. Growth in GDP fell from 7.1 per cent in 1996 and 5 per cent in 1997 to –6.7 per cent in 1998 (Ministry of Labour, 2000), before recovering to 10.7 per cent growth in 1999 (Ministry of Finance and Economy, 2000). Measured unemployment increased from 2.6 per cent in 1997, to 6.8 per cent in 1998 and a peak of 8.6 per cent in February 1999 (Ministry of Labour 2000; Park and Siengthai, 2000: 40), employment became insecure, and the structure of employment changed (Park, Duck Jay 2000: 7–9). Between 1997 and 1999, density rose slightly though membership remained stagnant (falling in 1998, recovering by slightly less in 1999). Thus the seeming improvement in density was due to falling employment (the denominator in the density equation), with union members being laid off in slightly lesser numbers than non-members during the financial crisis, discussed below. In 2000 and 2001 membership grew slightly, but by proprtionately less than employment, so density fell again.

Several reasons have been given for the post-democratization decline in density. For example, J. Lee (2000) cites the slowing of economic growth after 1990, though this is not persuasive in itself as, at least for the period 1990–96, the unemployment rate was consistently below 3 per cent and lower than in the 1970s or 1980s. Song and Suh (2001: 164) discussed how some authors believed the radical behaviour of unions post-democratization provoked reprisals that hampered union growth, while others implied unions were too successful as the gains they achieved 'mollified collective defiance' – again, a not persuasive view given that at least some studies, though by no means all, have suggested a positive relationship between higher wages and union membership growth (Bain and Elsheikh 1976; Kenyon and Lewis 1992).

We shall turn to other explanations shortly. But in this context, the other important phenomenon that we should note

is the near deunionization of female labour – despite the fact
that several international studies show women are no less likely
to seek unionization than men (e.g. Getman *et al*. 1976; Grimes
1994; Hammer and Berman 1981; Scoville 1971; Youngblood *et
al*. 1984). From 1973 to 1984 union density was higher amongst
women than amongst men. In these years 'the union movement
and union activity was dominated by women' (Broadbent 2003:
3). Yet by 1994 female union density was barely half that
amongst males and by 1997 it was just two-fifths the male rate.
Behind this was a transformation of female labour – from a location in labour-intensive mass-production industries (Song 1999:
11) to a peripheral employment ghetto. On the other hand, male
unionism was maintained by the growth of male-dominated
heavy manufacturing (Broadbent 2003: 3). There was little
change in the female employment share, which stood at slightly
over two-fifths through the 1990s, but the nature of that
employment changed significantly and with it the ability of
unions to recruit women. We explore this issue in the next
section.

Women and the rise of non-permanent workers

Peripheral employment – referred to in Korea as 'non-standard',
'non-permanent' or 'irregular' employment – encompasses
forms of work that depart from the traditional concept of full-
time, ongoing work with a single employer. Therefore,
non-standard employment is defined as encompassing part-time
worker, short-term or temporary worker (contract), temporary
work agency or dispatched employment, self-employment, and
workers employed by family (Betcherman and Dar 2000: 11).
Peripheral employees include all but the first of this group.
Women predominate amongst peripheral employees – in 2001
some 68 per cent of female employees were temporary or daily
workers. Accordingly, they represent a highly vulnerable part of
the labour force. As in other countries, women are concentrated
in traditional, female-dominated occupations. They face problems of unequal pay and harassment – for example, 67 per cent
of respondents to a 1997 KCTU survey reported experiencing
sexual harassment in the workplace (Interview, Ministry of
Labor official; Choi 2000.)

Even when they are permanent employees, women's jobs are insecure. During the financial crisis women were laid off more readily than men (e.g. Choi 2000). Hence between 1997 and 1998, the labour force participation rate amongst females fell 2.5 percentage points, from 49.5 per cent to 47.0 per cent, whereas amongst males it fell just 0.4 points to 75.2 per cent (KLI 2003). Employers took the view that they were more dispensable because they were not the primary breadwinners in their families – a not unrealistic reading of the patriarchal way Korean families are organized. (In a Korean household, for example, the eldest male is considered to be the head of the household, regardless of the seniority and abilities of his sisters and mother.) If both members in a couple were employed by one bank whose union we spoke to, the woman would be laid off and the man kept on during the financial crisis. When women kept their job, it was often as peripheral employees rather than as permanent workers (interview KWCTU[c]).

Largely as a result of their over-representation amongst peripheral employees, unionization is much lower amongst women than men – women account for two-fifths of workers but little over one-fifth of union members. Over the 1998–2001 period, on average up to 65 per cent of the difference in male and female densities could be explained simply by the greater incidence of peripheral employment amongst women employees – before taking account of other structural differences in their labour market situations including occupation, industry and workplace size (for example, 64 per cent of female employees work in establishments with five or less workers: Choi 2000). In industries such as finance, women are also under-represented amongst the officialdom in unions where they have substantial membership.

Other than one electronics enterprise trade union and one heavy industry, all unions we interviewed reported that the number of non-standard employees had increased during and after the crisis. Indeed, statistics indicate a remarkable growth in the use of peripheral employment in Korea over the 1990s. In 1993, peripheral employees accounted for 41 per cent of employees. Just six years later they represented 52 per cent of employees (KLSI 2001: 21). This included 33 per cent of employees who were 'temporary' employees (up from 27 per cent in 1993) and 18 per cent who were 'daily' employees (up from 15 per cent). Amongst female employees, the proportion who were peripheral employees rose from 59 per cent to 70 per cent in just the three years from 1996 to 1999, but men also suffered an increase in non-permanency, from 33 per cent to 40 per cent over this period.

The significance of this for unions should not be underestimated, as Korean unions have traditionally recruited virtually all of their members from the permanent workforce – typically, the rules of collective agreements, to which they are willing signatories, have precluded them from doing otherwise. A simple shift-share analysis will illustrate the impact this changing composition of employment has had on union density. Assume, for estimation purposes, that in 1993 all union members were permanent employees. As union density was 17.2 per cent in 1993, and permanent employees accounted for 59 per cent of the workforce, this implies union density amongst permanent employees was around 29.3 per cent. Let us now assume that density amongst permanent employees remained 29.3 per cent through the rest of the 1990s to 2001. Simply by virtue of the decline in the share of permanent employment to 49 per cent, aggregate union density would have fallen to 14.3 per cent by 2001. In fact, recorded union density was 14.5 per cent in 2001. In other words, the recorded decline in density between 1993 and 2001 could be fully explained by the growth of peripheral employment. As mentioned, the recorded decline is probably slightly understated, and therefore there is some small part of the real decline that is not attributable to this structural change in the labour market. Nonetheless, while it does not explain the initial recorded decline from 1989 to 1993 (a minority of which might reflect members shifting from recognized FKTU to unrecognized KTUC unions), it is clear that the shift to peripheral employment, and the failure of unions to recruit peripheral employees, is a critical factor in union decline in Korea. Small wonder, too, that union density amongst women has plummeted by comparison with that amongst men.

Central to explaining the importance of peripheral employees is the relative cost of permanent and peripheral labour. Figures varied, but typically unions and employers reported that non-permanent employees cost about 80 per cent of permanent employees; in one firm it was below 50 per cent. The initial surge in peripheral numbers took place during the immediate post-democratization period. Between 1985 and 1990 the wages share in GDP rose from 54 per cent to 59 per cent (a figure which it has not fallen below since). Large wage increases won by unions led to an unwillingness of employers to hire new staff. Unions complained of the intensification of work for members. Employers responded by saying they could not afford to take on new permanent employees but they could take on temporary employees, reducing pressure on permanent employees, and protecting employment security and pay. Ostensibly, at this time, lifelong employment was retained, at least for permanent employees. Unions representing permanent employees in effect acquiesced to this employer response (Interview, KEF). Temporary employees rose from 20 per cent to 29 per cent of the workforce between 1985 and 1990 (and total peripheral employment, including daily employees, from 37 per cent to 46 per cent).

The second surge in peripheral employment occurred as a result of the financial crisis, and changes in the political environment that followed. The state responded to the financial crisis with a programme of economic and social reform. This included accelerating capital market liberalization and banking system reform, removing foreign ownership restrictions, establishing a programme of corporate restructuring (Perkins, 1999: 140) and labour law reform. Three major areas of labour law change had an immediate impact: permission was granted for dismissal on the basis of 'managerial reasons'; permission was granted for employers to hire temporary workers and for temporary work agencies to be established (Park 2000: 5); and a Tripartite Commission was established to incorporate labour and management with government in managing change (Kim Sookon 1999: 197). In direct response to the economic downturn, employers cut the numbers of both peripheral employees and permanent employees, but when recruitment recommenced as recovery started, instead of resuming an employment model based on a lifelong learning model, employers sought workers who either had already acquired abilities or were expendable, cheaper peripheral employees. Aside from two in the electronics sector, all enterprise unions reported that a significant number of full-time employees lost their jobs due to crisis-driven company difficulties or government reform programmes.

The financial crisis also saw the end of lifelong employment, as employers sought, and obtained from government, the right to implement the new flexibilities referred to earlier. During and since the financial crisis, many companies 'spun off' parts of their enterprises (i.e. replaced employees with subcontracting arrangements, usually with the subcontractors employing the same workers but frequently on inferior pay and conditions). Employees in spun-off enterprises are ineligible to belong to the enterprise union in the host firm, as they are now employed by the subcontractor, a separate firm. Between 1996 and 2001 temporary employment rose from 30 per cent to 35 per cent of employees, but this time daily hire grew as well, from 14 per cent to 17 per cent, so total peripheral employment rose from 43 per cent to 51 per cent.

In part, then, the rise of peripheral employees reflected changes in the environment in which unions were operating, in particular the economic environment and employer behaviour. But we can already see how it also reflected union behaviour. We shall now turn to a closer exploration of unions themselves, and how their capabilities have shaped and been shaped by the rise of peripheral employment. We shall first examine the Korean unions' co-ordinating capacities.

Coordinating capacities of Korean unions

The union movement generally operates at three levels: (1) two national peak federations; (2) industry federations, with many industries having two federations, one affiliated with national peak federation; and (3) individual enterprise unions. Interposed in this are some newly created industry unions covering employees across multiple workplaces but rarely covering all unionists in an industry. This three-tiered structure is a result of a division in the labour movement created by the control exercised over organized labour by the developmentalist coalition between government and capital in the period from 1953 until 1987 (Park Se-il 1994: 78). Both the KCTU and the FKTU have contact with international organizations such as the ILO and NGOs in order to gather international support for Korean trade unionists (Interview, KCTU official, 7 June 2000 and FKTU official, 8 June 2000).

Perhaps partly as a result of historical instability in formal structures, and also because all unions have to be affiliated with one of the peak union councils in order to achieve legitimacy, there is a strong degree of articulation between the national, industry and enterprise levels. This articulation is most evident in wage negotiations. Both streams of the union movement follow essentially the same procedure. A target wage range is determined at the national level and passed on to the industry federations which, taking account of their circumstances, determine industry target wage ranges which set the framework for enterprise-level negotiations.

However, the FKTU and KCTU diverge on political strategies, reflecting in no small part their very different origins. The FKTU argues that union goals can be achieved with a policy of constructive engagement with employers at enterprise and industry levels, and with employers and government in the national Tripartite Commission. It encourages affiliated unions to avoid industrial action. For example, the FKTU did not take part in the 2000 nationwide general strike, and rather positioned itself for the 'new' industrial relations system it viewed as necessary for Korea. The KCTU, by contrast, argues that direct action is required to achieve goals. It withdrew from the Tripartite Commission as it believed that the commission did not give organized labour a channel for expressing views and that it only implemented decisions beneficial to employers. The KCTU's 1999–2000 campaigns included the 40-hour/5 day week campaign, a campaign to have the national social security budget expanded and a campaign to support peripheral workers. The tactics it uses include general strikes, demonstrations, rallies, and seminars and workshops to provide information to workers and the public. An example of different tactics used by the peak bodies is the 2000 May Day demonstrations. The KCTU organized street marches and demonstrations in major cities, and in Seoul there was police/demonstrator violence. The FKTU organized an indoor event in Seoul (Interview, KCTU officials; 7 June 2000). Relations between both peak councils and the government deteriorated after the jailing of the Daewoo union officials and subsequent arrests of other union officials.

Despite its suspect origins, the FKTU had clearly shifted from its prior position of high dependency on the state (though in 2000 it was alleged to be still receiving financial assistance from the government (Interview, KCTU Official, 7 June 2000)) and had to become more unionate in order to prevent membership loss and stem the flow of defections to the KCTU. An example was the FKTU's withdrawal from a meeting with President Kim to discuss bank reform (*Korea Herald*, 6 July 2000).

What of coordination at the industry level? In the metals and manufacturing sector, the FMKWTU^f was less militant than the KMWF^c and less likely to use strikes as a tool to achieve goals. Also, while the majority of FMKWTU^f affiliated enterprise trade unions are mostly in small and medium business, their largest unions are in enterprises where the company has weathered the financial crisis relatively well. The relationship between the FMKWTU^f and the KMWF^c was antagonistic. A KMWF^c interviewee described the FMKWTU^f as dependent on government for funding and hence not democratic or representative of members. Nevertheless, the two federations cooperated in an attempt to stop restructuring in 1998. While the attempt was unsuccessful, the two federations worked well together (Interview, KMWF^c official, 12 June 2000).

However, it is important not to generalize across all industries based on peak council behaviours. In finance, the roles were a reversal of the stereotype. The KFCFLU^c membership had problems in their relationship with the their peak body, the KCTU, resulting from the latter's perceived focus on issues to do with the large enterprise unions that are the backbone of the KCTU's power (auto and heavy industry) and the belief that the KCTU had 'knee-jerk' responses to government policy, rather than considering options and offering alternatives to government. The KFBFU^f, by contrast, had a more aggressive stance than most other FKTU-affiliated trade unions and in many respects may have been more militant than the KFCFLU^c. Its militancy arose from the way in which government reform affected the banking industry. As with the KFCFLU^c, the KFBFU^f enjoyed an increase in the number of affiliated enterprise trade unions as workers experiencing increased levels of employment insecurity formed trade unions. A general strike organized by the KFBFU^f against further banking industry reform took place on 13 July 2000. Its relationship with the FKTU soured when the KFBFU^f requested that the FKTU withdraw from the Tripartite Commission due to government reform policy. The relationship between the KFBFU^f and the KFCFLU^c was much less antagonistic than in other industries – they cooperated on issues such as restructuring protests and seeking to sue the IMF over reform outcomes in the financial sector, and both agreed it was likely they would merge at some point in the future (Interviews, KFCFLU^c official, 7 June 2000; and KFBFU^f official, 13 June 2000).

The Korean union movement therefore has both great

strengths and great weaknesses in its coordinating capacity. It has strong vertical coordination, particularly over wages, but horizontal coordination is very mixed, and more often than not competition gets in the way of coordination. The crippling effect this has is becoming increasingly apparent to union officials. Despite their different perspectives on tactics, we would not rule out the possibility of a future merger of the FKTU and the KCTU. For example, one KCTU official commented that his federation had a lot in common with the younger officials in the FKTU and could see a merger occurring in the future. The pressure for merger is probably stronger amongst the officials at the industry level who see the problems of competing industry federations. Merger at the peak level would enable industry level mergers to occur. Until then, the existence of a bifurcated union movement is a major impediment to united, coordinated action. In turn, this hampers the ability of the union movement to recruit and represent peripheral employees. Thus while the KCTU had sought to promote recruitment of peripheral employees, the much larger FKTU was inactive on the issue.

Discursive capacity

A further factor constraining unions' ability to undertake coherent, consistent strategies is turnover of leadership, reflecting an ongoing interpretation gap (Pizzorno 1968) between members expectations and leaders' actions. That is, Korean unions have major problems with their discursive capacity. Many unions we interviewed reported that their leadership changed at each election, usually held every three years. Each new leadership changed union policy and approach in an attempt to differentiate themselves from the previous leadership. One government respondent went as far as to argue that the reason for the withdrawal of the KCTU from the Tripartite Committee was that the present leadership believed that this was required to win the 2001 ballot (Interview, 14/6/00). With union leadership in such a fragile position, it takes a brave leader to argue to the permanently employed membership that they should broaden their church and embrace lower paid, peripheral employees – even though this may, in the long term, be necessary to preserve the bargaining position of the union.

Strategic capacity and competence

While economic and employer factors are important in explaining the growth of peripheral employment, a key factor has been union culture, and in effect a failure of unions' strategic capacity. Bray (1991) identified four potential responses from unions to atypical employees. They may ignore them; exclude and oppose them; limit and regulate them; or recruit and integrate them into union structures and processes. Korean unions initially pursued a different strategy – to encourage their growth as outsiders, through acquiescence to the employers' strategy of increasing peripheral employment in response to the high wage gains achieved by permanent employees. It was a short-term approach by unions – inevitably, the cost advantage of hiring peripheral employees over permanent employees would lead to the former displacing the latter.

Unions dealt with this potential problem by negotiating ceilings on the numbers of peripheral employees in Collective Agreements (CA). That is, in Bray's terms, they sought to limit and regulate peripheral employees. As mentioned, Korean unions have typically focused their attention on the 'insiders' – the permanent workers who form the core of their membership. They were accordingly happy to have peripheral employees excluded from coverage by the union, either by union rules or CAs. To cover peripheral employees would seemingly require that they have the same pay and conditions as permanent workers, and this would add to the company wages bill and undermine employers' capacity to pay high wages to permanent workers. Since then, many Korean unions have taken a 'can't do' approach to the unionization of peripheral employees, because they are excluded by rules and agreements and even, in some eyes, by legislation. Employers, of course, have been keen to maintain the non-union status of peripheral employees. Indeed, several employer and trade union respondents referred to the fact that peripheral employees would be dismissed if they sought to join or form a union. The trouble was, unions' capacity to maintain the ceilings on the number of peripheral employees was greatly weakened by the financial crisis.

The weaknesses of the Korean unions' approaches to peripheral employees owed much to the gendered nature of Korean unions. For women, according to Broadbent (2003: 4) the 'structure and culture of the union movement ... [is] exclusive and inhospitable'. Moreover, 'issues women considered important ... including sexual harassment and childcare were neglected/ignored by the union movement' (Broadbent 2003: 4). Even amongst permanent workers, women's wages are well below men's wages – the ratio of female to male regular wages was 67.1 per cent in 2001, with ever worse ratios for overtime pay and fringe benefits (KLI 2003) – but unions have only made scattered attempts to improve their representation of women and their interests. In one enterprise we looked at, the union had attempted to reduce the differential between male and female permanent workers' wages, by providing for smaller increments for men than for women. This has become a source of conflict within the union concerned. But unions' treatment of their regular female members was luxurious compared to that afforded peripheral female employees.

The failure of the 'ignore' and 'limit' approaches led to an attempt to adopt Bray's fourth response – to recruit and integrate peripheral workers. But the institutional framework that unions were happy to accept a decade earlier made integration highly problematic. The peak union bodies sought to encourage affiliates to unionize peripheral employees. The KCTU was more advanced than FKTU in this area. Three possible structural approaches emerged. We now examine those approaches. But to do this, we need first to understand the strengths and weaknesses of Korea's union structure.

Internal solidarity: structural and organizing capacity

A key element in the weakness of Korean unions in relation to peripheral workers is the way in which systems of internal solidarity have excluded peripheral employees. Of course, this exclusion has in turn weakened the effectiveness of internal solidarity because unions' bargaining power has been undermined by the growth of non-unionized peripheral employees. Central to this problem is the way in which Korea's union movement is structured on an enterprise basis. Yet there has been a growing recognition that enterprise unions are intrinsically weaker than industry unions, which might benefit from economies of scale and be more independent of the employer. Unions were significantly weakened during the financial crisis and have not regained all of their lost power. At the same time management in several of the companies we examined, sensing union weakness in a more competitive environment, has become more aggressive in relations with unions.

Another weakness and strength of the enterprise union structure is that the salaries of enterprise unions' paid officials ('dedicated union officers') are funded by the companies, regardless of whether they are in a KCTU or FKTU affiliate. Indeed, on the surface, this may seem to be a recipe for corporate control of the union – but it is not quite as simple as that. The payment of dedicated officers' salaries by employers occurs not through employer benevolence but as a requirement set out in collective agreements (CAs). It is thus like many other forms of union security provisions set out in agreements in industrialized nations. Union members pay dues on top of the amount that the employer pays for officials' salaries, and in the enterprises we studied these were at least 1 per cent of salary. So in theory at least, Korean enterprise unions could be quite well resourced. For example, one enterprise union we interviewed had eight dedicated officials for 1,500 members. However, it also makes unions potentially vulnerable when CAs are up for renegotiation. An employer can starve union officials of salary. This is not very common, though in one company we examined management, while not cutting off funds altogether, had taken a hard line, for example by not paying the salaries or allowances of 14 of the 55 union officers, not paying overtime to part-time officers, and not allowing the KCTU president on site. The union in return promised a strike and to demand a drastic increase in wages and welfare (Interview, H1^c Official, 29 June 2000).

While the Korean union movement may seek to recruit peripheral employees by trying to persuade them to join existing enterprise unions, this is made difficult by the coverage of CAs, the restrictions in union rules, and the culture that arose as a result of these arrangements. This culture has legitimized the notion that peripheral employees do not have a right to membership of an enterprise union and strengthened employer opposition and peripheral employee fear of dismissal. At each of the electronics workplaces we visited, the trade union planned to negotiate to stop management employing any further peripheral employees. E1^f planned to recruit peripheral employees and E2^f

planned to force government to follow the labour laws and transform peripheral employees into regular employees after they have been employed for more than one year. While their constitution allowed them to recruit peripheral employees, their CA did not. Thus, the union attempted to change this CA clause in the next round of negotiations. In a heavy industries union, H1^c, the union attempted to reduce the number of peripheral employees in the company in CA negotiations but believed that in the long-term an industry union would recruit peripheral employees. Fundamentally, the unionization of peripheral workers within the enterprise structure of Korean unions was almost impossible.

This led to the second, less problematic solution to the peripheral employee problem – establish industry unions, which peripheral employees would then be eligible to join. Indeed, the late 1990s saw a major reconsideration of the enterprise basis of unionism and a push amongst affiliates of both the FKTU and the KCTU to restructure along industry lines. This was for several reasons. Industry unions were seen as possessing stronger bargaining power, and to be better able to finance adequate training of workplace representatives. Industry unionism is seen as the only way by which unions could properly deal with the problem of the growth of peripheral workers. Amongst some officials at higher levels at least, there was a belief that restructuring unions along industry lines would reduce myopic decision making and enhance solidarity. Being organized along enterprise lines, many unionists were seen to only look at issues in terms of their own particular enterprise and fail to take account of broader industry or social concerns. However, given the ability of Korean unions to bring workers out onto the streets for demonstrations and general strikes – their organizing capacity is remarkably strong for a union movement with relatively low density – we would not want to make too much of this criticism. Most importantly, changes to labour laws foreshadowed by the government would fundamentally change the financial basis of enterprise unions and make many unviable.

To understand this last point, we must look again at changes in the political environment dating from the financial crisis. As part of a package of labour market reforms that followed the financial crisis, the government announced that the right to establish multiple enterprise unions would be established and the corporate payment of trade union officers' salaries would be prohibited. Driving this latter reform was employer opposition to the costs involved (despite the scope it may have given for corporate manipulation of union behaviour). Initially, the government announced in 1997 that from 1998 this practice would become illegal. Union opposition led to a partial backdown, with implementation delayed to 2002. Unions began to reorganize in anticipation of a funding crisis, for most enterprise unions did not believe that they could raise dues sufficiently to finance their dedicated officers' salaries. Interestingly, there was no sign that unions plan to build into future wage claims a component equivalent to the previous employer cost of officers' salaries, giving members the financial capacity to afford a significant rise in dues. Rather, more effort was put into organizing opposition to the reforms. Eventually, these efforts paid off, and in 2001 government announced that implementation of both measures would be further delayed to 2007. This was, in effect, a deal between the FKTU and employers: the FKTU wanted the continued payment of salaries for financial stability in the union movement and business wanted to maintain a single line for negotiation in an enterprise. The KCTU, still boycotting the Tripartite Commission, was not at the meeting at which this was formalized. Few people now believed that the reform would, in the end, see the light of day.

With the demise of the reforms to corporate payment of dedicated officers' salaries, much of the impetus towards industry unionism was lost, though the KCTU continued to push hard for it (along with the KFIU[f] in banking). A KCTU-affiliated taxi industry union was established in 2001. In metals manufacturing the KMWF[c] encountered resistance from members but had some support from enterprise union leaders themselves and undertook education programmes at the enterprise level for trade union officers and for members (Interview, KMWF[c] official, 12 June 2000). Each affiliate in autos and heavy industries reported support for an industry union among officials, but weak support among workers, and was running an education programme about the benefits of industry unions to employees. The H2[c] trade union official also noted that the repression of industry unions that occurred under Chun Doo-hwan has made unionists wary of industry unions. In ballots taken in 2001, several large enterprise unions voted to join the KMWF[c] but members at some key unions (including at Daewoo Shipbuilding and Hyundai Heavy Industries) voted against it. Member opposition in the large enterprise unions reflects huge disparities in wages between large and small firms (for example, wages in union E4^c reported that the average wage for their members was won 33,000,000 (Interview, E4^c union official, 5 July 2000), nearly twice the average for the industry (Ministry of Labor, 2000). Employers absolutely resisted any moves by unions towards industry bargaining, while employees in large companies feared a drop in pay if industry bargaining arose from industry unionism (though, as the Australian experience with enterprise bargaining indicates, the former is not inherent in the latter). Many officials from large enterprise unions fear a reduction in their bargaining power from shifting to enterprise unions, while in many enterprise unions there is also confusion as to the process of change. The loss of impetus, particularly amongst FKTU affiliates, for any shift to industry unionism left unresolved the many problems of enterprise unionism, most particularly the failure to accommodate peripheral workers within union structures.

Establishing new forms of internal solidarity: irregular workers' unions

In the face of the failure of widespread union restructuring, the only other way in which the Korean union movement can respond to the needs of peripheral workers is to establish new structures that are dedicated to peripheral workers, and create their own internal solidarities. This possibility would have become especially viable had the proposed laws enabling multi-unionism come into effect. If enterprise-specific peripheral worker unions were formed, these could later be merged with existing enterprise unions. Alternatively, and more realistically, multi-employer peripheral worker unions could be established and these unions, or parts of these unions, might then merge with future industry unions. This was, indeed, part of the strategy of the women's unions, discussed below. In autos, there was strong support amongst the enterprise unions for peripheral employees to form their own industry union or for peripheral workers to be recruited by the existing trade union, with little support for this second option from workers, and each union has education programmes in place to provide information about the benefits of NPE unions to employees.

But perhaps the most important development for female

representation in unions – and the most notable indictment of Korean unions' performance in regard to women workers up until now – has been the formation of women's unions. We identified two women's trade unions, both established in 1999: the KCTU-affiliated Korean Women's Confederation of Trade Unions (KWCTU^c), and the non-affiliated Korean Women's Trade Union (KWTU). (The FKTU has a women's department, but no women's union.) The KWCTU^c started off as Seoul based and spread nationally later in the year. Prior to reincarnation as the KWTU, the Korean Female Workers Association provided counselling to women workers, but became a union in order to increase its power. The KWCTU^c has 2,000 members (1,000 in Seoul) and the KWTU 1,000. Each union focuses on around half a dozen occupations. Both unions try to organize telemarketers and insurance sales workers (the main priority for the KWCTU^c). The KWCTU^c also attempts to organize insurance sales workers, credit card workers, hospice employees, hotel workers, delivery workers, tutors and child carers. The KWTU also tries to unionize cafeteria workers, copywriters, general office workers and golf caddies.

These women's unions are small operations. The KWCTU^c has three 'dedicated' staff in the Seoul region and one staff member per region. It operates out of cramped premises. Both unions rely on membership fees, and are financially weak, though the KWTU also has an unnamed sponsor as a benefactor. They do not see themselves as in competition with each other – the sphere of unorganized women workers is so large that there is plenty of room for both – but nor do they regularly meet or cooperate at an official level. Their growth plans are not ambitious – the KWCTU^c aims to have 3–4,000 members in the Seoul region in two years.

The ultimate goal of the KWCTU^c is to have all peripheral employees employed as permanent employees. The focus of the KWTU is on protecting the rights of peripheral employees, and of obtaining equal rights for female employees regarding pay, promotion, training, type of work, choice of work, and days off. Two major issues in the protection of peripheral workers' rights are, first, the enforcement of rights that already exist but are ignored (contract workers and dispatched workers) and, second, the recognition of some groups as employees rather than as self-employed.

A few examples illustrate the problems and issues facing

women workers and the women's unions. Many thousands of female insurance sales workers are classified as self-employed and are paid commission only. Not surprisingly, very few are unionized. In one company where the KWCTU^c had a presence, management refused to negotiate with the union as it claims the women were self-employed. The union sued the company for registering the women as business owners without the workers' approval. Aside from recognition as employees, the union tried to gain for these members base salary with increments, back-pay (when workers leave the company they are often not paid commission owing) and mobility rights.

In credit card companies, the dispatched workers law came into effect. This stated that if a worker is employed for more than 12 months they are eligible for a separation payment. The credit card companies responded by dismissing temporary employees after 11 months, then rehiring them. Other dispatch companies exchange staff between companies after 11 months or, in some cases, close the company when a majority of employees reach the eleven-month mark. For golf caddies, the KWTU tried to negotiate a collective agreement with a company and eleven caddies were sacked, though reinstated after union protestations.

The methods of the women's unions are necessarily innovative. They can usually only meet workers after hours as companies will not allow them to be approached on the premises. If a company finds that its peripheral employees have unionized they may fire them or even close down the company, starting again under a different name without the unionized staff. So workers are approached indirectly and if they join they do so secretly. A union official may go to a workplace and put contact details for the union on the doors inside the women's toilets. Information about the union may be spread by word of mouth amongst the workers. Both unions use campaigns and street demonstrations to gain publicity for their causes – for example, there is a weekly demonstration outside the insurance company mentioned above. The KWTU also provides counselling and advice for its members.

If sufficient workers from a particular sector – such as credit card workers or hotel staff – join it, the KWCTU^c plans to establish a separate women's trade union in that industry. That union could then merge with the relevant industry unions for permanent employees. This strategy reflects the KCTU affiliation of the KWCTU^c, and is dependent on support from the KCTU and affiliates for success. Some enterprise unions are cooperative but others are hostile to the KWCTU^c. In insurance, for example, there is a classic insider–outsider conflict: permanent workers belonging to an enterprise union take on a management role and seek to prevent peripheral employees who would be represented by the KWCTU^c from organizing. Enterprise union hostility to the KWCTU^c may therefore reflect members' desire to keep peripheral employees unorganized, or alternatively the enterprise union's wish to recruit peripheral employees itself. However, the KWCTU^c claimed all KCTU-affiliated unions support the organization of peripheral employees.

Conclusions

By looking at the power resources available to Korean unions, we can see areas of great strength alongside some fundamental weaknesses which explain unions' poor performance in relation to perpheral workers and the threat that the growth of a non-union peripheral sector poses to the ongoing strength of the union movement. Unions' vertical co-ordinating capacity is very strong as a result of the deep articulation between national, industry and local levels. Yet horizontal coordinating capacity is very weak, due to the bifurcation nationally, and in many industries, between FKTU and KCTU affiliated unions. Unions have high organizing and mobilizing capacity – they can get members on the streets for all manner of causes – but their discursive capacity is weak, leading to a destabilizing turnover in union leadership and poor long-term strategic planning and implementation capabilities. Unions' structural capacity is at best mixed, with a small number of well-resourced enterprise unions in large organizations doing well, but living beside a large number of smaller enterprise unions where bargaining power is weak, particularly in the more difficult, market-oriented climate that has emerged post-financial crisis. Enterprise union structures are typically unsuited to the needs of peripheral workers. Indeed they typically exclude them, but the large well-endowed *chaebol* unions preclude an effective restructuring along industry lines that may better accommodate the needs of peripheral workers – or at least, enable them to be taken on as members. What appears on the surface as strong internal solidarity is actually highly divisive, with several major lines of cleavage: between core and peripheral workers; between large and small enterprises; between FKTU and KCTU organizations; and, critically, between male and female.

Many Korean union leaders recognized the need for change – yet division and inertia in the union movement has stymied that change. Division and inertia cause and reflect limitations on strategic capacity within the union movement, and a culture that has prioritized permanent and male workers. There is nothing unique about this culture: it reflects the highly gendered nature of Korean society. One thing that is notable about it, however, is that it permitted some major strategic errors to be made – in particular, acceptance of the notion that non-union, peripheral employment should be allowed to grow as a buffer to prevent undue shocks to the pay and conditions of permanent, unionized workers. Union membership has collapsed amongst female employees – once the beachhead of Korean unionism. With that collapse, and the growth of non-union peripheral employment, has come a substantial weakening of the Korean union movement.

In the face of these structural and cultural problems, leaving many peripheral workers exposed to unconstrained market forces, new structures have emerged with their own specific union cultures: women's unions. It is unlikely that, in themselves, they will become the salvation of the workers who have been ignored for so long by mainstream unions. Their numbers are just too small, and the size of the peripheral worker problem so large. But they do represent a major challenge to the way in which mainstream union organizations think about and organize peripheral workers. One of them is integrated into the KCTU structure and has the capacity to directly influence the way in which that federation deals with female and peripheral workers. If the emergence of women's unionism can alter the culture within mainstream union organizations, and encourage a reevaluation of the strengths and weaknesses of the various power resources within the control of Korean unions, the latter may at last start to find an effective way of dealing with the growing peripheral worker 'problem'.

References

Allen, M. 2000. Presentation at 'Strategic Planning' Professional Development Meeting, AFL-CIO Education Department, Milwaukee, 13 April.

Bain, G. S. and Elsheikh, F. 1976. *Union Growth and the Business Cycle: An Econometric Analysis*. Oxford: Blackwell.

Betcherman, G. and Dar, A. 2000. 'Labour Adjustment, Non-standard Work and Employment Programs: Korea in an OECD Context', International Conference on Economic Crisis and Labour Market Reform: The Case of Korea, Session V, KLI and World Bank, Seoul.

Bray, M. 1991. 'Conclusions', in Bray, M. and Taylor, V. (eds.), *The Other Side of Flexibility: Unions and Marginal Workers in Australia*, Monograph No 3, ACIRRT, Sydney.

Broadbent, K. 2003. 'Sisters Organizing for Themselves: A Study of Women-only Unions in Japan and South Korea', *Reflections and New Directions*, Association of Industrial Relations Academics of Australia and New Zealand, Vol 1: Refereed papers, Melbourne, February, compact disk and www.mngt.waikato.ac.nz/airaanz/proceedings/Melbourne2003/Volume1_RefereedPapers/Broadbent.pdf.

Choi, Jang Jip. 1989. *Labor and the Authoritarian State: Labor Unions in South Korean Manufacturing Industries, 1961–1980*. Seoul: Korea University Press.

Choi, Sang-rim. 2000. 'The Reality of Korean Women Workers and the Activities of Korean Women's Trade Union', Koream Women's Trade Union, Seoul, at http://kwunion.jinbo.net/eng/data/0828Korea.htm.

Cummings, B. 1987. 'The Origins and Development of the Northeast Asian Political Economy: Industrial Sectors, Product Cycles, and Political Consequences', in Deyo, F. C. (ed.), *The Political Economy of the New Asian Industrialism*. Ithaca: Cornell University Press.

Deyo, F. C. 1989. *Beneath the Miracle: Labor Subordination in the New Asian Industrialism*, Los Angeles: University of California Press.

Getman, J. G., Goldberg, S. B. and Herman, J. B. 1976. *Union Representation Elections: Law and Reality*. New York: Russell Sage.

Grimes, P. F. M. 1994. 'The Determinants of Trade Union Membership: Evidence from Two Australian Surveys', PhD thesis, Research School of Social Sciences, Australian National Univesity, Canberra.

Hagan, J. 1983. 'The Australian Union Movement: Context and Perspective, 1850–1980', in Ford, B. and Plowman, D. (eds.) *Australian Unions: An Industrial Relations Perspective*. Melbourne: Macmillan.

Hammer, T. H. and Berman, M. 1981. 'The Role of Noneconomic Factors in Faculty Union Voting', *Journal of Applied Psychology*, 66, 4: 415–421.

Hyman, R. 1997. 'The Future of Employee Representation', *British Journal of Industrial Relations*, 35,3: 309–336.

Kenyon, P. D. and Lewis, P. E. T. 1992. 'Trade Union Membership and the Accord', *Australian Economic Papers*, 31, 59: 325–345.

Kim, Hwang-joe. 1993. 'The Korean Union Movement in Transition', in Frenkel, S. (ed.) *Organized Labor in the Asia-Pacific Region: A Comparative Study of Trade Unionism in Nine Countries*. Ithaca: Cornell University.

Kim Sookon. 1999. *Korean Industrial Relations System in Transition: Is Asian Value in Employment Practices Collapsing in the Korean Labour Market as a Consequence of Restructuring*, Conference Paper to Australia and Korea into the New Millennium: Political, Economic and Business Relations. Brisbane, Griffith University.

Kim Wan-soon. 1999. *Korea's New Role in the Regional and Global Economy: After the Financial Crisis*, Conference Paper to Australia and Korea into the New Millennium: Political, Economic and Business Relations. Brisbane, Griffith University.

Koo, Hagen. 2001. *Korean Workers: The Culture and Politics of Class Formation*. Ithaca: Cornell University Press.

Koo, Hagen. and Kim, Eun Mee. 1992. 'The Developmental State and Capital Accumulation in South Korea', in Appelbaum, R. P. and Henderson, J. (eds.), *States and Development in the Asia Pacific Rim*. London: Sage.

Korea Herald. 6/7/2000. 'Lunch between President, Labor Panel Canceled'.

Korea Labour and Society Institute (KLSI). 2001. 'GPN Global Labour Network Database: Korea', KLSI, Seoul, www.globalpolicynetwork. org/data/korea/korea-data.pdf.

Korean Confederation of Trade Unions. 1999. *What Is the Government's Response? Arrest, Arrest and More Arrests!*, www.kctu.org/, 18 May (accessed 26 February 2003).

Korean Labor Institute. 2003. *Monthly Labor Bulletin*, Seoul, February

Korean Ministry of Finance and Economy. 2000. *Korea Economic Update*, www.mofe.go.kr, 28 Sept. 2000.

Korean Ministry of Labor. 2000. *Major Labor-Related Statistical Tables*, www.molab.go.kr, 28 Sept. 2000.

Labourstart. 2003. *Korea: Worker Commits Suicide to Protest Anti-union Repression*, www.labourstart.org.

Lee, Joohoo. 2000. 'The Financial Crisis, the Search for Flexibility and Changes in Industrial Relations: The South Korean Case', Korea Labour Institute, paper presented to International conference on Transforming Korean Business and Management Culture, Michigan State University, USA, 19–20 September.

Lee, M. B. 1993. 'Korea', in Rothman, M., Briscoe, D. R., and Nacamulli, R. C. D. (eds.), *Industrial Relations Around the World: Labor Relations for Multinational Companies*. Berlin: de Gruyter Studies in Organization.

Leggett, C. and Kwon, Seung-ho. 1998. 'Labour in Developing Countries: Unions in Korea', in Hess, M. (ed.), *Labour Organization and Development: Case Studies*. Canberra: Asia Pacific Press.

Levesque, C. and Gregor M. 2002. 'Local Versus Global: Activating Local Union Power in the Global Economy', *Labor Studies Journal*, 27, 3: 39–65.

Moon, Chung-in and Kang, Mun-gu. 1995. 'Democratic opening and military intervention in South Korea: Comparative Assessment and Implications', in Cotton, J. (ed.), *Politics and Policy in the New Korean State: From Roh Tae-woo to Kim Young-sam*. Sydney: Longman Australia Pty.

Murray, G. 1998. 'Union Power and Strategy in the Canadian Automobile Sector, 1975–1995', Département des Relations Industrielles, Université Laval, Québec, Canada.

Park, Duck Jay. 2000. *Assessment of Labor Market Responses to the Labor*

Law Changes Introduced in 1998, conference paper to International Conference on Economic Crisis and Labor Market Reform, Seoul, Republic of Korea.

Park, Se-il. 1994. 'The Role of the State in Industrial Relations: The Case of Korea', in Niland, J. R., Lansbury, R. D. and Verevis, C. (eds.) *The Future of Industrial Relations: Global Changes and Challenges*. London: Sage.

Park, Young-bum. 1994. 'State Regulation, the Labour Market and Economic Development: the Republic of Korea', in Rodgers, G. (ed.) *Workers, Institutions and Economic Growth in Asia*. Geneva: International Institute for Labour Studies.

Park, Young-bum and Leggett, C. 1998. 'Employment Relations in the Republic of Korea', in Bamber, G. J. and Lansbury, R. D. (eds.), *International and Comparative Employment Relations: a Study of Industrialised Market Economies*. Sydney: Allen and Unwin.

Park, Young-bum and Siengthai, Sununta. 2000. *Financial Crisis, Labour Market Flexibility and Social Safety Net in Korea and Thailand*, Conference Paper to IIRA. Japan.

Perkins, F. 1999. *Korea Rebuilds: From Crisis to Reform*, conference paper to Australia and Korea into the New Millennium: Political, Economic and Business Relations. Brisbane, Griffith University.

Pizzorno, A 1968. 'Political Exchange and Collective Identity in Industrial Conflict', in Crouch, C. and Pizzorno, A. (eds.), *The Resurgence of Class Conflict in Western Europe since 1968*. London: Macmillan.

Pocock, B. 2001. 'Union Renewal: a Theoretical and Empirical Analysis of Union Power', Centre for Labour Studies, University of Adelaide.

Pocock, B. (ed.) 1998. *Strife: Sex and Politics in Labour Unions*. Sydney: Allen & Unwin.

Schein, E. H. 1996. 'Culture: the Missing Concept in Organizational Studies', *Administrative Science Quarterly*, 41: 229–240.

Scoville, J. 1971. 'Inflation and Unionization in the US in 1966', *Industrial Relations*, 10, 3: 354–361.

Song, Ho Keun. 1999 'Labour Unions in the Republic of Korea: Challenges and Choices', Discussion Paper 107/99, International Institute of Labour Studies, Geneva.

Song, Ho-Keun and Suh, Doowon. 2001. 'Korea', in Cornfield, D. and Hodson, R. (eds.), *Worlds of Work: Building an International Sociology of Work*. New York: Kluwer Academic/Plenum Publishers.

You, Jong-il. 1994. 'Labour Intitutions and Economic Development in the Republic of Korea', in Rodgers, G. (ed.), *Workers, Institutions and Economic Growth in Asia*. Geneva: International Institute for Labour Studies.

Youngblood, S., De Nisi, A., Mollestin J. and Mobley, W. 1984. The Impact of Work Environment, Instrumentality Beliefs, Perceived Labor Union Image and Subjective Norms on Union Voting Intentions', *Academy of Management Journal*, 27, 3: 576–590.

11

The rise of unions in semi-industrialized countries: the cases of South Africa and Zimbabwe

JULIANNE WHITELEY

Declining union membership and strike statistics in the advanced societies during the 1980s and 1990s resulted in both neo-liberal and some of their more pessimistic critics proclaiming the working class a thing of the past (Moody 1999: 9). The global market economy, increased international competition and the role of multinational corporations were well cited as reasons for the decline (Salamon 1998: 25; Wood 1999: 1). The most optimistic prognosis was that, unable to fight on, the organized working class would fall into a coma of co-operation with its former foes (Moody 1999: 9). Yet, while decline has proved a common fate of union movements in the advanced capitalist world, it has not been a universal experience (Kelly 1997). Pervasive industrial restructuring coupled with deepening international integration and the rise of international production systems have created a layer of nations that are partly industrial, increasingly urban and as internally uneven as the world in which they exist, yet situated somewhere above the rest of the third world by most industrial and economic measures (Moody 1999: 201). In contrast to the problems of diminishing membership and reduced political clout faced by unions operating in advanced societies, within industrializing and semi-industrialized countries, unions remain numerically robust and enjoy significant political influence. This chapter focuses on the experiences of the labour movements in South Africa and Zimbabwe. Both countries have a significant industrial sector, and a history of weak authoritarian rule and protectionism. In South Africa, authoritarianism gave way to democratization; in Zimbabwe, settler rule was followed on by independence and dominant partyism. The latter in turn has degenerated into a personality-centred autocracy. In the 1990s, both countries adopted broadly neo-liberal policy prescriptions, which resulted in painful periods of adjustment, particularly in the industrial sectors. In Zimbabwe, neo-liberalism has given way to elite-serving ad hoc policy measures. All these developments have posed serious challenges, whilst at the same time, opened up new opportunities for organized labour in both these countries.

Mobilization theory and trade union identity

Touraine (1991: 389) defines a social movement as 'a collective action aiming at the implementation of central cultural values against the interest and influence of an enemy which is defined in terms of power relations'. In uniting against a clearly defined opponent, unions can occupy a key role as a mobilizing force, typically pulling other organizations into the struggle (Moody, quoted chapter 10). 'Social-movement unionism implies ... that the strongest of society's oppressed and exploited, generally organised workers, ... mobilise those who are less able to sustain mobilisation: the poor, the unemployed, the casualised workers, the neighbourhood organisations' (Moody, quoted in chapter 10). In other words, the relatively strong bargaining position of their membership imparts a particular strength to organized labour vis-à-vis other popular movements.

Mobilization theory suggests that the capacity of unions to draw in and unite workers depends both on long-term trends in the capitalist economy and the effects of this on conceptions of deprivation. If the position of workers noticeably deteriorates, and management is partially 'blamed' for this, or if there seems a real possibility for improving material conditions, then the capacity of trade unions to mobilize workers will be relatively strong (Kelly 1998). Essential for collective action is a sense of illegitimacy: the conviction that an event, action or situation is unjust because it violates established rules or conflicts with widely shared beliefs and values (Kelly 1997). Thus, social movements can be seen as expressions of chronic deprivation (Tarrow, quoted in chapter 10). Collective action is thus explained by the existence of a grievance in which the actor is challenged by a fundamental social force in a conflict in which the general orientations of social lives are at stake: this will lead to a social movement (Klandermans in Rucht 1991: 24, 364). Yet, it is not enough for employees to feel aggrieved; they must also feel that there is a chance that their situation can be changed (Kelly 1997).

The sense of injustice must prompt the formation of a social group with a collective interest (Kelly 1997). Three processes are vital in bringing this about: attribution, social identification and leadership (Kelly 1997). An attribution is an explanation for an event or action in terms of reasons, causes or both (Kelly 1997). Collective action will arise from external, controllable attributions: workers must blame someone for their unhappiness in such a way that social identification with the categories 'us' and 'them' results (Kelly 1997).

Leadership is responsible for constructing the sense of injustice, promoting cohesion, encouraging workers to take action and defending the collective action undertaken (Kelly 1997). Each of these factors (attribution, social identification and leadership), are required for the mobilization of the labour movement to take place (Kelly 1997). If the workforce remains immobilized against opponents or if an opponent does not exist, membership decline could result (Kelly 1997).

The case of South Africa

The transition from authoritarianism to a social democratic typology: social movement unionism

The South Africa born out of the 1909 South Africa Act saw the establishment of a new state with power concentrated in an all-white parliament (Learner.org2; Silke 1997; Svanemyr 1998). The fact that black South Africans played no part in the founding of the Union of South Africa marked the start of a resistance to white minority political rule that waxed and waned in intensity for a period spanning eighty-five years (Silke 1997).

Until 1979 African unions were debarred from participating in the official industrial relations structure of South Africa. (International Labour Organization 1964: 29). Their exclusion from the statuatory industrial relations system exacerbated the systematic exploitation of the black labour force made possible through the colour bar, the pass laws, and other labour repressive legislation (International Labour Organization 1964: 15).

There were numerous attempts to organize African workers prior to the 1970s which, in spreading the idea of workplace collectivism, laid the foundation for a national mass-based unionism which concentrated its efforts on building shop steward structures in selected workplaces (Rosenthal 1996b: 60; Webster 1984 in South African Labour Review II:81; Webster 1985: xi, xii). These attempts included the ICU of the 1920s, the Federation of Non-European Trade Unions (from the late 1920s through the 1930s) and Council of Non-European Trade Unions (1941–55), and SACTU (founded in 1955) (Wood 2002). What each attempt had in common was a reliance on a few key leadership figures. However, SACTU was different to preceding initiatives in that it represented a specific brand of political unionism; the limited strategic options at the time resulted in a decision to closely link the fortunes of African unionism to the various struggles of the 1950s headed by the ANC (Wood 2002a, 2003).

SACTU fell victim to the wave of state repression in the 1960s, and, whilst never banned, was forced into exile. During SACTU's early years of growth, more conservative elements formed in reaction to the state such as the Federation of Free African Trade Unions of South Africa (FOFATUSA), with the backing of such disparate bodies as right-wing US unions and the Pan Africanist Congress. As with its rivals, FOFATUSA fell into the trap of relying on a few key activists, whilst neglecting shopfloor organization. (cf. Lewis 1984).

The repressive climate of the 1960s – to apartheid apologists a 'golden age', when it seemed that apartheid might possibly succeed in its objectives – led to a period of apparent labour quiesence, although it can be argued that the ANC and SACTU in exile, with their limited underground activity, kept alive the idea of a fairer society (ANC 1968; Kelly 1997; Svanemyr 1998).

The establishment of a number of worker service organizations by liberal students and former union officials in the early 1970s represented the start of a new wave of unionization; this gained momentum with the 1973 Durban strikes (Wood 2002a, 2002b). The scale and success of the latter represented not simply a product of new organizational resources, but also reflected the extent of real worker grievances. Wages in Durban had lagged behind most other industrial centres in the country, where real wages had begun to rise after a long period of stagnation (in response to changes in wage policy on the mines) (Wood

2002a). Following on the Durban strikes, the worker service organizations established a number of independent, mostly industrial, unions, despite the repressive political climate of their time. Examples included the Metal and Allied Workers Union (MAWU) and the Chemical Workers Industrial Union (CWIU). The growing strength of these organizations, their daily access to rank and file members and their location in strategic sectors of the economy, such as manufacturing, mining and transport industries, allowed them to mobilize effectively around economic aspirations (ANC 1977; Kelly 1997; Valentine 1986: 11; Webster 1985: xi). The wave of state repression that followed the 1976 Soweto uprising included the banning (an apartheid-era form of house arrest) of a number of union activists; it was only through an emphasis on shopfloor organization that the unions did not completely collapse. However, by the late 1970s, the independent unions had established a firm presence in many South African workplaces and by 1980, most had become coalesced into two federations, the Federation of South African Trade Unions (FOSATU) and the Council of Unions of South Africa (CUSA) (Wood 2002a). FOSATU, together with a number of non-aligned, and some breakaway CUSA unions, formed a super-federation, the Congress of South African Trade Unions (COSATU) in 1985 (Wood 2002; 2003).

It is something of a truism to state that workers had much to be discontented about (low wages, and the daily humiliations of apartheid) which served to enhance social identification amongst the working class and facilitate identification with the social categories 'us' (the black labour movement) and 'them' (the apartheid state); however, it was only in the 1970s that this translated into a capacity for sustained mobilization and collective action (Hawthorne 1999d: 68; Kelly 1997; Shopsteward Editors 1995b; Valentine 1986: 11). Social identification and attribution were deepened through poorly conceived state actions, which intensified existing attitudes, norms and values (Hawthorne 1997: 72; Kelly 1997; Svanemyr 1998). However, in contrast to the climate of 'little hope' of the 1960s, workers now had the organizational tools to mount a serious challenge to the status quo; the successful outcome of many factory level struggles highlighted the vulnerability of the status quo, and made union membership more attractive to previously unorganized workers, resulting in a self-reinforcing cycle of mobilization and collective action. Employer concessions – above all in terms of significant increases in real wages and cautious moves towards union recognition – served to inspire workers elsewhere.

During the 1980s, concentration on wage bargaining and the winning of union recognition, the decentralization of authority and power within organizations and the overwhelming impulse to unite against apartheid found concrete expressions in the principles of worker control, democracy, accountable leadership and open debate (Ray 1998: 67). Improved methods of organization and mobilization in reaction to the continued refusal of the apartheid state to accord meaningful political rights to black workers fuelled workplace militancy, despite the 1979–81 Wiehahn reforms that permitted African trade unions to participate in the statutory collective bargaining system (Webster 1984 in South African Review II: 80). As a result of increasing levels of state repression that led to the banning of a number of popular political organizations (most notably the United Democratic Front), the independent trade unions assumed a central role in opposition to the apartheid government by the late 1980s (Wood 2002a, 2003). Increasing linkages forged at this time with community and underground political organizations were to culminate in the Tripartite Alliance between the Congress of South African Trade Unions (COSATU), the African National Congress (ANC) and the South African Communist Party that followed on the unbanning of the latter two movements as part of the De Klerk reforms (Wood 2002a).

It must be born in mind that 1970s and 1980s union figures for South Africa under-report membership as African unions could not register until the Wiehahn reforms (only in 1981 were black migrant workers deemed employees at all). Many unions remained deeply suspicious of the statutory collective bargaining system, and deferred registration well into the 1980s. Nevertheless, in illustration of the steady growth and consolidation of unions during apartheid, despite the deterioration of the economy in 1970 and the economic recession of the 1980s, union membership expanded from 673,000 thousand in 1976 to just over 1.2 million members by 1983 (see figure 11.1), most of which took place after 1979 (Department of Manpower Annual Reports 1976–90). Membership continued to expand by a further 118,000 between 1983 and 1984 (Department of Manpower Annual Reports 1976–1990). Whilst some of this represented the belated registration of unions, it also reflected

Figure 11.1 Growth in South African union membership, 1976–90

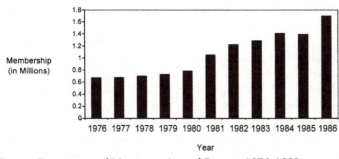

Year

Source: Department of Manpower Annual Reports 1976–1990.

the rapid growth of those unions that had opted for registration immediately after the Wiehahn reforms were promulgated.

This was followed in 1986 by a drop in membership of 15,000 people, possibly as a result of the Declaration of a State of Emergency that led to a large number of union and community activists being arrested or forced into hiding (Department of Manpower Annual Reports 1976–90). However, this was more than made up for the following year, in 1986, when membership again increased by 307 thousand members (Department of Manpower Annual Reports 1976–1990).

Collective action prior to 1994 in South Africa must be seen in the context of deep-seated senses of grievance (what Kelly refers to as blame) against the apartheid state, and, through close association, management (Klandermans in Rucht 1991: 24). However, 'sophisticated strategists for capital and the state [came] to realise that a certain form of trade union recognition could in fact facilitate a separation of 'economic' and 'political' struggle, and thus hope to weaken the role that organised workers could play in the popular struggle' (Webster 1985: 149). Nonetheless, the persistence of a racial division of labour underscored the close association with workplace injustice with that in the community; state repression against union activists and community leaders highlighted the common nature of the struggle. Union successes 'represented a combination of the increasing organisational strength of the unions and the institutionalisation of their role on the one hand, and the state's commitment to the near-total political exclusion of the Africans on the other' (Wood 2002a).

By the late 1980s, and against a backdrop of escalating state repression, COSATU 'assumed the mantle of the principal internal opponent of the apartheid regime' (Wood 2002). In doing so, the trade union movement established itself as a body that adopted a central role in opposing the Apartheid government by way of encouraging the political struggle for democracy. (Shopsteward Editors 1995a, 1995b; Wood 1998: 25). The result was a militant, community based unionism with open allegiance to the ANC (Shopsteward Editors 1995a). Its increasing power contributed to the fragmentation of the apartheid state, thereby facilitating the successful transition to South Africa's first democratic and non-racial government in 1994 (Learner.org3; Silke 1997; Van der Watt 1986: 56).

The challenges facing trade unions in South Africa's contemporary industrial relations arena

According to social movement theorists, the presence of conflict organises the actor, and links the organisation to the principle of opposition (Rucht 1991: 364). This implies that unions require a clearly identifiable opponent, linking the organization to the principle of opposition (Rucht 1991: 364). Union density has continued to increase, from 18 per cent in 1985 to 51 per cent in 1998 (see figure 11.2). Yet, apartheid was finally ended in the early 1990s; mirroring this, firms gradually phased out racial fordist production paradigms,[1] seemingly eliminating major sources of discontent. The persistence of militancy reflected persistent social and economic realities underlying contemporary South African society.

Figure 11.2: Union density in South Africa, 1985–98

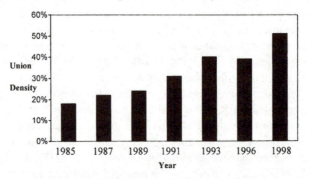

Source: Bezuidenhout, A. 2000. 'Toward Global Social Movement Unionism? Trade Union Responses to Globalisation in South Africa', Labour and Society Programme. Geneva: International Labour Organization.

Figure 11.3 Absolute poverty rates for the South African population, 2000

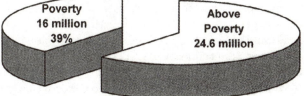

Source: Business Day. 2000a. Companies Expect to Shed Jobs, Survey Finds', 1 February, South Africa.

Social and economic concerns

Over a third of all South Africans are poor and can be considered labour market outsiders. Absolute poverty rates in South Africa are extremely high with an estimated 16 million South Africans, roughly 39 per cent of the population, living in poverty and food insecurity (see figure 11.3; Business Day 2000a: 8; Nattrass and Seekings 1996: 66).

South Africa's Labour Research Council points out that although South African government and business claim that much has been done since the 1994 elections, poverty and inequality has in fact increased since then (Labour Research Sevice (LRS) 2002: 44). The Gini index reflects that South Africa is among the countries with the highest levels of poverty in the world, with a 2002 Gini index of 59.3. This is higher than Zimbabe (Gini index of 56.8 in 2002). In the 1970s, whites accounted for 71 per cent of personal income and Africans for 20 per cent. By 1990, whites accounted for 54 per cent and Africans 33 per cent. Although these figures seem to confirm an evening out of wealth within the country, important to remember is that whites comprise 12 per cent of the population while Africans comprise 78 per cent. As long as more than 12 per cent of income goes to whites and less than 78 per cent goes to Africans, racial inequalities continue to grow. The increase in inequality, according to the South African Survey, is due largely to the growth of unemployment, which rose 59 per cent between 1995 and 2000 (LRS 2002: 44).

An estimated half of the population has insufficient food or is exposed to an unbalanced diet (Business Day 2000a: 8). Ninety-five per cent of all poor individuals are African with the poverty rates being much lower for whites than for any other racial grouping (Heintz and Jardine 1998: 18). Whilst union members represent a relatively privileged grouping of labour market insiders, they remain linked to more marginal categories of labour through the operation of extended informal networks of support. Half of all South African households depend on money from a family member who works (COSATU 1999). On average, one wage earner supports ten people (COSATU 1999). Whilst high unemployment may seem a disincentive to collective action, the operation of these networks places those within formal employment under intense pressure to improve their wages.

These facts underscore the point that, despite the ending of Apartheid, gross racial inequalities in material conditions persist. Webster makes the point that a strong culture of non-collaboration continues to characterize many South African workplaces; at least in part, this could reflect continued racial inequality and the domination of managerial ranks by whites. Furthermore, the existing gap between directors' earnings and workers' wages coupled with the fact that directors' earnings are increasing faster than workers' wages entrenches and deepens inequality in South Africa (LRS 2002: 44). This deepening inequality places a question over the 'trickle down' theory that economic growth will lead to job creation and thereby reduce poverty and inequality (LRS 2002: 44).

Although extended networks of support provide some linkage between labour market outsiders and union members, the unions have not yet succeeded in their objective of forging alliances with community based organizations that encompass such groupings (Desai 2002). This state of affairs has the potential to create divisions that could extend from the collective bargaining arena into the broader political arena. If left unattended, the poor's social discontent has the potential to formulate a new urban social movement that may react against both current union strategies and government policies.

South Africa's high unemployment rate also has the potential to jeopardize social cohesion. Unemployment in South Africa is primarily a structural problem, derived from the historical legacy of the apartheid economy (Bethlehem 1996: 57; Naledi 1998b: 20). The racial segmentation of the workforce, the systematic underdevelopment of skills and the dependence on low-wage, exploited black labour have all contributed to the current high unemployment figures (Focus on Nedlac 1997: 42, 45; Naledi

1998b: 20). Within South Africa unemployment is highly segmented, with women, youth and people living in rural areas facing a much higher probability of finding themselves unemployed (Naledi 1998b: 23). This has devastating implications for income distribution and the poverty rate (Naledi 1998b, 23).

According to statistics released by Statistics SA in April 2003, South Africa has an economically active population of 13.8 million, 30.5 per cent of whom are unemployed (figure 11.4; Department of Labour 2000a; 2000b). Between February and September 2002 unemployment rose from 29 per cent to 30.5 per cent. This increase also reflects a loss of over 350 000 jobs within the same period, thereby bringing the total number of unemployed to 4.8 million. (COSATU Weekly 2003a). The segment of the South African population worst affected by unemployment comprises the largest segment – the black population in which 43 per cent of all Africans are unemployed (figure 11.4; Department of Labour 2000a: n.p; Hawthorne 1999b: 64). In the face of such pressures, extended networks of support came under increasing strain. This may encourage individual trade union members to opt out of the networks completely, and the unions to adopt strategies and policies that more closely reflect the needs of labour market insiders. Critics of current COSATU leadership, such as Desai (2002), argue that this has already taken place.

This situation provides one of the many examples that highlight tensions between the ANC and COSATU, as the former implements neo-liberal macro-economic policies in accordance with IMF and World Bank prescriptions, which were ultimately

Figure 11.4 Incidence of unemployment within South Africa's economically active population

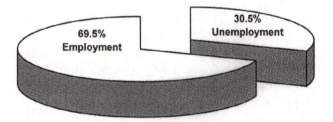

Source: Statistics SA.2003. *Incidence of Unemployment in South Africa's Economical Active Population 2003.*

embodied in the Growth, Employment and Redistribution (GEAR) policy agenda, which replaced the more interventionist Reconstruction and Development Programme (RDP) (Wood 2002a, 2002b). From an optimistic perspective, workers are, through the operation of extended family based networks of support (in the absence of an effective state social welfare system), closely linked to the most marginalized. This accounts for COSATU's continued willingness to actively promote meaningful economic redistribution, and challenge the ANC's conversion to neo-liberalism.

Nevertheless, COSATU campaigns continue to voice the concerns of the most marginalized, whilst ongoing initiatives seek (with some success) to organize hitherto unorganized categories of labour. As a 1998 survey of members shows COSATU has been successful in securing the active participation of unskilled, young and female workers in union affairs, and in impressing upon them a shared culture of democratic accountability (Wood 2002b). These workers are closely linked to members of COSATU unions via the above-mentioned informal networks of support which in turn grants a solid foundation for future organizational drives into areas where union presence is not as pervasive, such as in the informal employment sector (cf. Leibrandt et al. 2001: 73–86, Wood 2002a, 2002b).

A more pessimistic view suggests that union leaders have become politically incorporated into the new state elite; the unions remain wedded to the ANC Alliance despite its continued drift to the right. Whilst a truly independent mass based movement remains elusive, a new grassroots politics has already emerged, linked around independent civic associations, representing 'The Poors'. Strikes by rebel COSATU workers, such as the VW strike of early 2000, suggest that union leadership has lost touch with the grassroots (Wood 2002a, 2002b). These splits illustrate the constraints of COSATU's 'one-union, one-industry' policy, and the divergent interests of different constituencies (Wood 2002a). Although splinter organizations remain fairly small in their membership, if left unmanaged, they could coalesce into a new social movement opposed to all aspects of the status quo. This is most eloquently put by Desai (2002), who argues that:

> the multitude that brought down the Apartheid regime had a millennial faith in the exiled and imprisoned leadership of the ANC. The multitude that brought that ANC to power with

millions of acts of rebellion, from strikes to burning barricades to refusing to stay and pay and obey, became a (just slightly fractious) people under the ANC ... people that couldn't be bought were marginalized ... the living conditions of the poor rapidly worsened ... It was in these contradictory circumstances – with a government elected by the oppressed majority and using that power to carry out the programme of big capital – that people began defending their homes from the private security companies hired to effect the state's eviction notices ... Spaces for living that are not bonded to the dollar sign have been carved open and are jealously protected while new ways of struggling that value human needs and desires are being imagined.

Rising unemployment puts pressure on South African unions and COSATU to retain membership; quite simply, the pool of potential union members has got smaller. Widespread redundancies already have had a negative impact on union membership; simply to retain its current numerical strength, the federation is having constantly to recruit new members. This is reflected in measures undertaken by COSATU, such as the federation's insistence that job relief and poverty alleviation are to highlight the 2003 programme for the proto-corporatist Millennium Labour Council (COSATU Weekly 2003b).

The threat of job losses has led to COSATU calling periodic nationwide stayaways against redundancies and public sector reform. Although conventional wisdom holds that unemployment is a deterrent to striking; in South Africa the opposite is true; as noted earlier, the operation of extended informal networks of support placed immediate pressures on workers in employment to secure wage increases to sustain growing numbers of dependents.

Despite these pressures, there are a number of counter-tendencies, which have the effect of encouraging COSATU to remain within its alliance with the ANC. Whilst the latter remains generally committed to neo-liberalism, there have been a number of policy reduction interventions, including mass housing schemes, food shortage relief programmes and improvements in basic social services (above all, the provision of water, electricity and telephones). Indeed, government statistics show that between 1995 and 2000 the proportion of households living in formal dwellings increased from 66 per cent to 73 per cent (ANC 2002). Since 1994, the ANC-led government has built more than 1.3 million houses, investing more than R18 billion (ANC 2002). The proportion of households with access to clean water increased from 79 to 83 per cent (ANC 2002). Government figures show that since 1994, clean running water was provided to an additional 7.2 million people (ANC 2002). The proportion of households using electricity for lighting has increased from 64 per cent to 72 per cent, while around 2,700 villages have been provided with telephone connections for the first time (ANC 2002). The Statistics SA report also indicates a gradual increase over the five years in the use of public health care facilities and a gradual decrease in the use of private facilities (ANC 2002).

Worthy of note is that basic improvements in social services particularly in urban areas have directly impacted on the quality of life of COSATU members; this partially explains why COSATU has been willing to give the ANC government more room to manoeuvre than would otherwise be the case. This does leave COSATU in the tricky position of 'formulating coherent responses to the decay of still-hegemonic neo-liberalism, and of retaining political influence following the normalisation of politics' (Wood 2002: n.p). At the same time, critics have charged that union leaders have become politically incorporated into the new state elite; the unions remain wedded to the ANC Alliance despite its continued drift to the right. However, to many union activists, support for the ANC Alliance is conditional, and contingent on ongoing delivery (Wood 2002a, 2002b).

The South Africa employment market

Although the term 'globalization' is a contested one, it is generally recognized that the forces associated with this phenomenon include the rapid economic integration between countries driven by the increasing liberalization of international trade and foreign direct investment. (Hayter 1999: 58). Global processes entail a number of activities which include trade between countries in goods and services, capital flows, multinational enterprise, new production methods, networks and technology (Hayter 1999: 58). These processes, which have left neither industrialized nor semi-industrialized nations untouched, have placed considerable pressures on individual states to compete within world markets.

Isolation from global events prior to 1994 has led to an increased sense of urgency in reorganizing not only South African workplaces, but also the larger South African society, in ways that will facilitate global competitiveness. The internationalization of the labour market is not taking place without potentially adverse effects on the union movement.

The expansion of the service sector has resulted in women, a group traditionally difficult to organize, comprising an increasing sector of the labour force (Budlender 1997: 57). Atypical employment is augmenting and giving rise to an ever expanding dual labour force, in which the secondary sector remains underpaid, poorly regulated and under-organized (Department of Labour 2000a). Examples of forms of labour in the secondary labour market include employees of small enterprises, as well as those in the informal sector such as home workers, domestic workers and farm workers: in each instance, the workers are largely female, unskilled and unorganized.

South African unions have expressed cautious recognition of the dual labour market, and attempts have been made to grant coverage to these workers. Various attempts have been made to establish unions that cater for self employed women and domestic workers (e.g the Self Employed Woman's Association, established in 1994; the National Women on Farms Programme (NWFP); (Masangwane 1998: 59; Rees 1998: 52). The 1995 Labour Relations Act includes regulations designed to secure minimum wages and employment standards for all workers within South Africa's labour market. Yet, the problem proves to be one of implementing these regulations in such a way that employees in all sectors of the labour market can benefit from them (Department of Labour 2000a).

South African unions have not yet mastered a way of extending rights to these workers (September 1995). Urgency is required to master these processes given that firstly, these unprotected sectors of the labour force are becoming increasingly typical, and secondly, the informal sector has the potential to fragment the South African labour movement by organising social movements that are antagonistic to trade unions. South African unions need to search for a way to extend their agenda so as to incorporate an employment sector that generates workers who are removed from the outlook and values of the core South African labour movement (Crankshaw 1997:30).

Global pressures have resulted in the restructuring of industries in South Africa and this has brought about the demand for more highly skilled workers and the introduction of new technology. This is reflected in a shift in the composition of the labour force to an increasing proportion of white-collar workers who follow individual as opposed to collective strategies (Ray 1997: 27). Technology has evoked a militant response from workers who suffer job insecurity and fear job loss (Philips 1997: 50). To address these issues, unions have placed increased emphasis on training to upgrade the skills of the workforce so that they are compatible with the category of skill demand (Kraak 1997: 79). South African unions demand that adequate training be provided in such a way that it ensures the employment of workers displaced by restructuring (Kraak 1997: 79).

In organizing workers around such demands, the adverse effects of globalization (namely, the shift in demand to highly skilled workers, the introduction of new technology, and the restructuring of companies which leads to job shedding and retrenchment) have placed serious pressures on the union movement, fuelling centrifugal tendencies.

Still a social movement? The future role of South African trade unions

By the early 2000s, there were increasing signs of restiveness from the labour movement; COSATU has threatened to return to mass action if job losses flowing from the implementation of new technologies and work organization and from privatization continue (Business Day 2000b: 6; *Mercury* 2000: 8). For the workers, economic growth alone is no indication that poverty, mass misery, hunger and the disparities between living conditions of the rich and poor are being overcome (Sengenberger 1990).

Retrenchments have resulted in over 1 million people losing their jobs since 1990 (Business Report 2000c: 6). Since each worker supports ten people, '10 million people have suddenly become poor' since the 1990s, thanks to retrenchments and job shedding carried out on behalf of management and employers (SABC News 2002).

Managerial responses have continued to focus on the importance of securing competitiveness; critics have argued that managers have shown little willingness to make serious compromises with unions over redundancies and associated restructuring (Desai 2002). This unwillingness to compromise may have had the effect of reinforcing union solidarity, affirming the categories of 'us' (the labour force) and 'them' (management and employers) (Business Day 2000c: 11; Kelly 1997).

COSATU leaders insist that the unemployment scourge, negatively impacted upon by retrenchment and the unprecedented liquidation of companies 'has reduced workers to helpless spectators, and presents a national crisis' (Sowetan 2000: 6; Business Report 2000a: 25). In turn, it is necessary to focus renewed energy on building the workers' movement and an independent working-class agenda (Shilowa 1996). A high frequency of strikes indicates that labour leaders are active in encouraging workers to take action and defend this collective action accordingly, and that levels of solidarity remain high (Kelly 1997). Indeed, the South African strike rate is one of the highest in the world (Daily News 2000: 16).

The strength of South African unions in a seemingly adverse global climate underscores the relevance of mobilization theory; persistent inequalities, clear battle lines and recent memories of successful collective action feed into further militancy (cf. Kelly 1997). Again, 'COSATU remains a dynamic and effective federation by world standards on account of both its political role in the 1980s, and an historical emphasis on strong shop floor organisation' (Wood 2002a). The role that the unions played as a social movement during apartheid has been transferred to a present day context. Attribution of blame, social identification and effective leadership have been transferred from the context of opposition to the apartheid state, to opposition against employers and neo-liberalism today. In much the same way that South African unions were able to attract an increasing membership during the labour unfriendly apartheid era, they remain capable of mobilizing workers in adverse circumstances. COSATU unions retain a relatively strong and vibrant organisational base, enabling the South African unions to attract and retain members despite having to contend with the same range of broad pressures associated with globalization as unions in the advanced societies.

The case of Zimbabwe

A transition from independence to paternalism: the need for a social movement

The impact of Zimbabwean Unions on political policy is limited by historical weaknesses which arose prior to independence in 1980. At the time of independence there existed few industrial unions in Zimbabwe (Sachikonye 2001: 90). Although the coincidence of racial oppression and class exploitation provided explosive possibilities for worker mobilization, the marginalization of the trade union movement, by the military and rural character of the nationalist liberation movement resulted in a weak and divided labour movement that was ineffective in contributing to post-independence government policy (Adler *et al.* 1996: 86; Raftopolous and Sachikonye 2001: xix). The new ZANU-PF government created the Zimbabwe Congress of Trade Unions (ZCTU) which remained politically subordinated to the ruling party until the 1990s (Schwerdemsky 2001).

The result was a labour movement dominated by the ruling party, and unable to set its own independent agenda (Raftopolous and Sachikonye 2001: xix). Hence, unlike in South Africa, the liberation struggle in Zimbabwe bequeathed a weak union movement, for which conditions have not improved under a post-independence authoritarian state. Post-independence African workers increasingly faced African managers in their workplace and robust African nationalism in politics; racial fordism was never as deeply entrenched as was the case in South Africa (Adler *et al.* 1996: 86). This blurred class divisions and encouraged a unitarist approach to industrial relations that undermined opposition. Within this ideology, workers and managers could be portrayed as part of the same family, team and nation (86). Without an independent union presence in the factory, this system of seeming codetermination proved conducive to paternalism and subordination (86).

In the early post-independence years, conscious effort was made by the ZCTU, with the goodwill of the government, to amalgamate small, craft based unions into larger industrial unions, along the lines of 'one industry, one union' (Sachikonye 2001: 90). On the one hand, the introduction of the 1985 Labour Relations Act ('LRA', which replaced the pre-Independence Industrial Conciliation Act) precipitated a decade of union growth via the amalgamation and formal registration of unions representing specific industrial and service sectors (Sachikonye 2001: 90, 91).

On the other hand, whilst granting workers some rights, the 1985 LRA also preserved colonial era arbitration and grievance procedures (it prohibited strikes in most parts of the country) and granted the Minister of Labour extensive power to intervene in union affairs and negotiations. A battery of regulations and practices undermined free political activity and provided the basis for an authoritarian one party state (van der Walt 1998: 88). Still today ZANU-PF dominates parliament and controls the cabinet, thereby representing a formidable power in Zimbabwe (van der Walt 1998: 88). Nevertheless, economic growth and social redistribution sustained this patronage system and the state's hegemonic hold until the late 1980s (Sachikonye 2001: 102).

At the time, unions tended to emphasize bread and butter unionism and avoided direct political engagement, especially an oppositional role posing electoral alternatives to the de facto single party state (Adler *et al.* 1996: 86). This cautious attitude can in part be explained by state repression and by the lack of vision on the part of workers for a more fundamental workplace transformation (86). Workers did not see themselves as citizens capable of shaping the direction of development. They regarded this as the territory of politicians – a new state bourgeoisie whose interests were far removed from the reality of the shopfloor (86). These attitudes induced a measure of passivity: workers looked outward to politicians to produce wage increases and general development policies (Adler, Barchiesi and Gostner 1996: 86). This limited the political impact of the unions to centring around defensive struggles aimed at maintaining rather than expanding existing rights.

From the outset, most unions started out with a weak financial base (Sachikonye 2001: 96). Soon after formation, most unions charged monthly subscriptions of 10 to 20 cents per month, yet by the mid-1990s most monthly subscriptions were linked to the size of the pay packet (Sachikonye 2001: 96). Educational and skills levels of most unionists were also low at independence (Sachikonye 2001: 97). Educational programmes introduced soon afterwards concentrated on teaching workers about basic trade unionism, for example, labour regulations, leadership skills and so forth (Sachikonye 2001: 97).

Despite these enormous constraints, most unions gradually built up their membership base (Sachikonye 2001: 102). Although there is a scarcity of accurate and comprehensive data relating to union membership and industrial action in Zimbabwe, most evidence points to a doubling of union membership from around 12 per cent of the formal sector workforce at independence to an estimated 25 per cent by the end of the 1980s: a level which held firmly through the deepening economic crisis of the 1990s and the mounting scale of retrenchments (Sachikonye 2001: 102; Saunders 2001: 133).

The introduction of the government's economic policy programme of structural adjustments (ESAP) on Zimbabwean workers combined with the refusal of the government to dialogue with the unions on the modalities of preventing such impact saw a divide between the government and ZCTU as of 1989 (Schwerdemsky 2001). Although no definite link can be made, it appears that the educational programmes introduced in the early 1980s contributed to sharpened union militancy and self-consciousness in the mid-1980s (Sachikonye 2001: 98).

In 1985, the ZCTU adopted a critical attitude to the policies and restrictions on free collective bargaining and began to raise its social and political demands whilst at the same time trying to strengthen its own organization and build links with other popular sectors (van der Walt 1998: 89). New leadership within the ZCTU realised the need to acquire sufficient autonomy from the state and increased political engagement with the ruling party (Sachikonye 2001: 102; Schwerdemsky 2001).

Amendments to the LRA in 1990 permitted collective bargaining between management representatives and unions in industry based national economic councils (Adler *et al.* 1996: 86). The opening up of collective bargaining encouraged unions to organize on the shopfloor, build membership and become responsive to the needs of their affiliates (86; Sachikonye 2001: 102). These developments strengthened the union movement. As Sachikonye (2001: 94) describes it: 'It was a major advance from the era of unfettered state intervention in industrial relations through its regulatory wage determination ... the previous role occupied by a paternalist state was ceded to the bipartite partners – the union and employer organisations. '

The economic crisis of the 1990s coincided with the sharpening of union negotiation skills in areas of paid leave, housing and transport allowances, cost of living adjustment allowances and inflation (Sachikonye 2001: 94). From the mid-1990s, the bargaining process had become increasingly contentious and breakdowns in collective negotiations frequently erupted into strikes (Sachikonye 2001: 94). Strikes, in turn, have become the key means by which workers have positioned themselves in industrial relations and national political debates (Saunders 2001: 133).

During the 1990s, the mobilization of social forces initiated by the trade union movement resulted in state apprehension, particularly regarding the growth and power of ZCTU (Schwerdemsky 2001). The government, unwilling to dialogue with any group in society about political reforms, exerted oppressive measures aimed at fragmenting the ZCTU through surreptitious government schemes to form a rival national labour centre, through the Presidential Act which made stay-aways illegal and through violence: worker attempts to come out against racism and poor conditions and wages are often met by riot police who disperse the crowds, whilst the police and army arrest strikers, protect scabs and enable the victimisation of activists (Sachikonye 2001: 10; Schwerdemsky 2001).

As Mugabe neared the end of his second decade in power, Zimbabwe was marked by economic chaos, street protests and sharpening social divisions (BBC 1998). Inflation was 40 per cent, interest rates were at 50 per cent, and the price of petrol rose by 67 per cent in December 1998. (BBC 1998). A 22 per cent rise in food prices trigged riots, which when met by harsh security services and the army, forced people into submission (BBC 1998). Mass strikes staged in response to the rise in fuel prices were met by a temporary ban on such activities.

At the forefront of concerns toward the end of the 1990s was the issue of land reform: plans to confiscate farming land owned by the white minority. Most black farmers struggle to grow enough to eat on tiny plots, while the huge commercial farms growing tobacco, Zimbabwe's largest export, were largely in the hands of white Zimbabweans. What followed was rural violence: white farmers who had not already fled the country, were besieged and murdered by people waving machetes and demanding the redistribution of land to black Zimbabweans. The manner in which land reform was and continues to be carried out has led to an even wider loss of confidence in the economy and to falling food production.

In 2001, the ZCTU, made fresh demands on the government,

thereby blatantly raising issues generally seen as belonging to the political arena. One-day general strikes called by ZCTU shut the country down on two successive occasions. The first strike was marred by violence which left one person dead. Yet authorities did not meet any union demands. In turn, union demands, initially for lower prices and higher wages, extended to include a reduction in the money spent on military intervention in the Democratic Republic of Congo, a rescheduling of the national debt, freedom of information and a new constitution to be ready by 1999.

The July 2001 two-day strike called by ZCTU in reaction to a 70 per cent rise in fuel prices stopped virtually all industry and 80 per cent of commerce. After the government declared the strike illegal, thousands of police in riot gear were deployed across the capital, Harare, and other large towns, although the country remained generally peaceful. Hundreds of businesses remained closed, and traffic dropped by more than 50 per cent. The leader of the so-called war veterans, the shock troops of Mugabe's regime, issued a thinly veiled threat against supporters of the strike. 'We have already identified the companies and we know what we will do with the owners', Joseph Chinotimba said. 'If they are foreigners, let them go to Britain; they must leave our country.'

Continued state oppression created the impetus for the coalition of social forces that the ZCTU had brought together to seek alternative ways to effect political changes and eventually led in 1999 to the creation of a political party, the Movement for Democratic Change (MDC) (Schwerdemsky 2001). In the June 2000 general elections, the MDC campaign was conducted on the basis of the local structures of the trade union movement (Schwerdemsky 2001). State violence, intimidation and corrupt governmental policies proved effective in ensuring that the ruling ZANU-PF maintained a majority in the 2002 general elections (Schwerdemsky 2001).

Although unions have withstood extreme state repression thus far, the effects of state repression and the arrest of Morgan Tsvangirai, leader of the ZCTU is of concern. Whilst the Zimbabwean people have more than reasonable grounds for exasperation and rage, high levels of state repression could seriously undermine the labour movement; whilst social movement unionism often arises in response to authoritarian government, too much repression can make unionization impossible. In short, whilst Zimbabwean workers have much to be discontented about, and are likely to place much of the blame on the existing political order, the latter has proved relatively durable; if change seems difficult or impossible then resistance is likely to be low (cf. Kelly 1998).

Zimbabwe's unfavourable economic and political climate does indeed enforce the idea of the state as the primary opponent of the labour force. However, whilst Zimbabwean unions have worked hard to build up their financial base, and to increase and educate their membership, they face the determined opposition of the status quo. Nonetheless, the Zimbabwean unions have continued to attract membership despite the oppressive and labour unfriendly climate (COSATU2000; Filita 1997: 33, 38).

Challenges facing trade unions in Zimbabwe's contemporary industrial relations arena

State subordination severely limited the autonomy of the ZCTU during the first half of the 1980s (Raftopolous & Sachikonye 2001 :xvi). Nevertheless, acknowledgement of the state as opponent particularly during the 1980s, and the ongoing conflict between the state and the labour movement has continued to link the labour movement to the principle of opposition. As a result of the formation and amalgamation of industrial unions and the expansion of those unions that existed prior to independence, the growth of union membership has been remarkable and charts the trajectory of disunited and mostly ineffective unions in the 1980s to the evolution of a more coherent, focused and interventionist workers' movement at the turn of the century (Sachikonye 2001: 89; Saunders 2001: 134).

The labour movement in Zimbabwe has effectively transformed itself into a collective actor pitted against an oppressive authoritarian regime. Importantly, Zimbabwean trade unions are troubled by the same economic and social realities which exist in contemporary South African society, and attribute the blame for these circumstances to the current regime. With this in mind, effective leadership, the continued attribution of blame toward the state and ongoing social identification will continue to aggregate the Zimbabwean unions into an effective social movement.

Social and economic concerns

Since independence in 1980, Zimbabwe has made great progress in providing basic social services (health, education, water and sanitation, and emergency relief), but less progress in creating employment despite having one of the largest manufacturing sectors in sub-Saharan Africa (World Bank 1996: 2). The country is characterized by a highly unequal distribution of consumption and income, a legacy of the colonial period (World Bank 1996: 2).

Uptodate data covering Zimbabwean poverty and unemployment statistics is scarce to non-existent, and the reliability of what is available is dubious. But according to a 1996 World Bank survey, poverty in Zimbabwe is predominantly rural and is most prevalent in the country's communal farming and resettlement areas. As figure 11.5 indicates, in a survey conducted in 1992, 71 per cent of the population was rural and 29 per cent urban. When looking at the distribution of the poor in 1991, in figure 11.6, it can be seen that an overwhelming 77 per cent of the communal area population are poor. The prevalence of

Figure 11.5 Distribution of the total population, 1992

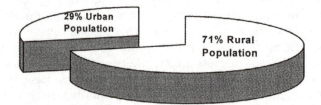

Source: World Bank. 1996. New York.

Figure 11.6 Distribution of the poor, 1991

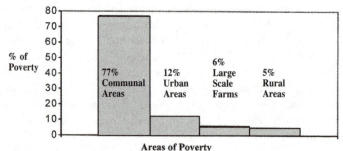

Source: World Bank. 1996. New York.

poverty was lower on large-scale commercial farms (6 per cent) and in urban areas (12 per cent). In large-scale farms, inequality is very high and poverty is concentrated among farm workers (World Bank 1996).

Poverty in Zimbabwe is mainly linked to two factors. First, the majority lack sufficient access to good land and reliable water (World Bank 1996: ii). Second, the country's manufacturing and commercial farming sectors have not historically generated sufficient employment (World Bank 1996: ii). In a study undertaken on Poverty and Human Resources in Zimbabwe in 1996, the World Bank concluded that after a period of stagnant growth, a painful adjustment period and several droughts, there now exist fairly good prospects for reducing poverty in Zimbabwe (World Bank 1996: v).

As indicated in figure 11.7, at the beginning of 1990 2.6 million or 25 per cent of Zimbabwe's 10.4 million strong population were estimated as unable to meet basic needs (World Bank 1996: 7). Of this 25 per cent, 31 per cent represents the rural population which comprises 71 per cent of the total population (World Bank 1996: 7). In 1996, 39 per cent of the population were living on less than $1 per day (World Bank 1996: 7). In 1990 the state introduced economic reform (ESAP) which coincided with one of the worst recent droughts in 1991–92. With 71 per cent of the population living in rural areas and dependent on agriculture for their livelihood, this constituted a major disaster. By 1995, the effect of AIDS was visible as many families had to assume increased support systems particularly for orphaned children. Inflation increased from 15 per cent in 1990 to 70 per cent in October 1999 in the face of

Figure 11.7 Absolute poverty rates for the Zimbabwean population, 1990

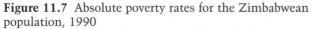
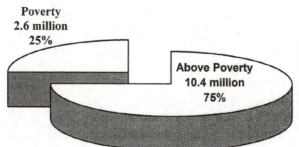

Poverty
2.6 million
25%

Above Poverty
10.4 million
75%

Source: World Bank 1996. New York.

retrenchment, the closure of businesses and rising unemployment.

Although the CSO reports that unemployment has decreased from 22 per cent in 1992 to 6 per cent in 1999 (see figure 11.8), it must be remembered that the definition of unemployment excludes students, homemakers, retired, elderly and others. Retired people are of interest here as many find themselves having to look after orphaned children. As a result, they are also actively seeking sources of income.

As in the case of South Africa, Zimbabwe's poor need to be linked to the collective organization in order to enhance social identification with the categories 'us' (the disadvantaged' and 'them' (the state). In particular, unions must forge alliances with the farming community who, although having no labour contracts to defend, have the potential to formulate a new group with an outlook removed from that of the labour movement. Sadly, baring in mind the destruction of large-scale commercial farming by the state, there are now very few farm workers left.

Furthermore, trade unions face considerable organizational constraints owing to the informal nature of this sector. The expanse of the territory to be organized requires considerably active and organized leadership as well as vast financial resources which Zimbabwean unions currently lack. Farm workers are unsure of the benefits of trade union representation and remain under the influence of the government which has maintained careful control of rural areas owing to the demographic advantage in doing so.

Arguably, organizing farm workers puts Zimbabwean unions

Figure 11.8 Zimbabwean unemployment rates, 1987–99

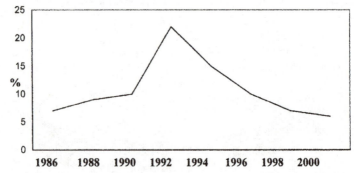

Source: Keogh E. 2002. *Unemployment in Zimbabwe: Statistics at Work.* Harare

at a crossroads. On the one hand, in assisting to forge alliances with a community with no formal working contracts, unions may be distracted from work-based issues (chapter 10). The initiative also over-stretches the already limited resources of Zimbabwean unions. Finally, by implementing an agenda that focuses on their members, they might be led to acting as a mechanism of domination (Deleuze and Guatari 1983; chapter 10). On the other hand, should farm workers remain under-represented, they could well form a social movement opposed to the principles of the union movement.

The Zimbabwean employment market

In 1990 the government introduced structural adjustment programme (ESAP) attempted to remove the incentives that favoured capital intensity and to stimulate export-led growth. The programme contained measures to liberalize markets, devalue the exchange rate and reduce fiscal deficit (World Bank 1996: ii).

From the point of view of the World Bank, adjustment programmes are typically controversial, but the programme in Zimbabwe has produced heated debate. There exist three reasons for this: First, the economy was not in a state of collapse before the programme began, which reduced the extent to which the need for reform was generally accepted. Second, the government has managed to implement only part of the programme. Its failure to reduce the fiscal deficit is inhibiting the growth that liberalization measures would otherwise be stimulating. Third, the government did not discuss the proposed reforms sufficiently with interest groups before implementation and failed to acknowledge publicly the fact that adjustment would involve inevitable costs (World Bank 1996: iv).

Two droughts in four years have compounded the economic effects of policy changes and persistent deficits. GDP grew by only 1.1 per cent per annum between 1990 and 1995. This is equivalent to an annual per capita decline of 1.4 per cent. Household incomes have declined during the 1990s. Real wages declined by 30 per cent between 1990 and 1994, accompanied by a sharp reduction in the number of available jobs (World Bank 1996: iii).

By the end of 1994 there existed 7 per cent more jobs in the formal sector that in 1990. Although an improvement, this represents an average employment growth of only 1.6 per cent per annum: far less than the 2.8 per cent per annum increase in Zimbabwe's population of working age. The growth of employment in the informal sector has been mostly low-profit, survivalist activities (World Bank 1996: iii). It can therefore be inferred that poverty prevalence has increased during the 1990s, and, according to the World Bank, in the eyes of the Zimbabwean public, adjustment is the principal cause of all the difficulties of the 1990s (World Bank 1996: iii). Of primary concern for unions is the fact that factors such as the decline in the formal sector, the economic crisis and the destruction of community farming have all resulted in fewer jobs to organize.

When examining ZANU-PF's main opponents it becomes clear that opposition encompasses not only a high degree of economic dissatisfaction but vociferous political discontent as well. Opposition to the ZANU-PF comes from three main constituencies. Firstly, disgruntled politicians from within and outside of ZANU-PF who protest against the structure of parliament and argue that polling arrangements need to be changed so as not to undermine the support for small parties. In other words, there is the desire to change the political arrangements of Zimbabwe's current authoritarian regime. Of interest is that opposition is also occurring within the party: Despite spiralling state sponsored violence, the ruling party appears less united than the monolithic apartheid state of the 1960s.

Secondly, the working class, students and peasantry represent the most effective opposition to ZAN-UPF and actively take to the streets to express dissatisfaction with political and economic conditions. Finally, workers have a strong sense of dissatisfaction and real grievances arising from a backward production process: low wages, large wage differentials, poor safety conditions, arbitrary management, limited collective influence over access to training and skills upgrading and few opportunities for meaningful collective bargaining exist (Adler et al. 1996: 83, 84). Economic structural adjustment programmes and neo-liberal policies have cost jobs and threaten the viability of industries. (83). Yet, there exists the concern that in representing part of the broader coalition, MDC is incapable of representing Zimbabwe's broad spectrum of workers (both in formal and informal employment) at the level required.

In the 1990s, unions forged vital links with other civil organizations, e.g. consumer and anti-poverty groups and later church, human rights and women's organizations which were consolidated in the period 1997–99. (Sachikonye 2001: 100). Russo and Corbin (1999) point out that alliances between community groups and unions have not always have been mutually beneficial, pointing to feelings of resentment when community groups have been used in an ad hoc way (see chapter 10). Alternatively, such links are made with the observation that the challenge of mobilizing civil society relates to the need for a counter-hegemonic ideology which would involve the construction of an alternative coherent ideology between differing groups within society (Sachikonye 2001: 100).

As predicted by mobilization theory, by uniting political and economic dissatisfaction amongst politicians, students, workers and unemployed with churches, human rights and women's organizations, Zimbabwean unions have come a long way toward forming a social group with a collective interest in changing the situation in which they find themselves for the better.

The move toward a social movement: the future role of Zimbabwean trade unions

The conviction that the current political and economic climate in Zimbabwe violates widely held beliefs and values in conjunction with the lack of government response to union demands has resulted in the Zimbabwean labour movement gaining momentum on its path of social movement unionism. The Zimbabwean labour movement has become a central medium for voicing a sense of illegitimacy and grievances against the Mugabe government and in doing so, it has placed itself as a central agency in the development of alternative political processes within the country (Raftopoulos and Sachikonye 2001: xv).

The government, in turn, has come to represent a fundamental social force in a conflict with a social movement in which the general orientation of social lives are endangered via police brutality, starvation and poverty. The sense of injustice fostered within opponent groups has prompted the formation of a social group with a collective interest in changing their current position and situation within Zimbabwe.

Within the workplace, post-independence Zimbabwean workers tended, until more recently, to develop a survivalist orientation that unfortunately encouraged close identification with the enterprise (Adler *et al*. 1996: 87). This attitude was reinforced by managerial paternalism and led workers to sacrifice to save the firm (87). However, grievances brought about by Zimbabwe's economic and political climate have reversed this situation and strengthened workers' confidence within the workplace. Massive dissatisfaction has contributed to a vision of opposition in the workplace on which a strategic perspective at the union level has been built (87). In this way, a collective sense of injustice has prompted the formation of a social group with collective interests.

In increasing their strength and anchoring their power on the shopfloor and in national politics through which workers interests can be expressed, Zimbabwean unions can maintain the ability to disrupt production. Zimbabwean unions have fostered a movement with a transformative approach, which has granted them the potential to influence politics and economic policy (Adler *et al*. 1996: 86). According to Kelly, the unions must continue to construct a sense of injustice, promote cohesion and encourage workers to take action and defend social action undertaken so as to entrench a common social interest and enhance social movement unionism.

The largest obstacle for Zimbabwean unions remains that of linking shopfloor structures to national organization and connecting the social movement with other constituencies threatened by structural adjustment (87). In particular, unions must link shared grievances and social ties of the peasantry, unemployed and farm workers with their activities so as to build up a class bound united front in such a way that social identification with the categories 'us' (Zimbabwe's disadvantaged) and 'them' (Zimbabwe's governmental regime) results. If this is achieved, union membership will continue to grow in spite of the authoritarian climate under Mugabe.

The few remaining farm workers, in particular, need to be convinced of the benefits of trade union representation and a clear alternative vision to the present political dispensation under whose influence they currently remain. Until this takes place, the possibility of formulating a cohesive social movement against the Mugabe regime remains questionable and sadly represents an obstacle for union growth.

Conclusion: the contemporary role and potential of unions in South Africa and Zimbabwe

South African unions have proved historically resilient to the effects of recession, and enjoyed an increase in membership during the recession of the 1980s. Even within the present day worldwide context of economic uncertainty, many unions continue to enjoy membership growth, although this trend is neither indefinite nor irreversible.

The role played by South African unions during the transition from confrontationism to multi-partyism vests the labour movement with a certain historical legitimacy – and capacity to mobilize – that has persisted into the post-apartheid era. Social movement unionism in South Africa is reinforced by recent memories of struggle and persistent injustice; whilst difficult strategic choices remain, the unions retain effective organizational structures, and the capacity to impact both at the workplace and at the central-political level.

Zimbabwean unions have assumed a political role that is in many respects similar to that played by the South African labour movement in the struggle against apartheid. In uniting with a range of other discontents – activitists, community groupings, students, the unemployed, churches, human rights and women's organisations, a social movement pitted against the Mugabe regime has formed. The largest obstacle to this movement remains the ability of the unions to attract support from those employed informally, and to convince the few remaining commercial farm workers of the benefits of trade union representation.

Nevertheless, in contrast to unions in advanced societies, Zimbabwe's unions have grown in strength and number, just as South African unions did in the 1980s. Given the scale of the recession and job losses, these gains may prove fragile. Yet, should this movement succeed in seeing Zimbabwe through a transition from authoritarianism to democratization, as occurred in South Africa, post-authoritarian Zimbabwe will be enriched by a dynamic union culture despite the constraints posed by prevailing economic realities, and the exingencies of future reconstruction.

The South Africa and Zimbabwe experiences underscore the need for unions to tailor their agenda to the contemporary employment market. In particular, the needs and concerns of employees in the informal economy and in other marginal categories of labour (which lie beyond the scope of any form of social, or de jure or de facto legal protection) need to be taken on board. In continuing to neglect those constituencies that comprise the informal labour market, unions are likely to be architects of their own downfall and run the risk of being replaced by other unions or new expressions of the workforce's latent collectivism (Boxhall and Haynes 1997: 570). By operating in the interests of all who work, and not merely those with permanent contracts, unions will increase their legitimacy and appeal not only to signed up members, but also to a far larger proportion of society.

Unions remain capable of coping with adversity in the external environment, if they prove willing to act both as vehicles for the defence and advances of narrow interests and as cultivators of more general interests (Hyman 1997: 326). The challenge for unions today is to represent all worker interests in a contemporary labour market characterized by divergent sectoral and occupational shifts in employment.

Note

1 That is, fordist forms of mass production combined with a racial division of labour.

References

Adler, G. Barchiesi, F. and Gostner, K. 1996. 'Unions without Comrades: Democratisation, Structural Adjustment and the Labour Movement in Zimbabwe', *South African Labour Bulletin*, 20, 3: 83–87.

African National Congress. 1977. 'Anti-Apartheid Year', South Africa.

—— 1968. 'We are at War', South Africa.

—— 2002. 'Research Highlights Extent of Poverty and Inequality', *Earning and Spending Report*, 2, 46. 15–21 November, South Africa.

ANC see African National Congress.

Baglioni, G. 1990. 'Industrial Relations in Europe in the 1980s', in Crouch, C. and Baglioni, G. (eds.), *European Industrial Relations*. London: Sage.

Baskin, J. 1996. 'Unions at the Cross Roads: Can They Make the Transition?', *South African Labour Bulletin*, 20, 1: 8–17.

Baskin, J. and Grawitsky, R. 1998. 'Year of Fire: Industrial Action in 1998', *South African Labour Bulletin*, 22, 6: 6–14.

BBC. 1998. 'Land Battle Sets Black against White', 21 November.

—— 1998. 'Political Conspiracy or Economic Mismanagement?' 1 December.

—— 1998. 'Mugabe's Long Shadow', 2 December.

—— 1998. 'Key Events in Zimbabwe's History', 3 December.

—— 2001. 'Zimbabwean Unions Step up Demands',. July.

Bean, R. 1995. *Comparative Industrial Relations: An Introduction to Cross National Perspectives* 2nd edn. London:Routledge.

Bendix, S. 1996. *Industrial Relations in the New South Africa*, 3rd edn. Cape Town: Juta.

Bethlehem, L. 1996. 'Re-Shaping Labour Market Policy in South Africa', *South African Labour Bulletin*, 20, 4: 57–65.

Bezuidenhout, A. 2000. 'Toward Global Social Movement Unionism? Trade Union Responses to Globalisation in South Africa', Labour and Society Programme. Geneva: International Labour Organization.

Boxall, P. and Haynes, P. 1997. 'Strategy and Trade Union Effectiveness in a Neo-liberal Environment', *British Journal of Industrial Relations*, 35, 4: 567–591.

Brand, S. 1986. 'Economical Survival', in Jacobs, G. (ed.), *South Africa: The Road Ahead*. Johannesburg: Jonathan Ball Publishers.

Budlender, D. 1997. 'The Woman's Budget', *South African Labour Bulletin*, 21, 1:57: 65.

Business Day. 1999a. 'Poverty Alleviation Vital for Regional Security – Selebi', 30 July. South Africa.

—— 1999e. 'SA Can Play a Global Role', 20 October. South Africa.

—— 2000a. 'Companies Expect to Shed Jobs, Survey Finds', 1 February, South Africa.

—— 2000b. 'Cosatu Strike will Cost R3.2 BN, says Sacob', 9 May, South Africa.

—— 2000c. 'Easter Recess', 3 May, South Africa.

Business Report. 2000a. 'Cosatu Sticks to Plans for May Strike'. *Business Day*. 25 February. South Africa.

—— 2000b. 'Erwin Punts Job Creation, Bemoans Casualisation', *Business Day*, 17 May, South Africa.

—— 2000c. 'Cosatu Gives May Deadline to Business'. *Business Day*, 13 April, South Africa.

Callinicos, A. 1992. *Between Apartheid and Capitalism: Conversations with South African Socialists*. London: Bookmarks.

Cardoso, C. 1996. 'Global Solidarity – Speech by Cardoso, International Secretary of CNM, Brazilian Metalworkers Union, to Numsa's fifth National Congress, 25–29 September', *South African Labour Bulletin*, 20,6: 84–86.

Collins, D. 1997. 'Globalisation: New Terrain, New Struggles', *South African Labour Bulletin*, 21, 5: 84–88.

Congress of South African Trade Unions. 1999. 'Cosatu's Job Crisis Campaign', South Africa.

—— 2000. 'What is Cosatu?', South Africa.

—— 2003a. 'More Vigorous Efforts to Create Employment Needed', *Cosatu Weekly*, 7–10 April.

—— 2003b 'Job Creation, Poverty Relief highlights LMC Programme this Year', *Cosatu Weekly*, 7–10 April.

COSATU see Congress of South African Trade Unions.

Cosatu Weekly. 2003a, 'More Vigorous Efforts to Create Employment Needed', 07–10 April.

—— 2003b. 'Job Creation, Poverty Relief Highlights LMC Programme this Year', 07–10 April.

Crankshaw, O. 1997. 'Shifting Sands: Labour Market Trends and Unionisation', *South African Labour Bulletin*, 21, 1: 28–36.

Crouch, C. 1982. *The Politics of Industrial Relations*, 2nd edn. London:Fontana.

Daily News. 2000. 'Protests May Worsen Job Crisis', 1 February, South Africa.

Delunze, G. and Guattari, F. 1983. 'Rhizome', in G. Deluze and F. Guattari (eds), *On The Line*. New York: Semiotext(e).

Department of Labour n.d. *A Framework for Labour Market Policy*. Pretoria.

—— n.d. *The Social Plan*. Pretoria.

—— 1996. *Working Together: An Accord for Employment and Growth*. Pretoria.

—— 2000a. *Labour Market Demographics*. Pretoria.

—— 2000b. *Staff Profiles*. Pretoria.

Department of Manpower. 1976–1990. *Annual Reports*. Pretoria.

Desai, A. 2002. *We Are the Poors: Community Struggles in Post-Apartheid South Africa*. New York: Monthly Review Press.

Dibben, P. n.d. 'Social Movement Unionism'.

Economic Strategy. 1996. 'Globalisation and the Neo-Liberal Agenda'. *The Shopsteward*, 5.2.

Farnham, D. and Pimlott, J. 1995. *Understanding Industrial Relations*, 5th edn), London: Cassell.

Filita, T. 1997. 'Cosatu: Marching Forward', *South African Labour Bulletin*, 21, 1: 36–42.

Focus on Nedlac. 1997. 'Nedlac's Social Plan', *South African Labour Bulletin*, 21, 6: 42–48.

Frege, C. 1999. 'The Challenges to Trade Unions in Europe: Innovation or Adaptation/Trade Unionism in Recession', *Work and Occupations*, 26,2: 279–281.

Grawitsky, R. and Boshiela, S. 2002. 'Labour Solidarity: The Case of Zimbabwe', *South African Labour Bulletin*, 26: 1: 10–11.

Hawthorne, P. 1997. 'Apologies of Apartheid', *Time Magazine*, 27 October.

—— 1999b. 'Across the Board, Black is Beautiful', *Time Magazine*, 24 May.

—— 1999d. 'Unity's Rainbow', *Time Magazine*, 24 May.

Hayson, N. and Webster, E. 1984. 'A Review of the 1980s', South African Research Service (SARS) (eds.), *South African Review II*. Johannesburg: Ravan Press.

Hayter, S. 1999. 'The Social Impact of Globalisation', *South African Labour Bulletin*, 23, 2: 58–63.

Heintz, J. and Jardine, C. 1998. 'Poverty and Economics: An Alternative Framework', *South African Labour Bulletin*, 22, 4: 17–23.

Hindson, D. 1984. 'Union Density', South African Research Service (SARS) (eds.), *South African Review II*. Johannesburg:Ravan Press.

Hirschsohn, P. 1998. 'From Grassroots Democracy to National Mobilisation: Cosatu as a Model of Social Movement Unionism', *Economic and Industrial Democracy*, 19, 4: 34.

Horn, P. 1997. 'The Informal Sector: West African Women Organise', *South African Labour Bulletin*, 21, 1: 90–94.

Hyman, R. 1989. *The Political Economy of Industrial Relations*. London:Macmillan.

—— 1994a. *Strikes*, 4th edn. London: Macmillan Press.

—— 1994b. 'Trade Unions and the Disaggregation of the Working Class', in Regini, M. (ed.), *The Future of Labour Movements*. London: Sage.

—— 1997. 'The Future of Employee Representation', *British Journal of Industrial Relations*, 35, 3: 309–336.

—— 1999. *An Emerging Agenda for Trade Unions?* Geneva: International Labour Organization.

ILO *see* International Labour Organization.

International Labour Organization. 1964. *Declaration Concerning the Policy of Apartheid of the Republic of South Africa and I.L.O. Programme for the Elimination of Apartheid in Labour Matters in the Republic of South Africa*. Geneva.

—— 2000. *Decent Work and Poverty Reduction in the Global Economy*. Geneva.

Jackson, M. 1992. *An Introduction to Industrial Relations*. London: Routledge.

Jarvis, D. 1998. 'The Organiser's Dilemma: Union Responses to Industrial Restructuring', *South African Labour Bulletin*, 22, 5: 27–34.

Jose, A. V. 1999. 'The Future of the Labour Movement: Some Observations on Developing Countries', *Labour and Society Programme: International Labour Organisation*. Geneva.

Keenen, J. 1984. 'The Recession and Its Effects on the African Working Class'. *South African Research Service: South African Review II*. Johannesburg: Jonathan Ball Publishers.

Kelly, J. 1997a. 'The Future of Trade Unionism: Injustice, Identity and Attribution', *Employee Relations*, 19, 5

—— 1997b. 'Industrial Relations: Looking to the Future', *British Journal of Industrial Relations*, 35, 3: 393–398.

—— 1998. *Rethinking Industrial Relations: Mobilisation, Collectivism and Long Waves*. London: Routledge.

Keogh, E. 2002. *Unemployment in Zimbabwe: Statistics at Work*. Harare.

Klaaste, A. and Siluma, M. 2000a. 'Rural Poverty Must be Tackled Now', *The Sowetan*. 11 February.

—— 2000b. 'Long Road Ahead for Democracy in South Africa', *The Sowetan*, 3 May.

Klandermans, B. 1991. 'New Social Movements and Resource Mobilisation: The European and American Approach Revisited', in Rucht, D. (ed.), *Research on Social Movements: The State of the Art in Western Europe and the USA*. Frankfurt am Main: Campus Verlag.

Kraak, A. 1997. 'The Right Balance: The Green Paper on Skills Development', *South African Labour Bulletin*, 21, 4: 74–82.

Labour Research Service 2002. *Annual Report 2002*. Salt River: Labour Research Service.

Lambert, R. 1998. 'Globalisation: Can Unions Resist?', *South African Labour Bulletin*, 22, 6: 72–78.

Learner.org1. n.d. 'Apartheid: the Beginning'. United States of America.

—— n.d. 'Human Rights for Everyone'. United States of America.

—— n.d. 'Resistance'. United States of America.

Leibrandt, M. *et al.* 2001. "Household Inequality and the Labour Market in South Africa', *Contemporary Economic Policy*, 19, 1: 73–86.

Lewis, J. 1984. *Industrialization and Trade Union Organization in South Africa 1924–1955*. Cambridge: Cambridge University Press.

Lipton, M. 1986. *Capitalism and Apartheid: South Africa, 1910–1986*. Aldershot: Wildwood House

Luckhardt, K. and Wall, B. 1981. *Working for Freedom: Black Trade Union Development in South Africa Throughout the 1970s*. Geneva: World Council of Churches.

Macridis, R. 1978. *Modern Political Systems: Europe*, 4th edn. New Jersey: Prentice Hall.

Maree, J. (ed.). 1987. *The Independent Trade Unions, 1974–1984*. Johannesburg: Ravan.

Marie, B. 1996. 'Giants, Teddy Bears, Butterflies and Bees: Ideas for Union Organisation', *South African Labour Bulletin*, 20, 1: 17–21.

Masangwane, S. 1998. 'Self-Employed Women', *South African Labour Bulletin*, 20, 2: 10–18.

Moll, E. 1990. 'From Booster to Brake? Apartheid and Economic Growth in Comparative Perspective', in Nattrass, N. annd Ardington, E. (eds.), *The Political Economy of South Africa*. Cape Town: Oxford University Press.

Moody, K. 1999. *Workers in a Lean World: Unions in the Internationl Economy*. London: Verso.

Munck, R. 1999. 'Labour Dilemmas and Labour Futures', in Waterman, P. (ed.), *Labour Worldwide in the Era of Globalisation: Alternative Union Models in the New World Order*. London: Macmillan

Naledi. 1998a. 'A Framework for Job Creation', *South African Labour Bulletin*, 22, 2: 18–19.

—— 1998b. 'Vision and Strategies', *South African Labour Bulletin*, 22,2: 19–25.

Nattrass, J. 1981. *The South African Economy: Its Growth and Change*. Cape Town: Oxford University Press.

Nattrass, N. and Seekings, J. 1996. 'The Challenge Ahead: Unemployment and Inequality for South Africa', *South African Labour Bulletin*, 20, 1: 66–73.

Nel, E. 1997. 'The Local Economy: No Hope for the Poor?', *South African*

Labour Bulletin, 21, 4: 10–13.

Parkin, F. 1971. *Class Inequality and Political Order*. London: MacGibbon & Kee.

Parsons, T. and Smelser, N. J. 1964. *Economy and Society: a Study in the Integration of Economic and Social Theory*. London: Routledge

Philips, G. 1997. 'Technological Change: Friend or Foe?', *South African Labour Bulletin*, 21, 6: 50–55.

Raftopolous, B. and Sachikonye, L. 2001. 'The Labour Movement: Politics and Economic Crisis', in Raftopolous B. and Sachikonye, L. (eds.), *Striking Back: The Labour Movement and the Post-Colonial State in Zimbabwe 1980–2000*. Harare: Weaver Press

Ray, M. 1997. 'Flexible Production: Shaping up to Globalisation', *South African Labour Bulletin*, 21, 5: 24–30.

—— 1998a. 'The Poor Paying the Price', *South African Labour Bulletin*, 22, 2: 6–14.

—— 1998b. 'Skills Development', *South African Labour Bulletin*, 22, 1: 39–41.

—— 1998c. 'Will Bigger be Better?', *South Africa Labour Bulletin*, 22, 3: 65–71.

Redman, C, 1999, 'In Gear for Growth', *Time Magazine*, 24 May.

Rees, R. 1998. 'We Want a Union: Finding a Home for Domestic Workers', *South African Labour Bulletin*, 22, 6: 52–58.

Rosenthal, T. 1996a. 'Restructuring: the Other Side of the Rainbow', *South African Labour Bulletin*, 20, 6: 51–57.

—— 1996b. 'Worker Control and Democracy', *South African Labour Bulletin*, 20, 3: 59–61.

Rucht, D. 1991. *Research on Social Movements: The State of the Art in Western Europe and the USA*. Frankfurt am Main: Campus Verlag.

Russo, J. and Corbin, B. 1999. 'The Concerted Voice of Labor and the Suburbanization of Capital: the Fragmentation of the Community Labour Council', in B. Nissen (ed.), *Which Direction Organized Labor?* Detroit: Wayne State University Press.

Sachikonye, L. M. 2001. 'The Institutional Development of Unions in Zimbabwe', Raftopolous, B. and Sachikonye, L. M. (eds.), *Striking Back: The Labour Movement and the Post-Colonial State in Zimbabwe 1980–2000*. Harare:Weaver Press.

Salamon, M. 1998. *Industrial Relations Theory and Practice*, 3rd edn. New York: Prentice Hall.

Saunders, 2001. 'Striking Ahead: Industrial Action and the Labour Movement Development in Zimbabwe', in Raftopolous, B. and Sachikonye, L. M. (eds.), *Striking Back: the Labour Movement and the Post-Colonial State in Zimbabwe 1980–2000*. Harare: Weaver Press.

Schwerdemsky, S. 2001. *International Dialogue on Trade Unions' Experiences of Political Engagement: a Comparison between Nigeria, Brazil, South Africa and Zimbabwe*. Nigeria: Friedrich-Ebert-Stiftung.

—— 2003. Personal Interview. Bonn: Germany.

Sengenberger, W. 1987. 'Vocational Worker Training, Labour Market Structure and Industrial Relations in West Germany', in Bergmann, J. and Tokunaga, S. (eds.), *Economic and Social Aspects of Industrial*

Relations: A Comparison between the German and Japanese Systems. Frankfurt: Campus.

—— 1990. 'The Role of Labour Standards in Industrial Restructuring: Participation, Protection and Promotion', *New Industrial Organisation Programme: International Labour Organisation.* Geneva.

September, C. 1995. 'Homeworkers: a New Trend in the World of Work', *The Shopsteward*, 4, 4.

Shilowa, S. 1996. 'How We Won a Historic New Constitution', *The Shopsteward*, 5, 2.

Shopsteward Editors. 1995a. 'Changing with the Times', *The Shopsteward*, 4, 6.

—— 1995b. 'Chronology'. *The Shopsteward*, 4, 6.

Silke, D. 1997. 'What Shaped South Africa?', *The South African Political Information Exchange*. Cape Town.

Sitas, A. 1998. 'The New Poor', *South African Labour Bulletin*, 22, 5: 16–23.

South African Broadcasting Corporation. (SABC) News Reports, Pretoria.

Sowetan. 2000. 'Government Action Needed to Create Jobs', 2 March, South Africa.

Statistics SA. 2003. *Incidence of Unemployment in South Africa's Economically Active Population 2003.*

Streeck, W. 1986. 'The Uncertainties of Management in the Management of Uncertainty: Employers, Labour Relations and Industrial Adjustment in the 1980s'. Berlin: Internationales Institut für Management und Verwaltung.

Svanemyr, V. 1998. *The Apartheid System*. Olso.

The Mercury. 2000. 'Call off the Big Strike', 2 May. South Africa.

Tilly, C. 1978. *From Mobilisation to Revolution*. New York: McGraw Hill.

Touraine, A. 1991. 'Commentary on Dieter Rucht's Critique', in Rucht, D. (ed.), *Research on Social Movements: The State of the Art in Western Europe and the USA*. Frankfurt am Main: Campus Verlag.

Trade Policy. 1996/97. 'Face to Face with Globalisation', *The Shopsteward*, 5, 6.

Tyson, H. 1996. *South Africa at a Glance*. Editors Inc.: Johannesburg.

Valentine, S. F. N. V. 1986. *The Image of African National Liberation Movements in the West German and Soviet Press 1972–1982*. Bonn: Rheinischen Friedrich-Wilhelms-Universität.

Valenzuela, J. S. 1994. 'Labour Movements and Political Systems: Some Variations', in Regini, M. (ed.), *The Future of Labour Movements*. London: Sage.

Van Der Walt, L. 1988. 'This Is Class Warfare', *South African Labour Bulletin*, 22, 5: 85–90.

Van Der Watt, I. 1986. 'South Africa: The Road Ahead', in Jacobs, G. (ed.), *South Africa: the Road Ahead*. Johannesburg: Jonothan Ball Publishers.

Visser, J. 1994. 'The Strength of Union Movements in Advanced Capitalist Democracies', in Regini, M. (ed.), *The Future of Labour Movements*. London: Sage.

Von Holdt, K. 1996. 'David or Goliath? The Future of the Unions', *South African Labour Bulletin*, 20, 4: 36–44.

Waddington, J. and Whitston, C. 1997. ' Why Do People Join Trade Union in a Period of Membership Decline?', *British Journal of Industrial Relations*, 35, 4: 515–546.

Waterman, P. 1998. *Globalisation, Social Movements and The New Internationalisms*. London: Mansell.

Webster, E. 1984. 'New Force on the Shop Floor', *South African Research Service: South African Review II*. Johannesburg: Ravan Press.

—— 1985. *Cast in a Racial Mould: Labour Process and Trade Unionism in the Foundries*. Johannesburg: Ravan Press.

Wood, G. 1998. *Trade Union Recognition: Cornerstone of the New South African Employment Relations*. Johannesburg: International Thompson Publishing.

—— 1999. 'Trade Union Governance and Democracy: A Comparative Analysis', Cranfield University. Centre for European Human Resources Management. Working Document.

—— 2002a. 'The Politics of Trade Unions in Transition: The Case of the Congress of South Africa Trade Unions', *Contemporary Politics*, 8, 2: 129–144.

—— 2002b. 'Organising Unionism and the Possibilities for Reconstituting a Social Movement Role', *Labour Studies Journal*, 26, 4: 29–50.

—— 2003. 'Solidarity, Representivity and Accountability: The Origins, State and Implications of Shopfloor Democracy with the Congress of South African Trade Unions', *Journal of Industrial Relations*, 45, 3: 326–343.

World Bank, 1996. Understanding Poverty and Human Resources in Zimbabwe: Changes in the 1990s and Directions for the Future. New York.

World Economic Forum. 2000. *1999 Global Competitiveness Report*. New York.

World News. 2001. 'Zimbabwe Unions Confront Mugabe', 5 July .

12

Social movement unionism

PAULINE DIBBEN

This chapter explores the role of unions as social movements. To do this, it begins by examining, firstly, the role of social movements more generally, before putting forward three propositions about what social movement unionism should entail. The first of these propositions is that social movement unionism should imply 'grassroots democracy', or at least close linkages with grassroots concerns either through formal democratic structures or more informal mechanisms to promote accountability. The second is that it should involve reaching out to other groups and seeking broad aims of social justice, and the third is that it implies a fight against the harmful aspects of international business and the current 'neo-liberal hegemony'. This fight does not imply 'fighting for its own sake', but protecting the weakest in society from the worst excesses of capitalism. The chapter then turns briefly to examine criticisms of trade unions as social movements, before turning to the experiences of Brazil, South Africa and the United States, as examples of the capacity of unions to recapture a 'social movement' role.

Social movements

A simple conception of the distinguishing features of social movements compared to other organizations is that, firstly, they mobilize their constituency for collective action, and, secondly, they do so with a political goal (Kriesi 1996). However a more careful analysis of social movements can include an examination of the extent to which they should be class based, their opportunities, and the threats to their sustained growth.

This first section therefore starts by examining what is meant by a 'social movement' (Tourraine 1981). In doing this, it examines the extent to which this means a class-based protest, or alternatively whether a social movement can be seen as the opposition to more general forces (Castells 1983; Della Porta 1999: 403). Moreover, some argue that collective identity is easier to establish around issues such as ethnicity and religion rather than social class (Tarrow 1998).

More generally, opportunities for social movements include what have been described as 'political opportunities' (Della Porta 1999; Tarrow 1998). At the same time, the chapter points to two particular issues that can threaten social movements. The first is the tendency for freeriding (Castells 1983; Kelly 1998; Olson 1965; Tarrow 1998), and the second is institutionalization (Tarrow 1998). For labour unions, the latter is particularly problematic (Tourraine 1981).

Social movements as class-based organizations

Should social movements be class based, as advanced in the Marxian tradition? Tourraine argues that conflict 'glues' social life together, and that social movements are the 'principal agents of history' (1981: 9). A social movement thus represents the embodiment of a particular form of struggle. Such struggles have four characteristics: backing by a committed population; an identifiable organizational base; a clear adversary that constitutes a distinct social grouping; and a focus on a general social problem rather than specific grievances. Castells (1983), on the other hand, places emphasis on the need for social movements to be progressive, but suggests that the particular adversaries of social movements are the bourgeoisie or capital, technocracy, and the state. Where the social movement seeks an improvement in collective, at the expense of private, consumption, the adversary may be the bourgeoisie or capital. To be successful, social movements must seek to challenge each of these adversaries, which in the current situation could be supranational (Della Porta and Diani 1999) and include the mass media, techno-scientific elites, educational and social welfare institutions and the entrepreneurial classes that control consumption.

Alternatively, some argue that class-based conflicts are not the only issues, that some conflicts actually transcend class lines. This suggests that targets of social movement protest are not always, or even usually, the traditional class enemies of capitalism. Della Porta (1999) refers to those since the 1970s that have focused on the environment, those that focus on women's rights and those that argue for human rights and peace, while Waterman (1993) adds ecology to this list.[1] Della Porta (1999) argues that trans-national social movements have expanded in reaction to these supranational forces (see also Munck 2002). Tarrow (1998) similarly suggests that social movements have a broader role. He emphasizes the need for a collective identity, and explains how social movements have been characterized as expressions of extremism, violence and deprivation. However he defines social movements as: 'collective challenges based on common purposes and social solidarities, in sustained interaction with elites, opponents and authorities' (Tarrow 1998: 4).

Because of this need for a deep-rooted feeling of solidarity and identity, Tarrow suggests that nationalism and ethnicity or religion have been more reliable bases for movement organization than 'social class'. However, some suggest that the emphasis of 'new social movements' on political rather than economic issues is misplaced. For example, the disability movement's rejection of purely economistic values while instead emphasizing a rights discourse, local–global affiliations and post-materialist horizons has meant that disabled workers still struggle with the effects of lean production (Roulstone 2002). In other words, political issues and economic issues cannot be separated.

Opportunities and threats

Social movements face both opportunities and threats. For instance, the internet has aided in establishing collective identity, mobilizing and networking (Aelst 2002; see also Munck 2002).[2] This presents a means of fighting the powerful 'network society' which excludes those who are not part of it, with 'informational guerrilla tactics' (Castells 2001),[3] although there are arguably limitations in terms of the extent to which use of the internet can build new social ties (Diani 1999). Political opportunities regularly emerge as a result of endemic divisions within elites (Kriesi 1996; Tarrow 1998). Della Porta (1998) suggests that more broadly, political opportunities include the degree of openness of the political system, electoral instability, the availability of potential allies, and tolerance for protest among the elite. Similarly, Tarrow suggests that: 'people engage in contentious politics when patterns of political opportunities and constraints change and then, by strategically employing a repertoire of collective action, create new opportunities, which are used by others in widening cycles of contention' (Tarrow 1998: 19).

If 'political opportunities' emerge, a relatively small social movement can seize the chance to grow in power; this in turn can open up further opportunities for other small-scale movements. Together, these movements have the potential to coalesce into a very much larger and more powerful force. However, there is a tension between the benefits of spontaneous social movements and the advantage of focusing on the same direction (Castells 1983). If political opportunities arise, then social movements have a chance to grow. If not, they may be relegated into playing a waiting game. This can lead to a state-focused analysis (Kohli and Shue 1994; Migdal 1994), a process that ignores the fact that social movements can be active in structuring their own political opportunities, for example in using the media (McAdam 1996b; McAdam et al. 1996). It also ignores the interaction between social movements and political forces and individual perceptions and motivations (Della Porta 1995). In addition, another criticism of the notion of 'political opportunities' is that it can be used as a 'sponge' to include every aspect of the social movement environment (Gamson and Meyer 1996: 275).

If they grow, social movements face potentially insurmountable challenges. These include the power of counter-movements (Voss 1996), freeriding (Tarrow 1998) and pressures towards co-optation and institutionalization (Tourraine 1981; Castells 1983). The larger the group, the more people will freeride on the efforts of individuals whose interest in the collective good is strong enough to pursue it. Some argue that rational people are guided by individual interest and will avoid taking action where they see that others can take it for them. However, this assumes that people only act out of individual self-interest and not in the group interest (Kelly,1998).

A second threat comes from social movement institutionalization, an issue that is arguably of particular importance in relation to labour conflicts (Tourraine 1981). Castells (1983) suggests that social movements should be both organizationally and ideologically autonomous of any political party. Kriesi (1996) argues that social movements can gain public recognition, access to decision-making procedures, and public subsidies by co-operating with authorities, but integration can limit the mobilization capacity of the social movement organization, and alienate parts of it.

Unions as social movements

There has been some discussion around what 'social movement unionism' should include. There is considerable variation in the cases of Brazil and South Africa on the one hand, and the more industrialized countries on the other (Von Holdt 2002). This section begins by examining three main propositions of 'social movement unionism', then assesses criticisms of a social movement role, before turning to the experiences of three countries to shed light on the feasibility of 'social movement unionism'.

'Social movement unionism': three propositions

In moving toward social movement unionism, one could argue that unions are returning to their roots (Waterman 1993) particularly in terms of grassroots democracy. Indeed, Von Holdt (2002) suggests that this is one of the key issues for social movement unionism. Alternatively, some claim that social movement unionism means reaching out to other groups, including non-traditional constituencies (Moody 1997). Yet others argue that unions form the most effective opposition to international business and the neo-liberal hegemony; their changing role reflects the challenges posed by 'globalization'.

Social movement unionism: going back to their roots, and grassroots democracy

In industrialized countries, the new strategies of organizing arguably recapture unions' roots (cf. Kelly 1997; Hyman 1997). Waterman (1993), for example, explains how Melucci's four characteristics of new social movements can be seen in the nineteenth-century labour movement: the centrality of information; new forms of organization that are informal, democratic and self-empowering; the integration of the latent and visible, the personal and the political; and a 'planetary' consciousness, or new kind of global awareness. Hyman (1997) suggests that the history of trade unionism can be traced back more than two centuries, and that there are five themes that characterize their formation and consolidation. Firstly, there are collective interests and a collective identity, and, secondly, a tension between fighting for all the oppressed and underprivileged, and defending the interests of the working class. Thirdly, unions assume a 'normal' employment relationship, one characterized by full-time and permanent contracts with employers, and where withdrawal of labour has a large impact. Fourthly, unions represent the general working class, and are embedded in national, not international societies. In the present times, unions have been threatened by globalization with cross-national competition, internationalized production chains, and financial deregulation.

It was mentioned above that Melucci's features of earlier trade unions included democracy, informality and self-empowerment, all of which characterize the new social movement unions. Moody (1997) similarly suggests that social movement unionism implies a grassroots democracy, the take up of class-wide issues even if the union's struggles originate in their own interests, and the reaching out to other social groups. Internal democracy is thus a source of power and broader social vision. More pragmatically, union members are unlikely to invest time and energy if they do not participate in decision making. Others, including both Waterman (1993) and Von Holdt (2002) similarly emphasize internal democracy, although it has been argued that this is an area that has been either neglected or misinterpreted in the case of South Africa (Von Holdt 2002).

Unions reaching out to other social groups, and fighting on broad issues

It can be argued that social movement unionism should not merely focus on those within the workplace but be extended to include broader issues. Social movements can be subdivided into three types: labour, collective consumption and political and human rights (Walton 1998). The labour movement has traditionally focused on the sphere of income and employment, whereas collective consumption is based around the availability of collective or public goods such as land, housing, transportation, education, health, water and electrification. Political and human rights action is around non-material issues of justice, representation, security, freedom from repression and democratization. However, these three spheres of action are often conflated. For example, austerity policies threaten both employment and subsidized food and transportation. Walton (1998) argues that collective action by the urban poor is more likely to take place around collective consumption issues and in non-institutional forms such as squatting and rent strikes than through institutional channels provided by trade unions, partly since the urban poor are often unemployed. This arguably means that trade unions should take a more proactive, and wider role. Moody (1997) for example, points to the key role of unions as the mobilizing force. Unions are a 'training ground' for workers, preparing them for greater struggles, but in major confrontation, it is typically the unions that pull other organizations into the struggle: 'Social-movement unionism implies an active strategic orientation that uses the strongest of society's oppressed and exploited, generally organized workers, to mobilize those who are less able to sustain mobilization: the poor, the unemployed, the casualized workers, the neighbourhood organizations' (Moody 1997: 276).

He adds that even where they only have a small membership, the unions' ability to mobilize broader sections of the class is greater than any other type of working-class or social movement organization. For example, unions can campaign for a general social safety net, strengthening the working class as a whole. Mass action in France in recent years, such as the strike of public sector workers in 1995 against the 'Plan Juppe', and more recent action against public sector pension reform, brought together workers from a wide range of occupations. Another example of unions extending their activities was the CGT (General Confederation of Workers) participation in demonstrations in support of women's rights. Again, in 1996 the French government sent police to remove African immigrants from a church in Paris in order to expel them from France. The CGT and other unions supported a protest march called by immigrants' rights groups.

Fighting international business and the 'neo-liberal hegemony'

Others have argued that the primary emphasis of new social movement unionism should not be on developing participation and outreach, but on challenging the negative consequences of 'globalization'. The 'new' adversaries of social movement unionism are arguably international business and the 'neo-liberal hegemony', and social movement unionism is the key to 'raising the forces necessary to confront international business and its allies' (Moody 1997: 4). Moody refers in particular to transnational corporations (TNCs), whose number and reach increased dramatically in the decades after the Second World War. These grew not only through building new facilities but also through taking over other companies, and bringing in new 'lean production' methods. This meant intensified work and longer working hours for most workers and shorter hours and lower wages for others. It also included outsourcing, just-in-time parts delivery that ties suppliers to assemblers, and a continuous search for marginal improvements in costs, both by adjusting the labour process and through management by stress. Unions are in the right place to be making an impact.

More generally, social movement unions can be seen in opposition to neo-liberal policies of deregulation, privatization, and cutbacks in government social programmes: '[Neoliberalism is] a mixture of neoclassical economic fundamentalism, market regulation in place of state guidance, economic redistribution in favour of capital, moral authoritarianism with an idealised family at its centre, international free-trade principles [sometimes inconsistently applied], and a thorough intolerance of trade unionism' (Moody 1997: 120).

The creation of a social movement role both challenges the

market dictatorship as well as the abuse of power by corporations and private investors. Such a movement is centred on the
premise that workers are not simple commodities but rather
people with rights that take precedence over market dictates
(Moberg 1999). Furthermore, some argue that the working-class
struggle should focus on governments that help to reinforce
exploitation, and are, in effect, 'the main conduit between
capital and the global market' (Wood 1997).

In common with business, unions also need to take an international response: 'If capitalism is now more global than ever,
so too is the working class it begets. Indeed, class formation is
now in many ways an international, if not really global, process'
(Moody 1997: 308). Waterman (1993) suggests that social
movement unionism should act globally, and refers to a 'new
global solidarity' that includes both labour and other activists,
with unions building relationships with other social movements
(1993: 255). He also suggests that it is not so much about focusing on one primary contradiction such as class, nationality or
gender, but recognizing the common democratic thread within
the many movements. Munck (2000) similarly refers to the need
for internationalism, but does not dismiss economic issues: 'all
labour struggles have an international context and ramifications
... economic globalization has created a common ground for
labour struggles in different countries' (Munck 2000: 385).
Munck suggests that the global neo-liberal consensus has been
broken, and that there can be a new reciprocal solidarity, with
workers uniting to challenge the social power of capital. For
example, full-time and permanent workers can build solidarity
with their less advantaged counterparts elsewhere to prevent
capital flight, thus accommodating both parties' interests.
However, he also draws attention to the current inequalities
between, for example the north and south, and the important
debates that have taken place around global social inequality,
protectionism and sustainability (Munck 2002).[4]

Lambert and Webster (2001) argue that unions are becoming
international, and moving toward 'global social movement
unionism'. They explain the development of SIGTUR, a
network of southern independent democratic trade unions from
Asia, Australia, New Zealand, Africa and Latin America that
arose as a result of neoliberal globalization, and point to successful organizing in Australia. In 1995, the government in Western
Australia threatened to undermine freedom of association

through legal amendments. Unions responded by organizing a protest march, and in South Africa and India there were boycott threats. The legislation was withdrawn.

Partnership with international business and support for neo-liberal policies

It could be argued that, to influence decision making, partnerships with business are necessary. The mass following brought about by social movement unionism could mean a heavier hand in negotiation and therefore more influence with both employers and the state. Waterman (1993: 267), for example, has suggested that social movement unions should be 'intimately articulated' with political forces (including states) with similar orientations. At the same time, there are those who recognize the tensions between working in partnership with employers and retaining a viable social movement role. Von Holdt (2002: 298), for example, suggests that in South Africa, trade unionism is characterized by a constant tension between movement and the institutionalization and routinization of industrial relations. More generally, it could be argued that 'partnership' can be problematic since it is difficult to work in partnership while simultaneously taking a critical approach to business: 'Union leaders who are ideologically and institutionally committed to the "competitiveness" of TNCs based in their own country through some kind of partnership program are unlikely to have the vision to overcome these very real stumbling blocks' (Moody 1997: 280). For example COSATU has been pressured to embrace lean production or European-style 'social partnership' (Moody 1997). More generally, Hyman (1997) suggests that 'partnership' with the employer and the state leads to agreements on wage restraint, the restrictions of labour law, and cutbacks in state provision. Such partnerships are not easily reconciled with social movement unionism, wherein unions campaign for rights, engage in 'contentious politics' and contest oppression, inequality and discrimination, often co-operating with other social movements. Indeed, how can a union work in partnership, and at the same time fight against injustice? To resolve this dilemma, some argue that unions should be 'economistic with a strong pragmatic focus' (Lambert and Webster

2001: 358). But is this selling out to those in power at the expense of the weakest? These issues are more fully dealt with in chapters 13 and 14.

Criticisms of social movement unionism

Various criticisms of social movement unionism have been advanced, some of which emphasize the outcomes for broader society. These include radical postmodern arguments that suggest that in taking a social movement role, unions may not be helping broader society, and other arguments that similarly criticize the behaviour of trade unions such as the 'aristocracy of labour thesis' (Moody 1997). Another critique, that will not be examined further here, could be described as 'conservative/ neo-liberal' , wherein the argument would be that trade unions, and social movement unions in particular, cause market imperfections and a loss of national competitiveness.[5]

A further area of criticism is that playing a social movement unionism role may distract unions from work-based issues. In addition, it could be argued that, in any case, the new forms of work and increasing diversity in effect prohibit or act against social movement unionism.

Social movement unionism: beneficial for society?

From a postmodern perspective, the underlying idea is that any large broadly based organization will become a tool of domination. In the case of unions, then, their narrow agenda that focuses primarily on their members, can lead to them acting as a mechanism of domination (Deleuze and Guattari 1988). Russo and Corbin (1999) come from a different perspective but acknowledge that alliances between community groups and unions have not always been mutually beneficial, pointing to feelings of resentment when community groups have been used in an ad hoc way. However they suggest that there is the potential for both community groups and unions to win, and suggest that institutional structures can provide needed resources, communication networks, legitimacy and support to grassroots groups. They point in particular to relationships between unions and the Catholic church and suggest that the revitalization of organized labour is contingent upon issues such as building a grassroots social justice movement, criticizing the individualistic culture, and reducing inequality (Russo and Corbin 1999).

Another criticism of social movement unionism that focuses on union behaviour is the 'aristocracy of labour' thesis. This, according to Moody (1997: 297), relies on the idea that unions are bureaucratic organizations with a narrow economic agenda, focused primarily on their members. Their interests are therefore different from those without jobs. A solution is for unions to shape their bargaining demands in a way that has a positive impact on other working-class people. Moody (1997) points, for example, to the Canadian Auto Workers (CAW) in 1996. Their collective-bargaining programme at the major auto companies was intended to increase employment in the industry and the country as a whole. The programme, included shorter working time, restrictions on outsourcing and guaranteed job levels for the communities in which each plant was located.

Social movement unionism: beneficial for unions?

Working with other groups can detract from the defence of working-class issues, and it can also lead to trying to do too much with limited resources. In other words, unions can neglect existing members' day-to-day workplace concerns, and non-worker interests in the community could hijack the movement. Indeed, expressing such fears, in the 1980s one of the two constituent strands of COSATU in South Africa preferred a 'workerist' agenda (Wood 2002b).[6] More pragmatically, Munck (2000) although acknowledging that unions should be both social and international, does caution that there is a need to understand their limited resources, since expansion in one area of struggle can be at the expense of another.

Another criticism is based on the need to appreciate local contexts and historical backgrounds. Ost (2002) suggests that in Eastern Europe, and particularly Poland, social movement unionism has led to a decline in trade unions. In the Polish, post-communism, context, it is only those unions that have

adopted what the author variously describes as business unionism, economic unionism, or servicing that have made a
comeback since social movement unionism has been interpreted
as having an alternative agenda, and not one that is intended to
help the workers, whereas business unionism is seen as progressive in promoting capital and the market economy rather than
communism. However, the government that Solidarity
supported went on to introduce 'harsh economic measures' and
did not defend labour's interests (Ost 2002: 42), a situation that
can have been something to do with their links with thirty right-
wing parties.

Social movement unionism: feasible in this age of diversity?

It could be argued that a social movement role is not feasible in
the context of an increasingly fragmented working class, and
rising instrumentalism. A variation of this argument can be
described as a 'post-fordist/new Labour' critique, which suggests
that new times have emerged with new technologies and more
flexible work forms, and that old working-class grievances have
become irrelevant.

It has been suggested that the new diversity of the working
class, or working-class fragmentation, leads to divisions, and
that these divisions have been largely ignored or played down
(Von Holdt 2002). However Moody (1997) suggests that most of
these arguments begin with the idea that there was a 'golden
age', when the working class was 'organically' united. He
suggests that outside, possibly, the Scandinavian countries there
never was a 'golden age', but does accept that diversity in the
workforce has grown (1997).

Two dimensions of the 'new diversity' are, firstly, gender
and, secondly, ethnicity and multiculturalism. Moody (1997)
suggests that women have grown as a proportion of the workforce, but particularly in part-time and other 'atypical' work and
on lower wages than men. However, workers of both genders are
similar in their relationship to capital. Colgan and Ledwith
(1996) point to how there can be the deliberate separatism of
women within the trade union movement to develop a feminist
consciousness and empower women. However, they suggest that
the majority would not want to vote for any measures that can

divide their union. In respect of ethnicity and multiculturalism there has traditionally been occupational segregation. This has persisted, but it is now more commonly seen in relation to immigrant workers from the third world, concentrated in low-wage manufacturing, electronics assembly, garment sweatshops, meat-packing and some construction jobs. These jobs are often casual and spatially segregated, but the following examples show how they can be organized (Moody 1997).

The first example is of agricultural workers in Texas belonging to the Union of Border Agricultural Workers (UTAF). This union recruited in both the US and Mexico and most of its members were undocumented immigrant workers since the growers preferred these to documented workers. Employer hostility and anti-immigrant sentiment among the local population made it difficult for UTAF, but working with organizations in both Mexico and the US, the UTAF won 'amnesty' status for all workers in the Texas and New Mexico chilli fields under the ICRA which meant that they became legally documented immigrant workers. However, there was no legal framework for union recognition for farm workers, so they carried out two strikes in 1990 and 1992 and waged a massive political campaign to change their legal status. The other example was the 1991 'Justice for Janitors' campaign in Los Angeles, involving mass actions and community support. It brought thousands of Mexican and central American immigrants into the Service Employees International Union (SEIU) Local 399. They organized a significant majority of the contractor firms in the relevant local labour market, recruiting through links with the immigrant communities. This contributed to rebuilding labour–community alliances, projecting labour activism and relevance in the media, defending the rights of immigrant workers, and highlighting the growing disparity between the working poor and the wealthy (Eisenscher 1999).

Social movement unionism: the experiences of three countries

This third section examines briefly the specific cases of Brazil, South Africa, and the United States. Particular attention is paid to the latter two of these three countries, due to the ongoing

debate about the extent to which unions exhibit a 'social movement' role.

South Africa and Brazil

The militarized state in late apartheid South Africa, military
rule in Brazil, and the crushing of the struggle in both countries
drew the unions and their activist supporters into political
conflict. In each country, Moody (1997) suggests that there was
a clear emphasis by the trade unions on class. This was at least
partly due to the marginalized position of the workers who often
lived in townships or favelas, which contrasted with the modern
factories where they worked. It should be noted, however, that
this class distinction can be too simplistic for South Africa,
where divisions have tended to be, and arguably still are largely
on racial grounds, referred to as 'racial fordism' (Munck 2002),
albeit that class has tended to correspond with race (Von Holdt
2002; see also Adler and Webster 1995).

   In both countries, however, neighbourhood groups, which
were often led by women not working in industry, arose to
demand basic infrastructure and basic freedoms of association
(e.g. many of the constituent organizations of the United
Democratic Front in South Africa) or even the right to occupy
the land (in the case of Brazil). The unions had close organic
linkages with these groupings, through the operation of
extended networks of support. In addition, in South Africa
COSATU (Congress of South African Trade Unions) shed the
reservations of its precursor organizations, and formalized
alliances with the neighbourhood Civics and other community-
based organizations in the UDF stable, while in Brazil, the
CUT (Central Unica dos Trabalhadores) sought alliances
with the residents' associations, of which there were over eight
thousand.

   Nevertheless, there were differences between the two countries. In Brazil, most of the opposition to the government was
either business-based, discredited or repressed. There was no
'hegemonic' group on the left to turn to, so the unions formed a
party of their own, the Workers' Party (Partido dos
Trabalhadores – PT). Their leader, Luis Inaciao da Silva, known
as Lula, a migrant from the impoverished, rural northeast, was

its head (Sader 2002). PT was 'aggressively socialist', and sought to represent and include all the working class based organizations. Lula had been the runner-up in presidential elections since 1989, before becoming president in 2002.[7] In South Africa, on the other hand, the African National Congress, a cross-class party, survived repression and remained the most prestigious opposition organization or party in the country, despite being outlawed for almost thirty years. Although there was, and still is, a debate within COSATU about setting up an independent workers' party similar to that in Brazil, the new unions chose to accept the leadership of the ANC in the anti-apartheid movement while maintaining the independence of the unions (Southall and Wood 1999). In the 1990s this became the formal alliance between COSATU, the ANC and the South African Communist Party (SACP).

COSATU has been criticized for not developing international links with other unions. This was recognized by COSATU in its Third National Congress in 1989 (Waterman 1998). The federation also has been hurt by a brain drain of union leaders to political positions at both national and local level (Von Holdt 2002). However, COSATU experienced steady growth from 1985 to 1993 with a peak of 3,272,768 members, although membership totals have now begun to tail off. More importantly, the neo-liberal direction of the new ANC government has created serious problems for COSATU and the other unions (see, for example, Moody 1997; Wood 2002b). The ANC gradually implemented neo-liberal macro-economic policies in accordance with IMF and World Bank prescriptions, largely within the Growth, Employment and Redistribution (GEAR) policy agenda. This replaced the more interventionist Reconstruction and Development Programme. COSATU did actively oppose the government in 1996 when it called a strike against restrictions on union rights. However, in general their support for the ANC has continued, including the run-up to the 1999 elections, when COSATU gave its backing to the ANC's manifesto (Wood 2002b).

Criticisms of COSATU's acceptance of the government's neo-liberal policies have continued, and one could suggest that this has resulted in a neglect of the real needs of local communities, referred to by Desai (2002) as 'the poors'. The 'compromise' that has arguably had to take place in South Africa during the transition period (Adler and Webster 1995) raises

questions as to whether social movement unionism can be
sustained in the 'post-struggle era'.

United States

In the United States, and indeed in many Western European
countries, a large proportion of the labour movement played a
social movement role in their early years (Wood 2002a). More
recently, it has been suggested that business unionism has been
prevalent. Business unionism, in focusing narrowly on job-
related matters and showing indifference to broader issues, acted
as a boundary between organized labour and community groups
(Russo and Corbin 1999). In addition, unions were reluctant to
organize among women, ethnic minorities, and those who
worked without wages, since they wished to be seen as offering
exclusive services to members (DeMartino 1999). Indeed, it has
been argued that 'consumerism had bought off the working
class' (Wood 1998).

More recently, the unions' ability to provide services has been
undermined by globalization, economic restructuring and neo-
liberal policies. Unions have faced an identity crisis and
therefore it has been argued that they need to move toward
social movement unionism (DeMartino 1999). Unions now
have to take account of people's broader concerns, as consumers,
citizens and family members, and take into account issues such
as immigration and environmentalism. Robinson (2001)
suggests that this is already happening, although through a
gradual process. He suggests that unions in the United States
are moving toward social movement unionism, but can be
currently characterized as social unions. They are becoming
more inclusive, but are still not generally critical of existing
economic and political institutions.

In contrast to this perception, Moody's description of the
AFL-CIO in 1998, with its emphasis on partnerships with business is more in tune with business unionism than with social
movement unionism (Moody 1998). However, at a more local
level, it has been suggested that the AFL-CIO Milwaukee
County Labor Council (CLC) has moved toward a social movement union role through encouraging activism in broader
societal issues, thus echoing the type of role apparent in the late
nineteenth century, where calls were made for shorter working
hours, free education for children and sanitary reform (Eimer
1999). In addition, the 'Justice for Janitors' experience showed

how a social movement union role was possible in America. Although the campaign was targeted at an immigrant low-wage workforce, scattered in many locations, and in many cases vulnerable to deportation, the campaign nevertheless worked.

Conclusion

The first section of this chapter examined more generally the role of social movements. In doing this, questions were raised about the extent to which social movements should be class-oriented, or whether they should instead take into account the broader issues that people are now concerned with. These broader issues include feminism, human rights, peace and ecology. Although social movements need to take into account broader issues, it is suggested that there are dangers for the weakest in society if economic issues are forgotten. Secondly, there was discussion of two fields of opportunity for social movements. One of these has generated much discussion, and revolves around the need for 'political opportunities' in order for social movements to emerge or grow. However, waiting for political opportunities puts social movements in a reactive role. The whole concept of social movements implies the idea of struggle. As such, social movements should not merely be reactive, but should also take a proactive role, at least insofar as speaking out for social justice is concerned. Another opportunity mentioned was the increased use of new means of communication, and most notably the internet. Although this can enable academic discussion, and links between leaders of some social movements, it should not be forgotten that in many places of the world access to the internet is still only available to those who are more powerful and possess adequate resources. Those who are on a low income, or indeed no income, and live in rural areas are often excluded. Threats to social movements were also examined. These threats can include counter-movements, but a more subtle threat comes from institutionalization. It is not the aim of this author to suggest that working in partnership is necessarily wrong. However, social movements have to beware of the compromises that they could be forced to make if incorporated into decision-making processes.

The second part of this chapter examined what is meant by

social movement unionism, and also pointed toward criticisms of this role. Three propositions were put forward for social movement unionism: firstly, that unions should aim for grass-roots democracy, secondly, that they should reach out to broader society and speak out for social justice, and, thirdly, that even if taking on 'partnership roles' they should not forget to fight the worst excesses of capitalism and neo-liberal policies. One could argue that, in fulfilling these three criteria, unions are neglecting their core activities, and that they are perhaps using other movements to justify their cause. However, in addressing the first, people do not solely exist in a work situation. In addressing the second, unions can be a powerful force for good, and if taking democracy seriously should address these broader needs and neither neglect nor smother them.

The chapter finally turned to briefly examine the experiences of Brazil, South Africa and the United States. Certain similarities exist between Brazil and South Africa, not least due to the history of repression of trade unions under an authoritarian regime, but, nevertheless, differences do still exist. One straightforward, but arguably key, difference is that in the first case, the leader of the trade union became the president, whereas in the second the trade union was one part of a tripartite alliance. However, in each case, the powerful needs of business are set against the clamouring of the poor for social justice. In South Africa in particular, in seeking long-term solutions the government does not appear to be addressing the needs of the weakest, but if this continues many of the weakest may not survive beyond the short term. Caution needs to be taken that the core objectives of the trade unions for social justice are not forgotten, and that social movement unionism does not become pure business unionism in these countries. The experience in the United States is somewhat different to the other countries examined. Here, according to some commentators, business unionism has apparently been replaced by social unionism, on the way to becoming social movement unionism. However, this optimism should probably be balanced by some scepticism. Unless unions take a more proactive role, questions remain around whether social movement unionism will be 'allowed' to emerge in a country where 'neo-liberal policies' reign supreme.

Notes

1 See also various publications by Lipietz.

2 An interesting alternative is texting, illustrated, for example, by pupils' anti war protests in the UK.

3 However, this has not gone unnoted by the 'establishment', and right wing hackers have persistently targeted progressive websites.

4 One suggestion, here, is the benchmarking of international labour standards on key issues such as wages and conditions, health and safety, and an equality agenda.

5 See chapter by Ian Roper in this volume.

6 See also Kelly (1998) who discusses injustice in the workplace as a key motivator for mobilization.

7 Although there have issues around the reassurances that he has made toward the business community. Time will tell if this will undermine his original championing of labour.

References

Adler, G. and Webster, E. 1995. 'Challenging Transition Theory: The Labour Movement, Radical Reform and the Transition to Democracy in South Africa', Paper presented at Albert Einstein Initiative Workshop, University of Witwatersrand, Johannesburg.

Aelst, P. 2002. 'New Media, New Movements? The Role of the Internet in Shaping the "Anti-Globalization" Movement', Paper presented at the Annual Convention of the American Political Science Association (APSA), Boston, August 2002.

Castells, M. 1983. The City and the Grassroots. London: Edward Arnold.

——2001. 'Identity and Change in the Network Society', Conversation with Manual Castells by Harry Kreisler, Institute of International Studies, UC Berkley.

Colgan, F. and Ledwith, S. 1996. 'Sisters Organizing: Women and their Trade Unions', in Ledwith, S. and Colgan, F. (eds.), Women in Organizations: Challenging Gender Politics. London: Macmillan.

Deleuze, G. and Guattari, F. 1988. A Thousand Plateaus. Minneapolis: University of Minnesota Press.

Della Porta, D. 1995. Social Movements, Political Violence and the State: An Analysis of Italy and Germany. Cambridge: Cambridge University Press.

Della Porta , D. and Diani, M. 1999. Social Movements: an Introduction. Oxford: Blackwell.

DeMartino, G. 1999. 'The Future of the US Labour Movement in an Era of Global Economic Integration', in Munck, R. and Waterman, P. (eds.), Labour Worldwide in the Era of Globalization: Alternative Union Models in the New World Order. London: Macmillan.

Desai, A. 2002. We Are the Poors: Community Struggles in Post-Apartheid South Africa. New York: Monthly Review Press.

Diani, M. 1999. 'Social Movement Networks Virtual and Real', Paper presented at 'A New Politics?' Conference, University of Birmingham, 16–17 September.

Eimer, S. 1999. 'From "Business Unionism" to "Social Movement Unionism": the Case of the AFL-CIO Milwaukee County Labor Council', *Labor Studies Journal*, 23: 63–81.

Eisenscher, M. 1999. 'Critical Juncture: Unionism at the Crossroads', in Nissen, B. (ed.), *Which Direction for Organized Labor? Essays on Organizing, Outreach, and Internal Transformations*. Detroit: Wayne State University Press.

Gamson, W. and Meyer, D. 1996. 'Framing Political Opportunity', in McAdam, D., McCarthy, J. and Zald, M. (eds.), *Comparative Perspectives on Social Movements: Political Opportunities, Mobilizing Structures and Cultural Framings*. Cambridge: Cambridge University Press.

Hagopian, F. 1994. 'Traditional Politics Against State Transformation in Brazil', Migdal, J., Kohli, A. and Shue, V. (eds.), *State Power and Social Forces: Domination and Transformation in the 3rd World*. Cambridge: Cambridge University Press.

Hyman, R. 1997. 'Trade Unions and Interest Representation in the Context of Globalization', *Transfer*, 3, 515–533.

Kelly, J. 1997. 'The Future of Trade Unionism: Injustice, Identity and Attribution', *Employment Relations* 19, 5: 1–19.

——1998. *Rethinking Industrial Relations: Mobilization, Collectivism and Long Waves*. London: Routledge.

Kohli, A. and Shue, V. 1994. 'State Power and Social Forces: On Political Contention and Accommodation in the Third World', in Migdal, J., Kohli, A., and Shue, V. (eds.), *State Power and Social Forces: Domination and Transformation in the 3rd World*. Cambridge: Cambridge University Press.

Kriesi, H. 1996. 'The Organisational Structure of New Social Movements in a Political Context', in McAdam, D., McCarthy, J. and Zald, M. (eds.), *Comparative Perspectives on Social Movements: Political Opportunities, Mobilizing Structures and Cultural Framings*. Cambridge: Cambridge University Press.

Lambert, R. and Webster, E. 2001. 'Southern Unionism and the New Labour Internationalism', in Waterman, P. and Wills, J. (eds.), *Place, Space and the New Labour Internationalisms*. Oxford: Blackwell.

McAdam, D. 1996a. 'Conceptual Origins, Current Problems, Future Directions', in McAdam, D., McCarthy, J. and Zald, M. (eds.), *Comparative Perspectives on Social Movements: Political Opportunities, Mobilizing Structures and Cultural Framings*. Cambridge: Cambridge University Press.

——1996b. 'The Framing Function of Movement Tactics: Strategic Dramaturgy in the American Civil Rights Movement', in McAdam, D., McCarthy, J. and Zald, M. (eds.), *Comparative Perspectives on Social Movements: Political Opportunities, Mobilizing Structures and Cultural Framings*. Cambridge: Cambridge University Press.

McAdam, D., McCarthy, J. and Zald, M. 1996. 'Introduction: Opportunities, Mobilizing Structures, and Framing Processes – Toward a Synthetic, Comparative Perspective on Social Movements', in McAdam, D., McCarthy, J. and Zald, M. (eds.), *Comparative Perspectives on Social*

Movements: Political Opportunities, Mobilizing Structures and Cultural Framings. Cambridge: Cambridge University Press.

Martinello, F. 1996. 'Correlates of Certification Application Success in British Columbia, Saskatchewan, and Manitoba', *Relations Industrielles*, 5, 3: 544–562.

Migdal, J. 1994. 'The State in Society: An Approach to Struggles for Domination', in Migdal, J., Kohli, A., and Shue, V. (eds.), *State Power and Social Forces: Domination and Transformation in the 3rd World*. Cambridge: Cambridge University Press.

Moberg, D. 1999. 'The US Labor Movement faces the Twenty-First Century', in Nissen, B. (ed.) *Which Direction for Organized Labor? Essays on Organizing, Outreach, and Internal Transformations*. Detroit: Wayne State University Press.

Moody, K. 1997. *Workers in a Lean World*. London: Verso.

——1998. 'Up Against the Polyester Ceiling: The "New" AFL-CIO Organizes Itself!', *New Politics*, 6, 4: www. wpunj.edu/~newpol/issue24/moody24.htm.

Munck, R. 2000. 'Labour and Globalization: Results and Prospects: Review Article', *Work, Employment and Society*, 14, 2: 385–393.

——2002. *Globalization and Labour: The New 'Great Transformation'*. London: Zed Books.

Olson, M. 1971. *The Logic of Collective Action*. Cambridge, Mass.: Harvard University Press.

Ost, D. 2002. 'The Weakness of Strong Social Movements: Models of Unionism in the East European Context', *European Journal of Industrial Relations*, 8, 1: 33–51.

Robinson, I. 2001. 'Neoliberal Restructuring and US Unions: Toward Social Movement Unionism?', *Critical Sociology*, 26, 1: 109–138.

Roulstone, A. 2002. 'Disabling Pasts, Enabling Futures? How Does the Changing Nature of Capitalism Impact on the Disabled Worker and Jobseeker?', *Disability and Society*, 17, 6: 627–642.

Russo, J. and Corbin, B. 1999. 'Work, Organized Labor, and the Catholic Church: Boundaries and Opportunities for Community/Labor Coalitions', in Nissen, B. (ed.), *Which Direction for Organized Labor? Essays on Organizing, Outreach, and Internal Transformations*. Detroit: Wayne State University Press.

Sader, E. 2002. 'Beyond Civil Society', *New Left Review*, 17: 87–99.

Southall, R. and Wood, G. 1999. 'The Congress of South African Trade Unions, the ANC and the Election: Whither the Alliance?', *Transformation*, 38: 68–83.

Tarrow, S. 1998. *Power in Movement: Social Movements and Contentious Politics*, 2nd edn. Cambridge: Cambridge University Press.

Tourraine, A. 1981. *The Voice and the Eye: An Analysis of Social Movements*. Cambridge: Cambridge University Press.

Von Holdt, K. 2002. 'Social Movement Unionism: The Case of South Africa', *Work, Employment and Society*, 16, 2: 283–304.

Voss, K. 1996. 'The Collapse of a Social Movement: The Interplay of Mobilizing Structures, Framing, and the Political Opportunities in the Knights of Labor', in McAdam, D., McCarthy, J. and Zald, M. (eds.), *Comparative Perspectives on Social Movements: Political Opportunities,*

Mobilizing Structures and Cultural Framings. Cambridge: Cambridge University Press.

Walton, J. 1998. 'Urban Conflict and Social Movements in Poor Countries: Theory and Evidence of Collective Action', *International Journal of Urban and Regional Research*, 22, 3: 460–481.

Waterman, P. 1993. 'Social-Movement Unionism: A New Union Model for a New World Order?', *Review*, 16, 3: 245–278.

——1998. *Globalization, Social Movements and the New Internationalisms*. London: Mansell.

——1999. 'The New Social Unionism: A New Union Model for a New World Order', Munck, R. and Waterman, P. (eds.), *Labour Worldwide in the Era of Globalization: Alternative Union Models in the New World Order*. London: Macmillan.

——2001. 'Trade Union Internationalism in the Age of Seattle', Waterman, P. and Wills, J. (eds.), *Place, Space and the New Labour Internationalisms*. Blackwell: Oxford

Wood, E. M. 1997. 'Labour, the State and Class Struggle', *Monthly Review*, 49, 3 (www.monthlyreview.org/797wood).

——1998. 'Capitalist Change and Generational Shifts'. *Monthly Review*, 50, 5 (www.monthlyreview.org/797wood).

Wood, G. 2002a. 'Organizing Unionism and the Possibilities for Reconstituting a Social Movement Role', *Labor Studies Journal*, 26, 4: 29–50.

——2002b. 'The Politics of Trade Unions in Transition: The Case of the Congress of South African Trade Unions', *Contemporary Politics*, 8, 2: 129–143.

13

Trade unions and political parties

PHIL JAMES

Trade union activities, internationally, extend beyond a narrow focus on the protection and furtherance of worker interests through the processes of 'industrial' representation and collective bargaining to encompass a range of political activities and associated objectives. However, the nature and extent of these activities vary, both between individual unions and national union movements.

In pursuing their wider political objectives, unions can utilize a number of different methods. These include lobbying political decision makers and parties, conducting publicity campaigns, organizing demonstrations and campaigning with other interest groups, such as community organizations and issue based pressure groups. They also include supporting the election of sympathetic parties, mobilizing union members in local and national government elections, collaborating with governments, notably via corporatist structures, and creating organizational linkages with political parties. Some of these methods have already been explored in other chapters. Here, attention is restricted to the last of those mentioned: namely, the linkages that exist between national union movements and political parties.[1]

The chapter proceeds as follows. Initially, attention is paid to the differences that can exist between unions and union movements with regard to the relative emphasis that they place on political activities in general. Following this, the various types of relationships that can exist between unions and political parties are explored and examples drawn from a number of developed economies, notably Germany, Great Britain, Sweden and the United States of America, are used to illustrate them. The factors that have acted to shape the particular configurations of party–union relationships are then discussed. Finally, some observations are made concerning the current and future trajectory of such relationships.

Unions objectives and the role of politics

It has long been acknowledged that unions can utilize a number of different methods to protect and advance the interests of their member, and potential members. Writing at the end of the nineteenth century, for example, the British Fabian socialists, Sidney and Beatrice Webb, argued that trade unions could pursue the 'common rule', or the establishment of minimum employment standards, through three methods: mutual insurance, in the form of 'friendly benefits; collective bargaining; and legal enactment (Webb and Webb 1897). In doing so, the Webbs, therefore, effectively acknowledged that the establishment of 'common' rules could encompass political, as well as labour market based activity.

In fact, internationally, union activities have invariably embodied a political dimension. At the same time, national labour movements, as well as individual unions within them, have varied historically in the importance attached to such activity. This has been usefully illustrated by Hyman's analysis of trade unionism in Britain, Germany and Italy (Hyman 2001).

In his analysis, Hyman distinguishes three ideal types of European trade unionism. First, a 'Business Unionism' orientation in which unions conceive of their role as being essentially concerned with labour market functions. Secondly, a conceptualization of unions as vehicles for 'raising workers' status in society more generally and hence advancing social justice' (Hyman 2001: 1–2). Thirdly, a view of unions as 'schools of war' in the struggle between labour and capital.

Hyman goes on to argue that union ideologies and identities are not normally exclusively based on one of these three different possible foci of trade union activity: class, society and labour market. Rather, in practice, all three 'typically have some purchase' and in 'most cases' unions have tended to incline towards 'an often contradictory admixture' of two of them (Hyman 2001: 4). Indeed, in his subsequent examination of trade unionism in Britain, Germany and Italy, he argues that the

British trade union movement has tended to operate between the market and class dimensions, the German between the society and the market ones, and the Italian between the class and society orientations.

Hyman's analytical framework therefore, for present purposes, serves to draw out an essential point, namely that union movements, and unions, have varied historically, and continue to vary considerably in terms of the nature and scale of their political objectives and activities. By implication, therefore, it also highlights the fact that similar variations exist with regard to the importance unions attach to links with political parties – a point that will be further highlighted below.

Unions and political parties: the potential relationships

In contrast to the extensive comparative literature that has developed in respect of the relationship between union movements and the state in advanced Western economies, there is a relative paucity of comparative analysis of the linkages that exist between unions and political parties. This is particularly so if attention is focused on studies that have sought to go beyond detailed description and establish broader analytical classifications or typologies of such linkages. For example, McIlroy (1998) has noted that while studies of union–party links are rare enough, typologies of such links are even rarer. Nevertheless, typologies of this sort have been developed by a number of authors.

Valenzuela (1992), for example, in a study of historical developments in the Americas and Western Europe has distinguished between five types 'of insertion of labour movements into national political processes', three of which are identified as existing under democratic regimes.[2] First, *social democratic*, in which the unions link up to form basically one national organization that, in turn, connects itself with a single, relatively strong party. Secondly, *contestatory*, in which the labour movement is divided into different ideological and partisan tendencies with a segment linked to the Communist party. Thirdly, *pressure group*, in which the unions link themselves with a pre-existing party, or fragments of it.

Rather differently, Ebbinghaus (1995), on the basis of an

examination of current and historical party–union links in twelve Western European counties, has distinguished five different ideal-typical clusters of union–party linkages that between them incorporate three fundamentally different scenarios: single party affiliation, multiple party affiliations, and the downplaying of union–party links. For example, in the *labourist* cluster, unions, such as in Britain and Ireland, are constitutionally linked to a 'labour' party that was created by the union movement, while in the *solidaristic*, as in Sweden, there is again a single focus of party affiliation, but in this case the party concerned played an active role in the development of the union movement. In contrast, in *segmented pluralism*, different party political affiliations exist, as in countries such as Belgium and the Netherlands, that embrace other 'socialist' and 'christian democractic' traditions and in *polarized pluralism*, which is seen to exist in France and Italy, a similar, but less institutionalized situation exists. Finally, in *'unity' unionism* party–union links are de-emphasized, as in Austria and Germany, in order to avoid previously existing disjunctions between 'socialist' and 'christian' ideological groupings within the union movement.

As can be seen from the above, the typologies of Valenzuela and Ebbinghaus aim to be all embracing in the sense that they seek to encompass union links with political parties, regardless of the ideological orientation of the latter. A further typology developed by Kitschelt (1994) is rather different in that it is concerned with identifying variations in 'union-socialist' bonding. In it, such bonding is seen to occur through three different 'structural configurations': those where labour unions dominate political elites; those where close communication exists between the major union confederation and the socialist party; and those where formal ties have been cut.

Kitschelt's model, although less wide-ranging, does have an important virtue in that it more explicitly acknowledges that union influence over political parties may arise not only through 'constitutional' linkages, but in other ways, such as through 'good communications'. This feature of his work has more recently been taken forward by Ludlam *et al.* (2002) in a typology based on two dimensions: organizational integration; and policy-making influence. On the basis of these two dimensions, which are seen as interrelated, the authors go on to distinguish the following four types of union–party links:

- an *external lobbying* type, where unions and parties have no formal organizational integration, and unions have little or no policy-making influence;

- an *internal lobbying* type, where there is little or no formal organizational integration, but unions are routinely consulted in party policy making;
- a *union–party bonding* type, where the special status of unions results in their occupying important governmental positions within the party, but not in domination of party policy making; and
- a *union-dominance* type, where unions both occupy important governmental positions within the party, and are able to dominate party policy making.

Unions and political parties: some examples

Two important points therefore emerge from the differing typologies detailed above. The first is that the relationships that exist between unions and political parties differ in terms of the extent to which they encompass formal 'organizational', or 'constitutional', linkages. The second is that, in the absence of linkages of this type, unions may still influence party political decision making in other ways. In what follows, each of these points is briefly illustrated by examples.

Constitutional linkages

The systems of union–party relationships that exist in Britain, Canada, New Zealand and Ireland provide, at least within developed Western economies, perhaps the best examples of situations where formal links exist between a large part of the union movement and political parties and these links focus on a single, 'labour', party. For present purposes, a brief description of those that exist in Britain will suffice to illustrate the type of arrangements that exist in these counties.

Under the rules of the British Labour Party, trade unions, as well as individuals and a number of other bodies, are allowed to affiliate to the party.[3] This they do through the payment of an annual affiliation fee, which is calculated on the basis of a payment per member affiliated. In 1994, 26 unions so affiliated over four million members and via these affiliation fees contributed 54 per cent of the party's income (McIlroy 1998).

Such a high level of funding in itself obviously provides a potential source of decision-making influence. However, such an indirect influence is bolstered by a number of other mechanisms. Thus, affiliated unions are able to send one delegate for each 5,000 members, or part thereof, for whom affiliation fees have been paid to the party's annual conference. In addition, union delegates, in combination, wield 50 per cent of conference votes – with the other 50 per cent being in the possession of constituency parties.[4] Furthermore, and more specifically, 12 of the 24 members of the party's national executive committee, who are themselves elected at conference, are reserved for affiliated unions.

These constitutional powers are supplemented by a number of others. These include, the right of trade unions to collectively to cast one-third of the votes in the election of the party leader and deputy leader, to nominate candidates for party treasurer and to be represented on the national constitutional committee, which is the party's disciplinary committee. They also include the right to elect 30 (out of around 143) members of the party's national policy forum and to nominate parliamentary candidates.

Other forms of influence

The above types of constitutional linkages that exist between unions and political parties, such as Britain, are invariably reinforced by less formal methods of influence. Such types of influence can, moreover, be of considerable importance. This can be illustrated by the role they play in two countries, Germany and Sweden, where there is an absence of any formal constitutional union–party relationships.

In Germany, the central trade union confederation, the *Deutscher Gewerkschaftsbund* (DGB), not only has no formal constitutional decision-making power within the social-democratic party, the SPD, but also, as a result of state funding of political parties, is able to exert little financial muscle over it: although financial contributions are on occasion made (Taylor 1989). Close personal relationships, however, often exist between DGB and SPD leaders and while the DGB does not play a direct role in party decision making, the constitution of the party includes a union council on which the heads of it, and the two other major trade union confederations, sit. Furthermore, the DGB's leadership is firmly in the hands of SPD members, many of whom occupy important party posts and hold a seat in parliament (Visser and Van Ruysseveldt 1996).

A similarly close relationship exists between the largest union confederation in Sweden, the *Landsorganization* (LO), and the Swedish social-democratic party, the *Sveriges Arbetarepartiet* (SAP) in Sweden. However, once again, in contrast to the British situation, the LO has no bloc votes at party congress, no guaranteed executive representation and no official say in the election of the party leader. In addition, as in Germany, the state funding of political parties means that meaningful influence cannot be wielded through union financial support (Taylor 1989). LO leaders, though, do sit on decision-making bodies. They have also frequently been elected to parliament, occupied ministerial positions in government and served on advisory government committees (Visser 1996).

Factors shaping union–party links

It needs to be recognized that the present-day links between trade unions and political parties are frequently the result of a number of historical shifts in them. In the case of Germany, for example, the current lack of a constitutional linkage between the DGB and the SPD stands in sharp contrast to the relationship that existed, prior to the destruction of the union movement in the inter-war period by the national socialists, between the social democratic party and the Allgemeiner Deutscher Gewerkschaftsbund (ADGB), the General Federation of German Trade Unions.[5] Such changes in union–party relationships, in turn, highlight a broader and more general point, namely that the current links that exist cannot be explained in the absence of a detailed understanding of the historical forces and processes that shaped them, particularly, in the case of most developed countries, those that exerted a formative influence during the latter part of the nineteenth and the early part of the twentieth centuries (Marks 1989).[6]

These historical forces and processes embody a host of differing, and interrelated, economic, social and political factors.[7] For example, in relation to the latter nineteenth and early twentieth century, they include the characteristics of the then subsisting labour and product markets, the occupational composition of the early union movement and and the relative emphasis it placed on political activity, the ideological leanings of key union and party leaders, and the degree to which the early trade union movement was the victim of repressive state policies and the period during which state policy moved from one of suppression to 'legitimization'. They also include the historical evolution of employer attitudes towards trade union organization, and the relative timing of the emergence of trade unions vis à vis social- ist inspired political parties, as well as the wider development of the political franchise.

In the context of the present chapter, it is not possible to do justice to the full scope of such influences, or the interrelation- ships between them. Consequently, the approach adopted here is to simply illustrate the role of some of the key ones through an exploration of the historical evolution of union–party links in one country, namely the United States: or to put this more specifically, through an examination of the evolution of the rela- tionship between the AFL (and its successor organization, the AFL-CIO,[8] on the one hand, and the Democratic Party, on the other.[9]

Unions and the Democratic Party

As will have already become clear in this chapter, in many developed economies strong relationships exist between the union movement and 'labour' or 'social democratic parties'. Indeed, as Ebbinghaus (1995: 51) has observed in relation to Western industrial democracies, the 'old siamese twins, working class party and labour unions, have a century-long history of their combined struggle to achieve political and industrial citi- zenship rights for the working class'.

In contrast, in the United States, no such clear 'twin-track' approach to the advancement of political and industrial rights emerged as a result of the failure to establish a stable and large- scale 'labour' party. Instead, what emerged during the early part of the twentieth century was a more 'arm's length friendship' between the AFL-CIO and the Democratic Party.

A variety of explanations have been put forward to explain this 'American exceptionalism', and the related business union- ism of the country's union movement (Marks 1989). One of those so identified, and convincingly so, has been the dominant role that craft unionism, and its focus on labour market regula- tion through controlling the supply of labour, played in the movement's early history and the length of the time period over which this dominance lasted. Yet, although this factor, because of the 'trade', rather than 'class', consciousness it encompassed (Hoxie 1923), does indeed appear to have an exerted an important influence, it is one that is in itself insufficient to fully explain US developments.[10]

In fact, at times craft unions in the US did support and engage in political activity, notably when faced with legal threats, or technological, or broader economic developments, that threatened their survival. However, unlike in Britain, where craft unionism was also predominant in the early stages of unionism, such circumstances failed to provide an impetus towards the creation of a 'labour party', notwithstanding attempts in some parts of the union movement to move in this direction. As a result, an explanation for the absence of such a party, and the AFL-CIO's subsequent concentration on links with the Democratic Party, also needs to take into account a range of other factors. These, according to Mark's insightful analysis, encompass doubts about the feasibility and value of establishing such a party given the nature of the country's political system, as well as the potential that at the same time existed to influence the existing political parties as a result of the early extension of the political franchise (Marks 1989). They also include problems associated with creating a separate 'working class' party within a highly heterogeneous labour force marked by significant ethnic divisions and divergences of the interest between industrial workers and those employed in a large agricultural sector, the unwillingness of some leaders of socialist organizations to engage closely with the union movement because of reservations about the utility of doing so,[11] given its strong commitment to business unionism, and the commitment of Samual Gompers, who led the AFL for a period of nearly forty years during the period 1886–1924, to this form of narrowly focused unionism.

At the same time, while after 1906 the AFL did view the Democratic Party as a 'friend', the nature of the relationship between the two organizations, including, after 1955, with the merged AFL-CIO, has varied substantially over the subsequent period and again, as a result of a range of factors. Thus, in a recent analysis utilizing the typology outlined early, Ludlam et al. (2002) have noted that initially this relationship involved an external lobbying role. However, it subsequently moved, via an internal lobbying one, to 'union–party bonding' from the 1940s onwards. A change that, in large part, stemmed from the need of the New Deal – Fair Deal wing of the party for material support from the unions and eventually resulted in union officials dominating party conventions and posts at all levels and the party pursuing union policy agendas, notably in respect of the 'Great Society' legislation pursued under President Johnson in the late 1960s.

Later though, the relationship underwent further changes. First, in the direction of a weaker, internal lobbying role, with the introduction of constitutional changes in the party aimed at reducing union influence and enhancing the power of other, 'more progressive', interest groups. Changes which led the AFL-CIO, but not all of its affiliates, to stay neutral in the 1972 presidential campaign. Secondly, against a backcloth of fears about the repercussions of a meltdown in union–party relations, back towards a 'bonding relationship'. This backward shift occurred after the signing, in 1979, of a 'National Accord' between the AFL-CIO that, among other things, gave the unions 35 seats on the Democrat National Committee, as well as 4 of the 25 executive committee seats.

Current and future trajectories

The history of the recent relationships between the AFL-CIO and the Democratic Party therefore demonstrates that union–party links are far from set in stone. This is particularly so if account is taken not only of the presence and nature of constitutional links, but also the degree of influence which unions are, in practice, able to exert over party policies. Thus, even though the formal relationship between the AFL-CIO and the Democrats has remained unchanged since 1979, it is clear that the former's influence over the policies pursued by the latter has declined significantly in recent years (Ludlam et al. 2002).

In fact, in a variety of countries a similar trend has been apparent.[12] For example, in Sweden, LO affiliates in the early 1990s stopped the previously existing practice whereby local union branches commonly affiliated members: in part, because of the party's desire to distance itself from the unions for electoral reasons and partly because of union dissatisfaction with the performance of the party when in government (Jenson and Mahon 1993). In a similar vein, the constitutional relationship between the British trade union movement and the Labour Party is noticeably weaker than that which existed prior to 1993 as a result of the latter's desire, once again primarily for electoral reasons, to obtain a greater degree of independence from the former.[13] Moreover, as this chapter is written, dissatisfaction with the current Labour government's policy agenda, is prompting debate within some unions as to whether they should reduce their funding to the party and, perhaps even disaffiliate (Maguire 2003).

Whether and how far such trends in the weakening of union–party relationships will continue are questions to which it is clearly not possible to give clear answers. However, against the background of increasing globalization, and a related competition among nations to attract and retain footloose internal capital, social democratic governments, albeit to differing degrees, have in recent years been pursuing neo-liberal economic agendas (Coates 2000). The adoption of such agendas has, in turn, acted to create growing tensions between unions and party. As a result, it appears reasonable to conclude that the strengthening of current union–party links is likely to be rare, not to say exceptional. At the same time, the long-standing nature of union–party links, along with the remaining relevance of the ideological beliefs that have informed them, suggest that it will also be rare for relationships to deteriorate to the point where a complete break in them occurs. Thus, as Ebbinghaus (1995) has observed: 'In times of change and crises, when we do not know what the future will bring, old ideologies often "go a long way"'.

Nevertheless, whether or not traditional union–party links remain, either in their current, or some revised, form, there are good grounds for believing that union engagement in political activities will not decline. Indeed, such activities may well become of greater importance. For example, it is unlikely that the needs of the growing numbers of workers, such as those working in small and medium sized companies and engaged on various forms of non-standard employment (see chapter 6), who currently fall outside the regulatory scope of trade unions and other channels of representation, such as works councils, can be adequately addressed through union organizing and collective bargaining alone. In addition, and more generally, government attempts across Europe to lower expenditures on state social

welfare systems, privatize public sector undertakings and dereg-
ulate labour markets clearly require a political response.

Yet, in a period in which nation states are faced with the twin
forces of increasing competition and the growing power of international capital, most notably in the form of multinational
corporations, governments are likely to be resistant to union
challenges to such policies. Attempts to combat this resistance
are consequently likely to require the paying of greater attention
to the establishment of trans-national regulatory regimes that
have the capacity to exert some control over the pressures for
reform arising from the process of globalization and government
responses to them.

In the case of the European trade union movement, as
Hyman (2001) has noted, the European Union provides a clear,
if far from straightforward, focus for international activity of this
sort. However, as he, along with Ludlam *et al.* (2002), has
pointed out, this agenda of international engagement is likely to
require not only greater cross-border collaboration among
unions, but also an increased willingness to join forces with a
wider range of interest and pressure groups. As a result, while
traditional national level union–party links may continue to be
viewed as worth preserving, it may also be postulated that the
relative role they play within the political activities of unions
will diminish.

Conclusion

National union movements, as well as individual unions within
them, have varied, in the extent to which they have historically
pursued political objectives and activities. They have similarly
varied in terms of the relationships that they have with political
parties.

A number of typologies have been developed to describe these
variations in union–party links. In combination, these reveal
differences in terms of both the ways in which these links first
developed and the factors that influenced both their establishment and subsequent development. For example, in Western
Europe, links between unions and labour and social democratic
parties arose both as a result of the party playing an important
role in the establishment of the union movement and, less

commonly, as in Britain, through the union movement creating the party.

More generally, a wide range of social, economic and political factors have shaped the nature and evolution of union–party links. In many developed economies those of most fundamental importance exerted their influence in the latter nineteenth and early twentieth century. Typically, such factors include the characteristics of the then subsisting labour and product markets, the occupational composition of the early union movement and the relative emphasis it placed on political activity, the ideological leanings of key union and party leaders, and the attitudes of employers towards trade union organization, as well as various features of the wider political environment. In some cases, however, such as in Germany and Italy, the current linkages, although informed by earlier arrangements, have stemmed in large part from decisions taken with regard to how the union movement should be re-built following periods of fascist rule.

In broad terms, the nature of union–party links has been examined along two, not mutually exclusive, dimensions. First, the presence (or absence) of formal constitutional linkages that provide unions with some direct say in party decision making. Secondly, the use of other, less formal, channels of influence, including close personal relationships between union and party leaders, the presence of union leaders on consultative or advisory bodies, and movements of personnel between the 'two wings of the labour movement'.

Overall, it was found that in the present day constitutional linkages of this type exist in only a minority of developed economies. At the same time, care must be taken not to see the presence or absence of them as providing a reliable indicator of the closeness of union–party relationships or the degree of influence that unions can exert within parties. It is difficult, for example, to conclude that the DGB and LO union confederations in Germany and Sweden exert a lower degree over the SPD and SAP respectively, than the AFL-CIO does over the Democratic Party in the US: notwithstanding that, in contrast to the AFL-CIO, they do not have any formal constitutional role. As a result, the influence that unions wield over parties can be seen to be affected by a range of, often interrelated, factors, including the degree of ideological congruency that exists between the union movement, on the one hand, and the party, on the other.

As regards the future of union–party links, these appear, in general, to be weakening. This weakening, in large part, appears to have been informed by two main factors: a desire on the part of political parties to distance themselves from unions for electoral and policy purposes; and a dissatisfaction, on the part of unions, with the performance of the parties they support when in government. Furthermore, but more tentatively, it seems unlikely that this trend will be reversed. At the same time, it may be that in a number of countries where such a trend has been apparent, union and party relationships will not continue to weaken, but stabilize around a new equilibrium. Nevertheless, it cannot be ruled out that in some countries it will become increasingly difficult to use the phrase the 'two wings of the labour movement' to describe the relationships that exist between unions and social democratic parties

Finally, and more generally, it seems likely that while individual unions and the union movements to which they belong will continue to engage politically, this engagement will come to embody a greater internal orientation. Consequently, insofar as traditional national level linkages with political parties remain, they may well become a relatively less important focus of trade union political activity.

Notes

1 It should be noted that this focus of attention does not extend to a consideration of the relationships that exist between unions and the parties they support when the latter are in government.

2 The two types distinguished in relation to 'authoritarian regimes' were the state-sponsored, in which both the unions and the parties are generated by political elites from the government but attain relatively broad acceptance among workers, and the confrontational, in which the leaders of the labour movement are predominantly in opposition to the government, but must rely principally on union organizations to resist its policies since the regime curtails the activities of the union-linked party or parties and the channels through which they normally manifest their influence.

3 The description that follows is based largely on the more detailed discussion of the links between trade unions and the Labour party contained in Ewing (2002).

4 It should be additionally noted that unions are also able to affiliate to local constituency parties and to exert an influence in this way.

5 This shift in relationships reflects the desire in the union movement after the Second World War to avoid the types of ideological fragmentation of

the union movement that had previously existed. It is for this reason that in Kitschelt's typology Germany is seen to provide an example of *unity unionism*.

6 The importance of this time period, in terms of shaping the nature of current relationships between unions and political parties, is less in those countries, such as Austria, Germany and Italy, where the trade union movements had to be re-built following their destruction under fascist rule.

7 The role of such factors is highlighted in several comparative studies of union–party links. See, for example, Ebbinghaus (1995), Marks (1989) and Valenzuala (1992).

8 The AFL was established in 1886 and from its outset, until the 1920s, was dominated by 'closed', predominantly craft, unions. In 1955 it merged with the Confederation of Industrial Organizations (CIO) which served as the main umbrella organization for more 'open', broadly based, industrial unions, and had traditionally favoured a higher level of political activity.

9 The analysis that follows draws heavily on Marks (1989) and Ludlam *et al.* (2002).

10 Indeed, it was not until 1906 that the AFL formally moved from a position of 'political neutrality' to one of explicit endorsement of the Democrats.

11 It should not be forgotten, in relation to this point, that the American Socialist Party received six per cent of the national vote in the 1912 presidential election, a share exceeding that received by any other socialist party in an English-speaking democracy before 1914 (Marks 1989: 198).

12 In addition to the examples of Britain and Sweden given below, a weakening of relationships between union movements and social democratic parties have been reported in a number of other countries, including Spain and New Zealand. See Gillespie (1990) and Walker (1989).

13 The constitutional changes introduced include a reduction in the unions' share of the vote in leadership elections from 40 per cent to 33 per cent, the termination of union sponsorship of Members of Parliament, and a lowering in the unions' share of the conference vote from 70 per cent to 50 per cent.

References

Coates, D. 2000. *Models of Capitalism: Growth and Stagnation in the Modern Era*. Cambridge: Polity.

Ebbinghaus, B. 1995. 'The Siamese Twins: Citizenship Rights, Cleavage Formation and Party–Union Relations in Western Europe', *International Review of Social History*, 40, 3: 51–89.

Ewing, K. 2002. *Trade Unions, the Labour Party and Political Funding – the Next Step: Reform with Restraint*. London: Catalyst Forum.

Gillespie, R. 1990. 'The Break-up of the Socialist Family: Party–Union Relations in Spain 1982–89', *West European Politics*, 13, 47–62.

Hoxie, R. 1923. *Trade Unionism in the United States*, 2nd edn. New York: Appleton.

Hyman, R. 2001. *Understanding European Trade Unionism: Between Market, Class and Society*. London: Sage.

Jenson, J. and Mahon, R. 1993. 'Representing Solidarity: Class, Gender, and the Crises in Social Democratic Sweden', *New Left Review*, 201, 76–100.

Kitschelt, H. 1994. *The Transformation of European Social Democracy*. Cambridge: Cambridge University Press.

Labour Research Department. 1997. *Trade Unions and Political Funding in Europe: A Report on Financial and Other Links between Trade Unions and Political Parties*. London: Labour Research Department.

Ludlam, S., Bodah, M. and Coates, D. 2002. 'Trajectories of Solidarity: Changing Union–Party Linkages in the UK and USA', *British Journal of Politics and International Relations*, 4: 2, 222–244.

Maguire, K. 2003. 'Union Goes to War with Labour', *Guardian*, 2 July, 1.

Marks, G. 1989. *Unions in Politics: Britain, Germany and the United States in the Nineteenth and Early Twentieth Centuries*. Princeton: Princeton University Press.

McIlroy, J. 1998. 'The Enduring Alliance? Trade Unions and the Making of New Labour, 1994–1997', *British Journal of Industrial Relations*, 36, 4: 537–564.

Taylor, A. 1989. *Trade Unions and Politics: An Introduction*. Basingstoke: Macmillan.

Valenzuala, J. 1992. 'Labour Movements and Political Systems: Some Variations', in Regini, M. (ed.), *The Future of Labour Movements*. London: Sage.

Visser, J. 1996. 'Corporatism beyond Repair? Industrial Relations in Sweden', in Visser, J. and Van Ruysseveldt, J. (eds.), *Industrial Relations in Europe: Traditions and Transitions*. London: Sage.

Visser, J. and Van Ruysseveldt, J. 1996. 'Robust Corporatism, Still? Industrial Relations in Germany', in Visser, J. and Van Ruysseveldt, J. (eds.), *Industrial Relations in Europe: Traditions and Transitions*. London: Sage.

Walker, S. (ed.). 1989. *Rogernomics*. Wellington, Wellington Press.

Webb, S. and Webb, B. 1897. *Industrial Democracy*. London: Longman.

14

Trade union democracy: the dynamics of different forms

MATT FLYNN, CHRIS BREWSTER,
ROGER SMITH AND MIKE RIGBY

Democracy is a noble aim, but it is one that few service-oriented organizations, even non-profits, try to achieve. So why is it so important to the trade union movement? Democratic structures are often thought of as facilitating dissent, and thus creating a drag on strategic management. The Automobile Association is far less democratic than trade unions, and yet is cited as far more effective in delivering both tailored service for, and political influence on behalf of, its customers (Bassett and Cave 1993). Why do unions try to be democratic when democracy produces so few obvious benefits?

Of course, democracy does benefit unions, and it is arguable that unions could not function without it. Unions are dependent for delivering their services on their members' willingness to volunteer their time and energy. Although only a small proportion of a union's membership takes part in most union activities, lay officers on the 'shop floor' deliver most union services. Dependence on the volunteerism of activists is particularly manifest in the UK where unions lack the state support enjoyed by their counterparts in much of the rest of Europe and have limited scope to pay full-time officers. If union members lacked the opportunity to influence union policy, it is doubtful whether they would devote as much effort to delivering its cause. Strauss (Firoito *et al.* 1991) labels the problem faced by unions as the *democratic dilemma*: that fine balance between giving members enough of a say in union policy to persuade them to help the union cause, while retaining an element of stability so that the national union can carry out its objectives. There is nothing new in the democratic dilemma. The Webbs (1897) foresaw the problem at the turn of the previous century when the union organizational model was transforming from small craft-based workers' organizations to large organizations representing wide ranges of workers in multiple sectors. Similar problems in the United States led the American Federation of Labor to exclude industrial workers in favour of a homogenous highly skilled membership. Pre-industrial unions were small enough to be intrinsically democratic, with a show of hands sufficient to generate consensus. Once unions became broad churches, national leaders faced the difficult task of managing a diverse range of competing views and aspirations.

Apart from their utility in formulating policy, democratic structures are also recognized as enabling a necessary check on national leaders' power. The accountability utility of democracy provides a necessary answer to Michels' 'iron law of oligarchy'. This theorizes that union leaders (once they get a taste for the privileges high office brings) will put the maintenance of the union structure before the immediate interests of members and, hence, will become divorced from the concerns of ordinary members (see Lewin 1980 for a useful description). Using democratic mechanisms, such as the election of national leaders, members can at one extreme influence and at another oust leaders who become too distant from problems on the work floor. The latter democratic remit has a regulatory influence on the union's hierarchy, by maintaining accountability of union leaders to active and ordinary members. An effective democratic structure should therefore channel union leaders to act according to the members' will, thus breaking Michels' iron law.

Definitions of democracy

Democracy, as it relates to trade unions, has then two major strands: (1) the issue of 'voice' – the influence which the ordinary member has over union policy, including the representation of differing constituencies within the union's membership; and (2) the issue of 'control' – how ordinary members exert influence over those responsible for implementing policy. Much of the academic literature and, to a large degree, trade union legislation in the 1980s and early 1990s, focused exclusively on the latter dimension, viewing democracy as regulating the interests of ordinary members against those of leaders. As we will discuss below, the Thatcherite union legislation had its greatest impact on the balance of power between union leaders and activists. British unions' experience since the late 1970s, however, indicates that a singular focus on the Michels problem glosses over the heterogeneity of members' interests. How are we to judge whether leaders are acting in the members' interest when members' interests are so diverse?

This is the reason why a focus on members' influence on not only control over policy makers and implementers, but also on the formulation of the policy itself, is an essential (but often overlooked) component of any analysis of union democracy. For ordinary members to keep their leaders accountable to their collective will, a degree of consensus must be developed about what that will is and there must be mechanisms through which that will influences those with power in the union. In turn, an effective democratic structure will ensure that union members with competing interests have a voice in policy development, and not be shut out by constituencies with greater influence. Here, democratic structures regulate relationships between constituencies to equalize power relations between groups of members.

The differing mandates of democracy in maintaining the accountability of union leaders to members on the one hand and ensuring all members have a voice over policy has led to confusion over analyses of democratic structures in unions. When Morris and Fosh (2000) ran a diagnostic on the democratic structures of a case study union using four theoretical models, they came up with four different answers to the question 'Is this union democratic?' Democratic mechanisms which keep leaders accountable to the membership (e.g. national ballots) may go a long way to resolving the Michels' problem, but attract criticism for bypassing the internal debate necessary for consensus building. Other structures (e.g. conference) may feature robust discussions, but be seen as the exclusive venue of a self-selected active elite. The debate over union democracy often becomes confused because of the lack of agreement over what democracy should achieve.

Our thesis is that since the early 1980s, the notion of democracy as control over leaderships has lost force and the notion of democracy as voice for partial constituencies has gained importance. We explore developments in these concepts of democracy below and return to this proposition at the end. This chapter, then, addresses each of these definitions in turn, indicating developments and providing examples, though paying more attention to the less studied issue of voice. We then draw some conclusions about the trends in democracy in the unions, illustrating our arguments with a UK case study of a predominantly public sector union having a need to represent private sector members.

Democracy as control of leaderships

Most attention, both in academic and political circles, has focused on resolving the Michels' problem: ensuring that the union leader does not lose touch with the ordinary members. While Michels discussed the benefits which high office brings, political and institutional power, as well as the influence of employers across the bargaining table, have been cited as more relevant seductions to the modern trade union leader. As will be discussed below, Thatcherite legislation requiring ballots over industrial action and the election of senior officers was drafted as an attempt to 'rein-in' union leaders who were perceived to have lost touch with the moderate tendencies of ordinary union members. The Trade Union Act 1984 was drafted in the hope that ordinary union members would restrain union leaders who aspire to take control of the levers of political and economic power. In many cases, such as the London Underground and firefighters disputes in 2002, however, ballots could be seen to add a layer of legitimacy, helping the respective leaders put paid to accusations of being out of step with their members.

In the 1960s and 1970s the left dominated the debate over union democracy, framing it as a struggle between ideological activists and business oriented leaders. While they recognized Michels' vision of the corruptible influence of power over union leaders, Marxists did not see revolutionary grandeur as the endgame of unchecked leadership, but, rather, the institutionalization of the union in the capitalist economic system (Hyman 1991). Because the union relies on the employer for indirect subsidies (e.g. workplace facilities, time off for lay officers, check-off facilities), as well as recognition and legitimacy, unions are seen as trading their responsibilities for organizing members for an institutional role tempering workers' dissent to protect the economic order. Marxist theory eschews liberal democratic principles based on national ballots and elections, preferring instead replication of the primitive democracy that enables active participation of all members at a grassroots level.

Fairbrother, for example, reflecting Marxist distrust of union leadership, argues that the locus of trade union democracy, as well as union activity, belongs at the local rather than national level (Fairbrother 1990). He notes that the shopfloor is where critical union services are delivered, citing privatization as the impetus for the development of local structures in hitherto centralized public sector unions (Fairbrother 1994). Local restructuring, he argued, was not the result of conscious national union policy. Rather, branch and shopfloor activists in the private sector could meet management practices alien to the public sector bred union leaders.

Whilst unions in the UK were used to criticism from the political left about a lack of democracy in their internal processes, particularly virulent during the 1970s, the period from the election of the Thatcher government in 1979 marked a more potent attack from the right. Government attitudes to the unions, and indeed the legislative programme aimed at reforming industrial relations, reflected the trenchant view of Norman Tebbit that 'by comparison with ... trade union leaders the late Duke of Wellington looks like a trendy liberal' (quoted in McIlroy 1995). This view reflected the belief that unions were dominated by unrepresentative activist cliques, executives, and paid officials, who exploited the passivity and moderation of the bulk of union members to pursue their own agendas of industrial and political militancy. Successive pieces of legislation during the early 1980s then proceeded to introduce compulsory secret ballots both for the election of senior union officers and as a necessary stage in the authorization of industrial action. Such secret ballots were also required periodically to approve the payment of affiliation fees to political parties (in effect, the Labour Party). In the face of this external attack, internal criticism about non-representativeness became more muted. Weakened by large-scale membership loss and political marginalization, the trade union movement at that stage seemed more willing collectively to accept Vic Allen's (1954) dictum that 'the end of trade union activity is to protect and improve the general living standards of its members and not to provide workers with an exercise in self-government'.

Initially, trade union leaderships and the TUC were almost uniformly hostile to the legal changes that were imposed on union organization and the conduct of industrial action. However, a largely unintended consequence of these changes was to *increase* the power of union centres. As legislation progressively rendered the taking of industrial action a legal minefield, unions had to rely on expert legal advice from solicitors or the increasing number of union legal officers, which could only be provided by the central services of the unions. Independent rank and file militancy could thus be more easily held in check. Furthermore, the organizational impact of the legal requirement for reliable and uptodate membership information, so that unions could comply with the strict new rules on balloting procedures, forced the development of a more professional and managerialist ethos within the unions, and the increasing use of centralized computer-based records.

These tendencies were strengthened from the late 1980s by union responses to continually falling membership rolls, which led to arguments in favour of the necessity for unions to reinvent themselves as 'consumer unions' (Bassett and Cave 1993). It was felt that traditional union structures and practices, dominated by a lack of strategic vision, were inhibiting the development of a more reasoned approach to finding solutions to political and financial crises. On this view, it was argued that professional officers and an expert full-time bureaucracy is best able to assess members' needs and how to advance them. Leaderships can represent members without constant consultation with often unrepresentative union committees, and members will judge their performance by the ends and outcomes they achieve. This 'servicing' or 'business' model, as it is sometimes also called, should develop direct methods of identifying membership priorities, through polling and consumer research, and then develop efficient mechanisms for their delivery. Many of these services, it is argued, will consist of *individual* advice and information, and will necessitate a switch of resources within the unions away from collective bargaining and towards the servicing of internal consultative mechanisms. Whilst not all unions adopted this new commercially driven and market-oriented approach with equal enthusiasm, tendencies towards greater managerialism were identified as a dominant trend (Kelly and Heery 1994). Though this did not prohibit internal democracy, it tended to augment the power of the full-time structure at the expense of activist groups.

Classic investigations of union democracy have often

identified the existence of *factions* (Lipset *et al.* 1956; Goldstein 1952) as indicative of successful resistance to oligarchical tendencies. Concern about the non-representativeness of activist factions became particularly acute during the 1980s, when unions were struggling to redefine their role. Worries about the penetration of the Labour Party by a variety of far-left political factions during the early 1980s, culminating in the purge of Militant by Neil Kinnock, a 'modernizing' leader, were reflected in the trade unions. Activist cadres and networks, openly encouraged within some unions in earlier years, now became more identified as part of the problem rather than its solution. Analyses of broader membership opinion, and particularly the views of non-unionized workers the unions were desperate to recruit, revealed that these groups felt that the unions did not adequately represent their views and interests. This was particularly paradoxical, given the attempts during the 1960s and 1970s to become more responsive to rank-and-file opinion.

In broad terms, during the 1980s and 1990s, trade unions in Britain have faced major problems evidenced in the decline in the number of union members and the resultant decline in income at a time when demands on their services, if anything, increased. At the same time, whether connected or not, many trade union leaders and officials have both assumed and accepted managerial responsibilities (Dempsey 2003).

The changes that have been introduced tend to strengthen the power of the centre. They include the following.

All member voting for general secretaries and national executive committees

Until 1984, different unions had different systems for choosing executives and their senior officer. Frequently election for these posts was indirect, by those already voted as representatives at annual conference or some other body, and all-member ballots for such positions were rare. Since the Trade Union Act of 1984, and the Employment Act of 1988, all unions have had the same system imposed on them, requiring elections to be by a secret postal ballot of all members. This has the effect of reducing the power of the annual delegate conference, and locates the legitimacy of senior post-holders much more firmly in the membership as a whole, resulting in what has been called the 'disenfranchisement of activists' (Smith *et al.* 1993).

Weakening the dominance of union conferences

Traditional analyses of union democracy have laid much stress on the functioning of the annual or biennial delegate conference, often defined by union constitutions as the 'supreme decision-making body' of the union. Concern began to develop during the 1980s, however, in an era of declining membership and revenues. Conferences were not only very costly to run, and often showed the union as apparently riven with dissent, but sometimes acted to prevent fiscally sensible policies proposed by executives, or to commit the unions to expensive and sometimes futile campaigns or other policies detrimental to broader union interests. Whilst union executives have always had the ability ultimately to ignore or delay unwelcome conference decisions, increasing sensitivity to the way conferences were perceived in the media (as sectarian and rancorous) led to attempts to conduct discussion in a less conflictual way. Arguably, the effect of Labour Party constitutional reform, reducing the power and significance of union delegations in the process of party decision making, has taken the heat out of many internal union disagreements.

Some unions, recognizing the alienating effect of procedurally dominated and confrontational conferences, have attempted to establish changes aimed at creating a different dynamic. There have been moves to have conferences meet less frequently, going to biennial or even less frequent conferences. There has been the development of 'discussion groups' to encourage broader delegate participation and avoid rostrum dominance by more conference-sophisticated members or oppositionalist cliques. For example, UNIFI introduced this approach from 1999. Others have developed different innovations. To escape the dominance of sectarian dominated conferences, the PCS executive can now ballot members directly when they feel conference decisions are not in the interests of the whole union.

Increasing appointment of FTOs

Unions have their own individual mechanisms for the selection of full-time paid officials who service the collective bargaining and other needs of branches. Direct and regular election of officials has been seen by many as the touchstone of union accountability, removing the risk that appointment by executives at national or regional levels results in the creation of closed elites of like-minded individuals. However, there has been an increased tendency for unions to move towards the appointment of officers. This has been fuelled by the recognition of the increasingly technical nature of the trade union officer role, requiring detailed knowledge of employment law, health and safety information, and well-developed communication skills to deal with a wider range of members and potential members, increasingly professionalized management and with the media.

The technician nature of the role has led to much greater focus within trade unions on notions of 'job descriptions' and 'person specifications' for officer posts, and with that a recognition that such expertise is more efficiently judged by selection rather than election procedures. Moreover, election of officials was noted from the early 1980s to have done little to broaden the profile of full-time officers to include women or members of ethnic or other minorities who were clamouring for greater recognition. Again, the achievement of broader social goals of equal opportunities has been more easily achieved by shifting the locus of selection away from election procedures dominated by localized concerns and personalities, to centralized mechanisms integrated with the achievement of broader and more long-term strategic goals.

Although unions have shifted from the election to the appointment of full-time officers, centralization has been moderated by the importance of lay activists in delivering union services. Heery and Kelly (1990), in particular, identified the influence lay activists' participation in union work has on how full-time officers prioritize activities, with activists' priorities having a stronger influence than the national union's strategic plan.

Centralization of budgets

Increasing centralisation in decision-making processes has been reflected in increasingly centralized management of funds. UK trade unions gain the vast majority of their incomes from membership subscriptions (a small amount may come from investments), and this proportion has been increasing since the early 1980s (Willman *et al.* 1993: 21ff.) The financial crises which resulted from rapidly falling membership rolls during the years of Conservative governments from 1979 were exacerbated by the fact that, in comparison with many other European countries, union subscriptions in the UK have always been at a low level. Moreover, McIlroy (1995) argued that 85 per cent of the income of the largest unions is spent on administrative costs, which are in the medium term relatively fixed. This administrative cost consists mostly of the costs of employing people and the unions have only reluctantly been forced into dismissals of staff. Membership loss (and therefore substantially reduced income), the reluctance of union conferences to raise subscription rates and the increasing demands of members facing redundancies which meant outgoings were hard to reduce quickly, put unions in an exposed position financially. These difficulties were particularly acute in the 1980s, and led to both union mergers to reduce overheads, and to the professionalization of budgetary control. Thus, when UNISON was formed in 1993 one of its first tasks was an attempt to centralize budgets. Many of the unions involved in this process have found a mix of branch funds which had substantial surpluses simply sitting in a current account earning no interest and others running a deficit. The effect of centralization of budgets was further centralization of authority. Willman *et al.* (1993) identified the significant role that the professionalization of the finance officer's role has had in centralizing the control of union resources. Automated subscription payment, subscription indexation and asset management have taken away the role of the conference in deciding how union assets are collected, invested and distributed. As assets became centralized, union branch, group and regional committees have become dependent on the centre for resources, significantly curtailing their autonomy.

Democracy as consensus building

Whilst attempts by the unions to build democratic structures in the sense of legitimizing and controlling leaders have in recent years been subordinated to the need to run the union in a cost-effective manner, the same crisis has led unions into attempts to build consensus amongst diverse constituencies. Consensus building in a democratic organization is an iterative process in which all members can influence union policy, which everyone then unites behind. The concept of ordinary members sharing an active role in shaping union policy has largely been overlooked in discussions of democracy. Union structures have largely been based on Schumpeterian (1976) ideals: seeing 'the masses' as largely inactive and disinterested in policy formulation, but capable of choosing between competing political candidates. As we discussed above, the Schumpterian model has largely sidelined ordinary union members, reducing union democracy to a struggle between leaders and their paid officers against unpaid lay activists.

Consensus building models, such as discourse theory, adopt the perspective that all citizens are capable of contributing to political dialogue, but are prevented from doing so because of unequal access to communicative networks. Breaking down barriers to membership dialogue is the aim: attaining what Habermas (1987) referred to as the ideal speech situation in which all members have an opportunity to raise or challenge assertions.

The answer to the Webbs' question of how large unions can take account of the views of a diverse range of constituencies while still presenting a united front has been far less explored, a point noted by Jahn (1988). This comparative dearth of literature is surprising, as consensus building is the more persistent challenge for trade unions. The trend from single-employer unions towards large, multi-sector, multi-grade unions has persisted over the past half century, but accelerated around the turn of the millennium, through mergers and the expansion of some unions into non-union workplaces. On Voos' (1983) argument that a union will seek to expand its membership base in order to increase its bargaining power with employers, it is logical that expansion would need to be coupled with an element of consensus to bring about this benefit. Drawing from the consumers' theoretical model, if groups of members do not believe their voices are being heard in the greater union, they will vote with their feet, rendering expansion fruitless and mergers tenuous. While less attention has been given by academics to democracy as a mechanism for consensus building, unions in recent times have focused resources into developing more pluralist democratic structures. As with the accountability side, these trends have resulted more from practical than from theoretical reasons. In trying to staunch the drain in union numbers since the late 1970s, unions have focused efforts on recruiting workers who had been historically under-represented in the trade union movement. As unions have sought to recruit new kinds of members, they have had to adapt their democratic structures accordingly. Some examples of this trend are as follows.

Developing special representation for women

These developments go back to 1979 and a TUC charter recommending the formation of Women's Advisory Councils within affiliated unions, and the provision of childcare facilities at conferences and meetings. This gradually developed into the provision of women-only courses and meetings, and of specialist union publications on women's issues. This phase of development has been characterized as unions following a *liberal* agenda (Kirton and Greene 2002) – that is, the structures and processes of the unions themselves remained relatively unchanged, and activity focused on creating equality of opportunity for women by developing their skills and experience so that they could compete more equally with men in standing for union office. Later developments in most large unions have shifted to a *radical* agenda, within which structures and procedures themselves have been identified as part of the problem of women's lower participation, and thus have been subjected to change. This phase has included target-setting for increased participation, and has involved reserved seats on executives and other internal bodies, and development of a women's TUC conference. Some unions have attempted to broaden the women's-issue agenda even further, like the GMB's campaign against domestic violence, the Daphne Project (Union 21 2002). In UNISON, the principle of proportionality was adopted on merger (McBride 2000).

Available evidence points to widespread adoption of these measures, and to what is generally accepted as progress, if still being far from full equality (Kirton and Greene 2002; Parker 2002). Many large unions have achieved parity or better on executives, and 7 of the 10 largest increased their number of women officials in recent years (LRD 1992; SERTUC 2000). Women's participation in union organization has become more visible, and union agendas are now reflective of a broader set of concerns. In this regard, union structures and processes can be seen to have become more democratic in terms of the fuller representation of interests.

Developing special representation for black workers

Recognition of the under-represented nature of ethnic minorities within trade unions resulted in the formation of the TUC Black Workers Charter in 1981, which launched a campaign to discover reasons for that under-representation, and to improve recruitment of black members. Over time advisory committees were formed in most of the big unions, but still tend to have only advisory status, unlike women's committees which tend to be sub-committees of executives. 'Positive action on gender and race has taken different forms. For women, it has commonly meant the creation of different forms of women's separate organizing. In contrast, the approach generally adopted in relation to black members is one of race-equality committees and conferences, rather than nationally endorsed separate black members committees' (Kirton and Greene 2002).

The greater reluctance by unions to support independent black organizing is reflected in the fact that the TUC Black Workers Conference still had many unions sending white delegates as late as 1996. An attempt to change rules so that only black members could be delegates was rejected because of quoted 'legal problems' relating to race discrimination legislation. The self-organization of black workers is still rare – only UNISON stands out as encouraging it. But three large unions (T&G, MSF, PCS) have reserved seats on their executives for black representatives. Problems are compounded by the fact that few unions have details of black membership, and few have black officials (LRD 1992). Moreover, this area of discrimination within unions has attracted nothing like the amount of attention from academic researchers that women's issues have.

Youth representation

The aim of increasing activity and representativeness in this area is more clearly centrally driven by union hierarchies rather than a response to well-organized and articulate minority demands. It is clearly motivated by the low and falling membership of young workers, particularly graduates (except in some public sector areas like teaching and the NHS), and the recognition of the serious demographic impact of this trend on the future development of trade unions. In the UK, for example, the proportion of 20 to 24-year olds in the unions decreased from 30 per cent to 19 per cent over the decade 1989–99 (LRD 2000). That this is not a uniquely UK problem is demonstrated by a recent European survey that showed the decline in membership of young people to be much more rapid than for older groups in most other European countries (Serrano Pascual and Waddington 2000).

The main explanation of this trend has been in terms of cultural change, and the increasing unwillingness of youth to get involved in collectivist organizations like political parties and trade unions. However, recent survey evidence for the UK concludes that it has been largely the failure of existing union organization to appeal to youth that is the main problem. 'There is broad support among young workers for the majority of the current trade union agenda. The problem for young workers is thus not primarily with the trade union agenda, but with the people who deliver it' (Waddington and Kerr 2002). Perceptions of the unions as being dominated by the concerns of the middle-aged, and talking in an archaic and procedurally dominated language, have had an alienating effect that unions, led by the broader strategic concerns of the TUC and modernizing organizations like Unions 21, have only recently begun to address.

Practically all unions now have reduced membership subscriptions for young members. Many have created youth sections, and youth conferences, but largely without connection to mainstream structures. Some unions with the particular problem of an ageing membership profile have gone further. For example, the GPMU has, as well as a conference for young members, also a reserved seat on the union's executive, reserved places on TUC and Labour Party delegations, and seats on branch committees. Other union initiatives include recruitment campaigns on university campuses; general promotional activities like organizing union stalls at music concerts; a joint UNISON/NUS website on information about employment rights to student part-timers; and a TUC organizing academy for young officers, with a specific brief to target the young (Waddington and Kerr 2002).

A large amount of trade union effort is now being expended in youth work and recruitment, though with little immediate effect on overall membership figures. The prominence and urgency with which union organizations are addressing this issue is testimony to their general willingness to increase the 'voice' of young people within unions, and to represent the concerns which they have. However, as in all attempts at internal representational reform, resistance will inevitably be met. Discussing the youth involvement programme in UNIFI, the organizer of a special conference noted, 'it is interesting and worrying to note that very few young members were nominated to attend [...] through existing union structures' (Kirton and Greene 2002).

Lesbian and gay representation

The gradual development of union concern about representing the interests of gay and lesbian membership began with the promulgation of the TUC Charter on Equality for Lesbian and Gay Workers in 1984, calling upon affiliated unions to develop policies supporting gay and lesbian rights. By 1992, unions covering 65 per cent of TUC membership had done so (LRD 1992). Sponsorship from the top can be seen to have initiated and supported much of this early development. This gives some support to arguments by Bok and Dunlop, (1970), Heery (1997) and Streeck (1988) that new initiatives aimed at broadening membership participation must frequently be driven by union centres, because local change is often not welcomed by local union leaderships, who fear shifts in the balance of power at that level. However, the capacity of activists to drive the agenda was demonstrated at the 1997 TUC conference, when despite opposition from the general council, delegates voted for the establishment of a motion-based lesbian and gay annual conference. This is now attended by delegates from the vast majority of affiliated unions, and is cited as evidence by one of the leading researchers in the field for her conclusion that a 'more supportive attitude to gay and lesbian issues ... has developed within the UK trade union movement as a whole over the last decade' (Colgan, 1999). Most large unions now have lesbian and gay advisory committees, though few have reserved seats.

Wider community involvement

Whilst labour history abounds with examples of unions mobilizing community support, this has generally been during the pursuit of long-term industrial action. Often, this has been when the normal mechanisms of industrial action have not been successful in achieving aims, and there has been a perceived need to galvanize other groups to shift wider public opinion more effectively, and improve fundraising. The Miners' strike of 1984–85, and the Liverpool dockers' strike can be seen as examples of this. However, the concept of developing wider community support as a strategic and long-term objective unconnected with existing strike action has been a more recent development in the UK.

The origins of this approach in the UK can be seen as being strongly influenced by the campaigning style adopted by some US unions, particularly operating in the public sector, and exemplified by John Sweeney, now President of the AFL-CIO (Sweeney 1999). The intention of this US strategy was to regenerate rank-and-file activism around a model of organizing which emphasized traditional union values of justice and dignity at work, and which targeted marginal and low-paid workers who had been hitherto largely neglected by unionization campaigns. Sophisticated methods of targeting likely organizations, 'workplace mapping' of potential recruits, and the identification and training of activist cadres inside the plant, supported by professional organizers outside, were all developed as parts of a more aggressive recruitment strategy. This was supported outside the plant by the development of new levers against unwilling employers, like consumer boycotts, lobbying shareholder meetings, galvanizing political and community support.

This model substantially influenced the foundation of the TUC Organizing Academy in 1998, where new young officers are now trained for campaigning roles. The spread of this approach in the UK has been limited, however. Heery *et al.* (2000), reviewing evidence on the practices of unions conclude that 'those aspects of the model which extend union organization into the community are reported in only a handful of cases'. Cited explanations for this include the resource intensity of the approach, and the consequent need to divert resources at a time of extreme financial stringency away from other activities, and internal resistance from existing post-holders who may fear that they lack the necessary skills for this more outwardly focused approach. That said, many of these same arguments were raised at the beginning of the previous century as the craft based trade union movements in the US and UK grappled with organizing industrial workers.

However, the approach may develop more widely in the future. This may be reflected in the finding of Heery *et al.* (2000) that the larger unions and those that had few restrictions (by trade or grade) on membership were the vanguard organizations as far as establishing internal mechanisms for representing diversity, and commitments to prioritizing recruitment of non-traditional workers. Examples of community-based action include:

- *TELCO/UNISON Living Wage Campaign* in East London – this is a broad coalition of community and union groups to pressure public bodies to ensure that external service providers are contractually obliged to pay a 'London living wage' of at least £6.30 an hour. This project has been organized as part of the union's 'Positively Public' campaign. Its dual purpose aims to develop a community good (highlighting the plight of low paid London workers) and direct benefits for UNISON members (challenging the outsourcing of public services by exposing working conditions in private sector workplaces).
- *ISTC campaign* – this works with schools, exploiting the fact that the footballer Ryan Giggs is a member of the union.
- *USDAW* is involved in campaigning work with the Asian community in North West England against the neo-fascist BNP.

Improving sectional representation in the union

The discussion thus far has been concentrated on the developments which unions have made in their internal representative structures which have been a response to an increasing acceptance of *social differentiation* and the development of *group identities* in the membership as a whole. However, there have also been developments for some unions in terms of increasing workforce differentiation through sectional development, aimed at reducing the risk that the interests of members of smaller groupings within a union may become marginalized.

Large conglomerate unions like the TGWU and the GMB have dealt with the problem of marginalization in the past by the formation of trade groups and industrial conferences. The aim of these sectoral bodies has been to provide a focus for the development of relevant policy making, and also to act as an organizing base for the exercise of influence and the guarantee of sectoral voice within broader union structures (Salamon 2000). It is also true to say that they served a marketing function in terms of facilitating mergers with unions representing new sectors (McIlroy 1995).

Whilst unions have in the past developed mechanisms successfully to prevent small sections from marginalization, the privatization of public utilities in the 1980s and 1990s presented new challenges.

Developing a theoretical basis for the voice utility of democratic structures

As we noted above, much of the academic attention has focused on developing a theoretical basis for analysing the effectiveness of democratic structures in maintaining the accountability of union leaders. Critical factors have included the existence of factions (Lipset *et al.* 1956); contestable elections (Edelstein and Warner 1975); constraints on leaders to tolerate opposition (Martin 1968), local and regional autonomy (James 1984), and constitutional checks and balances (Undy and Martin 1984). What would be considered major elements of a consensus building democracy which aims to give voice to under-represented groups? Unfortunately, no one has created a comprehensive shopping list, but we can perhaps draw together some of the major elements identified both within and outside the industrial relations literature.

It is against the general background of the consolidation and strengthening of central union power that more recent initiatives to increase the voice of particular minorities within union structures must be seen. 'It can be argued that democratic organizations, such as trade unions, are better able to promote social justice for all if different social groups are included in decision making. In other words, social group difference can be drawn upon as a resource if inclusive mechanisms are developed through which the diverse social groups can be heard' (Kirton and Greene 2002).

Many years of declining membership and political influence led to calls for union 'revival' approaches, but these agendas, whilst often expressed in terms of making unions more representative, have been driven largely by concerns about recruitment (Heery 1997). Thus, mechanisms to increase the voice of various under-represented groups (women, ethnic minorities, youth, gay and lesbian members) can be seen as the result of two potentially conflicting currents within the unions. First, pressures exerted by groups of members to persuade mainstream trade union organizations to incorporate within their policies issues relating to broad societal discrimination against particular social groups. And second, emanating from union centres, the view that highlighting social issues pertaining to particular categories of members, and even creating special internal union representative mechanisms, could be used as a marketing tool to aid the recruitment of further members in those social categories. As one recent survey has expressed it, 'Although membership issues were viewed as being of considerable importance by respondents, the primary emphasis was not ... upon decentralising the union structure and enhancing membership participation. The unions were concerned above all about membership levels, and therefore most of the responses related as to how to improve recruitment' (Rigby, Smith and Lawlor 1999).

This is not to say that the new representative bodies that have been created in many unions are only there for window dressing and tokenistic purposes, and that the union centres are able to manipulate them *purely* as marketing tools. They are the products of multiple agendas, operate in contexts of competing power interests, and one must exercise caution in reading off greater genuine internal representativeness simply from the *existence* of such bodies. It is in this context that we propose elements of a theoretical framework for analysing the effectiveness of internal representation. These elements are drawn from the larger field of political theory.

Dialogical approach to reasoning

Lewin (1980) discusses the process of dialogue between leaders and membership to bring a consensus building dimension to describing union democracy. Rather than taking a Schumpterian perspective on the actions of ordinary members, Lewin sees them expressing parochial interests. The role of leaders is to interpret the will of the membership and organize diverse interests into a coherent consensus. By articulating that consensus to the membership, leaders ignite a 'public spirit' which generates active membership participation: understanding and contributing to union policy beyond parochial interests to articulation of values. This interaction between leader and member defines the robustness of democracy.

Lewin's approach also differs from traditional liberalism by adopting a dialogical approach to reasoning, focusing on how an individual comes to embrace certain values, rather than how those values are imposed on the collective masses. For example, whereas a monological approach to union policy on unemployment would start with macro-economics and the management of the wider market, a dialogical approach would focus first on individual union members' experience with work and unemployment, how that experience translated into values; and how the individual fed those values into the larger dialogue. From a researcher's perspective, a dialogical approach has metatheoretical implications, favouring an abductive approach over deductive reasoning, since there is not an apparent proposition which can be tested.

A recognition of formal structures as both facilitators and barriers to dialogue

Feminists have written the largest body of literature on the barriers to dialogue of oppressed constituencies. Their interest arose from the impact male dominance has had on unions' bargaining agenda. Feminist theorists have identified union structures as sources for protection of the status quo as much as facilitators of debate. Since structures have been identified as sources of the problem, many of the potential solutions to gender inequality have focused on the formal bodies without women officers; and women officers are constrained in shaping equal opportunity policy by their role in representing constituencies structures.

As we have noted, unions have sought to improve representation for women through reserved seats, equality committees and the formalization of self-organized groups. Feminist theorists have debated whether, for the purposes of union structures, women should be treated as a distinct gender group or as an oppressed social group. Taking the former approach, unions should guarantee seats for women on governing bodies, such as the national executive, but would have no real prescription about what policies women officers should support. The latter position would prescribe efforts to guarantee that women's issues are included in union policy making: for example, assembling a women's forum which reports to the national executive. However, McBride (2000) notes that recent union experience indicates both approaches are necessary. It is difficult to get women's forums to give attention to governing in a gender neutral manner.

Policy networks as a medium for exchange

The issue of how informal networks impact on union democracy has been largely unexplored, but could offer useful insight into the process of policy making, particularly where formal democratic structures prove inadequate in representing groups of members. In the political science field, the study of policy networks has cast light on public policy formulation outside formal governing bodies. Policy network theory is generally recognized as more descriptive than normative, but has drawn attention to processes that had hitherto been unexplored.

Within the policy network field, there are two general theoretical approaches: corporatist and pluralist theories. Corporatists tend to focus on the influence interest groups, companies and other organizations have on public policy, with a particular emphasis on power relationships, and exchange theory (Jordan 1990; Rhodes 1990; Rhodes and Marsh 1992). Interest groups exchange tangible and intangible resources in order to maximize utility. For example, Rhodes and Marsh identified 'assets' which interest groups possessed and exchanged with the government of the day in exchange for influence. These included technical expertise (e.g. from motoring organizations). The corporatist model says very little about how consensus is built, relying on a rational actor model to personify interest groups. Organizations know what outcomes they desire and use their assets to achieve their aims. Accordingly, the corporatist model says more about policy making within a 'market' of resources than it does about democratic processes such as dialogue and persuasion.

This is not to say that the corporatist model has no descriptive value. On the contrary, it can help to identify how and why constituencies have varying degrees of influence, and the barriers which are put in place to prevent groups of members from raising concerns. Willman *et al.* (1993) note that unions often pursue policies of expanding into unorganized workplaces despite the fact that the cost of servicing new members outweighs any returns from subscriptions. They conclude that new constituencies must produce intangible benefits to the union (for example, prestige or political influence) which cannot be quantified in an economic model. How new constituencies use these intangible assets may speak volumes about how they gain influence within the union as a whole.

Policy networks as social construction

In contrast to the corporatist perspective, pluralists see networks as media through which actors (in this case, individual actors rather than corporations or interest groups) make sense of their respective environments (Jordan 1990, 1994; Rhodes and Marsh 1992; Wilks and Wright 1987; Wright 1988). Sense making emerges through interaction between actors, and the advice, information, representations, etc. which are exchanged. The pluralist model is a much more finely woven network of exchanges, crossing organizational boundaries.

A union wishing to develop policy networks through a pluralist model would probably emphasize the communication networks, facilitating the interaction of union representatives seeking advice and information, with dialogue as a positive byproduct. Many unions, for example, have established electronic bulletin boards on their websites to support lay representatives in exchanging ideas and practical skills on campaigning on specific workplace issues. Recent efforts of unions to develop lifelong learning programmes have also aimed to improve communications between members through interaction in a classroom setting.

Situated learning

Much of the sociological and anthropological research around situated learning speaks to the issue of representation of atypical community members. Lave and Wenger's model of learning through peripheral participation (1997) is premised on the reasoning that learning is as much a process of joining a community as learning new skills. The development of a shared language and shared understanding empowers the 'outsider' by enabling her or him to articulate her or his unique perspective to the rest of the community in a meaningful way: moving towards Habermas's ideal speech situation. Gould (1996) discusses the importance of minority inclusion in building social networks to develop voice; while Orr (1996) notes that situated learning can facilitate individuals to build their own networks based on common language and understanding. The literature on situated learning may speak particularly well to the dilemma we posed above as to whether new representative bodies enable underrepresented constituencies to get their voices heard or are merely window dressing. The dilemma is based on the fact that most representative bodies are created by central leadership (although some have their origins in self-organized groups (Humphrey 2000). Situated learning may be one piece of the puzzle to learn how under-represented constituencies use mechanisms in order to get their views articulated. Again, an abductive approach would provide the best epistemology.

Community based research

Little has been written, in a trade union context, about how minority constituencies research their own workplace situations and feed that knowledge into policy formulation at a higher level of the union. The use of knowledge as a resource for breaking into the policy-making arena is a central pillar of critical theory and an important part of what Habermas envisioned as an ideal speech situation (Comstock and Fox 1993). While little has been written about this in a trade union context, there are many examples of research carried out with oppressed groups as a means of gaining influence (Park 1993; Rahman 1985).

Critical theory takes a subjective epistemological perspective, basing knowledge on the internalization of the individual. While there are different levels of knowledge, experiential, practical and propositional (Heron 1998), which can serve different purposes, knowledge formulation cannot be divorced from the intent of the researcher. Accordingly, there is always a political dimension to research. Sociological research can serve as a tool for oppression or emancipation. The critical theorist metatheoretical stance may prove a useful complement to other models for consensus building democracy. In particular, where feminist theorists have focused on structures as barriers to dialogue, critical theory can cast light on how knowledge hoarding is used as a means of preventing groups from raising wider awareness of their situations.

An example: PCS – representation of privatized members

Around one in ten public sector jobs in the UK has been transferred to the private sector as a result of compulsory competitive tendering, market testing, PFI and other forms of privatization. As a detailed study sponsored by the Equal Opportunities Commission (Escott and Whitfield 1995) has confirmed, privatized workers are amongst the most vulnerable in the workforce, with particular risks to their pay, pensions and working hours.

The Civil Service union, PCS, took a strategic position in its organizational plan to expand its membership in the private sector through the retention of ex-civil servants and recruitment of new members engaged directly by private companies. The union's outlook reflected a combined recognition of the stagnant (or shrinking) market for union membership in the Civil Service and the potential for growth in largely non-union private companies that provide services to government departments.

Although the union calls itself the Public and Commercial Services union, civil servants still account for more than nine out of every ten PCS members. Recruiting non-civil servants (not only private sector employees, but also the growing number of quango employees, staff in the aviation industry and staff of devolved governments), poses significant challenges to the union. PCS was formed in 1997, the end result of a series of mergers which, over the previous decade, had amalgamated four unions (five, if you count the staff association formed in GCHQ following derecognition) into one. The predecessor unions were structured to meet the needs of Whitleyism: an industrial relations system unique to the Civil Service which historically involved national pay scales, routine consultation on workplace issues, and exclusive employee representation through union channels. Although the predecessor unions' largely centralized structures were well suited for representing civil servants under Whitleyism, they appeared alienated and unresponsive to members who were privatized during the Thatcher and Major years.

PCS, largely in response to Civil Service changes in the 1990s, is a less centralized union than its predecessor organizations. In 1994, the Major government abolished national pay bargaining, leaving it to the (now) 153 departments and agencies to negotiate directly with the unions. As a result, considerable negotiating powers have shifted since the 1990s from the national to 'group' level, structured according to employing departments. However, delegation on the union side only occurred organically where the structures were in place below the national level to take on negotiating responsibilities. Most of the private sector constituency in PCS is divided by contract, and lacks a sufficient number of representatives to make it feasible to service members to the same level as their Civil Service counterparts. In PCS's largest employer, EDS, for example, four thousand members are divided into ten contracts with different pay scales.

Recognizing that the existing structure was unable to meet the representational needs of private sector members, full-time officers and lay representatives have sought to use alternative means of giving private sector members a voice in union policy:

Dialogical approach to reasoning

One of the most difficult challenges for PCS, a challenge shared with almost all British public sector unions, has been reconciling its policy against privatization with its strategy of expansion within private companies. The organizations in which PCS has members are mainly contractual service providers with a significant presence in the public sector. For PCS, delivering the right message has meant ensuring that an anti-privatization message does not denigrate the work of those people the union is trying to recruit. One of the ways in which it has sought to address this conundrum has been to ensure the representation of private sector representatives on the national committee responsible for taking forward the union's public sector campaign. Private sector representatives have helped fine-tune the union's campaign, for example by highlighting issues such as the two tier workforce and diminution of pension rights post-privatization which both public and private sector members can campaign against.

A recognition of formal structures as both facilitators and barriers to dialogue

One of the fundamental ways in which sectoral expansion differs from efforts to widen representation along gender or ethnicity lines is on the focus on formal structures. Much of the effort of unions since the 1980s in making unions more inclusive to women and minorities has concentrated on modifying existing structures to make them more representative, as discussed above. Where a union endeavours to break into new workplaces, most efforts go into building new structures, where none had previously existed. This often involves running branch level elections, often in the hope of getting even one nomination.

Building new structures presents separate challenges to unions apart from modifying existing ones. The high cost of servicing members without a fully developed lay structure means that for a long period of time 'established' constituencies subsidize new ones. As Willman (1989) points out, the subsidization issue can dissuade union members from supporting expansion. In addition, where unions break into atypical workplaces, a balance needs to be struck between ensuring the structure is relevant to the workplace, while also being able to give members an effective voice in the rest of the union.

PCS took a different approach to representing private sector members than its counterparts in other parts of the public sector. UNISON, Britain's largest union with members in areas such as local government and the health service, for example, has opted to keep privatized members in public sector structures. PCS, by contrast, established separate branches for its largest private sector constituencies, as well as creating an internal association for private sector members. The differences in approaches reflect how the private sector constituencies of the two unions are distinct. Much of the Civil Service privatization occurred in IT services, with large blocks of work transferred to large multinational IT companies, raising challenges for these groups of members unique to PCS. Accordingly, the union's priorities lay in ensuring that private sector representatives have the structures to learn from one another's experience with large multinationals. In UNISON, many employees who were privatized worked in support services: catering, cleaning and security services within public buildings. They share common issues with public sector colleagues, and it was felt that uniting public and private members would be the best approach to representing them.

PCS faces a unique challenge insofar as the Civil Service is the one part of the public sector without national pay bargaining. Not only do departments and agencies have their own pay systems but, as a consequence, their contracts with private service providers do as well. In EDS, for example, the largest government contractor conducts ten separate pay negotiations with the union. This division of the workforce has implications for organizing members within each employer. Development of employer-wide structures has been hampered by the absence of a negotiating remit. In EDS, branch representatives have used pay harmonization, the European Works Council and organizational issues as a means of developing cross-employer organization in the form of a sectoral committee. While it is recognized that the committee cannot negotiate directly with the employer, it does co-ordinate the process of harmonization, an effort being driven by both union and employer sides.

In other workplaces, the imperative has been recruiting activists to represent members and to organize them within their respective employers. One of the greatest challenges has been representing support staff such as security staff, administrative staff and cleaners. One of the largest support service contract stretches geographically from Norfolk to Cornwall, with members dispersed in twos and fours across the regions. Because the company would not recognize Civil Service lay representatives, the union was forced into organizing the lay structure into six regional shops, recruiting activists to represent dispersed members.

Doubtless, the construction of new lay structures in privatized areas is borne of necessity, as ex-civil servants find themselves in workplaces without representation. The significance, from a representation perspective, is how private sector reps use the opportunity to break their workplaces from traditional structures built around Whitleyism. One rep spoke of his exasperation at being a part of a private sector rump of a public sector union, but added, 'It's exciting to have the opportunity to build a part of the union from the ground up.'

Policy networks as a medium for exchange

PCS efforts to ensure that private sector members' views are represented at national level do follow the mould set by the trade union movement in representing women and minorities. Although private sector members do not have reserved seats on the national executive, the NEC did put a proposal to the last national conference for reorganization of the executive which included reserved seats. The proposals were rejected, largely for reasons separate from the issue of private sector representation.

A national Commercial Sector Association (CSA) has recently been established with elected officers from the main sectors in which PCS has members: IT, support services and the finance sector. The association's official responsibilities are limited to organizing an annual forum of private sector lay representatives. However, it has wide discretion in drawing up its agenda, and officers have sought to identify issues relevant to their constituencies which would not necessarily be picked up by the rest of the union. One of the key issues is that of pensions, as many of the private sector employers are closing their defined benefit pension schemes. The CSA is organizing a seminar for commercial sector representatives on protecting pension rights aimed at both local representatives and employee pension trustees. The Civil Service is one of the few employers which has negotiated improvements in its pension benefits.

Situated learning

When PCS's predecessors first broke into the private sector, the basis on which they approached workplace representation was Whitleyism: most union representatives of privatized employees were themselves transferred from the Civil Service. As time passes, reps move on or adapt to new workplaces, the reproduction of the Civil Service brand of industrial relations decreases. Representatives in private sector workplaces are developing their own identities through taking new approaches to representation. For example, workplace representatives in large IT companies have been trailblazers in the union in using intranet, email and internet facilities to communicate with members and with one another. Their experience, drawing from their own IT knowledge, has influenced the union's national strategy.

Community based research

The private sector constituencies have used primary research on workplace issues more often than other parts of the union. For example, the union commissioned two workplace surveys to gauge members' views on working life, their jobs and PCS as their workplace representative. The survey was conducted jointly between lay and full-time officers and contributed to the union's organizational strategy in the private sector. Part of the reason is the nascent form of formal structures, and the need for alternative means of listening to ordinary members. Because the research was shared within the union, the process of conducting the surveys helped facilitate discussion about PCS's identity as a representative of private sector employees.

Early indicators in the commercial sector

Although the Civil Service has experienced privatization since the 1990s, it is only in the past few years that PCS has begun to develop a strategy for representing privatized members. While many of the structures are still new, PCS's experience speaks to how constituencies generate a voice in wider union policy. What appears to be of equal importance to the establishment of structures is how they are used by the representatives. As the chair of the CSA noted, the association is picking issues to campaign on which, while not important to civil servants now, may be important to them in the near future. The closure of pension schemes, globalization and the casualization of employment are all issues which affect privatized members more directly than those in the public sector, but which public servants are recognizing as bearing down increasingly on their employment. The CSA has emphasized in its literature, for example in its 'Commercial sector toolkit', its value to the majority in providing expertise on these issues.

Conclusions

This chapter has focused on the tensions between two models of union democracy which have elsewhere been described as 'representative' and 'participative' models (Hyman, 1994). The pressures on unions from the dramatic collapse of membership numbers since 1979 had a dual effect as far as union democracy is concerned. It led to an increase in the centralization of the way the unions are managed; and it also persuaded the unions to diversify their memberships. This latter drive in turn required the unions to look for new ways to enable under-represented groups to participate in union activities.

We began this chapter by presenting two alternative models of union democracy: accountability and voice, positing that differences in perspective between the two models account for the confused dialogue on what union democracy is there to achieve. While the connection between the two models is concealed, it does exist and is significant. As unions become more diverse through expansion into new workplaces and mergers, democratic structures are being adapted to ensure that members have voice not only in the workplace, but also within the union. Although this chapter has dealt solely with internal union democracy, the issue of membership voice will also be important to unions' role in works councils as the Information and Consultation directive is transposed into UK law. If British unions are to be stakeholders in, and not supplanted by, works councils, they will need to demonstrate that they are conduits of the views of ordinary members. What Habermas described as the ideal speech situation not only achieves fairness between constituencies, but also effectiveness in maintaining accountability of full-time officers to the union membership.

From a chronological perspective, the birth of the new millennium is seeing unions re-examine some very traditional concepts of participative democracy, with unions seeking to link membership involvement in union activities to involvement in decision making. This re-examination is not retrograde: the evidence which we have reviewed above suggests that unions have recognized the weaknesses in many of their structures and have put resources into making union activities more accessible to a wider range of members and potential members. Neither could it be seen to be primarily ideological. Most initiatives are born from practical necessity: ensuring there are union representatives in place to service newly organized members. In other words, the precipitous decline in union membership numbers which led to a centralization of services, is now resulting in the development of new lay structures.

In sum, while there has been comparatively less theory building from the industrial relations field on the inclusion of under-represented groups in policy formulation, we can draw theory from other political schools. The one common element of the theoretical framework outlined above is the linkage between democracy and participation. There is an affinity here to the radical perspective linking democracy with activism. The key to involvement in democratic decision making is the active involvement of groups of workers in order to articulate their views. In other words, it is not just the formal representative bodies which determine whether democracy is real or window dressing, but how the under-represented groups can and do use them in both structured and unstructured ways.

References

Allen, V. 1954. *Power in Trade Unions: A Study of Their Organization in Great Britain*. London: Longman.

Bassett, P. and Cave, A. 1993. 'Time to Take the Unions to Market', *New Statesman and Society*, 6, 268: 16–17.

Bok, D. C. and Dunlop, J. T. 1970. 'Labor and the American Community', Anonymous (ed.), *The Protection of Minority Interests*. New York: Simon and Schuster.

Cockburn, C. 1983. *Brothers: Male Dominance and Technological Change*. London: Pluto.

Colgan, F. 1999. 'Recognising the Lesbian and Gay Constituency in UK Trade Unions: Moving Forward in UNISON?', *Industrial Relations Journal*, 30: 444–463.

Comstock, D. and Fox, R. 1993. 'Participatory Research as Critical Theory: The North Bonneville USA Experience', in Park, P., Brydon-Miller, M.,

Hall, B. and Jackson, T. (eds.), *Voices of Change: Participatory Research in the United States and Canada*. Westport, Conn.: Bergin and Garvey.

Dempsey, M. 2003. 'Trade Union Managers: Invisible Actors in Trade Union Governance', Working Paper, Cranfield School of Management, Cranfield.

Edelstein, J. and Warner, M. 1975. *Comparative Union Democracy*. London: Allen and Unwin.

Escott, K. and Whitfield, D. 1995. *The Gender Impact of CCT in Local Government*. Manchester: Equal Opportunities Commission.

Fairbrother, P. 1990. 'The Contours of Local Trade Unionism in a Period of Restructuring', in Heery, E. and Fosh, P. (eds.), *Trade Unions and Their Members: Studies in Union Democracy and Organization*. London: British Sociological Association.

——P 1994. *Politics and the State as Employer*. London: Mansell Publishing.

Fiorito, J., Gramm, C. and Hendricks, W. E. 1991. 'Union Structural Choices', in Strauss, G., Gallagher, D. and Fiorito, J. (eds.), *The State of the Unions*. Madison: Industrial Relations Research Association.

Goldstein, J. 1952. *The Government of British Trade Unions*. London: Allen and Unwin.

Gould, C. 1996. 'Diversity and democracy: Representing differences', in Benhabib, S. (ed.), *Democracy and Difference: Contesting the Boundaries of the Political*. Princeton: Princeton University Press. Princeton, N.J.: Princeton University Press.

Habermas, J. 1987. *The Theory of Communicative Action: Vol.2 – Lifeworld and System: A Critique of Functionalist Reason*. Boston: Polity.

Heery, E. 1997. 'The New New Unionism', in Beardwell, I. (ed.), *Contemporary Industrial Relations*. Oxford: Oxford University Press.

Heery, E. and Kelly, J. 1990. 'Full-time Officers and the Shop Steward Network: Patterns of Co-operation and Interdepedence', in Heery, E. and Fosh, P. (eds.), *Trade Unions and Their Members: Studies in Union Democracy and Organization*. London: British Sociological Association.

Heery, E., Simms, M., Simpson, R. and Salmon, J. 2000. 'Organizing Unionism Comes to the UK', *Employee Relations*, 22: 38–57.

Heron, J. 1998. *Co-operative Inquiry*. London: Sage.

Humphrey, J. 2000. 'Self-organization and Trade Union Democracy', *Sociological Review*, 48, 2: 262–282.

Hyman, R. 1991. 'A Future for American Unions?', in Strauss, G., Gallagher, D. and Fiorito, J., (eds.), *The State of the Unions*. Madison, Wis.: Industrial Relations Research Association

——1994. 'Changing Trade Union Identities and Strategies', in Hyman, R. and Ferner, A. (eds.), *New Frontiers in European Industrial Relations*. Oxford: Blackwell.

Jahn, D. 1988. '"Two Logics of Collective Action" and Trade Union Democracy: Organizational Democracy and New Politics in German and Swedish Unions', *Economic and Industrial Democracy*, 9: 319–343.

James, L. 1984. *Power in a Trade Union: The Role of the District Committee in the AUEW*. Cambridge: Cambridge University Press.

Jordan, G. 1990. 'Sub-Governments, Policy Communities and Networks: Refilling Old Bottles?', *Journal of Theoretical Politics*, 2: 319–338.

———1994. *The British Administrative System: Principles versus Practice*. London: Routledge.

Kelly, J. and Heery, E. 1994. *Working for the Union*. Cambridge: Cambridge University Press.

Kirton, G. and Greene, A. 2002. 'The Dynamics of Positive Action in UK Trade Unions: The Case of Women and Black Members', *Industrial Relations Journal*, 33: 157–172.

Labour Research Department (LRD). 1992. *Out at Work: Lesbian and Gay Workers' Rights*. London: LRD.

———2000. *Special Issue Bargaining Report, September 2000*. London.

———2001. *Labour Research, August 2001*. London.

Lave, J. and Wenger, E. 1997. *Situated Learning*. Cambridge: Cambridge University Press.

Lewin, L. 1980. *Governing Trade Unions in Sweden*. Cambridge, Mass.: Harvard University Press.

Lipset, S. M., Trow, M. and Coleman, J. 1956. *Union Democracy: A Report of the Bureau of Applied and Social Research*. Glencoe, Ill.: Free Press.

McBride, A. 2000. 'Promoting Representation of Women within Unison', in Terry, M. (ed.), *The Role of Unions in the Public Sector: Unison and the Future of Unions*. New York: Routledge.

McIlroy, J. 1995. *Trade Unions in Britain Today*. Manchester: Manchester University Press.

Martin, R. 1968. 'Union Democracy: An Explanatory Framework', *Sociology*, 12: 205–220.

Morris, H. and Fosh, P. 2000. 'Measuring Trade Union Democracy: the Case of the UK Civil and Public Services Association', *British Journal of Industrial Relations*, 38: 95–114.

Orr, J. 1996. *Talking About Machines: An Ethnography of a Modern Job*. New York: Cornell University Press.

Park, P. 1993. 'What Is Participatory Research? A Theoretical and Methodological Perspective', in Park, P., Brydon-Miller, M., Hall, B. and Jackson, T., (eds.) *Voices of Change: Participatory Research in the United States and Canada*. Westport, Conn.: Bergin and Garvey

Parker, J. 2002. 'Women's Groups in British Unions', *British Journal of Industrial Relations*, 40: 23–48.

Rahman, M. 1985. 'The Theory and Practice of Participatory Action Research', in Fals Borda, O. (ed.), *The Challenges of Social Change*. Beverly Hills, Calif.: Sage.

Rhodes, R. 1990. 'Policy Networks: A British Perspective', *Journal of Theoretical Politics*, 2: 293–317.

Rhodes, R. and Marsh, D. 1992. *Policy Networks in British Government*. New York: Oxford University Press.

Rigby, M., Smith, R. and Lawlor, T. 1999. *European Trade Unions: Changes and Response*, London: Routledge.

Salamon, M. 2000. *Industrial Relations Theory and Practice*. London: Pearson.

Schumpeter, J. 1976. *Capitalism, Socialism and Democracy*. London: Allen and Unwin.

Serrano Pascual, A. and Waddington, J. 2000. 'Young People: The Labour Market and Trade Unions', in *Report prepared for the Youth Committee of the European Trade Union Confederation*. Brussels: ETUC.

Smith, P., Fosh, P., Morris, H. and Undy, R. 1993. 'Ballots and Union Government in the 1990's', *British Journal of Industrial Relations*, 31, 3: 365–382.

Sneade, A. 2000. 'Trade Union Membership 1999–2000: An Analysis of Data from the Certification Officer and the Labour Force Survey', *Labour Market Trends*, 433–444.

South East Region Trades Union Congress. 2000. *New Moves Towards Equality: New Challenges*. London: SERTUC.

Streeck, W. 1988. 'Editorial Introduction', *Economic and Industrial Democracy*, 9: 307–317.

Sweeney, J. 1999. 'Protect Employees to Protect Prosperity.' *Observer*, 7 February.

Undy, R. and Martin, R. 1984. *Ballots and Trade Union Democracy*. Oxford England: Basil Blackwell Publishers.

Union 21. 2002. *Innovations*. London: Union 21.

Voos, P. B. 1983. 'Union Organizing: Costs and Benefits', *Industrial and Labor Relations Review*, 36, 4: 576.

Waddington, J. and Kerr, A. 2002. 'Unions Fit for Young Workers?', *Industrial Relations Journal*, 33: 298–315.

Webb, S. and Webb, B. 1897. *Industrial Democracy*. London: Longmans Green.

Wilks, S. and Wright, M. 1987. *Comparative Government–Industry Relations: Western Europe, United States and Japan*. Oxford: Clarendon.

Willman, P. 1989. 'The Logic of "Market-Share" Trade Unionism: Is Membership Decline Inevitable?', *Industrial Relations Journal*, 20: 260–270.

Willman, P., Morris, T. and Aston, B. 1993. *Union Business: Trade Union Organization and Financial Reform in the Thatcher Years*, Cambridge: Cambridge University Press.

Wright, M. 1988. 'Policy Community, Policy Network and Comparative Industrial Policies', *Policy Studies*, 36: 593–612.

15

Trade unions, social partnerships and national business systems

KAMEL MELLAHI AND GEOFFREY WOOD

This chapter explains how national business systems influence trade unions' choices of social partnership. It explores the reasons behind the origins and persistence of social partnerships within different categories of business system, the extent to which they constitute an inherently unstable form of exchange, and their capacity to resolve systemic crises.

The period since the 1970s has seen an acceleration of cumulative change which is transforming the position of unions and labour in Western societies. Unions in most Western countries (see for example: Stuart and Lucio (2002) for the UK, Rigby (2002) for Spain, Cooney (2002) for Australia) have turned to programmes of social partnership with governments and employers to promote, in theory, employment, productivity and skill development.

Social partnership is a disparate concept. It means very different things in different national cases. Ackers and Payne (1998: 532) noted that 'the best guide to the meaning of contemporary British social partnership is its rhetorical usage by the major political and industrial sectors, but we need conceptual tools to decipher the various semantic threads and criss-crossing definitions'. We believe this statement is also valid for other Western countries. The aim of this chapter is not to untangle the concept of social partnership and unions but to try to explain the reasons behind different national approaches by unions towards social partnership in different business systems, and changes thereto, in the 1990s and early 2000s. We argue that the different forms of social partnership reflect the characteristics of national business systems, looking at the case of compartmentalized – Anglo-American, and co-operative ones – North European. The type of social partnerships, with labour and unions, that is initiated or reconstituted reflects the characteristics and contradictions of a specific national paradigm. Further, within the same system, partnerships are dynamic and subject to change over time. We suggest that in collaborative business systems, partnerships tend to be in the form of national level accords. Since the 1980s, the central problem has been that of introducing a degree of decentralization within a broadly co-operative framework – i.e. to achieve greater numerical flexibility, whilst retaining the high degree of functional flexibility/high trust that characterizes collaborative systems.

In contrast, in compartamentalized business systems, the central problem of partnership is that of trust, especially in the aftermath of decades of aggressive downsizing. Engendering this will facilitate functional flexibility; such trust has been eroded by the strong emphasis on numerical flexibility within such systems. Here, the resultant partnerships tend to be firm and/or local community centred. In short, in compartmentalized systems, social partnership represents a response to internal contradictions. In contrast, social partnerships represented a defining feature of collaborative systems that has been the subject of adjustment in the face of external shocks. In this chapter, we provide a general introduction to social partnerships, locate this within business systems theory, and then explore the characteristics of social partnerships within specific national paradigms.

Definition of partnership: one word – a variety of meanings

Precise definitions of partnership remain elusive (Caroll 1999). As Guest (2001: 101) notes, partnership 'is one of those warm words, that can mean all things to all people'. Researchers have also decried the absence of good conceptual frameworks for understanding how to manage a social partnership (Halal 2001), an absence which may account for the different interpretations of social partnership and what it entails. Above all, social partnerships represent attempts to balance the needs of individuals (and communities) with those of firms. Partnership in organization typically is discussed in terms of the benefits of the variety of stakeholders. Traditionally, social partnerships have been associated with what is referred to as the 'Rhineland model' of neo-corporatism, inferring long-term state support for representative trade unions, an affiliation to collective bargaining, and the establishment of long-term strategies between government, business and organized labour (Beardwell and Holden 2001: 489; Iankova 1996).

More recently, within certain national business systems, social partnerships have been taken to entail a recognition that, as members of an economic community, key stakeholders have a legitimate interest in an enterprise. However, the latter manifestation of social partnerships tends to also be predicated on the assumption of mutual gains. In this chapter we explore the relationship between specific business systems and patterns of social partnership, and the extent to which the latter are adjusted in the light of long-term fluctuations in the global capitalist economy.

Social partnerships with unions can only be realized through unions making appropriate contributions for mutual benefit, which, in turn, is only possible through an 'environment of relative equity and fairness' (Beardwell and Holden 2001: 489). In short, what is sought is a situation of 'mutual advantage' (Huxham and Vangen 2000). Underpinning contemporary notions of a social partnership are a desire to provide some protection for individual employees and their collectives, but within a context that retains many of the key manifestations of the neo-liberal orthodoxy, including flexibility, general deregulation and an emphasis on ensuring competitiveness (Beardwell and Holden 2001: 489).

Social partnerships are not necessarily characterized by an absence of conflict; rather, conflict becomes institutionalized, with established mechanisms for conflict resolution that do not endanger the existing social order (Kirichenko and Koudyukin 1993: 43). In other words, the emphasis of social partnerships is on fairness, inclusivity, economic growth and social progress rather than order at all costs. Waddock (1988) argues that partnerships will only succeed if a degree of flexibility is incorporated. In implementing a partnership, key issues include the anticipated fragility of any deal made, the time needed to develop a partnership, the degree of co-operation present, staff support, and the expectations of the various partners (Waddock 1988).

Business systems and social partnerships

Whitley defines business systems as 'particular ways of organising, controlling and directing enterprises ... particular arrangements of hierarchy–market relations which become institutionalized and relatively successful in particular contexts' (Foss 1999a). Business systems theory seeks to explain 'the "stamp" in terms of the modes of organizing and managing that belonging to a certain country leaves on firms, and second, how firms interact and compete' within a specific institutional context (Foss 1999a). It aims to transcend purely economistic analyses that focus solely on the regulative aspects of institutions, by also looking at the cognitive and normative aspects thereof, and the manner which the latter may influence resource allocation (Foss 1999b). In other words, specific institutional configurations – which may be characterized by partnerships of varying strengths – represent the product not only of direct economic pressures, but also factors such as trust that may, in turn, impact on economic outcomes.

Whilst individual industries can develop their distinct 'business recipes', internal economic factors 'will not generate highly dissimilar business systems' within a similar national context (Pedersen and Thomson 1999). As Foss (1999a) notes:

> They combine preferences for particular kinds of activities and skills to be co-ordinated authoritatively with variations in the degree of discretion exercised by managers from property rights holders and in the ways in which activities are co-ordinated. They also exhibit differences in extent and manner in which activities are co-ordinated between economic actors. Thus the nature of firms as quasi-autonomous economic actors, their internal structures and their interdependencies are all interrelated and differ significantly between institutional contexts.

Whitley (1999) identifies a number of distinct patterns of business systems. Inter alia, these include 'compartmentalized' business systems and 'collaborative' ones; these are somewhat broad categories, and a number of sub-categories may be identified. The former is dominated by adversarial competition, short-term marketing and contracting, similarly short-term employment relations, large and highly integrated ownership units, and 'efficient' external labour markets (Whitley 1999: 43). Ownership is indirect, and is exercised via financial markets (Whitley 1999). In contrast, collaborative business systems are characterized by higher levels of collective organization and co-operation within sectors. They are characterized by higher levels of employee–employer interdependence, and higher levels of trust (Whitley 1999: 44). Moreover, there are commonly corporatist relations within such systems, involving tripartite deals between labour, business and the state. The level of trust in an economy affects the level of inter-firm co-operation; a key determining issue is the strength of social institutions that generate and guarantee trust between relative strangers (Whitley 1999: 51).

Business systems developed interdependently with dominant social institutions; particular forms of economic organization thus tend to predominate in particular institutional contexts (Whitley 1999: 47). Moreover, 'the distinctiveness and cohesion of different business systems reflects the extent to which dominant institutions are integrated and their features mutually reinforcing' (Whitley 1999: 47). Collaborative systems can have the effect of restraining self-interest, socializing 'good' citizens, and restraining rational, rent-seeking individuals from destroying productive resources in the pursuit of short-term gain, enhancing mutual cooperation and trust (Friedman 2000). Thus, a greater diversity is likely to be exhibited within and between 'lower-trust' compartmentalized business systems than 'higher-trust' collaborative ones.

While like any other mode of social organization, business systems are prone to periodic shocks, most of the past research focuses on static levels of relationships ignoring, or underestimating, the different patterns of conflict that might occur over time. Because of the cyclical nature of the economy and dynamism of the current competitive environment, it may be more relevant to consider how much and when, rather than if, the factors affect partnership change. Business systems theory, for instance, is somewhat sketchy in areas such as how stable individual systems are, and the manner in which they cope with crises (Foss 1999a). However, it tends to see disturbances as a product of technical and/or economic factors. Nonetheless, the kind of social action that leads to disturbances is sometimes more simply conditioned by the prevalent regulatory norms and institutions, but may sometimes seek their transformation (Foss 1999b). However, social action is not the monopoly of the weak; employers may also mount sustained attacks on particular institutional configurations. Thus, agitation can be seen as 'as a companion to regulation allows us to see changes in the labour process (and in other aspects of capitalism) as the outcome of strategic initiatives, which do not necessarily indicate a new phase of the system' (Friedman 2000).

Two forms of crises may be identified. The first, commonly associated with collaborative systems, involves minor fall-outs between the principal players. For example, a neo-corporatist social accord involving centralized wage setting may be suspended or even abandoned, but will subsequently be reconstituted. A good example would be Norway, where several social accords have failed owing to union leapfrogging of wage claims and/or employer intransigence, but ultimately have been replaced by new ones. In Sweden, the degree of centralization of bargaining, whilst generally high, has tended to fluctuate albeit in a somewhat more moderate fashion than is the case in Norway (Iverson 1999: 9).

Secondly, there are the more serious 'crises of existence', triggered off by fluctuations in long-term economic waves; more specifically, a downturn is likely to result in severe problems of adjustment, necessitating some adjustments in social institutions. Collaborative systems face the problem of a lack of dynamism; collaborative processes can easily become ossified, given the need to restrict individual or interest-group 'freeriding' – the pursuit of fractional group interest – to the detriment of the social whole. Conversely, compartmentalized business systems face problems of trust, which in turn, may exact a heavy toll in terms of productivity. The situation is depicted in table 15.1.

Table 15.1 Problems of adjustment in different business systems in the 1990s and early 2000s

Business system type	Country example	Issue
Collaborative	Austria	Recognition and control of decentralization
Dynamic collaborative	Sweden	Consolidation of reform
Compartmentalized	USA	Creation of legitimacy
Compartmentalized	United Kingdom	Creation of trust

Sources: Casey B. and Gold, M. 2000. *Social Partnerships and Economic Performance.* Cheltenham: Edward Elgar. Harcourt, M. and Wood, G. 2003. 'Under What Circumstances Do Social Accords Work?', *Journal of Economic Issues* (in print). Whitley, R. 1999. *Divergent Capitalisms: the Social Structuring and Change of Business Systems.* Oxford: Oxford University Press.

In all the above cases, attempts to ameliorate the relevant challenges have, in part, included efforts to develop social partnerships and/or to reconfigure existing ones. As Rao and Sita (1993) note, 'the interactive relationship leading to mutual problem solving and benefits has been variably referred to as a collaborative or participative strategy', becoming a social partnership when issues and efforts of a broader scope are encompassed. Much of the literature on social partnerships focuses on possible long-term relations between the unions and management (see Beardwell and Holden 2001; Guest 2001). However, social partnerships can also encompass deals reached between governments, unions and employers at a centralized level (e.g. corporatism), or agreements between employers and communities (cf. Rao and Sita 1993). For example, a social partnership arrangement may develop between a multinational company and a host community to, say, reduce levels of environmental pollution. Similarly, a broadly based social partnership could provide community-based development organizations with the necessary resources and backing to 'undo the damage of business flight and racial animosity that plague poor communities' (Rubin 1993: 428). Thus, social partnerships may be focused on the two central groupings within the firm, employers and employees – with varying degrees of state involvement as well – or have a more explicitly community focus, involving one or more local groupings (Waddock and Post 1991).

As noted earlier, collaborative business systems are more closely associated with neo-corporatist-type deals. In contrast, the kind of social partnership that emerges in compartmentalized systems tends to be more localized. The situation is depicted in table 15.2. Neo-corporatist accords-based partnerships are likely to emerge when the principal social actors – and, this is predicated on the presence of coherent 'encompassing organizations' (i.e. employer associations and unions) with broad social footprints) (Olson 1982) – perceive a strong mutuality of interest, and few conceivable options other than co-operation. Chapter 3 provides a critical assessment of the role of social accords in promoting democracy and social equity.

Should levels of trust be very low, and 'encompassing organizations' – particularly unions – be weak or decentralized, the firm may seek to build partnerships with community organizations. However, if the crisis of trust is less severe (and owing to

Table 15.2 Business systems and forms of partnership

Business system	Country example	Form of partnership
Stable collaborative	Austria	Social accords/neo-corporatism
Dynamic collaborative	Norway	Social accords/neo-corporatism, but with periods of devolved bargaining
Moderate compartmentalized	United Kingdom	Partnerships between employers and unions at firm level
Compartmentalized	United States	Partnerships between employers and community organizations.

persisting institutional constraints, the firm is less able to wield the 'iron whip of hunger', ensuring employee compliance through extremely insecure tenure), partnerships may be geared towards securing the involvement of employees. In the case of the latter, trust is enhanced at workplace level, which, it is hoped, will lead to higher levels of employee co-operation and trust, whilst retaining relatively dynamic external labour markets.

Social partnerships in compartmentalized systems: the Anglo-Saxon model

Starting in the early 1980s, the rules of the game changed in Britain and the US. The competitive environment of the 1980s, and liberal government policies significantly reduced the role of traditional institutions such as unions. The key thesis of the co-operative paradigm within the Anglo-Saxon business system, is that firms, employees, customers, distributors and the wider community are interdependent on each other for critical resources in the current intense global competitive environment. The new paradigm is underpinned by the belief that the game is not zero sum but that organizations are one well integrated organism in which sharing resources co-operatively could create more payoffs for all parties. In the new context, corporations seem to be the primary agent facilitating and often benefiting from the inclusive partnership-based paradigm.

The answer to why firms engage in such partnerships is not

clear. Some scholars have suggested that many firms enter such partnerships to improve their strategic position by learning new skills or acquiring tacit knowledge (cf. Donaldson and Dunfee 1999; Freeman 1984; Finnie *et al.* 1998) or to increase legitimacy. We believe, in spite of a lack of empirical evidence, it is fair to suggest that some social partnerships are a product of the bandwagon effect in which firms succumb to isomorphic pressures and mimic other firms that have entered a partnership. Halal (2001) argues that four elements make up the relationship between stakeholders and the corporation: conflict resolution (Jones 1995), equitable treatment (cf. Adams 1963), market penetration (Bolman and Deal 1997), collaborative problem-solving (Donaldson and Dunfee 1999; Finnie *et al.* 1998; Freeman, 1984; Spagnolo 1999). Furthermore, the issue of whether social responsibility pays in business terms is not clear. While a number of studies show a positive correlation between social responsibility and corporate performance, a host of studies show little relationship between the two (Aupperle *et al.* 1985; Cochran and Wood 1984; Harrison and Freeman 1999; McGuire *et al.* 1988). However, it is evident that, at least in part, social partnership initiatives in compartmentalized business system represent a response to crises of trust.

It must be noted that these forces that are bringing firms to interact with their stakeholders are not the same as those which determine *how* the firm will interact – behave – with its partners. We believe that the latter is shaped by prior ties and experiences between the parties involved as well as the current economic, political and social contexts. That is, the behaviour of the firm in these partnerships is dynamic and evolves as new realities emerge and new contexts are formed. A firm's behaviour in the partnership is thus the result of both its own experience in social partnerships, the behaviour of other partners and reaction to emerging realities. For instance, while Marks & Spencer was long held as an exemplar of partnership with its employees, customers, suppliers and the wider community (Mellahi *et al.* 2002), the company changed direction in the late 1990s and early 2000s after the company was hit by a crisis (see Burt *et al.* 2002). It reconstituted its relationship arguing that it needed to amputate its partnership structure to win its battle for survival. In short, because, from managers' viewpoint, economic realities are considered fundamental to survival, when the 'going gets tough', concern for profit and survival drives out social consideration (Halal 2001). Halal (2001: 40) notes that 'The prevailing rules of institutional conduct for capitalist economies demand financial success, whether we like it or not, and the hard reality is that corporations are economic institutions that must compete successfully in an increasingly turbulent marketplace.'

This partnership, however, creates a paradox for the different partners. The key question here is whether the goals of the different partners are compatible? On the one hand, partnership could offer the potential for co-operative behaviour from the different partners and mutual gains. On the other hand, the potential exists for firms to reap extraordinary profits at the expense of weaker and compartmentalized employees. For instance, if firms and unions are each potentially useful to the other, yet each contain features antagonistic to the other. Thus, because the two parties have different aims and responsibilities, it is not surprising that their objectives also differ. In the extreme, the positions of unions and managers are mutually exclusive and incompatible, because each focuses on a diametrically opposite objective.

Nevertheless, what explains the different manifestations in social partnership in the United States and Britain? Or is there simply diversity within both contexts? In other words, reflecting the characteristics of fragmentation, are 'managers simply behaving in short-term, contradictory and opportunistic ways' or is there a strategic linkage whereby managers use partnerships to underpin changes necessitated by specific national systemic characteristics (Bacon and Storey 2000: 409).

There is an extensive US literature on mutual gains enterprises (see, for example, Kochan and Osterman 1994) which in some respects seems to echo the 'soft pluralist' British tradition (Bacon and Storey 2000: 409). A contemporary manifestation of this would be social partnerships centring on building relationships – and trust – between employer and employees. As many writers have correctly pointed out, the willingness of unions to commit themselves to such partnerships – in effect, helping management pull their chestnuts out of the fire – is a product of union weakness (cf. Bacon and Storey 2000). However, at the same time, such partnerships are not possible should unions be totally absent and/or the workforce is highly compartmentalized and individualized.

Alternatively, there are social partnerships that focus on

building relationships with communities. This would, in part, reflect neo-unitarist thinking – employers and employees form a coherent team, or at least, employees and unions are so weak that it is hardly worth concluding a partnership with them at all. Here the real challenges are building relationships between the firm and the broader community. This does not necessarily mean that in compartmentalized systems with weak unions, community partnerships will emerge as a means of plugging a trust gap. Managers are unlikely to be interested in a partnership at all if they completely have the upper hand, and are able to shape their relations with employees and society to their will.

For the firm, such partnerships would engender tolerance and support for its activities and a favourable market response for its products. Again, one can find examples of such practices in both the US and Britain. However, given the greater relative strength of the British union movement vis-à-vis its US counterpart, and an accumulated body of pluralist practices in the former, social partnerships between managers and employees seem to receive particular emphasis in Britain (see Bacon and Storey 2000: 407). In contrast, in the US, the weaker position of labour – and even less secure employment contracts than Britain – has led to considerably more emphasis being placed on partnerships with communities. On the one hand, US firms are in a stronger position to unilaterally reorganize work. On the other hand, in a highly competitive external market, the kind of advantage that can be secured through community support (or at least tolerance) may be of great value.

In a highly compartmentalized system, partnerships can pave the way for new alliances, 'expanding capacities beyond an organization's resource base ... alliances allow organizations greater flexibility and the opportunity to leverage competencies, improve customer service, and create a wider geographic reach' (Sagaw and Segal 2000). Community partnerships can help attract and retain skilled workers to a specific locale, help build a team of workers from those who live in different neighbourhoods (some deeply disadvantaged), and provide a firm with greater insights into what is possibly its immediate marketplace (Sagaw and Segal 2000). Moreover, the US federal system, with the devolution of much power to states and local authorities, does mean that it makes economic sense for firms to have local and regional communities on their side (Currie and Skolnick

1988: 38). However, it should not be assumed that a stronger emphasis in the United States on community partnerships than in Britain purely reflects immediate profit motives; social practices become institutionally embedded over time. The US has a more deeply entrenched tradition of corporate philanthropy than Britain (the case of the Quaker firms in the latter notwithstanding). In the US, firms have historically assumed some responsibility for 'good work' partially to reduce pressures for governmental interference and to justify demands for a minimalist state (see Currie and Skolnick 1988: 40–5). In contrast, in Britain, unions have tended to be in a stronger position than their US counterparts; the greater political clout of unions (at least until the 1970s) has meant that many British employers have, quite simply, become accustomed to dealing with unions as a matter of course (Hyman 1975). This explains the stronger emphasis placed on community partnerships in the US and vice versa in Britain. At the same time, it must be recognized that these national models are not totally divergent. There are many examples of British firms seeking to build links with communities (e.g. Marks & Spencer) and US firms with unions or employee teams (e.g. Steelcase).

The US paradigm: community-based social partnerships and firm-level counterparts

As noted earlier, social partnerships need not necessarily focus on deals between employers and employee representatives. Indeed, social partnerships may form part and parcel of corporate efforts at 'good citizenship' within the community. Social responsibility represents 'the obligation a business assumes toward society ... to be socially responsible is to maximise positive effects and minimize negative effects on society' (Ferrell *et al.* 2000: 6). Classic corporate social responsibility represents an attempt by the firm to divert a proportion of revenues to 'good to worthy causes, as well as finding creative ways to improve the quality of life of the firm's employees and the local community' (Ferrell *et al.* 2000: 278). However, any outreach is very much on the firm's terms; assistance is seen as a 'free gift' to be extended or revoked at will; the firm does what it sees as socially desirable, taking only limited account of the views and interests of the subject. Community-linked social partnerships are based on a recognition of the limits of classical corporate social responsibility initiatives; here the views of key stakeholders are considered and brought aboard, making for more sustainable and ultimately successful outreach initiatives.

This form of social partnership has become a central element of the contemporary organizational landscape within the United States. Sagawa and Segal (2000: 105) note that 'almost anywhere you look you can find evidence of stepped-up business–social sector interaction'. Halal (2001: 28) notes that the 'two concepts central to the conduct of business – corporate profitability and social responsibility – have co-existed in an uneasy tension through industrialisation'. Prior to this, the history of firms and their relationship with their primary stakeholders and the wider community was generally characterized by conflict in the firm–stakeholder relationship. Consequently, past studies on the determinants of firm–stakeholder relationship tended to focus on power, regulatory stance, and level of influence related parameters such as unions' and managers' bargaining power. These studies were underpinned by bargaining and transaction cost theories. Although the conflict adversarial based view did not exclude some elements of co-operation and partnership (cf. Bowen 1953; Carroll 1977; Carson and Steiner 1974; Heald 1957; Johnson 1971; McGuire 1963; Walton 1967), it was dominated by the assumption that the relationships between the firm and other stakeholders were a bargaining zero sum game in which each party could use the balance of power to gain a larger share of benefit. In such a context where objectives are not only perceived to be different, but can be incompatible, it is often implied that the process to achieve them is incompatible as well. Consequently, each party sought self-interest with guile in a highly adversarial context. Goal incongruity and stake asymmetry between firms and unions, for instance, often shaped the bargaining process as well as the outcome of the bargain.

During the 1980s and 1990s, the pendulum swung in the opposite direction as the firm–stakeholder relationship started incrementally shifting from confrontation to co-operation – although this model was introduced in the 1960s, it did not take off until the mid-1980s. Social partnerships are resurfacing as a critical yet complex issue attracting the attention of both academics and practitioners. Contemporary community-based social partnerships represent a more developed form of corporate social responsibility – not only does the firm simply 'do good works' in the community, but it acts in concert with community groupings to ensure that its outreach activities have maximum impact. For example, the revitalization of the urban centre of Cleveland in the United States in the late 1980s represented the outcome of ongoing partnerships between business and community organizations (Austin 1998). Proponents of such deals argue that a win–win situation is likely to result; again, overall social prosperity is promoted as well as a more attractive environment in which to do business. However, the rationales for such deals are again rather complex when viewed from a business ethics perspective; in entering such agreements are firms motivated by the desire for self-preservation and advancement, or by genuine moral concerns? Alternatively, it could be argued that community-linked social partnerships represent little more than a re-warmed version of classical corporate philanthropy – limited 'good works' done in order to make the relentless pursuit of profit more socially acceptable.

It could further be argued that many community-linked partnerships represent little more than a form of marketing by other means. Corporate assistance for community development may result in favourable exposure for the firm, both through formal and informal mechanisms. Again, partnerships to promote a green agenda – for example, alliances or linkages with NGOs to promote or facilitate more environmentally sound production methods – may provide a ready opportunity to advertise a firm's green credentials. For example, critics have charged that US ice-cream firm, Ben and Jerry's social responsibility initiatives represented a cynical attempt through 'save the world marketing' and through 'a series of feel-good stunts to sell high-price ice cream' (Ferrell *et al.* 2000: 280). However, many utilitarians would have little problem with such developments, as long as they result in a general improvement in the social condition, or, indeed, that of the biosphere.

An alternative, and somewhat bleaker view of corporate social responsibility – particularly in its more holistic partnership manifestations – is provided by David Korten. Korten asserts that, given the predatory nature of contemporary capitalism, with its emphasis on short-term profits, any company that acts in a socially responsible fashion is automatically placed at a weakness: 'corporate managers live and work in a system that is virtually feeding on the socially responsible' (quoted in Ferrell *et al.* 2000: 279).

Despite insecure employment contracts and the relatively

weak position of organized labour in the US, managers may still in some cases be under pressure to develop some form of workplace partnership. This would particularly be the case in industries seeking to develop competitive advantages through new forms of work organization. In turn, the latter may be facilitated through placing a greater emphasis on securing the consent of employees.

Literature suggests that the partnership between employers and employees is based on the 'new psychological contract' which is based on commitment and trust. Paradoxically, a large body of research also suggests that organizational downsizing is likely to be a permanent feature of the modern organizational landscape; this is particularly the case in compartmentalized business systems (Cameron *et al.* 1991). This begs the question: are commitment and trust a one-way street? Several authors argue that downsizing results in the death of corporate loyalty (Economist Editors 1993; O'Neill and Lenn 1995). Mone (1997) notes that 'more often than not, employees remaining following organization downsizing trust the organization and their managers less and experience guilt, lower morale, increased stress due to both job insecurity and increased workloads, lack of concentration, and reduced satisfaction' and survivors exhibit 'lower morale and commitment to the organization, increased absenteeism, tardiness, theft, and overall, lower work productivity'. Similarly Brockner *et al.* (1987) found that the survivors of downsizing may reduce their level of commitment to the organization, because they identify with the loss of respected co-workers and friends. Mone (1997) argues that much of the literature on the new psychological contract is found in organizations following downsizing (quoted in Mone 1997; Hakim 1994). O'Reilly (1994) urges employees to 'rely on no one but themselves' and not to be 'committed to the organization, because it cannot commit to you'.

The British paradigm – firm-level social partnerships: underpinnings and benefits

Waddock (1988) argues that firm-level social partnerships can accrue meaningful benefits to all parties. Critical in the creation of partnerships is the existence of a problem that can only be solved through mutual interaction; 'including organizations and individuals holding a stake in the problem to be solved is central to partnership success' (Waddock 1988).

Successful social partnerships have often been upheld as one of the benefits of corporate success. However, much trumpeted partnership agreements have often failed to rescue companies from subsequent financial crises, good examples being Hyundai and Rover (Guest 2001: 103).

Whilst firmly committed to the neo-liberal policies of previous Conservative governments, the Blair Labour government in Britain attempted to temper some of its worst excesses through promoting social partnerships. Certainly, this does not entail a return to the 'Rhineland model': indicative of this is that the word 'partnership' receives considerably more emphasis than the traditional term of 'social partnership' (Beardwell and Holden 2001: 489). What is envisaged is an emphasis on the mutual responsibilities of employers and employees, with unions and managers engaging in ongoing dialogue 'to introduce change, improve productivity and resolve disputes' (Beardwell and Holden 2001: 490). This desire is advocated in the Fairness at Work legislation, the Employment Relations Act 1999 (ERA), and through the 1999 Partnership Initiative, the latter providing some funding for new partnership arrangements (Guest 2001: 104; Smith and Morton 2001).

Social partnerships in Britain have received broad backing from the labour movement (Bacon and Storey 2000; Undy 1999; Beardwell and Holden 2001: 490). However, this may simply reflect the vulnerability of unions, and the desire to retain some vestiges of support from the state and employers (Bacon and Storey 2000; Beardwell and Holden 2001: 490). However, it can be argued that union members do have a strong interest in areas outside the traditional scope of collective bargaining; surveys of union members indicate that employees place a high premium on job security, quality of work and job fulfilment (Beardwell and Holden 2001: 490). Given this, it can be argued that unions have little option but to express support for social partnerships if they are to accurately represent the needs of their members. In the case of management, meaningful concessions will be necessary if any partnership deal is to get off the ground; management cannot endlessly repeat a stated commitment to partnership without, at the very least, broadening the scope of consultation.

Critics of the British social partnerships have argued that such deals are more likely to be motivated by the exigencies of profitability rather than fairness (cf. Breitenfellner 1997). Instead, social partnerships should centre on a broader social agenda, straddling national boundaries if need be. However, the latter is only likely to take place if labour unions are capable of co-ordinating their activities internationally, and through concerted action by individual national governments; essentially a form of super neo-corporatism would be the desired policy outcome (Breitenfellner 1997).

As Guest (2001: 101) notes, the attraction of partnerships for unions includes the fact that they represent one of the few viable routes through which they may be valued by employers, and yet still retain an independent voice. However, the cost entailed from any social partnership is that they may simply become a device for incorporation by management (Guest 2001: 101). Indeed, it can be argued that 'despite its connotations of mutuality and mutual gains', it may in practice be weighted towards the company, with other partners contributing much more to the company's success than the company gives back to individual employees, collectives and communities (Guest 2001: 101). Employers may use partnerships as a means of pre-empting efforts by unions to broaden the scope of collective bargaining; if unions are ideologically committed to the notion of partnerships, they may be forced to accept a restriction on negotiation and the expansion of consultation (Beardwell and Holden 2001: 490).

Metcalf (1995) argues that, in Britain, traditional collective industrial relations 'is crumbling', possible outcomes being new forms of workplace-centred partnership, or authoritarian forms of workplace governance. However, whilst the former may result in greater productivity, they may undermine existing relationships between employers and unions that have been built up over many years. Indeed, it is a common perception that practices often turn out to be primarily for the benefit of the company; what employees can do for the firm is given a far higher priority than what the firm can do for individuals or communities (Beardwell and Holden 2001: 101).

Moreover, there is considerable evidence to suggest that even those firms which might be expected 'to be on the leading edge of best practice' are still likely to be associated with low levels of trust, especially in terms of management trusting trade unions (Guest 2001: 101). Trust is only possible if all parties have a shared vision (Ferrell *et al.* 2000: 149). This has led Kelly (quoted in Beardwell and Holden 2001: 490) to argue that 'it is difficult, if not impossible to achieve a partnership with a party who would prefer that you didn't exist; the growth of employer hostility is a major objection to the case for union moderation'. In other words, given the strength of management and governmental ambivalence, there is little reason for employers to enter into truly meaningful partnerships, when they are capable of exercising their prerogative independently (Beardwell and Holden 2001: 490). Moreover, it can be argued that unions have had far more success in extracting genuine concessions from employers through traditional collective bargaining, especially when backed up with the threat of collective action from the shop floor (Beardwell and Holden 2001: 490).

Finally, despite the Blair Labour government's strong emphasis on 'partnership', it seems that partnership agreements – even those only directly involving employers and unions – only gained a foothold at a small minority of British workplaces (Guest 2001: 102). Indeed, as Guest (2001: 103) notes, many partnerships seem to be borne out of a notion of crisis (just as was the case with the 'Rhineland model' partnerships). Partnership has become formally institutionalized in Britain through various governmental initiatives, but these have yet to gain broader practical support (Guest 2001: 104); one of the few exceptions to this general rule being the Low Pay Commission (Metcalf 1999). Moreover, partnership only represents one of a plethora of alternative policy options open to the contemporary labour movement (see Hyman 1997).

Theoretical implications

As Foss (1999a) notes, business systems are characterized and differentiated by the following constituent features:

1. The different ways of organizing and coordinating transactions, where what is different across different systems is the mix of hierarchical and market-organized transactions.
2. Different types and levels of specialization ('preference for particular kinds of activities and skills').
3. The degree of separation between ownership and control, that is, the mode of corporate governance.
4. Organizing principles that influence firm routines and capabilities through their influence on authority relations, organizational structures, relations between the professions, and so on' (Foss 1999b).

It is evident that social partnerships can directly shape the first, second and the fourth features, the former through differing mechanisms of wage setting and labour market governance, and the latter two through the extent of direct workplace participation, and national deals on skills development and involvement. Moreover, collaborative business systems are characterized by high levels of co-operation within sectors, and alliance-based configurations of ownership and control (Whitley 1999: 44). Such characteristics may be strengthened through centralized social accords, which may provide greater incentives for co-operative forms of corporate governance (cf. factor 3; see also chapter 14).

There is little doubt that many different forms of business system are viable (Foss 1999b), and that different institutional mechanisms may successfully regulate endemic crises. Efficiency should always be defined relative to context (Foss 1999b); specific forms of social partnership may have greater utility in one system than in another. As Schneiberg (2001) notes:

> The institutions of capitalism tend to cohere in a limited number of stable configurations, profoundly shaping firms' capacities to pursue flexible specialization or diversified quality production. In the contemporary period, global competition and technological change have rendered mass production strategies increasingly ineffective, while placing a premium on strategies and structures that support innovation, variety and rapid adaptation.

Such strategies can include skills development, initiatives to enhance workforce commitment, wage stability, and, indeed, 'the enhancement of collective institutions that restructure competition' (Schneiberg 2001). As we have seen, many of these strategies can be partially realized through some or other form of social partnership; even the most modest form of philanthropic partnership incorporates a systemic dimension. 'Different institutional environments encourage the development of contrasting kinds of firms with varied governance structures and organizational capabilities' (Whitley 2000), resulting in differing partnership outcomes.

The nature and extent of partnerships will be shaped by changes in the global economy, technological development, and associated institutional fluctuations. As Friedman (2000) notes, shifts away from classic fordist methods of production have had the following consequences: 'The fundamental compromise between a national collection of large companies and national trade unions breaks down; as does the national commitment to demand management, full employment, social security and the principle of public provision of collective needs.'

In the case of collaborative business systems, given a potential institutional lack of dynamism, the former pressure has been most visible. This has led to attempts at reform and controlled decentralization, whilst retaining key aspects of neo-corporatism. In compartmentalized business systems, where such a compromise has generally been lacking, the latter process has been more visible. In return, this has exacerbated problems associated with trust; more flexible forms of production may be facilitated by high levels of numerical flexibility, but they also require higher levels of employee commitment and skills in key areas. In return this has led to firm-based partnerships, and attempts to build bridges with other stakeholders in society.

The central concerns of regulating endemic crises, 'available analytical frameworks and sets of resulting policy prescriptions are inexorably concerned with questions of power' (Coates 1999). Social partnerships are thus not just about agreeing – in the case of neo-corporatism – on macro-economic targets, but also in reconfiguring power networks. The latter is about seeking to identify where power lies, and blockages rest, in the determination of growth trajectories at both firm and system levels (Coates 1999). Power triggers/blockages can be seen as anchored either in particular institutional mixes or in particular balances of class power (Coates 1999); whatever the explanation, it is evident that partnerships concern both material concerns and power. In both cases, they are, however, about regulation and sustainability; even the most narrow community-level social partnerships do entail both power and material concerns and objectives.

Conclusion

The diverse manifestations and changing nature of social partnerships in the late 1990s and early 2000s reflects specific forms of systemic crisis. Within collaborative business systems, the challenge has been to reconstitute long-established forms of social partnership to facilitate greater labour market flexibility in the face of increased global competition, yet retain the former's best features. The latter would include a strong commitment to skills development, cooperative forms of workplace organization, and high levels of trust, as well as a commitment to a basic degree of equity. In contrast, compartmentalized systems face an increasing crisis of legitimation and trust in an age of insecure contracts, volatile financial markets, and limited managerial accountability. If employees and their collectives are extremely weak, managers may first focus their attentions on securing the consent of other stakeholder groupings that are in a position to impact on the future of the firm; hence community partnerships. In contrast, should there be a deeply embedded tradition of pluralism – or semi-pluralism in the workplace, employers may first seek to develop partnerships with employee representatives. In both cases, however, the resultant partnerships will be more locally based, and constrained in form and consequences; they are unlikely to serve as a basis for genuinely broadening workplace democracy on a sustainable basis.

References

Ackers, P. and Payne, J. 1998. 'British Trade Unions and Social Partnership: Rhetoric, Reality and Strategy', *International Journal of Human Resource Management*, 9, 3: 529–550.

Adams, S. 1963. 'Toward an Understanding of Inequity', *Journal of Abnormal and Social Psychology*, 65, 5: 422–436.

Apeldoorn, B. 2000. 'Transnational Class Agency and European Governance: the Case of the European Round Table of Industrialists', *New Political Economy*, 5, 2: 157–181.

Aupperle, K. E. Caroll, A. B. and Hatfield, J. D. 1985. 'An Empirical Examination of the Relationship Between Corporate Social Responsibility and Profitability', *Academy of Management Journal*, 28,2: 446–463.

Austin, J. 1998 'Business Leadership Lessons from the Cleveland Turnaround', *California Management Review*, 41, 1: 86–106.

Bacon, N. and Storey, J. 2000. 'New Employment Strategies in Britain: Towards Individualism or Partnership?', *British Journal of Industrial Relations*, 38, 3, 407–427.

Beardwell, I. and Holden, L. 2001. *Human Resource Management: A Contemporary Approach*. London: Prentice Hall.

Bolman, L. G. and Deal, T. E. 1997. *Reframing Organizations*. San Francisco: Jossey-Bass.

Boulding, K. 1963. *Conflict and Defense*. New York: Harper and Row.

Bowen, H. R. 1953. *Social Responsibility for the Businessmen*. New York: Harper & Row.

Breitenfellner, A. 1997. 'Global Unionism: A Potential Player', *International Labour Review*, 136, 4: 531–555.

Brockner, J., Grover, S. L., Reed, T. F., DeWitt R. L. and O'Malley, M. N. 1987. 'Survivors' Reaction to Layoffs: We Get By with a Little Help for our Friends', *Administrative Science Quarterly*, 32: 526–541.

Burt, S. L., Mellahi, K., Jackson, P. and Sharks, L. 2002. 'Retail Internationalisation and Retail Failure: Issues from the Case of Marks & Spencer', *International Review of Retail, Distribution and Consumer Research*, 12, 2: 191–219.

Cameron, K., Freeman, S. J. and Mishra, A. 1991. 'Best Practices in White-Collar Downsizing: Managing Contradictions', *Academy of Management Executive*, 5: 57–73.

Carroll, A. B. 1977. *Managing Corporate Social Responsibility*. Boston: Little, Brown.

—— 1999. 'Corporate Social Responsibility: Evolution of a Definitional Construct', *Business and Society*, 38, 3: 268–295.

Carson, J. J. and Steiner, G. A. 1974. *Measuring Business's Social Performance: the Corporate Social Audit*. New York: Committee for Economic Development.

Casey, B. and Gold, M. 2000. *Social Partnerships and Economic Performance*. Cheltenham: Edward Elgar.

Coates, D. 1999. 'Why Growth Rates Differ', *New Political Economy*, 4, 1: 77–96.

Cochran, P. L. and Wood, R. A. 1984. 'Corporate Social Responsibility and Financial Performance', *Academy of Management Journal*, 27, 1: 42–56.

Cooney, R. 2002. 'The Contingencies of Partnership: Experiences from the Training Reform Agenda in Australian Manufacturing', *Employee Relations*, 3: 321–335

Crouch, C. 1993. *Industrial Relations and European State Traditions*. Oxford: Clarendon.

Currie, E. and Skolnick, J. 1988. *America's Problems: Social Issues and Public Policy*. Glenview: Scott, Foresman and Company.

Donaldson, T. and Dunfee, T. W. 1999. *Ties That Bind: A Social Contracts Approach to Business Ethics*. Boston, Mass.: Harvard Business School Press.

Economist Editors. 1993. 'The Death of Corporate Loyalty', *Economist*, 3 April: 327–364.

Ferrell, O., Fraedrich, J. and Ferrell, L. 2000. *Business Ethics: Ethical Decision Making and Cases*. Boston: Houghton Mifflin.

Finnie, W. C., Sellew, R. Uselton, J. C. and Vehige, R. 1998. 'Strategic Partnering: Three Case Studies', *Strategy and Leadership*, 26, 4: 18–22.

Flanagan, R. 1999. 'Macro-Economic Performance and Collective Bargaining: An International Perspective', *Journal of Economic Literature*, 37: 1150–1175.

Foss, N. 1999a. 'Preface: Perspectives on Business Systems', *International Studies of Management & Organization*, 29, 2: 3–18.

—— 1999b. 'The Challenge of Business Systems and the Challenge to

Business Systems', *International Studies of Management & Organization*, 29, 2: 9–24.

Freeman, R. E. 1984. Strategic Management: A Stakeholder Approach. Boston, Mass.: Pitman.

Friedman, A. 2000. 'Microregulation and post-Fordism: Critique and Development of Regulation Theory', *New Political Economy*, 5, 1: 59–76.

Gebert, D. and Boerner, S. 1999. 'The Open and Closed Corporation as Distinctive Forms of Organization', *Journal of Applied Behavioral Science*, 35, 3: 341–359.

Guest, D. 2001. 'Industrial Relations and Human Resource Management', in Storey, J. (ed.), *Human Resource Management*. London: Thomson Learning.

Hakim, Cliff. 1994. *We Are All Self-employed: The New Revolution*. New York: Berrett-Koehler.

Halal, W. E. 2001. 'The Collaborative Enterprise: A Stakeholder Model Uniting Profitability and Responsibility', *Journal of Corporate Citizenship*, 2: 27–42.

Harcourt, M. and Wood, G. 2003. 'Under What Circumstances Do Social Accords Work', *Journal of Economic Issues* (in print).

Harrison, J. S. and Freeman, R. E. 1999. 'Stakeholders, Social Responsibility, and Performance: Empirical Evidence and Theoretical Perspectives', *Academy of Management Review*, 42, 5: 479–485.

Heald, M. 1957. *The Social Responsibility of Business: Company and Community, 1900–1960*, Cleveland, O.H.: Case Western University Press.

Huxham, C. and Vangen, S 2000. 'Ambiguity, Complexity and Dynamics in the Membership of Collaboration', *Human Relations*, 53, 6: 771.

Hyman, R. 1975. *Industrial Relations: A Marxist Introduction*. London: Macmillan.

——1997. 'Trade Unions and European Integration', *Work and Occupations*, 24, 3: 309–331.

Iankova, E. 1996. 'Labour Relations and Political Change in Eastern Europe', *Industrial and Labor Relations Review*, 50, 1: 177–186.

Iverson, T. 1999. *Contested Economic Institutions*. Cambridge: Cambridge University Press.

Johnson, H. L. 1971. *Business in Contemporary Society: Framework and Issues*. Belmont, Calif.: Wadsworyh.

Jones, T. M. 1995. 'Instrumental Stakeholder Theory', *Academy of Management Review*, 20,2: 404–437.

Kirichenko, O. and Koudyukin, P. 1993. 'Social Partnerships in Russia: The First Steps', *Economic and Industrial Democracy*, 14: 43–55.

Kochan, T. and Osterman, P. 1994. *The Mutual Gains Enterprise*. Boston: Harvard Business School Press.

McGuire, J. B., Sundgren, A. and Schneeweis, T. 1988. 'Corporate Social Responsibility and Financial Performance', *Academy of Management Journal*, 31: 354–72.

McGuire, J. W. 1963. *Business and Society*. New York: McGraw-Hill.

Marshall, M. 1996. 'The Changing Face of Swedish Corporatism', *Journal of*

Economic Issues, 30, 3: 843–882.

Mellahi, K., Jackson, P. and Sharks, L. 2002. 'An Exploratory Study into Failure in Successful Organisations: the Case of Marks & Spencer', *British Journal of Management*, 13, 1: 15–30.

Metcalf, D. 1995. 'Workplace Governance and Performance', *Employee Relations*, 17, 6: 5–20.

—— 1999. 'The Low Pay Commission and the National Minimum Wage', *Economic Journal*, 109, 453: F46–F66.

Mone, A. M. 1997. 'How We Got Along After the Downsizing: Post-Downsizing Trust as a Double-Edged Sword', *Public Administration Quarterly*, 21, 3: 309–336.

Mueller, F. 1997. 'Organized Industrial Relations in Europe: What Future?', *Organization Studies*, 18, 2: 344–348.

Oberman, W. 2000. 'The Conspicuous Corporation: Business, Public Policy, and Representative Democracy', *Business and Society*, 39, 2: 239–244.

Olson, M. 1982. *The Rise and Decline of Nations: Economic Growth, Stagflation and Social Rigidities*. New Haven: Yale University Press.

O'Neill, H. M. and Lenn, D. J. 1995. 'Voices of Survivors: Words That Downsizing Should Hear', *Academy of Management Executive*, 9: 23–34.

O'Reilly, Brian. 1994. 'The New Deal: What Companies and Employees Owe One Another', *Fortune*, 13 June: 44–52.

Pedersen, T. and Thomsen, S. 1999. 'Business Systems and Corporate Governance', *International Studies of Management & Organization*, 29, 2: 42–59.

Prechel, H. 1999. 'Fighting for Partnership', *Work and Occupations*, 26, 4: 539–540.

Rao, A. and Sita, C. 1993. 'Multi-national Corporate Social Responsibility', *Journal of Business Ethics*, 12, 7: 553.

Rigby, M. 2002. Spanish Trade Unions and the Provision of Continuous Training: Partnership at a Distance, *Employee Relations*, 24, 5: 500–505.

Rubin, H. 1993. 'Understanding the Ethos of Community-Based Development', *Public Administration Review*, 53, 5: 428–448.

Sagawa, S. and Segal, E. 2000. 'Common Interest, Common Good: Creating Value Through Business and Social Sector Partnerships', *California Management Review*, 42, 2: 105–122.

Schneiberg, M. 20001. 'Contemporary Capitalism: The Embeddedness of Institutions', *Organization Studies*, 22, 1: 173–182.

Sisson, K. 1999. 'The New European Social Model: the End of the Search for Orthodoxy or Another False Dawn', *Employee Relations*, 21, 5: 1–54.

Smith, P. and Morton, G. 2001. 'New Labour's Reform and Britain's Employment Law: the Devil is not only in the Details but in the Values and Policy Too', *British Journal of Industrial Relations*, 39, 1: 119–138.

Shaguolo, G. 1999. 'Social Relations and Cooperation in Organizations', *Journal of Economic and Social Behavior*, 38, 1: 1–25.

Stuart, M. and Lucio, M. M. 2002. 'Social Partnership and the Mutual Gains Organization: Remaking Involvement and Trust at the British Workplace', *Economic and Industrial Democracy*, 23, 2: 177–201.

Undy, R. 1999. 'Annual Review Article: New Labour's "Industrial Relations Settlement": The Third Way', *British Journal of Industrial Relations*, 37: 315–336.

Vartianen, J. 1998. 'Understanding Swedish Social Democracy: Victims of Success?', *Oxford Review of Economic Policy*, 14, 1: 19–39.

Visser, J. 1998. 'Two Cheers for Corporatism, One for the Market: Industrial Relations, Wage Moderation and Job Growth in the Netherlands', *British Journal of Industrial Relations*, 36, 2: 269–292.

Waddock, S. 1988. 'Building Successful Social Partnerships', *Sloane Management Review*, 29, 4: 17–24.

Waddock, S. and Post, J. 1991. 'Social Entrepreneurs and Catalytic Change', *Public Administration Review*, 51, 5: 393–413.

Walton, C. C. 1967. Corporate Social Responsibilities. Belmont, Calif.: Wadsworth.

Whitley, R. 1999. *Divergent Capitalisms: The Social Structuring and Change of Business Sytems*. Oxford: Oxford University Press.

——2000. 'Editorial', *Organization Studies*, 21, 5: v–x.

16

Engagement or disengangement? Unions and a new politics

GEOFFREY WOOD

A central strategic issue facing organized labour is that of engagement. Many years of membership decline in the advanced societies has cast a question mark as to the future of trade unions. To their proponents, possibilities of firm-level partnerships with employers provide unions with both a welcome space to regroup, and a clearly delineated future role in a rapidly changing world. Yet, many such partnerships have failed to deliver meaningful concessions to employees. This chapter explores the possibilities for alternative forms of engagement and the extent to which this could contribute to a regeneration of the European social model.

Reformist forms of engagement

There are a number of potential levels of engagement with management through which unions and employees may gain a real say on work organization, industrial strategies and, indeed, the wider society. At plant level, it has been argued that new forms of partnership may allow for the real democratization of working life (see chapter 15). Such partnerships may be facilitated by new technologies and associated changes to work organization.

Although the term 'post-fordism' is widely deployed, to more 'optimistic' writers it represents a clean break from deskilled and authoritarian workplace environments of the fordist era of mass production (Hirst and Zeitlin 2001: 505). Employees gain a greater degree of autonomy, as work becomes reskilled in response to both changes in markets and technology. Work becomes less bureaucratic, and more human centred. The old confrontational system of industrial relations is replaced by a more participative one, allowing for employees to gain a real say in a wide range of areas (Belussi and Garibaldo 2001: 466).

More ambitious postmodern accounts tie fundamental changes in work organization to broader social transformation; not only do old forms of work centring on the production line become less common, but so do long-standing social cleavages. Society dissolves into an 'ecstatic' morass of consumerism; old struggles are devoid of meaning in an age where even reality is blurred (Baudrillard 1990).

In addition to the limitations of this model outlined in chapter 2, some argue that the operation of contemporary capitalism is considerably more complex than 'optimistic' post-fordists would suggest. Many of the central characteristics – and contradictions – of classic fordism extend into more flexible forms of work organization. Within core firms, the need for high levels of integration of tasks and stages makes it difficult to individualize reward systems; it is not possible to totally individualize work within the modern organization. Hence, there are strong counter-tendencies reinforcing workplace collectivism (Gough 2001: 484). Moreover, the privileged position of skilled core workers is enhanced by a tendency to under-invest in training and development; this and the high cost of technologically advanced machinery opens up new opportunities for collective action by employees (484).

Whilst firms may seek to weaken the position of employees by more flexible employment contracts (eroding security of tenure), this is counterbalanced by the inevitable loss of cumulative knowledge, as more experienced, costly, and less pliant workers are gradually weeded out (485). Even greater insecurity and lower investment in training on the periphery reduces organizational commitment and undermines the quality of production. In short, the weakening of collective forms of representation may result in employees making increased use of the exit option; voice is replaced by more fractured and individualistic forms of workplace protest.

An offshoot of 'optimistic' perspectives of post-fordism is the 'third way' perspective of workplace participation and democracy, as promoted by the Blair government in the United Kingdom (see chapter 2). Distinct from classic accounts of industrial democracy this approach aims to marry industrial competitiveness with more humane approaches to working life (Beardwell and Holden 2001: 489). One could argue that union members do have a strong interest in areas outside the traditional scope of collective bargaining; surveys of union members indicate that employees place a high premium on job security, quality of work and job fulfilment (Beardwell and Holden 2001: 490). In the circumstances, unions have little option but to express support for social partnerships if they are to accurately represent the needs of their members. In the case of management, meaningful concessions will be necessary if any partnership deal is to get off the ground. Managers are unlikely to gain employee buy-in through endlessly repeating the partnership mantra without, at the very least, broadening the scope of consultation.

However, as Moody (1998) notes, the actual track record of firm-level partnerships is patchy at best. There are numerous cases where firms have used partnerships to gain a short-term advantage, later switching to aggressive anti-union policies, as happened at General Motors, Caterpillar and Boeing. In practice, moves towards lean production and high performance are often underwritten by harsh workplace regimes, 'the road to competitiveness being paved on the backs of workers' (Moody 1998). As Mitchell (1999) notes, trust relations in partnerships are extremely fragile; should one side break its promises, any cohabitation soon degenerates into meaninglessness.

There are certain reasons why firm level partnerships may extend across workplaces, and diffuse across an economy. If parties are uncertain of each other's intentions, they will be mistrustful of any information provided by the other (Marsden 1998: 186). Moreover, external shocks may make full reciprocity difficult or impossible; this may lead to a breakdown of any form of co-determination. This may encourage both parties to form alliances across firms; employers via employer associations, and employees via unions (187). This provides a mechanism whereby each side may escalate retaliatory action, but, similarly increases the costs of doing so; each party will have a strong interest in weeding out ill-advised disputes (187). This may vest firm level forms of participation with a broader importance; meaningful industrial citizenship may be diffused across an economy. Broader external pressures on firms may preclude them from seizing the short-term competitive advantage a partnership affords, then reneging on the deal. Of course, trust is a two-way street; low levels of trust at firm level cannot be remedied entirely by wider alliances. As Mitchell (1999) argues, 'if trust is not engendered within the individual corporation, it is difficult if not impossible to imagine how it would be sustained at this inter-firm level'. Nonetheless, empirical evidence would suggest a close relationship between meaningful levels of participation at the workplace and wider institutional context (Dobbin and Boychuck 1999). Countries with strong neo-corporatist traditions are likely to be associated with higher levels of employee autonomy at individual workplaces (1999).

Disengagement

It can be argued that, given the present malaise in democratic politics alluded to in earlier chapters, an 'unholy union between corporate and political estate' (Tinker 2000: 1), alternative means have to be found for impacting on events. Large corporations have hopelessly commodified the political sphere of the liberal democracies; the only alternative is via the politics of the streets (1). The latter could coalesce around a 'peoples alliance' or 'historical bloc', with unions playing a leadership role (1).

There are two broad strands within the disengagement camp. The first is ultra-leftism; it is assumed that crises and adjustment in fordism reflect a reinforcement of existing tendencies in monopoly capitalism, necessitating a vanguardist response (Jessop 2001a: xxi). The existing economic order and associated political superstructure is so heavily loaded in the interests of capitalism that no meaningful gains are possible short of the total overthrow of capitalism by revolutionary struggle (Callinicos 1997).

A major limitation of Trotskyist tradition is that its founder believed that many of the contradictions of capitalism concerned its own expansion; the universalization of capitalism would be short-circuited by its own demise (Meiksins Wood 2002). These assumptions were echoed in the writings of Lenin. However, capitalism has indeed become universal; it has proved both remarkably durable, and capable of breaching all geographical limits. Nonetheless, Meiksins Wood (2002) argues that this has opened up the possibilities for a new era of struggle; this universalism is both a show of strength and a reflection of 'disease'.

Capitalism's inherent conflicts and contradictions have also become universal; it is thus hardly surprising that new universalistic forms of struggle such as the anti-globalization movement have come into being. This leads us to the second strand of the disengagement school of thought; one that highlights the emergence of a new politics of social movements and action.

It is argued that the inherent tensions within capitalism open up the possibility for a new democratic response based on more incorporative forms of political activity. Just as forms of industrial governance and market structure are prone to periodic crises, failure and changes in modes of policy, so are broader governance mechanisms (Jessop 2001b: 438). As formal party politics in liberal democracies becomes increasingly devoid of meaning, new forms of opposition emerge; the enervated state of formal political institutions opens up a space for new forms of activism and protest.

As Moody (1997: 305) notes, there are many forms of union struggle and organization; the broad social movement role played by unions in many parts of the developing world stands in contrast to the more established role played by many unions in the advanced societies. Unions in the latter overwhelmingly remain bureaucratic institutions fashioned for collective bargaining and corporatist politics (305). Meanwhile, in the former, unions have to match their social movement activities with day-to-day struggles for recognition and related workplace rights, even if a 'virtuous circle' of successful militancy within and without the workplace is possible. Confrontation rapidly switches to 'competitiveness' and the desire to save jobs, and collective bargaining to partnership deals (305). As a result, commitments to genuine social transformation, or even to decisive struggles, are often sacrificed (306). Yet, grassroots initiatives, such as Workers' Centres in North America, rolling strikes, and spontaneous strike action by the rank and file, may impel organized labour in a more radical direction. As Gindel points out, the search for progressive alternatives is not just about new policies, but also new politics (308). Moody argues that capitalism is unable or unwilling to even deliver modest reforms on the lines suggested by proponents of the 'third way'. Given the resurgence of more radical strands of unionism in both the advanced and developing world, he suggests that the possibility exists for forwarding a more radical agenda than would be possible through cautious engagement (308). This would reflect the fact that despite the existence of powerful centripetal tendencies around race, region and gender, workers are increasingly united in terms of the pressures they face, from an unstable and rapidly changing system, that constantly degrades both working life and society (179).

MacEwan (1999: 228) argues that small struggles over environmental and social issues can advance the agenda for democratic change. Civil society actors 'can provide small wedges that can enlarge political space and provide the political experience that may form a foundation for a democratic economic development strategy' (MacEwan 1999: 230). In their most advanced form, calls for a new politics amount to an extended political ecology (as adverse to political economy), with social movements (including regenerated unions) and allied organizations as the agents of change, with not just capitalism, but also established variants of industrialism the targets (Jessop 2001a: xxi), the latter an issue about which trade unions would be ambivalent. Moreover, political ecology recognizes that there are limits to development; a universal adoption of the Western model of industrialization would bring about the final ruin of the biosphere; rather there is a need for hybrid models drawing on both Western and indigenous forms of knowledge (Lipietz 2000).

Political ecology is thus about making hard choices that may be unpalatable to organized labour. On the other hand, it does broaden the appeal of a progressive project, which runs the danger of being marginalized in view of the shrinking of the traditional industrial working class and the global failure of socialist experiments. Strategically, political ecology would have considerably broader appeal than traditional Marxism, which battled to co-opt oppressed groupings other than the industrial (male) proletariat, without lapsing into authoritarianism (Lipietz 2000). As De Angelis (2000: 153) suggests: 'the interaction among these social subjects on the various occasions of struggle creates alternative modes of thinking, which are increasingly able to root the multidimensionality of human needs and aspirations in the universalism of the human condition'.

Moreover, it seeks to accommodate the increasing diversity of the workforce, which incorporates both 'knowledge workers' and the unskilled, salaried workers and those in insecure, temporary employment (153). To Lipietz, the construction of a truly progressive red-green coalition, bringing together traditional working-class collectives with representatives of other oppressed groupings may be a compromise that entails a difficult 'reflective (re)definition of needs', but also holds the best promise of a communitarian future (153). As De Angelis (2000: 178) notes, the problems of the present human condition are not just questions of growth (in the sense of more health services, better public space, more employment, more structures addressing basic needs, more democracy), but also of less (less arms production, less superfluous packaging, less commercialization of social life, less working time, and so forth).

Jager and Raza (2001) argue that much contemporary writing on political ecology has focused on ecological distribution conflicts, mainly on north–south lines. However, political ecology deserves broader consideration. Neither money nor the environment can be manipulated at will; inevitably fracture lines will show, sparking conflicts at a range of different levels: within (in the form of disputes over the regulation of property rights), between, and across (in the form of alliances) classes. This includes not only conflicts centred on the process of production, but also the usage and the allocation of space in both urban and rural areas (Jager and Raza 2001).

Towards new forms of class compromise?

But, what form should a progressive alternative take? Is it realistic strategy to seek to extract genuinely meaningful compromises as milestones towards a more desirable future, founded on equity and sustainability? Wright (1999) argues that there are three interpretations of class compromise. The first is when unions or other working-class organizations make gains that promise real benefits to their members, which prove empty; class comprises are in the end capitulations in favour of capital.

The second is that of 'negative' class compromise – both sides fight each other to mutual standstill, with an uneasy peace being maintained in exchange for meaningful concessions by both sides. For example, workers could agree to abstain from militancy for a fixed period of time (but only for a fixed period of time) in return for wage or other concessions. The third is a 'positive' class compromise. Here, through various forms of actual co-operation, both parties improve their relative positions.

The third position would be at odds with both conventional neo-liberal and Marxist theory. The former would see any gaining of working-class strength as a labour market distortion, whilst the latter would believe that any gains by workers would naturally diminish the efficacy of a system premised on exploitation. Wright (1999) however, suggests that an inverse J relationship might exist, as per figure 16.1. The left hand half of figure 16.1 would be very much according to conventional wisdom; as working-class power increases, that of capitalists decreases, and vice versa (Wright 1999). However, once a critical threshold is reached, working-class associational power is beneficial to capitalism (1999). This is owing to gains in productivity and profit rates, as a result of high levels of bargained co-operation, skills upgrading and job training, increased problem-solving capacity and a greater willingness to accept technological change (1999).

Figure 16.1 Conflicting utopias

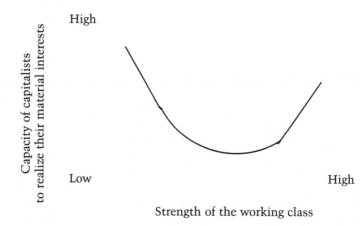

Source: Wright, E. O. 1999. 'Working Class Power, Capitalist Class Interests and Class Compromise'. Madison: Department of Sociology, University of Wisconsin.

Furthermore, Wright (1999) argues that there are three possible sites of class compromise; not just in the sphere of production, but also in the spheres of exchange (including labour market governance) and politics. Compromise is not about empty gestures, but is when *both* sides give away something of value. As Przeworski notes, a class compromise is only such when workers have a reasonable certainty that future wages will increase as a function of current profits (1999), and not empty promises of consultation or participation.

But, what drives class compromise? It is commonly assumed that 'bad' policies – such as unrestrained neo-liberalism – simply do not work. However, as Chomsky (1996) notes, such policies may prove highly functional for extended periods of time in furthering the interests of a small politically powerful minority, even if it brings misery to the bulk of society. Bad ideas may be bad for their subjects, but good for the planners and elites associated with them (1996).

In practice, neo-liberalism is really about 'for you, not me, except for temporary advantage'; powerful vested corporate interests continue to invoke state protectionism, whilst the weak must do without (Chomsky 1996). Thus, the distinction between neo-liberals and their critics is not about state intervention, but where it should be directed; more pure forms of the free market are reserved for weaker client governments in the third world. In the advanced societies, domestic policy is invariably about protection against 'unfair' foreign competition, and spending on defence, which, in creating conditions for renewed growth, also entails massive transfers of funds to private power without significant redistribution taking place (1996). Given this attractiveness to powerful minorities, how, then, may alternatives to 'Pentagon-style' neo-liberalism be brought about?

Within the mainstream radical tradition, it is assumed that class compromise is forced by collective action. A development of this is the social structures of accumulation (SSA) school of thought, that assumes that SSAs stabilize conflict and channel it in ways that are not too disruptive; this may be via repression or a compromise whereby groups 'share the fruits of the accumulation process' (Kotz, quoted Wright 1999). In other words, long-term co-operation (or positive class compromise), underwritten by specific institutional configurations, may provide the basis for regulating contestations, underpinning a stable growth trajectory, in contrast to the intermittent trench warfare of negative class compromise.

Positive compromise may not only be impelled by the threat of persistent outbreaks of collective action; it may also reflect the nature of alternative ideas. As noted earlier, 'bad politics' are retained when they are profitable to elites. When they cease to work even for a small minority, pressure for change becomes overwhelming; if neo-liberalism (even in its most bastardized 'pentagon' manifestations) has demonstrably failed in delivering even to the privileged, then even the most selfish members of the latter are forced to consider alternatives. The adoption of Keynsian policies in the advanced societies reflected not just the increasing strength of organized labour both in the workplace and in the polity, but also the loss of confidence of business interests in the aftermath of the Great Depression. Again, the immediate pressures for economic and social reconstruction, and the pressing need for political stability, in much of Western Europe after the Second World War forced capital into far greater compromises than would have otherwise taken place. Of course, as Marx cautioned, severe crises may not necessarily result in more progressive alternatives; a descent to 'barbarism', in the form of totalitarianism, or an imploded state and society, is another potential outcome.

Positive class compromises are only likely to take place when all alternatives have been exhausted (Harcourt and Wood 2003), and where state institutions remain relatively functional and/or when totalitarianism is firmly off the agenda. In other words, when both sides face the mutuality of external pressures be they for national reconstruction or imminent economic collapse. Ireland's experiment with neo-corporatism represents a good example of the latter, and, as noted earlier, post-war Western Europe the former. The durability of the capitalist system is partially underpinned by the primacy of the profit motive; the strongest ideological commitments of social elites have time and again been sacrificed in the interests of accumulation.

This does not mean that positive class compromises are possible in less drastic sets of social circumstances. As such compromises become institutionalized, and the benefits palpably visible to both parties, it is likely that deals will be renewed. However, when a large component of society finds itself outside their ambit, then their existence is likely to be threatened (Casey and Gold 2000). A good example of the latter would be the Austrian consensus following on the rise of the far right in the late 1990s. Moreover, positive compromises may be made in response to less pressing short-term crises. However, such deals are likely to be fragile and undermined by freeriding, unless both sides are forced into line either by some or other form of coercion (be it fear or the law), or through a deeply embedded culture of mutuality.

In short then, meaningful positive compromises are likely to be founded either on effective collective action and/or severe crises. As Arrighi notes, transitions in accumulation are characterized by a proliferation of financial investment, given the limited options for profitable productive investment and the need for liquidity in a time of uncertainty (Jager and Raza 2001). In turn, this contributes to further cost-cutting by manufacturing firms, and, investment bubbles that inevitably face deflation.

Indeed, the deflation of the stock market bubble over 2001 and 2002 has laid bare the severe contradictions of the late Pentagon age. Brenner (2002) argues that the deflation of the stock market bubble has begun to propel the world backwards into full blown recession. Should equity prices fall below a certain level, the US will no longer be a safe haven to foreign investors, placing downward pressure on the dollar (2002). Investment necessary to fund the deficit would only be reattracted through interest rate increases, which would result in a domestic credit crunch, causing further declines in equity prices and consumer demand; the 'meltdown scenario' (Brenner 2002). The inevitable has been – and may continue to be – temporarily staved off by renewed bouts of hype and speculation. But, the rickety props supporting a veritable Potemkin village are increasingly visible (Wood 2002), whilst the tried-and-trusted remedies of the Reagan era – centring on deficit-funded defence spending – seem no longer functional.

If the resultant crisis cannot be solved within existing structures, it represents a 'great crisis' about regulation. In the latter case, the political situation is more open; social actors are forced to abandon old norms, and develop new strategies for dealing with the crisis (Brenner 2002).

This may result in both old and new forms of social contestation, allowing for creative forms of protest. A good example of the latter would include the anti-globalization movement, founded on rainbow alliances, bringing together organized labour and a range of community organizations, bridging national divides (see also chapter 12). As De Angelis (2000: 153) notes: 'A process of the recomposition of radical claims and social subjects has been underway, a process that is forcing every movement not only to seek alliances with others, but also to make the struggles of other movements their own, without any prior need to submit the demands of other movements to an ideological test.' The apparent stifling of the anti-globalization movement after the events of September 11, 2001 revealed both its inherent strengths and weaknesses. On the one hand, it revealed the tentative nature of progressive politics, given the neo-liberal hegemony over the established media and political discourses. On the other hand, the problems faced by the anti-globalization movement reflected the nature of gains made. Increasingly, contentious global economic forums have been forced to flee to peripheral locales, reinforcing the image of large corporations as global outlaws, forced to carry out their global manipulations in areas far from the public eye.

The hysterical reactions whipped up through the 'war against terrorism' against any form of dissent, is one prompted by chronic weakness not strength. Although the lack of high profile confrontations may have starved the anti-globalization movement of some of the oxygen of publicity, it opens the way for new rounds of campaigning, forcing global capital constantly onto the offensive. The resilience of global capitalism is partially due to the increasing interdependence of capital, state, culture and the family; 'globalization' is propelled by, and impacts back on all four (Waterman 1999: 249). Although the cultural embeddedness of the contemporary order is a source of strength to the status quo, it is also a weakness. Cross-class and non-class struggles over human rights, the environment, gender, sexual orientation and cultural issues assume a new importance given the multi-faceted nature of the reproduction of the capitalist order (249).

Moreover, if the existing growth regime proves increasingly incapable of delivering to even a small group of privileged insiders, then the latter are likely to be more open to new forms of compromise. This, and a broad social movement base, opens up new possibilities for 'radical engagement' (Waterman 1999). Wright (1999) depicts the nature of strategic alternatives as shown in figure 16.2. In the case of a 'great crisis' of regulation, the choices may be very much starker (figure 16.3).

In such cases, where the present ceases to deliver even for the elite, two outcomes are possible. The first is a drift towards 'bloody neo-fordism', highly numerically flexible forms of workplace organization, backed up with increasingly overt

Figure 16.2 Strategic alternatives

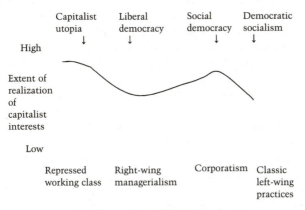

Source: Wright, E. O. 1999. 'Working Class Power, Capital Class Interetss and Class Compromise'. Madison: Department of Sociology, University of Wisconsin

Figure 16.3 Stark alternatives

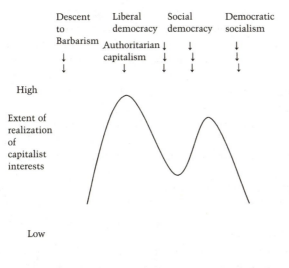

authoritarianism both within the workplace and polity. Should this fail to deliver, a further drift towards 'barbarism' is possible. What Martin Jacques (*Guardian* 10 Oct. 2002) refers to as an 'age of selfishness' – encompassing a range of social dysfunctions, from the loneliness of individuals adrift in communities, to the struggle to balance working and social life, to deeply corrosive advertising – fulfils a real economic function, underpinning the present consumer spending driven growth. However, as basic relations of trust and 'good faith' are eroded, commercial activity becomes more difficult, unless backed up by the (inefficient) use of power (cf. Bachmann 1998: 316). Given the closely intermeshed nature of social, political and economic life, what has short-term utility in promoting consumer demand and numerical flexibility, may ultimately undermine all spheres; there are no winners from a descent to barbarism.

This underscores the importance of effective collective organization in impelling a society towards a more sustainable, and more equitable, growth regime and associated institutional configurations, towards the second possible outcome, revived social democracy. The situation may be depicted as per table 16.1.

There is a second dimension to the role of social movements in helping tip the balance towards a more progressive – and sustainable – outcome. Whilst neo-corporatism has many merits (see chapter 3), it also has certain inherent limitations. In such a system, grievances and themes 'that do not fall under the purview of peak interest organizations' are systematically marginalized (Steinmetz 2001: 129). This leads to a potential surplus of peripheral grievances that the system cannot address (129). On the one hand, there is a danger that, vested with organizational clout, such groupings may consistently undermine social accords, leading to the ultimate collapse of the system. On the other hand, the linkage of peak interest organizations such as organized labour, with other more peripheral groupings, in rainbow coalitions, allows both for the bargaining table to be broadened at central level, and for grievances that are not systemic threatening to be voiced at a range of levels.

Such coalitions can link peak interests with the network of organizations 'subsumed in everyday life', allowing for both formal messages to be articulated centrally, and informal messages to be realized through everyday actions (Steinmetz 2001: 129). These are only sustainable, however, if organized labour positions itself not as the senior partner, but as a facili-

Table 16.1 Alternatives and the importance of collective
organization

	'Capitalist utopia'	Revived social democracy
Polity	Hegemony of large corporations/'hollow democracy'/gradual drift to authoritarianism	Social accords
Labour market	Radical deregulation	Focused regulation
Workplace	Bloody neo-fordism	Co-determination/ conduct underpinned by central accords

Source: Wright, E. O. 1999. 'Working-class Power, Capital Class Interests and Class Compromise', Madison: Dept of Sociology, University of Wisconsin.

tator, opening the way for a range of collective voices to be expressed and accommodated with emerging institutional frameworks (cf. Breitenfellner 1997); in other words, a relationship expressed through an organic network, rather than via a formal hierarchy (cf. Waddock and Post 1995), underpinned by multiple nodes of activism and possibilities for collectivism. Whilst this may lead to a certain unwieldiness and instability, it can be argued that this represents a very much better alternative to senior/junior partner relationships, such as is common between firms and unions in the United States.

The desirable outcome would be a system that can accommodate pressures from below, allowing for a greater resilience through flexibility, in contrast to the ossified – and brittle – centralization associated with countries such as Austria (cf. Casey and Gold 2000). Whilst such pressures may periodically result in the collapse of neo-corporatist deals, the underlying institutional features of collaboration between the principal groupings in society persist. Such features would include union federations and employer associations with broad social footprints, and deeply embedded institutional precedents for collaboration. Harcourt and Wood (2003) refer to such a system as 'jagged' collaboration. In essence, a revived form of social democracy would seek to incorporate the flexibility – and fluctuating nature – of Nordic experiments in neo-corporatism, but with a crucial difference. Periodic bouts of decentralization in countries such as Norway are commonly forced by individual

Table 16.2 Alternative outcomes: the case for revived social democracy

Level	Capitalist utopia	Revived social democracy
Business system	Extreme compartmentalization[a]	Advanced collaborative[b]
Workplace	Bloody neo-fordism. Low trust/low levels of mutual commitment	Industrial citizenship, workplace participation linked to centralized social accords. High trust/high commitment
Financial system	Capital market based financial systems, principal emphasis on shareholder value	Credit based financial systems, long-term relations of interdependence between borrowers and firms
Interfirm relations	Low levels of trust, high levels of opportunism. Low levels of collaboration between competing firms	High levels of trust, low levels of opportunism, high levels of collaboration within sectors
Labour market	Deregulated. Low investment in skills	Reregulated; emphasis on role of collectives in enforcing both individual and joint rights. High investment in skills
Community	Age of selfishness	Multiple levels of participation; networks of solidarity uniting diffuse interests
Polity	'Hollow democracy' Formal political participation increasingly devoid of meaning, given power of large corporate interests	Jagged social accords. Periodic discontinuities, with institutional underpinnings of system persisting

Sources: Harcourt, M. and Wood, G., 2003. 'Under What Circumstances Do Social Accords Work?', *Journal of Economic Issues* (in print). Whitley, R. 1999. *Dangerous Capitalisms: the Social Structure and Change of Business Systems.* Oxford: Oxford University Press. Sako, M. 1998. 'Does Trust Improve Business Performance?', in Lane, C. and Bachman, R. (eds.), Trust Within and Between Organizations. Oxford: Oxford University Press.

Notes: [a]Compartmentalized' business system is the term Whitley (1999:43) uses to describe the Anglo-American model, with adversarial competition and short-term contracting with suppliers, customers, and employees' deregulated labour markets (Whitley 1999: 43). Ownership control is in the form of the pressures generated by the buying and selling of shares. This system is characterized by low levels of trust (Harcourt and Wood 2003; cf. Whitley 1999). [b]The classic example of 'collaborative' business systems would be the Rhineland model, underpinned by a system of social accords, with a relatively high degree of collective organization and co-operation between sectors. Ownership control is via alliances of groups of owners, with shares often closely held, rather than regularly traded on the stock market. Again, ownership integration of production chains is high, with considerable collaboration between firms within sectors, and some co-ordination of production chains by alliances of firms. Collaborative business systems are characterized by high-trust relations; skilled labour provides a major source of competitive advantage (Whitley 1999). Labour markets are heavily regulated; however, losses in numerical flexibility are offset by gains in functional flexibility, made possible by effective public training systems (Harcourt and Wood 2003; cf. Whitley 1999).

unions in a time of general economic growth and low unemployment (cf. Dolvik and Stokke 1998).

In contrast, the 'jaggedness' implicit in a new form of social democracy could also be the result of grassroots pressures by social movements representing minority cross-class interests. Grassroots pressures may be mediated by network relationships between national-level social actors and smaller community organizations; whilst these relationships may periodically break down, reflecting the contradictions of relationships between working-class and cross-class organizations, there are strong pressures towards reconstitution. The basic fundamentals of the system could persist owing to beneficial outcomes for the bulk of society, and the absence of credible alternatives. The nature of potential outcomes, drawing on the experience of European accords-based social democratic systems, are highlighted in table 16.2.

As Dobbin and Boychuck (1999) argue, meaningful improvements in working life at plant level are inherently bound up with broader systemic realities. Social change must, perforce be conceived at a range of institutional levels, allowing for multiple forms of mobilization, engagement, and alliance. Institutions are 'nested' at a range of levels: sectoral, regional, national and trans-national (Boyer and Hollingsworth 1997: 470). There are multiple levels of political mobilization, challenge and strategic engagement. Focusing on a single level neglects the multi-faceted nature of contemporary capitalism and the possibilities for creative response by unions (cf. Radice 2000).

Conclusion

This chapter makes the case for a new form of 'radical engagement' drawing on the experience of European social democracy, and the potential afforded by emerging network alliances between social movements, linking unions with a wide range of grassroots organizations (cf. Lillie 2000). It is suggested that a more accountable, flexible – and ultimately more durable – version of the European social model is possible through alliance politics linking a wider range of community organizations at both the grassroots and commanding heights. Whilst potentially destabilizing, it may allow for greater dynamism and inclusiveness. However, a new form of social democracy is only possible if corporate interests are impelled in this direction through the mass mobilization of new social movements and/or if all credible alternatives are exhausted.

References

Bachmann, R. 1998. 'Trust: Conceptual Analysis of a Complex Problem', in Lane, C. and Bachmann, R. (eds.), *Trust Within and Between Organizations*. Oxford: Oxford University Press.

Barbrook, R. 2001. 'Mistranslations: Lipietz in London and Paris', in Jessop, B. (ed.), *Regulation Theory and the Crisis of Capitalism, Volume 1: The Parisian Regulation School*. Cheltenham: Edward Elgar.

Baudrillard, J. 1990. *Revenge of the Crystal*. London: Pluto.

Beardwell, I. and Holden, L. 2001. *Human Resource Management: A Contemporary Approach*. London: Prentice Hall.

Belussi, F. and Garibaldo, F. 2001. 'Variety of Pattern of Post-Fordist Economy', in Jessop, B. (ed.), *Regulation Theory and Crisis of Capitalism, Vol. 3: Regulationist Perspectives on Fordism and Post-Fordism*. Cheltenham: Edward Elgar.

Boyer, R. and Hollingsworth, J. R. 1997. 'From National Embeddedness to Spatial and Institutional Nestedness', in Hollingsworth, J. R. and Boyer, R. (eds.), *Contemporary Capitalism: The Embeddedness of Institutions*. Cambridge: Cambridge University Press.

Breitenfellner, A. 1997. 'Global Unionism: A Potential Player', *International Labour Review*, 136, 4: 531–555.

Brenner, R. 2002. *The Boom and the Bubble: The US in the World Economy*. London: Verso.

Callinicos, A. 1997. 'Where Does Political Power Lie?', *International Socialist Review*, 206: www.isf.org.uk.

Casey, B. and Gold, M. 2000. *Social Partnerships and Economic Performance*. Cheltenham: Edward Elgar.

Chomsky, N. 1996. 'New Wine in Old Bottles: A Bitter Taste', *Electronic Journal of Radical Organizational Theory*, 2, 1: 1–9.

De Angelis, M. 2000. *Keynesianism, Social Conflict and Political Economy*. London: Macmillan.

Dobbin, F. and Boychuck, T. 1999. 'National Employment Systems and Job Autonomy: Why Job Autonomy is High in the Nordic Countries and Low in the United States, Canada, and Australia', *Organization Studies*, 20, 2: 257–291.

Dolvik, J. and Stokke, T. 1998. 'Norway: The Revival of Centralized Concertation', in Ferner, A. and Hyman, R. (eds.), *Changing Industrial Relations in Europe*. Oxford: Blackwell.

Gough, J. 2001. 'Where's the Value in Post-fordism?', in Jessop, B. (ed.), *Regulation Theory and the Crisis of Capitalism, Volume 3: Regulationist Perspectives on Fordism and Post fordism*. Cheltenham: Edward Elgar.

Guardian (London/Manchester).

Harcourt, M. and Wood, G. 2003. 'Under What Circumstances do Social Accords Work?', *Journal of Economic Issues* (in print).

Hirst, P. and Zeitlin, J. 2001. 'Flexible Specialization and Post-fordism: Theory, Evidence and Policy Implications', in Jessop, B. (ed.), *Regulation Theory and the Crisis of Capitalism Volume 3: Regulationist Perspectives on fordism and Post-Fordism*. Cheltenham: Edward Elgar.

Jager, J. and Raza, W. 2001. 'French Regulation Theory and Political Ecology: A Proposed Framework for Integration with an Illustration in Urban Studies'. Vienna: Departments of Urban and Regional Development, and Economics, Vienna University of Economics and Business Administration.

Jessop, B. 2001a. 'Series Preface', in Jessop, B. (ed.), *Regulation Theory and the Crisis of Capitalism, Volume 5: Developments and Extensions*. Cheltenham: Edward Elgar.

——2001b. 'The Regulation Approach, Governance and Post-fordism', in Jessop, B. (ed.), *Regulation Theory and the Crisis of Capitalism Volume 5: Developments and Extensions*. Cheltenham: Edward Elgar.

Kelly, J. 1999. *Rethinking Industrial Relations: Mobilization, Collectivism and Long Waves*. London: Routledge.

Lillie, N. 2000. 'Book Review – Munck, R. and Waterman, P. (eds.): Labour Worldwide in the Era of Globalization', *Industrial and Labor Relations Review*, 53, 3: 536–537.

Lipietz, A. 2000. 'Political Ecology and the Future of Marxism' (www.perso.club-internet.fr/lipietz).

MacEwan, A. 1999. *Neo-Liberalism or Democracy?* London: Zed.

Marsden, D. 1998. 'The Role of Interfirm Institutions', in Lane, C. and Bachmann, R. (eds.), *Trust Within and Between Organizations*. Oxford: Oxford University Press.

Meiksins Wood, E. 2002. 'Back to Marx', International Socialist Forum: www.isf.org.uk.

Mitchell, L. 1999. 'Trust and Team Production in Post-Capitalist Society', *Journal of Corporate Law*, 24, 4: 869.

Moody, K. 1997. *Workers in a Lean World*. London: Verso.

——1998. 'Up Against the Polyester Ceiling: The 'New' AFL-CIO Organizes – Itself!', *New Politics*, 6, 4: www.umi.com.

Radice, H. 2000. 'Responses to Globalisation: A Critique of Progressive Nationalism', *New Political Economy*, 5, 1: 5–19.

Sako, M. 1998. 'Does Trust Improve Business Performance?', in Lane, C. and Bachmann, R. (eds.), *Trust Within and Between Organizations*, Oxford: Oxford University Press.

Steinmetz, G. 2001. 'Regulation Theory, Post-Marxism and New Social Movements', in Jessop, B. (ed.), *Regulation Theory and the Crisis of Capitalism, Volume 5: Developments and Extensions*. Cheltenham: Edward Elgar.

Tinker, T. 2000. 'Sleepless in Seattle: Farewell Democracy, Hello WTO!', *Electronic Journal of Radical Organizational Theory*, 6, 1: 1–3.

Waddock, S. and Post, J. 1995. 'Social Entrepreneurs and Catalytic Change', *Public Administration Review*, 51, 5: 393–413.

Waterman, P. 1999. 'The New Social Unionism: A New Union Model for the New World Order', Munck, R. and Waterman, P. (eds.), *Labour Worldwide in the Era of Globalization*. London: Macmillan.

Whitley, R. 1999. *Divergent Capitalisms: The Social Structuring and Change of Business Sytems*. Oxford: Oxford University Press.

Wood, G. 2002. 'Book Review – Robert Brenner: The Boom and the Bubble', *African Sociological Review* (in print).

Wright, E. O. 1999. 'Working Class Power, Capitalist Class Interests and Class Compromise'. Madison: Department of Sociology, University of Wisconsin.

17

Conclusion: broadening democracy and the labour movement

GEOFFREY WOOD

The economic pressures associated with the unification of markets, the deregulation of financial services, the homogenization of consumer taste and the scaling back of tariff barriers have placed specific pressures on both emerging and established democracies. To Perry Anderson (2000), these two developments have led to a contradictory situation, where well-established autocracies from Indonesia to apartheid South Africa have been dismantled, yet democracy has been weakened at its core. In new and established democracies, corporate interests are moulding and confining the political discourse within increasingly narrow limits (Hertz 2001).

In both these contexts, unions have to cope with far-reaching changes in the nature of work and political discourse. At workplace level they have to face the challenge of broadening the democratization of working life in an age of insecure tenure and assertive managerialism. Beyond the workplace, they have to cope with the weakening of the public sphere and the ideological hegemony of neo-liberalism. Despite these challenges, unions remain of vital importance both as agents for the broadening of democracy, and as potential representatives of both the factory floor and more marginalized groupings in society.

Internal versus external democracy revisited

Contrary to conventional wisdom (cf. Lipset 1977), the various contributions to this volume have emphasized that external and internal democracy are by no means contradictory, but, rather, are mutually self reinforcing. As noted in chapter 4, the rise of effective and representative trade unions facilitated the broadening of the wider political discourse, and the emergence of the welfare state and associated moves to promote greater social equity. Again, new unionization initiatives aimed at drawing in and voicing the concerns of the unorganized may help place the concerns of highly marginalized groupings more firmly on the national agenda, promoting greater inclusiveness in both emerging – and mature – democracies (chapter 12). Conversely, unions' effectiveness is contingent on their capacity to enhance employee rights both within and beyond the workplace, and the quality of working life (chapter 5).

Vibrant internal democracy makes unions more attractive to potential and present members, and enhances their capacity to engage in effective collective action. The latter gives unions more clout at both centralized and workplace levels, broadening the basis of participation in decision making both over day-to-day workplace governance, and in setting macro-economic policy.

A difficult road?

But, which is the most desirable way forward for organized labour? Much of the contemporary literature has focused on the limits and possibilities of the organizing strategy (Frege 1999; Gall 2003; Moody 1997). There is little doubt strategic choice is vital in determining the fortunes of unions (Hyman 1992, 1997; Kelly 1997); this accounts for the greatly uneven performances of individual unions both in hostile climates such as the United States under the Bush II administration, and more favourable environments, such as post-apartheid South Africa. Quite simply, methods of outreach matter.

However, of equal importance are devising mechanisms for realizing core union objectives for expanding the base and quality of firm-level recognition and in working towards broader social justice, once recruitment targets have been met. The organizing strategy seeks to rediscover the social movement role played by Western unions during their early years of existence (Hyman 1997), and aims to infuse the union discourse with a stronger sense of justice and inclusiveness. However, it remains rather vague as to the most desirable strategies for redressing grievances and advancing the general cause of organized labour.

As Fung and Wright (2003a: 285) note, those committed to broadening democratization and bringing about a fairer society remain divided over means. On the one hand, unions can seek to enhance their role and influence through alliances with established political parties and/or or via collective bargaining at a range of levels (Valenzuela 1992). On the other hand, unions may seek to broaden their appeal and capacity through the use of informal methods such as protest and disruption (Desai 2002; Fung and Wright 2003a: 285; Rachleff 2002). The waning influence of organized labour within the advanced societies, and its search for a new role in newly democratized emerging markets brings a particular urgency to this debate, and whether there is room for a middle ground.

Unions, democracy and social justice: the possibilities and limits of formalism

Central to the rise of trade unions was the fight for recognition. Above all the latter represents an effort to limit arbitrary managerial power, binding managers to specific procedures for conduct; it represents an industrial peace treaty, and at the same time a source for rules and terms of contracts of employment, for the distribution of work and for the stability of jobs (Farnham and Pimlott 1992: 293). To workers, the employment relationship would be unattractive in the absence of clearly demarcated limits on their obligations to employers (Marsden 1999: 31). In the other extreme, endless and ongoing bargaining would be highly unstable for employers; sequential spot contracting would preclude both flexible decision making and long-term planning. Increasing union power results in employers – and employees – agreeing to sets of rules that are both efficient and enforceable (32).

Pluralist theory holds that the existence of a democratic state does not override the rights of individuals to form their own associations, which represent their interests, and to pursue their objectives. Pluralists hold that it is neither feasible nor desirable to have a situation where individuals are not free to form their own collectives to pursue their specialized interests. Inter alia, this would include the right of individual workers to form their own associations to specifically voice their interests within the workplace, and, potentially, within the wider society as well. In short, recognition is not just about rules, but also about the entrenchment of the rights of individuals and their collectives. Collective bargaining represents an inherent democratization of working life, in that employers recognize that power and decision making in a range of critical areas has to be shared with workers in the interests of stable workplace governance (Flanders 1975).

Centralized bargaining at industry level can provide the basis for effective and strongly entrenched industrial citizenship. Through their representatives employees are able to reign in the power of all employers operating in the sector, even over those, who, at plant level, possess the will and capacity to implement labour-repressive policies. At the same time, industry-wide bargaining can fall prey to over-formalization, and result in reduced levels of grassroots accountability (cf. Giddens 1981: 179). In many cases, centralized bargaining may depend on state intervention to reign in freerider behaviour, and underwrite basic systemic rules (cf. Salamon 1987). Although state intervention can be a great source of strength to unions, it can make them over-dependent on official or state-underwritten mechanisms and encourage them to devote increasingly less attention to keeping in touch with the needs of their members. In South Africa, for instance, a whites-only labour movement, which had mounted a popular, albeit racially motivated, insurrection in 1922 had by the 1960s degenerated into a self-perpetuating, ineffective oligarchy (Wood and Harcourt 1998). Similarly, the New Zealand system of compulsory union membership and arbitration bred a complacency that made the labour movement particularly ill-equipped to withstand the assaults of the neo-liberal National Party government in the early 1990s (Wood 1996).

The limits and possibilities of centralization are further pronounced at a corporatist level. Dependent on the operation of basic democratic freedoms, such as that of association, and emphasizing compromise and mutual gain, neo-corporatism does incorporate a strongly democratic dimension (see chapter 13). However, under centralizaton, groups with disproportionate interests and power will inevitably try to constrain the actions of others (Bardhan 2000: 263). This may result in a significant component of society finding themselves outside the corporatist tent (Casey and Gold 2000), giving rise to extremist anti-systemic politics, perhaps typified by the Pym Fortuyn and Jorg Haider phenomena.

Unions and the streets: the possibilities and limits of informalism

As a result of persistent economic crises from the 1970s onwards, and associated changes in the global economy, the economic footing of the Keynsian state was undercut, and, in its place, the 'competition state' has emerged (Green 1999: 21). The latter sought to control or discipline organized labour, in an attempt to compete for increasingly mobile investment capital. To conservatives, this 'taming of labour' was to be welcomed in that it fostered greater consensus and coalition building around an emerging neo-liberal agenda, allowing for the expansion of democratic rule into the third world, and a curtailing of the activities of the interventionist 'nanny state' in the advanced societies (21).

In contrast, it can be argued that there is a need 'to confront and transcend the limitations of capitalism', democracy being not only about representation, but also about the right to contest and refute the ideological hegemony of neo-liberalism (cf. Habib and Taylor 1999: 119). Contrary to predictions, the latter did not give rise to a new pervasive, yet tolerant post-historical era built around an emerging consensus to political and economic problems (cf. Fukuyama 1992), but, rather, to both intolerant micro-nationalisms, and a new conservative interventionism. As expounded by the Bush II administration, the latter encompasses substantial increases in defence spending, protectionism, and the implementation of a variety of measures to reign in the 'undeserving poor', ranging from the increased outsourcing of social relief to private charitable institutions, to coercive work-fare schemes.

In her classic treatise on revolution, Arendt (1963) argues that democracy has clear spatial limits. In the modern state, the currency of politics is persistently one of 'rulership' (1963). Communication between public representatives and their constituents is never one of a delegated agent reporting back and soliciting the wishes of the principal, but rather between those who govern and those who consent to be governed (1963). Although organizations representing the interests of the working classes may, in theory, allow the masses 'to recruit their own elites', in practice, the divide between the few who constitute the public space, and the many, 'who remain outside in obscurity' persists. Thus, both within larger trade unions, and in the broader polity, there is an inevitable tendency away from democracy towards rulership and clientism.

The increasingly unappealing nature of formal politics, and the chronic weakness of established unions within the advanced societies, has added a new currency to Arendt's arguments. These concerns have led to increasing interest in a unionization of the grassroots, autonomously operating at community and plant level, and in coalition with similar localized clusters of activists. As international financial organizations and the WTO relentlessly press for the marketization of basic social services, the active redistribution of resources from the poor to the rich that has characterized much of neo-liberal policy since the late 1970s has become increasingly flagrant (Wood 2003). Desai (2002) argues that only the groupings of activists drawn from communities at the receiving end of such unrestrained marketization can halt this tendency. To proponents of the new unionism of the grassroots, the creativity and richness of community counter-attacks is deeply inspiring in an age where formal politics have become moribund and meaningless (Desai 2002; Rachleff 2002).

However, grassroots activism does make for a certain lack of strategic vision. Too often, the resultant contestations have been isolated affairs, in which alliances across communities and regions have been fragile and constantly open to co-optation by elites. Even while they can represent a new *focoism*,[1] epitomizing hit-and-run attacks that debilitate the status quo and excite communities for the next struggle, they can also make for factionalism and fragmentation (Wood 2003). Are we seeing the start of a renewed challenge working towards a more equitable future, or desperate and isolated responses by workers and communities under constant assault? In other words, are we seeing the emergence of a new politics based around community activism or a kind of 'anti-politics' driven purely by reaction (Wood 2003; cf. Fergusen 1990)?

These questions are particularly important given possible

responses; resistance to the imposition of neo-liberal style governance inside or outside the workplace may result in broadening industrial citizenship by the state, or a further reduction of collective rights, abandoning workers to the discretion of managers at plant level. More broadly speaking, one could argue that the proliferation of an inherently postmodernist anti-politics may weaken collectivist projects at national and trans-national levels in an age where collectivism can still make valuable gains. In many countries, corporatist and semi-corporatist arrangements continue to preserve the earlier gains of organized labour. Localist movements may link together diverse interests in communities, united in poverty and exclusion (Desai 2002), or an intolerance where identity is founded on a rejection of even more vulnerable groupings.

Unions and 'participatory governance'

There is little doubt that, in the developing world, organized labour has fallen on 'dark times' (Wallerstein 1998; cf. Arendt 1973); the successes of new strategies for representation and outreach represent rays of light in what remains a bleak era. As Jacobi notes, the tendency of neo-liberal theorists to suggest that the status quo represents the inevitable order of nature is ahistorical and discounts the possibilities for new ideas and actions underaken by both individuals and collectives (Soron 2001: 206). Nonetheless, progressive responses remain fragmented, vacillating between wild optimism fuelled by small gains in the face of major setbacks, and a kind of debilitating pessimism (206–209).

The relationship between objective forces and social action remains a two-way one, whereby each remoulds the other (206–209; Wallerstein 1998). In short, any progressive project has to make institutions more responsive to the potentially liberating interventions of individuals (Arendt 1963). Thus, the future of organized labour is contingent on an ability to broaden dialogue and democracy both within and beyond the labour movement (cf. Fletcher and Hurd 1999; Frege 1999; Moody 1997; Roberts 1999). Indeed, contrary to conventional wisdom democracy within the wider polity can be reinforced by internal union democracy. Internal democracy can make for more vibrant and popular unions. It can strengthen the countervailing power to elite interests, and inject a wider range of perspectives into the broader discourse.

As Fung and Wright (2003b: 4) note, the left's defence of the affirmative state – founded on the assumption that the state has a central role to play in righting the worst excesses of capitalism – has become weaker in recent years. It is commonly suggested that the privatization of the public sphere represents the inevitable outcome of the present developmental trajectory (cf. De Haan and Sturm 1999). However, it can be argued that the problem centres more on the design of institutions, than their potential.

The latter possibility has led Fung and Wright (2003b: 5) to suggest that the most desirable way forward lies in *empowered participatory governance* (EPG). The latter represents the creation of new democratic forums for ordinary people to directly participate in decisions that affect their lives. Participation becomes more meaningful, in that discussions are closely followed on by action. EPG can seek to remedy both the failure of state agencies, and 'restructure democratic decision making more generally' (6). Although primarily conceived of as a mechanism for reviving governmental structures, EPG is a model explicitly designed to have relevance for adoption in different institutional contexts and other areas of social life (15). Decentralized decision making can be supported by state structures (16). Again, state structures are colonized, revitalized and transformed by such initiatives. As with other social collectives, trade unions can play a vital role both in reining in Caesarist or populist tendencies that can emerge from extreme devolution, and, in turn, be themselves renewed by giving individual activists a greater stake in the labour movement's well-being.

The concept of EPG draws on a long tradition in critical thought, most notably that associated with the later Frankfurt school, as well as writers such as Lessing, Benjamin and Arendt (see Benjamin 1978; Crook 1991; Jay 1984). Habermas (1990) argues that through opening up new opportunities for dialogue – not necessarily confined to the speech act – structures of governance can be rendered more accountable and brought more closely into line with the grassroots. In contrast, a withdrawal into fragmented individualism may allow room for creative expression in personal areas of endeavour, but represents a serious loss to the collective world (Arendt 1973: 12).

Fung and Wright (2003a: 282–284) argue that countervailing power is not easily strengthened through supportive public policies instituted by governments, or by established adversarial organizations, such as political parties. When the existing order serves little more than a tiny elite, 'the world may become so dubious that people ask little more of politics' and established political actors, other than a desire to be left alone (Arendt 1973). This has been reflected in declining popular participation in formal party politics.

In this context, effective challenges to the status quo are most likely to emerge from the grassroots, or through the slow transformation of 'traditional adversarial organizations', such as trade unions. Revitalization of the latter should centre on the granting of greater autonomy to regions and affiliates that possess the necessary understanding and competencies for dealing with specific local challenges, as and when they arise (Fung and Wright 2003a: 285). This does not necessarily solve the perennial conflict between grassroots democracy, and national unity and clout; however, through EPG, a new dimension is introduced, forcing leaders to think beyond top-down governance.

By opening up new forums for participation, EPG can revitalize formal governance structures, adding a greater legitimacy to centralized, formal decision-making processes; the idea being to enrich the public sphere, rather than prescribing rigid policy alternatives (cf. Habermas 1990; Arendt 1963). Broadening democracy can strengthen accountability, developing ways of supplementing rather than undermining structures for representation or negotiation (285). Again, whilst seeking to tap into grassroots sentiments, it seeks to transform activism currently centred on protest and disruption (Fung and Wright 2003a: 285).

The EPG approach would be seemingly critical of formalized mechanisms for broadening the scope of union input into industrial and macro-economic governance, such as neo-corporatism. However, it can be argued that such forms of co-operation rarely exist in isolation; rather greater flexibility can be imparted into centralized deals through an overt or tacit recognition that they are likely to be adjusted, reinterpreted or topped up by more localized bargaining. The most durable and best performing examples of neo-corporatism are characterized both by regular fluctuations in the degree of centralization and bargaining practice, and in the persistence of specific institutional features, including union federations and employer associations with broad social footprints, and deeply embedded institutional precedents for collaboration (Harcourt and Wood 2003).

Collaborative governance at centralized level alone is likely to result in stronger interests, more capable of collective action, capturing weaker groupings; this exacerbates tendencies towards weak feedback loops (from leadership to grassroots) and long lines of accountability and report-back. On the other hand, regulation of individual employers would not necessarily empower workers, unless the latter possess effective countervailing power (Fung and Wright 2003a: 264). This explains why labour law geared towards protecting the rights of the individual has tended to be rather less effective than collective labour law in upholding employee rights (Wood *et al.* 2003). De-collectivisation makes monitoring and reinforcement extremely difficult (2003). Again, where specific transgressions of individual rights are both widespread and deeply embedded, legal efforts at curtailment are likely to face active opposition or passive non-compliance, necessitating active enforcement (Olson and Kahkonen 2000: 32).

In its purest form, EPG tends to be most closely associated with experiments in local government, service delivery and environmental management (cf. Fung and Wright 2003b). However, there does seem to be some evidence of a correlation between effective unionism, room for active participation at a range of levels, and a certain systemic dynamism that can accommodate both centralized deal-making and localized campaigning. EPG would not mean a system that allowed for meaningful workplace participation, centralized bargaining or a shift in emphasis in labour law away from individual and towards collective rights. Rather, it would suggest moves towards a system that embodied all these features, operating in a mutually reinforcing manner.

Olsonian theory would suggest that such systems are unsustainable and that workable centralized bargaining would necessitate reining in grassroots pressures (Olson 1982). However, there is ample empirical evidence to suggest that the operation of national and industrial level bargaining structures is not contingent on the curtailment of other forms of participation. Rather, such structures have proved ultimately more durable when the system imparts sufficient flexibility to allow supplementary bargaining at other levels, and, even, for the temporary breakdown of centralized deals.

For example, post-apartheid South Africa has a labour movement that has retained high levels of internal democracy and militancy and has functional centralized bargaining structures (Wood 2003). The latter has included both the widely respected industry-wide Bargaining Councils, together with proto-corporatist structures such as NEDLAC and the Millennium Council. Again, in Sweden, Denmark and Norway, corporatist deals regularly break down in the face of grassroots pressures, yet are equally regularly renewed; widespread popular support for the underlying system persists (Harcourt and Wood 2003). Nonetheless, 'jagged corporatism' is characterized by relatively robust macro-economic performance (2003; Wood and Harcourt 2001).

Such systems are characterized not so much by 'encompassing organizations' ability to reign in dissent, but rather their ability to manage it; the relationship between grassroots democracy – and spontaneous outbreaks of conflict – and centralized bargaining can be potentially symbiotic, rather than contradictory (cf. Habermas 1990). In such instances, participatory collaboration is high, but so is the efficacy and vibrancy of countervailing power (cf. Fung and Wright 2003a: 265). The situation can be depicted as in table 17.1.

Table 17.1 Towards participatory governance in labour relations?

Governance institutions	Degree of countervailing power	
	Low	High
Top-down adversialism	Bloody fordism	Union struggles for recognition during years of union growth
Participatory collaboration	Employer-driven partnerships	'Jagged corporatism', and/or multi-level bargaining

Source: Based on Fung, A. and Wright, E. O. 2003a. 'Countervailing Power in Empowered Participatory Governance', in A. Fung and E. O. Wright (eds), Deepening Democracy: the Real Utopias Project, Vol. 4. London: Verso.

Conclusion: unions as agents for broadening the democratic agenda

The malaise in formal democratic politics in the advanced societies and the decline of organized labour reflect changes in the global economy, and the increasing hegemony both of neoliberal ideologies and the corporate interests they serve. Viable policy alternatives are unlikely to emerge and be placed on the policy table in the absence of countervailing power. Although the new politics of the streets has undoubtedly represented a source of inspiration to progressives battered by decades of marginalization, it faces the risk of endemic fragmentation and/or an incapacity to move beyond protest. Social collectives, such as unions, can play a vital role in channelling and focusing spontaneous popular upsurges, yet be revitalized through greater internal democracy and decentralization, geared towards accommodating diverse constituencies, comprised of both core and peripheral categories of labour. At the heart of any revival of the labour movement lies democratization both in the manner in which unions conduct their affairs and as an expression of their aspirations in wider society and the polity (see Fletcher and Hurd 1999; Gall 2003; Moburg 1999; Moody 1997). Even though the new organizing strategies and rich internal debates within unions provide grounds for optimism for the future of democracy, persistent assaults on the labour movement worldwide since the late 1970s make it extremely difficult for unions to move beyond the immediate exigencies of survival.

Note

1 The revolutionary strategy pursued by Che Guevara and Fidel Castro during the Cuban revolution, 'focoism' represented a specific form of guerilla action, centring on small armed units mounting highly conspicuous attacks on representatives of the status quo. Such attacks would raise popular awareness of the nature of the struggle, whilst the inept and heavy handed response of the authorities would act as an even more effective mobilizing device. Focoist strategies need not necessarily centre on the use of violence.

References

Anderson, P. 2000. 'Renewals', *New Left Review*, 1, 239: 5–24.

Arendt, H. 1963. *On Revolution*. New York: Viking.

——1973. *Men in Dark Times*. Harmondsworth: Penguin.

Bardhan, P. 2000. 'The Nature of Institutional Impediments to Economic Development', in Olson, M. and Kahkonen, S. (eds.), *The Not-So-Dismal Science: A Broader View of Economies and Societies*. Oxford: Oxford University Press.

Benjamin, W. 1978. *Reflections*. New York: Harcourt Brace Jovanovich.

Casey, B. and Gold, M. 2000. *Social Partnerships and Economic Performance*. Cheltenham: Edward Elgar.

Crook, S. 1991. *Modernist Radicalism and its Aftermath*. London: Routledge.

De Haan, J. and Sturm, J. 2000. 'On the Relationship between Economic Freedom and Economic Growth', *European Journal of Political Economy*, 16, 2: 215–241.

Desai, A. 2002. *We Are the Poors: Community Struggles in Post-Apartheid South Africa*. New York: Monthly Review Press.

Farnham, D. and Pimlott, J. 1992. *Understanding Industrial Relations*. London: Cassell.

Fergusen, J. 1990. *The Anti-Politics Machine*. Cambridge: Cambridge University Press.

Flanders, A. 1975. 'Industrial Relations: What is Wrong with the System?', in Barrett, B., Beishon, J. and Rhodee, E. (eds.), *Industrial Relations and Wider Society*. Drayton: Collier-Macmillan.

Fletcher, B. and Hurd, M. 1999. 'Political Will, Local Union Transformation and the Organizing Imperative', in Nissen, B. (ed.), *Which Direction Organized Labor?* Detroit: Wayne State University Press.

Frege, C. 1999. 'The Challenges to Trade Unions in Europe', *Work and Occupations*, 26, 2: 279–281.

Fukuyama, F. 1992. *The End of History and the Last Man*. London: Hamish Hamilton.

Fung, A. and Wright, E.O. 2003a. 'Countervailing Power in Empowered Participatory Governance', in Fung, A. and Wright, E. O. (eds.), *Deepening Democracy: The Real Utopias Project, Volume 4*. London: Verso.

——2003b. 'Thinking about Empowered Participatory Governance', in Fung, A. and Wright, E. O. (eds.), *Deepening Democracy: The Real Utopias Project, Volume 4*. London: Verso.

Gall, G. 2003. 'Introduction', in Gall, G. (ed.), *Union Organizing: Campaigning for Union Recognition*. London: Routledge.

Giddens, A. 1979. *Capitalism and Modern Social Theory: An Analysis of the Writings of Marx, Durkheim, and Max Weber*. Cambridge: Cambridge University Press.

——1981. *The Class Structure of the Advanced Societies*. London: Unwin.

Green, D. 1999. 'The Lingering Liberal Moment: An Historical Perspective on the Global Durability of Democracy after 1989', *Democratization*, 6, 2: 1–41.

Habermas, J. 1990. *Moral Consciousness and Communicative Action*. Cambridge: Polity.

Habib, A. and Taylor, R. 1999. 'Daring to Question the Alliance', *Transformation*, 40: 112–120.

Harcourt, M. and Wood, G. 2003. 'Under What Circumsances do Social Accords Work', *Journal of Economic Issues* (in print).

Hertz, L. 2001. *The Silent Takeover: Global Capitalism and the Death of Democracy*. London: Heinemann.

Hyman, R. 1989. *The Political Economy of Industrial Relations*. London: Macmillan.

——'Trade Unions and the Disaggregation of the Working Class', in Regini, M. (ed.), *The Future of Labour Movements*. London: Sage.

——1997. 'Trade Unions and Interest Representation in the Context of Globalization', *Transfer*, 3, 515–533.

Kelly, J. 1997. 'Trade Unions and the Disaggregation of the Working Class', *Employee Relations*, 19, 5: www.emerald-insight.co.uk.

Jay, M. 1984. *Adorno*. Cambridge, Mass.: Harvard University Press.

Lipset, M. 1977. *Union Democracy*. New York: Free Press.

Marsden, D. 1999. *A Theory of Employment Systems: Micro-Foundations of Societal Diversity*. Oxford: Oxford University Press.

Moburg, D. 1999. 'The US Labor Movement Faces the Twenty-First Century', in Nissen, B. (ed.), *Which Direction Organized Labor?* Detroit: Wayne State University Press.

Moody, K. 1997. *Workers in a Lean World*. London: Verso.

Olson, M. 1982. *The Rise and Decline of Nations: Economic Growth, Stagflation and Social Rigidities*. New Haven: Yale University Press.

Olson, M. and Kahkonen, S. 2002. 'Introduction: The Broader View', in Olson, M. and Kahkonen, S. (eds.), *The Not-So-Dismal Science: A Broader View of Economies and Societies*. Oxford: Oxford University Press.

Rachleff, P. 2002. 'The Current Crisis of the South African Labour Movement', *Labour/Le Travail*, 47: 151–169.

Salamon, M. 1987. *Industrial Relations*. New York: Prentice Hall.

Soron, D. 2001. 'Back to the Future: The Contemporary Left and the Politics of Utopia', *Labour/Le Travail*, 47: 203–216.

Valenzuela, J.S. 1992. 'Labour Movements and Political Systems', in Regini, M. (ed.), *The Future of Labour Movements*. London: Sage.

Wallerstein, I. 1998. *Utopistics, Or Historical Choices of the Twenty-First Century*. New York: New Press.

Wood, G. 1996. 'Deregulating Industrial Relations: The New Zealand Experience', *South African Journal of Labour Relations*, 20, 1:41–58.

Wood, G. 1998. *Trade Union Recognition: Cornerstone of the New South African Employment Relations*. Johannesburg: International Thompson.

——2003. 'Book Review: Ashwin Desai, *We are the Poors*', *Labour/Le Travail* (in print).

Wood, G. and Harcourt, M. 1998. 'The Rise of South African Trade Unions', *Labor Studies Journal*, 23, 1: 74–92.

——2001. 'The Consequences of Neo-Corporatism: A Syncretic Analysis',

International Journal of Sociology and Social Policy, 20, 8: 1–22.

Wood, G., Harcourt, M. and Harcourt, S. 2003. 'The Effects of Anti-Discriminatory Legislation on Workplace Practice: A New Zealand Case Study'. Working paper, Middlesex University/Waikato University.

Index